A Painful Reminiscence of a Dignified Soul

by Zhong Da

The contents of this work, including, but not limited to, the accuracy of events, people, and places depicted; opinions expressed; permission to use previously published materials included; and any advice given or actions advocated are solely the responsibility of the author, who assumes all liability for said work and indemnifies the publisher against any claims stemming from publication of the work.

All Rights Reserved
Copyright © 2020 by Zhong Da

No part of this book may be reproduced or transmitted, downloaded, distributed, reverse engineered, or stored in or introduced into any information storage and retrieval system, in any form or by any means, including photocopying and recording, whether electronic or mechanical, now known or hereinafter invented without permission in writing from the publisher.

Dorrance Publishing Co
585 Alpha Drive
Pittsburgh, PA 15238
Visit our website at *www.dorrancebookstore.com*

ISBN: 978-1-6480-4000-9
eISBN: 978-1-6470-2648-6

A Painful Reminiscence of a Dignified Soul

THE STORY OF MY CHILDHOOD is a story of sadness, bitterness, and tears. I am not an orphan but maybe I can call myself a para-orphan or a semi-orphan. I have received very rare care and love from my parents, let alone from my grandparents. My father passed away when I was only two years old and my mother followed him three years later. They left me when I was most vulnerable, most pitiful, and most in need of love and care. I know nothing of my parents' kisses and hugs, nor their character, their temperament, or hobbies. I do not remember what they look like, their faces, or their figures, for there was not a single their photograph left. I even do not know my mother's first name. I only know her surname as Ying for at that old time, people always called married women as that nee surname and never mentioned their first name.

The one and the only thing I can remember of my father, however, is rather a happy occurrence. One evening, while I was tottering in the room, my father returned home from customs office. He put his portfolio on a desk, took out something from it, and sat on an armchair. Then he waved me to come to him. I staggered to his place with a face full of smile. He showed me a truck-shaped transparent glass bottle of sweets, waving it right and left to lure me. At that time cars and trucks were still rare things. The queer shape struck me a great deal. Furthermore, the sweets within the bottle were unusual. They were grains of different colors shining with silk luster. I was extremely delighted and eagerly reached my hand for it. He did not give me and said with a grin, "You are too young to hold it. You would drop and break it." He opened the bottle, took out a red grain of sweet, and put it in my mouth. It was delicious and I enjoyed it very much. I asked for more. He gave me another one and put the bottle on the top level of a cabinet, which I could not reach. He patted my head tenderly and told me, "Whenever you want it, tell the adults." With this word he turned back to his desk to do his own things. As the shape of the bottle was so unique and the candy was so pretty and sweet, it left a deep impression that made me remember it forever. I cherish it highly for it is the only connection between my father and me in my memory.

The one and the only thing I can remember of my mother is a very sad recollection.

Shortly after my father's death, my mother got womb cancer. Most of the time she was lying in bed, unable to work, and tended by my sister-in-law. She could no longer accompany me and take care of me. At that time, I almost knew nothing about disease, suffering, sorrow, or sympathy, so I did not know I should keep company with her, console her, and take care of her. I just played myself and rarely went to see her. Her disease went on over two years and often had excruciating pang. Though my eldest brother Da Yi had done his best to help her, sending her to the hospital, searching for the best doctor to heal her, providing highly nutritious food to her, constantly soothing and solacing her, her disease showed no signs of getting better and became worse and worse. As a last resort, my eldest brother escorted her to go to Shanghai for treatment. She had been hospitalized for a long time to take cobalt-beam therapy, which was said to be the most advancing method to deal with the cancer. My mother suffered a lot from all the treatment, yet still got no cure. My brother had to carry her back home. My mother refused any further medical treatment, peacefully waiting for her last day. My eldest brother did not agree, but he could do nothing without my mother's cooperation.

One bad evening, my mother's situation became quite emergent. Her pulse was very weak, her breath was slow, her heartbeat was hardly felt and her eyes kept closing. She seemed to be in the demarcation of life and death. My eldest brother judged that her last time was coming. He summoned all our family members gathered in my mother's bedroom. My mother had six sons. The eldest and I were living with her, the second one was working at a bank in Xuzhou County, the third was studying in a university in Shanghai, and the fourth and the fifth were studying in boarding school. Now all my brothers except the second one had already been at home. My eldest brother arranged us kneeling down in front of my mother's bed in three rows. Our maid servant, who always took a share in our joys and sorrows, also knelt in the last row. As I was the youngest son, my eldest brother put me closest to my mother. I was kneeling just by her bedside facing her face. I clasped her hand and looked straight at her. Two years of suffering had drained her. Her face was white and her arms were like two reeds. What struck me most was that her belly was dented as deep as a basin. Her eyes were closed. Suddenly, my mother strained all her effort to open her eyes. When she saw all of us

A Painful Reminiscence of a Dignified Soul

kneeling before her, she beamed a very faint smile. She looked rather pleased, but her brows still remained slightly knitted. She seemed not to be satisfied completely and closed her eyes again. We kept kneeling there without a word. The room was deadly silent and the air was intense and still. After a while, she tried her hardest to half open her eyes again, scanning around us as if searching for something. She could not keep eyes open long; her eyelid soon dropped again. It seemed she was quite ready to bid farewell with us, yet still loathed to part with us right away. My brother did not know what she was thinking and could not help her.

Suddenly our front door was flung open and my second elder brother burst in. He rushed toward my mother, knelt down, grasped my mother's hand tightly, and asked her pardon for his late coming. He explained that his work was very busy and he was unable to take leave earlier. He was hurrying home by taking an express train that day. Though my mother had almost lost all her consciousness and did not understand what he said, she was still able to open her eyes and stare at him straightly with a very faint satisfactory smile on her face. She seemed striving to open her mouth, but she could not. This sight only lasted few seconds. Her eyes suddenly closed and her head fell on one side. All colors were drained from her face and her body was motionless. We remained silent and did not know what to do. After a decent interval, my eldest brother rose to his feet and walked to the bedside. He put his hand to my mother's nostrils to feel her breath. There was no breath at all. He put his hand above her heart, there was no beating there. With tears in his eyes, my eldest brother painfully declared that my mother was dead.

At once, all the family but I burst into loud cries. At that time, I still did not know the full meaning of death. I could not quite distinguish death from sleep. I thought she was sleeping again, so I did not feel sad and cried. But when all the family was crying bitterly, I felt it was wrong not to cry. I tried hard to force me to cry, but my tears just would not come out. Fearing to be blamed by my brothers, I buried my head on the bed, pretending to cry, and loudly. The crying went on and on and showed no sign of stopping. At last, the maid servant swept tears from her face and reminded my eldest brother that we had to refrain crying for a while, that we must change her clothes quickly before her body became cold and stiff. As her words were quite reasonable and convincing, everyone reluctantly stopped crying and stood up. They went to my mother's bedside, touched her hand, gazed at her face for a moment, bid a last farewell to her, and left the room. I still stayed by the bedside. My sister-in-law went to the wardrobe to take out my mother's grave clothes, a set of brand-new, purple colored ones. She asked me go away and with the maid servant's help they changed my mother's clothes hurriedly.

The next morning, my brothers set a plank bed in the main hall of our house, which is in the middle of two rooms, and then they moved my mother's body from her bed onto the plank bed. In front of the plank bed was a long table covered with white cloth on which there were plenty of sacrificial offerings and white flowers. All the family was dressed in mourning clothes, hempen garments, and was wearing a white cap on which a cotton ball was stitched.

In the afternoon, a mourning service was held in the main hall. Several Buddhist monks wearing yellow patchwork vestments were walking slowly around the long table, chanting the sacred Buddhist scripture which are meant to expiate the sins of the dead, to save the soul of the deceased from hell, and to offer the spirit an eternally peaceful rest. Another monk was sitting at the corner of the hall, ringing a bell and beating a wooden fish— a percussive instrument— to create a rhythm accompanying the chanting of the scripture. We brothers and my sister-in-law stood beside my mother's body, keeping silent and bowing our heads with profound grief. The atmosphere of the hall was so grave and solemn that the air seemed still and frosted.

The swift happenings of that day made me a new child. I got to know some new senses—the sense of sorrow, of grief, of regret, of shame. I looked at my mother's body, a cold, stiff, motionless corpse, quite different from living creatures. I clearly knew then what death means. My mother was not sleeping. She would never wake, never hold my hand, and never talk to me again. Feeling an unspeakable impulse, my tears were trickling down my face. I regretted I didn't cry the night before. I was ashamed that I was not a good son. I felt remorseful that I hadn't kept company with her more often, hadn't soothed her pain when she was alive. Though I want to dedicate my love to her, now I'll never be able to do that.

At night, I just couldn't go to sleep. All the troubled thoughts were lingering in my mind. I was constantly thinking about how I could make up for my faults. In the long search for the way, suddenly it seemed I got a good idea and I was happy. Every person must have a house to live in and every dead person also must have a house to live in. The dead person's house is a coffin, which will be buried deep in the earth. It must be very strong. If I can buy a remarkable coffin for my mother as her last home, I will be able to atone that it was all my fault.

A Painful Reminiscence of a Dignified Soul

With this excellent idea, I happily set out of my house. I wandered the streets looking for a coffin store. After turning many corners of the streets, I finally find a coffin store and I entered in it excitedly. There are a lot of coffins with various colors piled up high one upon another against the walls. I examine each coffin carefully, tapping its wall to hear the sound, rubbing its surface to see if it is smooth. Finally, I choose a pitch-black one, strong, pretty, with a raft of beautifully carved patterns on its lid. I take the coffin down from the top of that pile. Of course, I have no money to buy it, I have to steal it. But I cannot take such big a thing out without being seen by the storekeeper. I improvise another excellent idea. I begin to chant some magic words, order the coffin to shrink smaller and smaller. When it reaches the size as small as a matchbox, I stop my chant. I triumphantly put the "matchbox" in my pocket and strut out of the store. I am hopping back all the way excitedly. After returning home I go to my mother's body, staring at her face for some time with mixed feelings—sad for her death, happy for I get a nice house to her. I make three deep bows to her body sadly, solemnly first, then I elatedly tell her that I have bought a new house for her. I take out the "matchbox" from my pocket and put it on the floor in front of her. I chant the magic word again in order it to restore its proper size. Very soon a big, pretty coffin appears in front of my mother. I seem to see a vision of my mother's smiling face in my eyes and I am immensely delighted. I feel satisfactory that I have redressed my fault and I am the best son in the world. But my satisfaction did not last long, for the clamor of morning traffic suddenly awoke me. The entire exciting thing was but a dream. I felt sad and disappointed, yet I liked that strange and fascinating dream. It has come back to my memory over and over again. It is the one and the only dream I have remembered for all my life.

After my mother's passing away, I found myself even more lonely and deserted. My eldest brother was working at the custom house. He was very busy, going out early in the morning and coming back late in the evening six days in a week. In addition, he had to take care of his weak wife and a baby, for his wife had just given birth to a daughter. I was always staying alone, nobody played with me, nobody talked to me. Usually I stayed in my room gloomily. Occasionally I would go out of the door to look the scene of the street or to go to my neighbor's house to play with their children. When I saw children walking in the street, clinging their hands to their parents', or when I watched my neighbor's children lying on the green lawn under the tranquil starry sky listening an intoxicating fairy tale told by their grandmother during the summer night, I always admired and envied them. They had good luck, they were happy, but I never had that delighted experience, I could not enjoy such affection from my parents. I complained about my fate and felt miserable.

Maybe my eldest brother noticed my mood, one night he came to my room and had a talk with me.

"How are you these days? Now is summer vacation, a new school term will begin soon. I want to send you to school. Would you like to go to school?"

Hesitating for some time, I answered, "School is an enchanting place. Of course, I would like to go there. I always admire those pupils. But children usually go to school at six years old and I am only four and a half. I am afraid I cannot catch up with the lessons."

"Yes, you are a little young for going to school, but you are clever. You can certainly catch up the lessons if you work hard. Don't mind that."

"I am also afraid of the big boys who might bully me. They would hit me."

"Ha ha, you are wrong. They are kind and warm. They are big brothers and big sisters. They will take care of you and play with you. You can make many friends there. Don't worry about that. Going to school is better than staying home alone."

"Well, I'll go to school. I'll try. If I cannot follow the lessons, if they don't like me, I'll return home." I thought a while and agreed.

"Alright, tomorrow I'll take you to the school to enter your name in the roll. Before going, clean yourself carefully and wear your nice clothes. Be polite to the teachers. If they ask you something, just tell them the facts. Don't be afraid. Now go to bed. Have a good sleep tonight." he patted my shoulder and left my room.

The next morning, my brother led me to a primary school not very far from my home. The name of the school is "MinCheng 敏成". I did not know the words. My brother explained: "敏 means quick, 成 means getting success. The name means this school will cultivate you and help you become a talented person fast."

I am delighted and like the name. My brother held my hand and we entered the school. He asked a female teacher to register my name in the students' roll.

She cast a glance at me and said, "He is too young to enter school."

My brother told her "He is clever. He can catch up the lessons. If you find he cannot, you can ask him to go back home."

The teacher took out a sheet of white paper and a pencil. She drew a square and asked me to draw a square; she drew a circle and asked me to draw a circle;

A Painful Reminiscence of a Dignified Soul

Then she wrote a word "天" (that means sky) and asked me to write the same word. I did the work all right. The teacher smiled, touched my head slightly, and entered my name in the register. We thanked her and left the school.

Then my brother took me to a stationery shop. He bought a few pencils, a pencil sharpener, an eraser, a pencil box, and a notebook for me. Then he asked me to choose a school bag or school suitcase by myself. There were many beautiful things there. I liked them all and I was fastidious. Finally, I selected a small yellow leather suitcase. Everything was prepared. I was happy and felt proud that I'll soon be a pupil, waiting for the day the school begins. I expected the time to go quickly.

At last the great day arrived. I was excited. But unexpectedly, my brother told me that he was busy and could not escort me to school, asking me to go there myself.

I was terrified and said, "I am afraid."

My brother encouraged me, "You should foster the ability of self-dependence from the beginning. Don't be afraid. It is not very far from here. Be brave!"

I could not disobey his word. I had to go to school myself. I never walked a long way by myself before, so I was very nervous. I walked slowly. It seemed that everybody and everything on the street was a threat to me when I reached near the school gate, facing the huge buildings and the great crowd of students, who were all bigger than I. All the smaller pupils who were first attending school had their mother accompanying them. Frightened by the sight, I turned around and went back. While I was walking, I thought that playing truant was wrong. I would be blamed by my brother. I stopped and then I went to school again, but when I reached near the school gate, my heart beat faster and faster. I dreaded to meet the teachers and big boys. Before I knew what came about, I ran away. After running forty or fifty paces, I stopped again. I was wondering whether I should go to school or go back home. Hesitating two or three minutes, I began to blame myself that I was too timid and weak-minded. I began to gather my nerves and decided to attend school. I strode confidently to the school, but when I was near the gate, a ring for the beginning of class sounded. I was horrified and stood still. Even if I was bold enough to enter the classroom, it was too late now and I would be scolded by the teacher and sneered at by my classmates. Being scolded before all the students is a great shame. I could not bear it. I turned back again.

I wanted to return home but I did not dare go that either. I wandered along the street uneasily. It seemed that everybody in the street was looking at me. It was school time and I carried a school suitcase roaming the street. They must think that I was playing truant and I was a bad boy. I decided to go to a quiet place and hid my school suitcase somewhere. I thought of the park that is along the side of Yangtze River. At this time of morning, the park would be very tranquil and have few people. I staggered to the park that was not far away. In the park, I walked along the narrow path slowly to find someplace to hide my school suitcase. There are many flowering shrubs there. I hid my suitcase in one of the shrubs, but later I found that when there was a gust of wind, the suitcase would be revealed. I took out the suitcase and continued to search for the right place. Suddenly, I saw a pile of wood by a building and I believed it was a safe place. I went there and hid the suitcase among the wood.

Relieved from worrying, I roved about the park aimlessly. For the time being I forgot the wrongdoing I had made and enjoyed the beauty of the park. Everywhere were trees and colorful flowers. The leaves of the trees were green and dense. The flowers gave off a fragrance and I sniffed it lightly. Sparrows were twittering and hopping merrily on the trees and the butterflies fluttered their wings among flowers. There are very few people now and the park was quiet and still except for the rustle of leaves. I breathed the fresh air deeply and stretched my body and limbs.

Later, I took a seat on a bench facing the Yangtze. The river is very wide. There seems to be no end of it. Its water and the sky are fused at the horizon, misty and blurred. The water was flowing smoothly. Many boats were bobbing on the river gently and some ships were running fast and steadily. Birds were rising and dipping in their flight over the sky. It was really a beautiful scene, but I wasn't in a good mood to appreciate it. A sense of fault was constantly lingering in my mind.

The time was flying and the sun was moving toward the west. I began to feel tired. Furthermore, I was very hungry and thirsty. I thought I had to go back home. Though I was afraid of returning home, I had no other choice. Reluctantly, I stood up and went to the pile of wood to take back my school suitcase. To my great horror, I could not find it anywhere among the wood. Someone had stolen it. I stood there dumbstruck. I did not know what to do. I dare not go back home, but staying in the park overnight was much more terrible. I was crying bitterly, sitting on the wood. The sun was setting lower and lower. I had to make a decision. After a long time of consideration and hesitation, I decided to go back home. After all, home is my family. To say the worst, I would be scolded or beaten by my brother. It was much safer than staying in the park. I returned home in great fear and sneaked into

A Painful Reminiscence of a Dignified Soul

my room silently, did not greet my sister-in-law. I sat in a chair dumbly and prepared to be blamed or beaten.

When my brother returned home from work, he came into my room and asked me, "How are you feeling today? Do you like your school?"

I did not know how to reply. I kept silent.

"How many classes do you have today? What lessons did your teachers teach you? Are you interested in them?"

I still kept silent.

"Who sits beside you? A boy or a girl? What is his or her name?"

I still kept silent. I felt extremely nervous.

My brother found it strange and said, "Don't be shy. Just tell me the facts and what you think. Maybe you are unhappy, I guess."

I still kept silent.

My brother said, "Give me your notebook. I want to know what the words your teacher taught you today."

Perceiving nowhere I could retreat, I burst into tears, confessing my mistakes and telling him all the facts, "I didn't go to school, I was afraid and my school suitcase was stolen by somebody."

I sobbed and braced myself for being scolded or beaten. But my brother just kept staring at me without saying or doing anything for a long time, seemingly contemplating something deeply.

Finally, he shook his head, heaved a deep sigh, and said, "Don't cry. This event is due to my negligence. You are indeed too young to go to school alone. I should have accompanied you to go there. It doesn't matter much. Tomorrow I'll go to school with you to explain to your teacher why you missed the class today and I'll buy you a new school bag. Don't worry about that. Go to sleep now. Good night!"

He soothed me and felt my hand and then returned to his room. I was quite relieved and deeply grateful to my brother for his kindness. I went to bed at ease.

The next morning my brother bought another set of stationery for me and took me to go to school. He found the teacher who was in charge of my class. The teacher was a young woman named Yang. My brother introduced himself to the teacher and explained why I hadn't attended school yesterday. He apologized that he did not accompany me to school. He asked the teacher to excuse me, telling her I was a very unfortunate child for I had lost both my father and mother and he hoped her to take good care of me. I could not help but sob bitterly. Teacher Yang held my hand closely, promised my brother that she would not blame me and would take good care of me always. My brother was gratified with her words and gave her a hearty thanks. Then he said goodbye to her and went to his office.

Taking me by hand teacher Yang led me to the teacher's room. She was very kind and warm. She told me that a school is like a big family. All the teachers and students are friends, brothers and sisters, and I need not be afraid of them.

Then she informed me what they did yesterday, "In the morning we had a school-opening ceremony. The headmaster made a speech of which the main point was: 'The object of our school is not only developing your skills of reading and writing and teaching knowledge, but also introducing you the art how to behave properly and speak politely, how to live together harmoniously and peacefully. In addition, we'll teach you how to maintain good health. In short, we'll guarantee that you will be well developed morally, intellectually and physically. You must study hard, respect teachers, be friendly with classmates, and observe school rules. We hope you all will grow up healthily and happily since your early ages.' After the ceremony, I brought the new students to look around the school, so that they would know the right place they want to go. In the afternoon, we started the first class. I taught the students of your class a few simples Chinese characters."

At the end of her talk, she took out a sheet of white paper and wrote those characters on it and taught me to learn them patiently. After helping me to make up my missed lessons, she led me to our classroom. She introduced me to my classmates and arranged for me to sit in a seat in the first row, for I was the shortest and the youngest one in the class. Sitting beside me was a girl who was nice and welcomed me. When everything was settled, teacher Yang began to teach the new lessons.

As school was a totally new thing for me, I was still nervous and in a great panic that I might do something wrong, so I was sitting on my seat straight, did not make a single move, fixed my eyes on the teacher, and listened to her teaching, trying to be deemed a good pupil.

After class was lunch time. My desk mate took me to the dining room. We ate at the same table. While eating, we exchanged each other's names and the family affairs. She has a grandmother, parents, and two elder brothers. I admired her very much and told her my parents had passed away. She felt sorry and showed deep sympathy for me. As her age is greater than mine, she said she would often get together with me and play with me. She talked and acted as if she were my elder

A Painful Reminiscence of a Dignified Soul

sister. I was pleased with her word and I had my first friend. I thanked her earnestly. After lunch, she showed me where the playground was and promised to teach me how to skip rope and kick the shuttlecock later.

In the afternoon we had a math lesson. The teacher is a young man in twenties. He was tall with a smiling face and big eyes. He taught us how to write and speak the numbers: "one, two, three..." He also told us how to use them in our daily life.

He showed us three pencils and asked, "How many pencils are there?"

We all shouted out "three".

Then he stretched out his right hand and asked again, "How many fingers in my hand? Write down on your notebooks." He walked between the lines of the desk and examined our writings.

I found the character "5" was not easy to write and scribbled a figure like a chicken claw. The teacher smiled at my writing and held my hand to write a regular "5". My face flushed with shame.

After school, we all hastily left the classroom to go back home. Outside the school gate, I saw many women who were waiting there to pick up their children and many of our classmates were running towards their mothers. They were all talking happily, holding hands, and walking away briskly. I admired their fortune and felt sad. They were all older than I, yet they still had somebody to accompany them, but I hadn't had anyone to accompany me. I was staggering lonely, silently along the apathetic street and thought of my poor mother, my tears could not but stream down in torrents.

Gradually I no longer had fears and led a regular student's life, learning lessons earnestly and playing with classmates happily. I began to love and adore my school. Our teachers were very kind and responsible. Whenever we had difficulties or made some small fault, they would help us to solve the problems or gave us some good advice.

One day I faced an awkward thing. Some classmate took my pencil sharpener without telling me and did not return it to me. Despite my many announcements, no one responded. Since it was an important thing for me and I often needed to use it, I got angry.

One day, I stood on my stool and yelled, "Who has taken my pencil sharpener? I hope he returns it to me. Just put it back on my desk. I do not want to know his name."

Suddenly I saw Teacher Yang was entering the classroom and staring at me. I immediately stepped down the stool and felt quite embarrassed and ashamed.

Teacher Yang did not blame me. She just advised me to be more patient. A couple of days later, still no one returned it to me. I gave up hope and was unhappy. To my surprise, one afternoon Teacher Yang gave me a sharpener privately. I refused shyly but she insisted and said, "It is only a small gift." Finally, I received it and gave her a hearty thanks. Yes, it is indeed only a small thing, but it left me a long remembrance.

In the third grade in school, I got in trouble with math, for my marks for math tests were always low. I was disconcerted about it. Sometimes when I couldn't solve a math problem, I would get upset. At times when I was unable to complete my homework, I might even put aside my pen, tear up my paper, and walk away to my bed and wallow in self-pity, trying to abandon the math lesson. Fortunately, my math teacher noticed my mood and encouraged me to go forward confidently. He often gave me remedial course after school. I myself also made great assiduous effort. Before the end of that school term, I achieved some advance. Then I had more faith in myself. Sometimes when my classmates came to help me to solve a difficult math problem, I would refuse them politely and thought of the problem again and again. Usually I would solve the problem myself and found them not too hard after all.

In our class, students often made fun with each other. One day several female students measured each other's mouth with a rule. They found classmate X's mouth is the biggest, and classmate Y laughed loudly and said, "Afterwards I will just call you 'big mouth'." X didn't mind that, thinking she was merely making a joke. Next morning when X came into the classroom, Y called "Big Mouth, you are coming!" Many students looked at X. X went to her seat with tears in her eyes and decided she would never give heed to Y. Some students told Teacher Yang. Teacher Yang had a long talk with Y, telling her that everyone must have good manners and must respect others' feelings. She advised Y to make an apology to X. Teacher Yang also advised X to have a large heart and excuse Y.

In another case, a female classmate C and D were good friends. One day D went to classmate E's home to play. C was angry and told D, "You have got a great new friend, I am not worthy of being your good friend. You need not play with me afterwards." D was vexed and reported the thing to teacher Yang. Teacher Yang felt C's childish manner very funny and her mind narrow. She advised C, "One should have more good friends, not one good friend; just as one should have more good books, not only one good book. Jealousy is a bad mental attitude; we should throw it away." C felt shy and promised to correct her fault. Not long afterwards, C and D resumed their good friendship. C and E also became good friends. In short, our teachers paid great attention to moral education, not like under Mao's rule, which just stressed political education.

Apart from teaching knowledge, our teachers also organized many extracurricular activities to enrich our lives. In the spring, our teacher usually took us out for an outing. My first outing was going to the countryside. It was a vast expanse of farmland, among which were scattered the peasants' thatch huts. They were all dim and low. The azure sky was bright and balmy. The air of the country was fresh and permeated with the fragrance of the plants. Wisps of morning breezes caressed and cooled our faces. It was quite comfortable. On all sides of the village, near and far, spread the trees and bamboos. Many trees were covered with tender buds. The willow wands tinged with faint yellow. The slim trunks of the bamboo grow so close together that their leaves were a half-transparent yellow-green in the sunlight. We walked along the small path which meandered among the field. Beside the path were weeds and wildflowers. Everything was strange to me and fascinated me very much. Whenever we saw a plant, the teacher would tell us its name and some knowledge about it. Teacher also took us to visit a peasant's family. An old peasant received us warmly. We asked him something about the villager's lives and how they grew their crops and domestic livestock. He answered our questions simply and briefly. Then he led us to visit his vegetable garden and courtyard. In his courtyard there is a pigpen in which was a pig. There was also a tender and sturdy peach tree there, its blossoms were flaming red and its green leaves are exuberant. Many chickens were hopping around pecking grains and pests. After the visit, we thanked the old peasant and waved goodbye to him. On our way back home, the teacher asked us to write a composition about this journey. The outing enlarged our vision and increased our knowledge. I thought it had many good effects for us. I liked it.

Another outing that left me a deep impression was to visit Mountain Jiao. Mountain Jiao is the one and the only island which can be used as a scenic site for tourists on the about three thousand kilometer Yangtze River. It is one of the most important protected scenic spots of the nation for it has great historic and cultural attractions. As it is in the middle of the river, we had to take a ferry to get there. The mountain is grand and majestic, simple and elegant, covered by exuberantly verdant trees and grass. Among the green bamboos and trees are many ancient pavilions and a temple. A female tour guide led us to see the most admirable scenic spots and the ancient, historical attractions and made some explanation about them. She told us Mountain Jiao is renowned for its four ancient things. First, an old temple built in the Song Dynasty one thousand years ago. Second, numerous old trees, including some ginkgo trees and locust trees, aged several hundred years, some of them with queer shapes and forms and third, countless old tablet inscriptions written by famous calligraphers of successive dynasties. For this reason, the mountain is also called "the mountain of calligraphy". Forth, an old stand of artillery built in the Qing Dynasty because Mountain Jiao was an important military point in the past. She also informed us that as the mountain is so beautiful, the most famous emperor Qianlong of the Qing Dynasty had visited it eight times and lived there five times and wrote many poems to praise it. There are also many ancient relics there such as imperial robes and jade belts worn by ancient high-ranking officials. While we toured the mountain, occasionally we could see some small animals like wild rabbits running here and there. Weeds spread untrammeled along the road, wide flowers bloomed with their hidden scents, and beautiful trees provided us with deepening shade. When we turned around and looked at all directions, we were environed by the rolling water of the mighty Yangtze as if we were embraced by a dear mother. All of the scene and atmosphere were really refreshing to our minds and pleasing to our eyes. Though we were lingering at this wonderful place and reluctant to part, the sun had slanted to the west, we had to ferry back. Through the tour I was filled with wonder and pride. Ours is a great country with an ancient civilization.

In one winter, there was a great snow in our city. It was a rare thing, so we were very pleased. The teacher in charge of our class organized a snowball fighting. She divided the students who were willing to take part in the play into two groups and asked each group to select a commander who should plan a strategy and direct the operation. The fighter who was hit by one snowball was meant to be lightly wounded, hit by two balls was heavily wounded, and hit by three or more balls was dead and had to withdraw from the fighting. Then the two groups discussed their battle plan separately and secretly. I was in the second group. Our commander was intelligent. He designed a special scheme and divided our group into three parts. The first part's job was to make the "cannonball". The second part's job was to transport the ball. The third and the main part were the fighters. Our opposite group did not divide into three parts. All of them were fighters. Each fighter had to fetch snow and make the "cannonball" himself so their combat effectiveness was less than ours. During the fighting, the fighters ran after their enemies wildly, trying best to hit their target accurately and the rivals would try their best to dodge the ball. After the end of the fighting, the judge counted the number of the balls that had hit the soldiers. The group whose soldiers were hit less balls was the winner. Our group won the battle. I was "heavily wounded", being hit by two snowballs. The snowball fighting was really interesting. It tested out physical ability and our will for we were playing on the very cold weather and bad conditions.

Even the songs we learnt during those days were of great worth. They were not only pleasant to hear, but also conveyed the truth or moral values, telling us what we should do, what we should not do, what we should love, and what we should hate. For example, in my first grade I learned a song titled "Holding the Hoe in Hand, Hoe the Weeds":

> Holding the hoe in hand hoe the weeds,
> While the weeds were being hoed away,
> The seedlings will sprout well.
> Yiyahai Yahuhai
> While the weeds were being hoed away,
> The seedlings will sprout well.
> Yahuhai Yiyahai

The song was so simple, but taught me to love labor and labor hard to discard the dross, protect valuables, and to attach great importance to agriculture. Another example is "The Song of Fishing Light":

> The clouds float in the sky over the sea,
> Fishes are hidden in the water.
> Drying fishnet under the sun in the morning,
> Wild sea winds blow across our faces.
> Fishes are difficult to be caught,
> Taxes are heavy.
> Generations after generations,
> The descendants of the fishermen are always poor.
> Taking good care of the broken fishnet left by grandfather,
> On which we still have to rely for another winter.

This song taught me to hate those who exact the heavy taxes and feel the deep sympathy for the sufferers. Another song also left me a deep impression. Its title is "The Song of Building Highway":

> Let us all shed our blood and sweat,
> In spite of the scorching sun and the pang of bones and muscles.
> With concerted efforts we pull the rope to the road roller denying sloth,
> Even though the road roller is as heavy as a mountain,
> ....
> As if marching to the front line to battle the enemy,
> We had to charge ahead without retreat.
> Bearing the heavy duty, we march forward formidably,
> The big road of freedom will soon be completed.

There were still many other songs filled with such quality-oriented teachings we had learned such as "We are the Vanguard of Opening the Road" and "The Fresh Flowers of the Month of May" (several important movements happened in May), many of which I still remember and often sing even now. I repeated those old songs here just to illustrate the fact that I had received a good education in the primary school in the past. Not like the children under Mao's rule, who were just instructed to seek a will-o-the-wisp of communism, to absolutely obey the Communist Party, and to blindly participate in the class struggle ruthlessly. All the party emphasized were political things, empty things.

The two kinds of education can be obviously observed in the sharp contrast between the two children songs: "The Song of Scouts of China" I sang in my childhood and "The Song of Young Pioneers" the children sing under the Communist rule. You can make a judge yourself which one is better. The words of the two children songs are as follows:

A Painful Reminiscence of a Dignified Soul

The Song of Scouts of China

The scouts of China, scouts, scouts,
We are, we are young soldiers of the Three Principles of the people.
Though we are young,
Our spirit is true.
Dedicate our body,
Dedicate our heart,
Dedicate our strength to the masses of the people.
Strengthen the spirit of our heart with
loyalty,
Filial piety,
Benevolence,
Love,
Faith,
Righteousness,
Peace,
And justice.
All of us march forward unitedly.
March forward!
March forward!
The blue sky is high,
The sun is bright.
Dadi, Dida,
Dida, Dida

The Song of Young Pioneers

We are the successors of the communism.
Carry forward the glorious traditions of the revolutionary martyrs.
Love our country,
Love the people.
The bright red scarves flutter on our chest.
Fear no difficulties,
Fear no enemies.
Study diligently,

Struggle ruthlessly.
Facing the victory,
We march forward bravely.
We are the successors of the communism.

We are the successors of the communism.
Pioneer is our proud name.
Prepare at any moment,
Perform great feats.
Eliminate completely
All the enemies.
For the realization of the lofty ideal,
We march forward bravely.
We are the successors of the communism.

Contrasting the two songs of the children, we can see the aim of the "Song of Scouts of China" is to cultivate the children to be the adults who will devote their whole life to pay close attention to the "nationalism, democracy and the people's livelihood" of the country with perfect moralities—the eight characters: loyalty, filial piety, benevolence, love, faith, righteousness, peace, and justice. On the other hand, the "Song of Young Pioneers" is full of empty slogans. It will train the successors of communism. But what are the content and the form of communism? Nobody tells them and nobody knows. The song calls on the children to fight and destroy all the enemies. But who is the enemy? During Mao's era, he assigned landlords, rich peasants, counterrevolutionaries, bad elements, rightists, capitalist roaders, and reactionary academic authorities to be enemies. But the assignment was completely wrong and later even the Communist Party itself rehabilitated all the victims in the 1980s. Then who is the enemy now? All these questions nobody tells the child. The children only learn an illusion, to be slaves of communist party, and fight blindly and cruelly against any people whom the party named as the enemy.

Similar to the "Song of Scouts of China" America's scouts also stress the morality. "The Scout Law" of America is "A scout is trustworthy, loyal, helpful, friendly, courteous, kind, obedient, cheerful, thrifty, brave, clean and reverent." "The Scout's Creed" of America is "On my honor I will do my best to do my duty to God and my country, and to obey the Scout Law, to help other people at all

A Painful Reminiscence of a Dignified Soul

times, to keep myself physically strong, mentally aware, and morally straight." I was fortunate that all the things I had learned in the primary school were promoting clean, simple, plain, thrift, diligence, and encouraging us to help, care, respect each other and to be a being of virtue. Unlike the children under Mao's rule who were just taught to be blind political beings.

I have mentioned too many digressive words. Now let me return to my childhood life.

My life at home was rather monotonous at that time. I felt lonely without the love and care of mother and father. I lamented my misfortunes. But in certain circumstances, bad things can yield good results. Just as the proverb goes, "Make up on roundabouts what one loses on the swings." Because I had less company, I had plenty of time to dispose of by myself. I had to find something to do. In my home there were a great many books and books of all kinds, which my five elder brothers had read. I began to touch them and very soon the bookcase became a place of my bliss. I spent most of my time reading. I became an addict of books. My lonely situation pressed me to form a good habit, which, I believe, was the thing I "made up on the roundabout".

At first, I read the picture books, which helped me to learn many Chinese characters. As my grade went up, I began to read children books. I not only found those books interesting, but also very useful. For example, the book *Aesop's Fables* taught me many valuable ideas through short, interesting stories, such as honesty is the best policy, pride comes before a fall, and slow and steady wins the race. The book *Robinson Crusoe* gave me a good lesson. A shipwreck cast him to an uninhabited island. As no passing ship to rescue him for many years, he decided to make a boat himself to sail back home. The work was indeed extremely painstaking. But when the boat was completed, he found no way to carry the boat to the sea. If he dug a canal to lead the water to the boat, it needed a very long time and he could not live so long, so all the hard labor he had done was but beating a dead horse. That lesson told me that we must think twice before you act.

When I entered the fourth and fifth grade, I read adult books. There are four great classical novels of Chinese literature. I read three of them during that period and each one gave me a lot of delight and lessons. *The Journey to the West* is a comic novel based on the actual pilgrimage of the Buddhist monk Xuanzang to India in search of sacred texts. Its main character is Sun Wukong, also known as the Monkey King, who accompanies and protects the monk on the journey to the west. He is a mythological figure who acquired supernatural powers through Taoist practices. He is able to lift ten thousand kilograms staff with ease and travel twenty thousand kilometers in one somersault. He knows seventy-two transformations, which allow him to transform into various things. Each of his hairs possesses magical properties, capable of being transformed into clones of the Monkey King himself or into various weapons and other objects. He is rather mischievous but very, very loyal, always risking himself to help his master Xuanzang to complete his mission. Loyalty is a very important quality. I like the Monkey very much.

Water Margin tells stories of a group of heroes. There are one hundred and five men and three women in all. They are oppressed by the corrupt and unjust official and then rise up and struggle bravely against the evil. These stories describe various vivid, tangible pictures of farmers uprising full of the contrast between virtue and vice, love and hate, beauty and ugliness, kind and enmity, and many intimately tied friendships. The heroes do lots of good deeds to help the poor and weak by withering the evils. Among them there is a hero called Wu Song. When he crosses a mountain pass, he meets a tiger. While fending off the beast and having no weapon to defend himself, he ends up slaying the tiger by pinning it to the ground and raining its head repeatedly with his bare fists. He is really brave. I admired all those heroes in the fighting against the evils and I decided to do the same in the future.

Romance of the Three Kingdoms is a historical novel set in the turbulent years towards the end of the Han Dynasty. The novel, part historical, part legend, and part mythical, describes romantically and dramatically the plots, personal and military battles, intrigues, and struggles of three states—Cao Wei, Shu Han, and Eastern Wu—each of them wants to achieve dominance. The novel is among the most beloved works of literature in East Asia. Among so many notable characters I admired Guan Gong and Zhuge Liang most. Guan's deed and moral qualities is to be prized. He is the epitome of loyalty and righteousness. There were even many Guan Gong temples in China. Zhuge Liang is a chancellor of the state Shu Ham. He is recognized as the greatest strategist of his era and an accomplished scholar and inventor. They are my examples.

Another one of my favorite books is *The Story of Yue Fei*. Yue Fei was a national hero of the Song Dynasty. In his day, minority nationalities on the northern border such as the Jins often invaded central China. Yue Fei, as a valiant and wise commander, often defeated the enemy. But Yue's success annoyed the capitalist

A Painful Reminiscence of a Dignified Soul

Qin Hui, who wielded real power at court. He resorted to false accusation to eliminate the war party and finally had Yue Fei sent to prison and executed. Yue Fei was known not only for his military successes, but also for his high ethical standards. Confronting the invade of Jins, Yue faced a dilemma: On the one hand he wanted to battle the invaders and defend his country, but on the other hand he also wanted to stay home and take care of his elderly mother. Torn between the competing Chinese virtues of loyalty to nation and filial piety to mother, he did not know what to do. Noticing her son's hesitation, his mother asked Yue Fei to take off his shirt. She tattooed four Chinese characters on his back: "精忠报国" which means "serve one's country with unreserved loyalty" With his mother's action, now Yue Fei could fulfill both his mother's desire and his duty to the country. He promptly went to the front line. Yue's deed so deeply touched me that I read that book twice.

Except for those famous books, of course I read many other books. Especially I enjoyed reading allegories and martial arts novels for I wanted to be a generous and gallant man.

The five years I spent in the primary school and stayed at home, from age five to nine, were a critical time in forming my character. My experience during this period yielded permanent effects in my life. I like and treasure that kind of life which I hope will continue. But unfortunately, my peaceful life suddenly ended.

There came the July 7 Incident of 1937. The incident happened near Lugou Bridge in Hebei Province, so it is usually called "Lugou Bridge Incident". The Japanese infantry there often conducted surprise maneuvers at night. One night they conducted the maneuver very close to a contingent of Chinese military forces. Surprised by the maneuver Chinese directed small fires, The Japanese fired back. The skirmish may have ended there thorough talks. But the Japanese used the minor thing as a flimsy excuse to invade China. A few days later, they began shelling Wanping County with heavy artillery and then both armies committed to all-out war.

Before that incident, I had learned from our history lesson that Japan had occupied our northeast three provinces on September 18, 1931. Now it wanted to occupy more of our territory. I was very angry and exasperated. I hoped our government would resist it resolutely, no longer retreat. At the same time, all the Chinese people were excited and made an appeal for the resistance against Japan. The radio stations broadcasted "March of the Volunteers" every day and I sang the song every day. The song really stirred and roused the heart of every Chinese person:

> Arise, Ye who refuse to be slaves!
> Let's build our new Great Wall with our flesh and blood!
> Chinese nation is at its most perilous moment.
> Everyone is forced to give the last thundering roar!
> Arise! Arise! Arise!
> Braving the enemy's gunfire, we march on as one!
> Braving the enemy's gunfire, march on!
> March on! March on! March on!

Finally, the voice of people received positive answer of the government. The Second Sino-Japan War started.

On August 13th, the Japanese Army landed in Shanghai. Counting on the superior training and equipment of its army, Japan had anticipated to occupy Shanghai in a few days. But quite out of its expectation, its army met dogged resistance in Shanghai. It was a fact that our soldiers had to rely primarily on small weapons against an overwhelming air, naval, and armored forces, but they had strong will and determination. They fought Japanese troops bravely on the sea shore and beaches of the Yangtze in a suburb of Shanghai. The most heroic battle of the defense was at the Four Bank's Warehouse. The eight hundred heroes there, led by regimental commander Xie Jinyuan, that pledged to fight to the last man. They held out the position against numerous attacking waves of Japanese forces. Their best weapons were machine guns with which they covered the retreat of our remaining forces till the last soldier. A famous song "The Song of Eight Hundred Heroes" was composed to praise them and widely spread throughout the country. I was so moved by their heroic action that I sang the song every day with confidence:

> China will not perish, China will not perish,
> Look at our national hero Colonel Xie.
> China will not perish, China will not perish,
> Watch the eight hundred heroes of the lone battalion
> Fight for every inch of land.
> From four sides come the gunfire,
> From four sides come the wolves,
> They would rather die than retreat,
> They would rather die than surrender.

A Painful Reminiscence of a Dignified Soul

....
Comrades, arise! Comrade, arise!
Let's answer the call to arms,
And follow the example of the eight hundred heroes.
China will not perish, China will not perish!
Will not perish! Will not perish! Will not perish!"

After holding firmly to the city of Shanghai for three months, our army finally retreated due to the inferior equipment. Though Shanghai fell in the end, the tenacious, stubborn resistance of our forces provided a great morale-lifting effect to the Chinese army and people and demoralized the Japanese army dramatically

While the war was going on in the battlefield, Japan also made air-raid over the cities near Shanghai. My city, ZhenJiang, was one of their targets of bombing. For safety, many organizations built air-raid shelters. Our school also dug one under the playground. To prevent a stampede during an air-raid, our headmaster made a speech instructing us how to enter and leave the shelter quickly and orderly. After the speech an exercise was practiced. As the air-raid warning—the bell of our school—was sounded, the students of the first grade ran first into the shelter, following them were the students of the second grade, third grade, and so on. The teachers were the last. We stayed underground quietly for over ten minutes. As the bell sounded again, we left the shelter calmly. The exercise was successful.

My family could not dig a shelter, but we also take some measures. We put two very strong square dining tables together on which placed two thick cotton-padded quilts. When air-raid warnings were sounded we hid under the table. Our house was a single-story building. Even if the roof toppled, we would still be safe.

Japan's ambition was boundless. After taking Shanghai, its army continued to advance. My city is only about two hundred miles west of Shanghai, so inhabitants of our city became nervous. What would the Japanese army be doing? Would they kill our men and rape our women? As Japanese army came closer and closer to our city, many people escaped the city to seek refuge somewhere. We were also anxious and did not know what to do.

One evening about six o'clock, my eldest brother rushed home and gasped out loud, "The Japanese troops are only a few miles away from our city. Our commissioner has ordered me to evacuate immediately and to report for duty at the next customs office in Hankou, Hubei Province. Pack your things quickly. We must leave here in half an hour."

"Oh my! What a surprise! Within half an hour... Run away... and with three small children, aged nine, four, and two. Impossible!" exclaimed my sister-in-law, her eyes brimming with tears.

Yet with no time to debate, she and my brother began to collect things in a rush. I was also told to collect my things as soon as possible and my things must be as light as possible. I was astounded. I loved my home and could not bear to leave it, especially the large collection of books and the many rare antiques my father gathered with all his mind and energy in his life. Books had helped me forget my loneliness and bestowed me great happiness. Without them how could I spend my spare time, I wondered. Yet all these lovely, valuable things I had to abandon now. I felt distressed. I loathed to part with them. Nevertheless, there was nothing else I could do. Hesitatingly, I began to gather my best clothes and some articles of everyday use hastily and put them into a bundle. Then I stared at the gleaming glass bookcases sadly and stroked them affectionately. My brother and sister-in-law were in a frantic rush, jamming their things into two leather suitcases and a knapsack. Our supper had already been prepared, a big pot of hot porridge in the kitchen was waiting for us to serve, but we had no time to enjoy it. Finally, we were ready to leave. My brother carried a knapsack on his back and a suitcase in his hand. My sister-in-law carried her two years son on her back and a suitcase in her hand. We were filing out of the room one by one. Before my brother locked the door, I turned around to the few chickens in the courtyard and whispered goodbye to them pitifully, "Sorry, I can no longer feed you. Take care of yourselves. Bye!"

The first stop of our journey was Wuhu, the native city of my sister-in-law. We stayed at her parents' house. The next day, my brother went out and tried hard to get steamship tickets to go to Hankou. But he failed because there were too many refugees. We were anxious because the Japanese army was advancing quickly. Fortunately, when my sister-in-law's father heard our trouble, he came to help. He owned a small soap factory and had some connection with the steamship company. Through the back door, he finally got the tickets for us. What a relief it was!

In the evening we were to board on ship, my brother and his wife were busily preparing for the departure. An atmosphere of misery and graveness was enveloping the house. All the adults had complex feelings, hating to part with each other but also hurrying to get away. Yet we three children were still not disturbed. I could

A Painful Reminiscence of a Dignified Soul

offer no help. My nephew and niece, who were too young to know what the emergency meant, were playing happily and often causing troubles, sometimes crying for candy, sometimes grabbing toys with each other. My sister-in-law had to spend time to appease them.

After a long agonizing moment, at last we were ready to set off on our risky journey. My sister-in-law's parents insisted on seeing us off at the pier, for they feared they might never see us again. There were no means of transport at that time so we had to walk along. My brother carried a heavy trunk and had a big knapsack on his back. My nephew was riding on his mother's back and I was holding my niece by the hand. My brother and his wife could walk fast, but the young and the old couldn't, so my brother had to stop and wait for us from time to time. On a November night, the weather was very cold and the wind was piercing. We trudged on and on tenaciously. At last, we reached the bank of the Yangtze River. We all heaved a sigh of relief. But with a closer look, to our great dismay, we found that the ship had already left the pier. We were behind schedule because we had spent too much time at home and along the way. The ship was so crowded that all the decks were full of passengers. We watched the ship plodding slowly and laboriously up the river and regretted that we hadn't been able to board the ship. How disappointed and anxious we were! My sister-in-law was so nervous that tears were streaming ceaselessly down her face. We kept standing there numbly and aimlessly until the ship disappeared from our sight. Finding no other alternative, we reluctantly turned our back and headed home.

That night my brother couldn't sleep. He thought of the gravity of the situation. The enemy's troops were pressing near and we could find no way to flee. What would happen if the enemy occupied the city and he could not report for duty at the customs office in Hankou? He tried hard to find a way out but he couldn't seek a solution.

Early the next morning, as usual, my brother went out to get a newspaper to see how near the enemy's troops were. But to his astonishment, instead of the news of the progression of the war, a story of a tragic incident was plastered on the front page: "The Enemy Bomber sank the Steamship to the Bottom". The steamship was the very ship we had missed! The story related that the ship sank and all the passengers, except for a few very good swimmers, were drowned. We were horrified by the news. What a terrible catastrophe! How pitiful were the hundreds of passengers who lost their lives! We were very sad and compassionate for them.

Yet, insofar as we ourselves were concerned, we felt how fortunate was our lot! Our anxiety of missing the ship turned into rejoicing of missing it. Had we caught the ship in time, we would already have gone to Heaven certainly, for none of us were good swimmers.

There is a Chinese proverb: "When the old frontiersman lost his horse, who could have guessed it was a blessing in disguise." This proverb comes from an ancient story. An old frontiersman lost a horse and was sad. Later, his lost horse returned accompanied by another finer one and he rejoiced. When the man's son gladly mounted the newly acquired steed, he was thrown down and broke his leg. The old man was grieved again. Before long a war broke out, many young people were conscripted and killed during the battle, but the old man's disabled son was unfit for military service and remained to look after his father. Doesn't our experience in 1937 corroborate the proverb exactly?

Despite all the twists, we finally were able to take another ship to arrive in Hanko and my brother worked there for a short time. Not long after that, as Japanese army still pressed on and was close to our city, my brother was instructed by the commissioner to flee to Hong Kong as the first step, then wait for further instruction. A few days later, we boarded a train from Hankou to Guangzhou. In the middle of the journey, a Japanese plane circled over our train. The train stopped immediately and all the passengers rushed out to the fields, prostrating on the ground. The plane did not bomb the train and soon flew away. We were enormously relieved and went back on the train. The train started again and we arrived in Guangzhou without any further trouble.

Finally, we reached Hong Kong. We stayed in a hotel. Compared with my native city, it was much more modern and beautiful. It was the first time I saw the tall buildings, the big department stores surprised me a great deal. My brother told me Hong Kong originally belonged to China, but after the Opium War this territory was ceded to Britain. It is now controlled by Englishmen.

I was angry and said, "Japan occupied our three northeast provinces. Britain occupied our Hong Kong. It was a shame. We must recover them in the future."

My brother agreed and said, "That is why we are now engaged in the war of resistance against Japan and Britain will return Hong Kong to us in due time, for we have a ninety-nine-year lease with it."

Though I complained of Britain's occupation, still l admired its work. Under its control, Hong Kong became such a prosperous city and an important commercial and trade center. There were so many good and valuable things there.

A Painful Reminiscence of a Dignified Soul

While waiting for the instructions from his superior, my brother took us to tour the city, to go to the theaters and parks. After a long, hazardous journey of seeking refuge, these few happy, leisurely days were really a nice compensation.

At last an order came. My brother was to be transferred to the customs in Fuzhou, the capital of Fujian Province. My brother found himself in a difficult condition. Fuzhou is a coastal city. After the war started, many China's coastal cities like Shanghai and Tianjin had already been occupied by Japan. Fuzhou was very likely the next coastal city Japan intended to land. If we had just moved to Fuzhou and Japanese army came, we would have to take another refuge. We had three small children and had suffered enough from fist refuge. Can we stand up the second one? It would be very dangerous. My brother pondered the question again and again. He did not want to repeat the hardship and risk once more. After consulting with his wife, he decided to go to Fuzhou alone to report for duty and left us all in Hong Kong for the time being. He will make a further decision later according to the development of the war.

When my brother told me the arrangement, I felt sad and tears welled up in my eyes. I have already pitied myself for being without the love of father and mother and now I shall lose my brother's love? Then who will love me? Who will take care of me? I kept drawing my hand through the tearing eyes without a word. My brother stroked my head lightly and consoled me tenderly.

"It is war time now, everything is uncertain. I cannot help but leave you for a time. It is for your safety and good. You have experienced the hardship and danger yourself not long ago. You know the pain of it. Whenever the situation is allowed, I'll come to take you immediately. After my leaving, your sister-in-law will take good care of you. Don't worry about that. Your sister-in-law is also in difficulty now. She has to bring up three children alone. If you like, you can help her to do some chores at home. At the same time, you should do more reading. Though I am not here, I'll be thinking of you all the time. I'll write to you very often. Cheer up, my dear."

With these words, I felt better. What he said was factual and reasonable. I did experience the hardship myself, I no longer complained. I seized his hand and promised to help my sister-in-law as much as possible. Then I asked him to send me to school before he left. He told me that it was in the middle of this school term; I could not enroll now. I had to wait till the next term. I was disappointed, but I knew we could do nothing about it, I had to wait. To alleviate my dismay, my brother took me out for a walk. He bought me some books, lots of candies, a pair of leather shoes, and a set of high-quality jacket and pants that matched my figure well. I felt warm. How nice is my brother!

Shortly after the talk, my brother rented an apartment for us to live. It had two bedrooms with beautifully decorated walls, a tiny but very nice kitchen, and a bathroom. We liked it very much. For several days, my brother and sister-in-law were busy with cleaning the rooms and arranging the things. I took care of and played with my niece and nephew. After everything had been settled down correctly, my brother left Hong Kong for Fuzhou.

For a long time I was in a bad mood, as if I had lost something precious and delicious. But I knew I should not wallow in the valley of sorrow, so I strove to pluck up my spirit and courage. Gradually, I recovered my normal state of mind. I began to read books and to do some housework. I swept the floor and wiped the table every day. My sister-in-law was happy, for she had more spare time. Later, step by step, she taught me how to wash dishes, how to clean vegetables and cut meat, and so on. At last she taught me how to cook rice. It is a difficult job. How much water is needed for an amount of rice? How much time it would be cooked and I must take away the firewood in time. I had failed for several times, but finally I became an expert at rice cooking. At first, I only did those jobs occasionally and most of kitchen work was still done by my sister-in-law.

My sister-in-law is a woman of extroverted disposition and very soon made lots of friends in the neighborhood. Some of her friends were addicted to mahjong and often invited her to take part in their play. Gradually, my sister-in-law also became a fanatic mahjong player. At first, she went to the play once or two a week. Then she went out more often and left large part of house work for me to do. At last she went to her neighbors with her child almost every day. Her only housework was buying food and frying dishes and all the other kitchen work and chores were to be done by myself. I felt angry and exasperated, thinking that I was a member, not a servant, of the family. I was eating my brother's food, not her food. I was only ten years old, why should I do so much work? I believed that I was ill-treated. I wanted to protest or argue with her, but I was afraid. I hadn't other relatives or friends here. Many times, my mouth was about to open to file a grievance, but I was cowed by her stern look and shrank back.

There was another reason that I was not getting along well with my sister-in-law. She loved her children dearly, kissing them, hugging them, and giving them

A Painful Reminiscence of a Dignified Soul

candies and cookies all the time. This is natural, I understand. But why was she so cold to me? She rarely talked with me or gave me candies and snacks. She never gave me pocket money. Admittedly, I was gluttonous of sweets and I believe that it is a child's natural instinct. When I saw my niece enjoy a candy, my mouth could not help watering.

One day, I suddenly thought of a ridiculous idea to quell my thirst for candies. I could get some candies from the confectionery shop. Of course, I had no money to buy any candy. But at that time, in every confectionery shop in front of each kind of candy or preserved fruit was placed a small tray with some sample in it for customers to taste. One day I put on the new high-quality jacket and the leather shoes my brother bought me and walked gently and steadily into a confectionery shop as if I was a child from a rich family. I surveyed every kind of candy carefully. Then I stopped at a small tray and took a piece of the sample into my mouth confidently, contemplating for a while and then shaking my head slightly to show my dissatisfaction. I continued my searching and took a second or a third sample with the same manner. Finally, I would strut my stuff and leave the shop with a knitted brow. Yes, it was a nice trick, but I could not repeat the play again and again, for the shop assistants would soon discover that I was a swindler. After I visited two or three confectionery shops, I felt shy with this base job. I stopped the game soon and continued to bear the suffering of the thirst for candy and snacks.

The exhausting work and the lack of love made me feel more and more dismal. With no mind in work, I dropped or clattered everything I touched, I slit my finger as I cut meat. Hence more blame of my sister-in-law fell on me. I was distressed. I could not sleep well or cried out in a nightmare. I thought I was abused and I must find some way to comeback. But what could I do? Refuse to eat? Quarrel with her? It was no use, she would punish me. I thought of running away, but where could I go? Where could I get food and sleep? I found no solution and concluded that I had to endure all the suffering. That was my fate.

One day I read a report in a newspaper which interested and excited me. The story goes like this: When Japanese troops were about to enter a city in Jiangsu Province, the inhabitants of the city were worried and horrified. One inhabitant, fearing the killing and looting, escaped into a distant forest on a mountain. Being isolated from the outside world, he knew nothing about the situation of the war and did not dare to go back home. He stayed on the mountain for over twenty days, having nothing to eat, merely drinking spring water. At last he could not bear the hunger any longer, thinking that he would rather be killed in a minute by Japanese soldiers than dying of hunger in the lingering sharp pain. So, he risked his life to go back home.

The story encouraged me a lot. A man can keep alive for over twenty days without food, simply supported by water. In Hong Kong there are fountains in every park, I can drink there freely. Twenty days is a long period during which I was confident that I would meet some kind person who would take me as an adopted son or I would be hired as a child labor by some manufacturer. A fancy picture flickered into my head and smile returned on my face again. I decided to run away.

One morning, after my sister-in-law had gone to the market to buy food, I put the residual four buns and two books in my small school bag and went out, waving a goodbye reluctantly to my dear apartment. I roamed the streets aimlessly, gazing at window displays here, listening to the broadcast of advertisements there. Toward midday I went to a park, drank water from the fountain and ate a bun. In the afternoon, sometimes I wandered the park, enjoying the trees and flowers. Sometimes I sat on a bench, watching the children who were playing on the grass. Very soon, the dusk was drawing close and the park was almost empty. I began to feel nervous and quickly went back to the busy streets where people were bustling to and fro and neon lights were shedding warm glow. I was at ease again, but the peace time did not last long. The lights and the people were gradually diminishing and I wondered where I should sleep. I was getting more and more anxious and panicked. At a time, I was even tempted to go back home. But at the same time, I was not going to be jeered by my sister-in-law as a boy without backbone. I wandered on, looking for a place to sleep. Finally, I came to an archway of a high building, where was quiet. Believing it was a good place to stay, I entered into it and sat down against the wall. I was very tired and hungry. I wanted to have another bun. But thinking that I still have a tomorrow and the day after tomorrow, I refrained myself from eating it. It was in deep night now, no pedestrians in the street, the eerie silence and the bizarre emptiness frightened me. I hoped there were some people nearby, yet I also feared there were any people too for who knew they were good ones or bad ones and maybe they would drive me out of here. In all these mixed feelings, I was gradually conquered by tiredness and fell asleep.

The next morning, I got up early before anyone found me out. I went to the park again. I drank some water and ate one bun. Then I did some physical exercises, jumping about on the floor, stretching my arms and legs, and twisting my body into different positions. After that, I felt much refreshed and sat on a bench, considering what I was going to do next. Suddenly an idea struck me that I could try to get some work at a factory. I stood up and left the park to search for a factory. I walked along the less busy streets slowly, carefully noticing the sign on each door. After roaming an hour or more I saw a long short wall along a street, in the middle of which was an iron gate. After reaching the gate I found it was a food manufacturer. I walked toward the gatehouse, but a nameless fright made my heart beat fast. I took a few steps back. I stayed there for a while, composing my mind and gathering my courage. Then I bid my lip and went straight to the gatehouse. At the window I talked to the doorman timidly.

"Uncle, does your factory need any labor? I want to work here."

The doorman seemed to be surprised and puzzled, waving his head slightly and said, "No, we do not need any labor. You ought to go to a school, not a factory."

"But I am an orphan. I cannot afford to go to school."

"Then you can go to an orphanage, they will help you."

"But they said that I am too big. They only take small children. Beg you to take me. I am hungry and cold," I entreated him desperately and my tears streamed down.

The doorman seemed to feel sympathy for me, stroking my hand tenderly and consoled me, "I understand your difficulties. I really would like to help you, but it is just impossible. This factory does not need any more workers now and even if it needed, it could not hire you, for hiring child labor is illegal. Maybe you can find some family which needs laborers. Maybe they can help you. What do you think? My poor little thing."

Recognizing I was impossible to get a job here, I thanked the doorman for his kindness and I left the factory. Dismally, I returned the park that was my home now. After drinking some water, I lay on an open bench. I was too tired and soon fell into sleep.

When I woke up, the sun was already setting low. I got up hurriedly and went to the fountain to drink water. Facing the bun, I did not know what to do. Eat it or leave it? Hesitating for a long time, I reluctantly had another precious bun. Yet it helped little, I was still very hungry. Watching at the last remaining one, a fierce conflict thought tortured me. My empty stomach urged me to eat it right now, the need of tomorrow asked me not to do that. Finally, my will triumphed and I put the last bun back in my school bag. I returned to the street, where I rambled for three or four hours.

When it was near midnight, I went back to the archway. Hovering around it until there were no people on the road, I entered into it and lay down beside the wall. Though extremely tired, I could not sleep. My mind was full of trouble things. I had roved the city for two days and there still wasn't the slightest hope. I had no food and became weak, had I to die of hunger? What should I do? What can I do? I thought about all the questions, trying to find a way out, but I couldn't. I concluded what I could do was to wait and see, resigning myself to my fate. With a miserable and desperate heart, I sobbed myself to sleep.

As the brilliant light of the early dawn was glinting the city, it seemed to bring forth some courage to me to explore my chance. I went straight to the park to drink water and finished the last bun. After doing some exercises, I wandered absently around the park. More and more people came in the park. I paid attention to everyone, trying to find a kind person who would like to help me. But it is difficult to judge a person's mind on his outward appearance. For a long time, I did not approach anyone to strike up a conversation. Later, I saw a lady in her thirties with a slim figure and bright eyes. She was seated on a bench, watching her little girl playing on the green lawn. Her dress was simple and her face seemed very kind and gentle. I stared at her secretly for a long time and guessed that she might like to adopt a boy as her daughter's playmate. I timidly went to the bench and sat beside her. Perceived my motion she turned her head. Finding it was but a boy, she looked at me with a faint smile and asked, "You are also playing here. Where are your parents?"

This question embarrassed me. I replied awkwardly, "They haven't come. I am playing here myself."

"You do not go to school?" She felt strange.

Hesitatingly I replied, "I have fallen ill. I am on sick leave." I fabricated a lie to meet the exigencies.

She turned her head and kept looking at her girl. I expected she would talk to me again but she did not. She must recognize I was telling a lie and took me as a truant. Feeling ashamed that I had told a lie and had been despised, I snuck away. Having taken this lesson, I decided not to do that thing again. They would regard me as a bad boy.

I was very, very hungry now. My abdomen was dented deep and my intestines were twisting. I could not bear the pang and was conscious that I must search for

A Painful Reminiscence of a Dignified Soul

something to eat now. I began to plod along the street with my weary body, trying to find some food. Restaurant was my first objective, where there might be some leftovers discarded by the customer. I entered several restaurants, waiting for the leftovers, but the waitpersons found me not a customer and drove me away as a beggar. I was disappointed, but their suspect reminded me, if I am willing to be a beggar, I might be able to get some food or money. I had a fierce mental conflict. Shall I become a beggar or not? After having weighed the alternative in my mind for a long time, I decided I would rather die of hunger than become a beggar. I hated to downgrade myself to that degree.

I continued to drag my feet alone the street laboriously until I came to a high school. On the two sides of the gate there were several food stalls, by one of which crouched a young man who was eating sandwiches. I stood beside him gazing at his sandwich with an air of admiration. I hoped he would drop some leftovers and I could take them.

Seeing me rooted there like a stake, he laughed and raised his sandwich, saying, "Do you want to have it?"

I nodded shyly and said, "I am hungry, but I am not a beggar. I want to take your leftovers."

The man bought another piece of sandwich and gave it to me. It was quite out of my expectation. He is so generous!

I received it reluctantly and made a deep bow to him and said, "Thank you very much!"

"Don't mention it. I like you." he patted me on the shoulder and strode away after he finished his meal.

I wolfed the delicious food ravenously and felt much better.

At night, I returned to the archway again. I was more and more worried. I no longer believed that story in the newspaper. A man can keep alive for twenty days without food. I myself had already experienced the taste of hunger. Before I ran away, I thought I could find work at a factory or adopted by a kind person. But now it was evident that no factory could hire a child labor and it seemed nobody would take me as an adoptee. What would be my future? Must I starve to death in the open air of the park? I began to be afraid and chills were crawling up my spine. I was trembling and sobbing into my dreadful dream again.

Next morning, I regularly went to the park. After drinking water, I thought about what I should do now. I did not like to wander the streets aimlessly. I was very weak and I must save my scant energy. I took a seat on the bench, trying to think of a definite objective to go. I pondered deeply what else way I was able to take. Can I go to the shop to ask for a job? Maybe the shopkeeper can employ child labor, but the hope is very thin. Perhaps I can visit the residents, maybe they need servant, but people usually employ adult women to do housework. They could not hire a boy. That is not a good idea either. Going to the government for help? No, they will send me back to my sister-in-law. I wrestled with the question again and again but could not find any good idea. Suddenly my empty stomach reminded me that my present key question was to find food for survival.

Hesitantly, I stood up and dragged my feet, step by step, to the streets. I cruised about the city. I was greatly debilitated by lack of food. I was really very weak now, yet I did not want to yield. I struggled on. I staggered one street after another wearily. One or two hours later, I approached a huge building, which was now used as a refugee camp. In front of the building is a broad open ground where a crowd of refugees was forming a line for food. It was lunch time. After they got food, each family found a place to sit down and had their meal. I surveyed them, trying to find someone who looked kind and would be willing to share some food to me. Finally, I chose a family composed of a couple, a girl and a boy, I walked slowly toward them.

Standing before the man, I made a deep bow and begged earnestly, "Uncle, would you please share me a bit of food? I am really hungry. I haven't eaten anything for a long time."

"You haven't a home of yourself?" he asked in surprise.

The boy and the girl also turned their heads and looked at me.

I felt awkward and did not know how to reply. I did not want to tell a lie again. I regretted I had told a lie in the park, but I also shy to say I was a fleer.

"Tell me the truth. Don't be afraid."

"I am running away from home," I admitted.

"Why?"

"I only have a sister-in-law and she treated me very bad," with these words, tears brimmed in my eyes.

The man pulled me to sit down by him and asked me to have a meal together with them. We talk no more and began to eat. I had only a little food and stopped. I did not dare to share too much of their food.

"Why stop? You can eat your full. There is no food limit in the camp. We can take as much food as we need. I can go to the counter to take more food."

A Painful Reminiscence of a Dignified Soul

I was pleased and took meal again until I ate to my heart's content.

After the meal, the man took me into the building. They lived in a big room with many other refugees. There was no bed there, all were seated or laid down on the floor. The family had a long talk with me in the afternoon.

The man advised me to go back home, saying, "Leading a vagabond life for a boy is very dangerous. You can't be sure you are able to find food to eat and find a place to sleep every day. You are too young to work, no one would employ you. How can you keep your living? However cruel your sister-in-law might be, she is your family member. She would provide you food and lodging at least. It would be better than hunger and roaming the streets. What do you think?"

I agreed with all his words and I already had the exact experience myself, but I still hated to go back home. I told them all the details of my daily life and my anguish, not only the physical pain but mainly the psychological pain. I thanked his advice and concern, yet I told him I still do not want to live with my sister-in-law. He made no more admonition. It seemed he had deep sympathy with me and understood my feelings. He kept silent for a long time and appeared he was contemplating something.

Finally, he talked with me again, "You mustn't wander the streets all the time. It is too agonizing and perilous. I think of a way now. You can stay here for the time being until you would like to return home or find a job. You can eat and sleep with us. We will take good care of you. You can play with my children. Are you willing to live with us?"

What a good idea! It was completely out of my expectation. I was so touched by his kindness that my eyes welled with tears of joy. I thanked him and told him I was glad to live together with them. I congratulated myself on my good luck—having a new "home" so quickly.

I stayed in the camp with the family happily. The man was a businessman who had taken refuge to Hong Kong from a city of Hubei Province when Japanese army occupied it. He wanted to find a job here. Sometimes he and his wife would tell me stories and I would play with his daughter and son, aged eight and six respectively. I regarded his family as my own, calling the man "uncle", his wife "aunt".

My life was happy, but following happiness came many problems. My clothes became dirtier and dirtier and I had no clothes to change into. In addition, my uncle told me that he had no extra quilt to share me and felt sorry for seeing me suffer from the cold at night. He suggested I go back home to take a quilt and some clothes out. I was in a dilemma. I thought it was a good idea, yet I feared to go for I was afraid of being caught by my sister-in-law. After considering the question for some time, I decided to take a risk. My sister-in-law usually go shopping for food at nine o'clock and return at ten o'clock in the morning. If I slipped back home at that period of time, it might be safe. Uncle agreed with my idea and let me have a try.

The next morning, I arrived at my home about nine twenty. Seeing no commotion outside or inside the house, I unlocked the door, hurrying into my bedroom. I crammed into a big cloth bag a quilt and as many my clothes as I could carry. Putting the bag on my shoulder, I strode towards the door. Just as I reached it, the door was opened and my sister-in-law entered. I was frightened and darted out, but my sister-in-law gripped me hastily and tightly. I struggled fiercely to free myself, but I failed. She dragged me into the sitting room. I thought certainly she would scold me seriously or beat me, but she did not. On the contrary, she seemed to be quite happy and relieved.

She let me sit beside her on the couch, holding my hand in hers and said gently and affectionately, "Where were you going these few days? Why should you run away? You naughty boy! You must have been suffering a lot."

I kept silent.

"Since you left home, I have been extremely anxious. I went out to buy food earlier each morning. After putting food on the kitchen table, I wandered the streets all day long, hoping to encounter you by chance, but in vain. I was getting warier and warier. I cannot eat and sleep well. You should not run away."

I understood her great predicament and anxiety. If my brother knew I was lost, what would he do with his wife, who bore the responsibility for the event? She must have been frightened badly. Perhaps she suffered more than I had during those days. I snickered in my mind and even had a certain compassion on her.

She stood up and fetched many candy and cookie to me, then asked me to go to the kitchen with her to prepare lunch.

From then on, on the one hand, she took greater precautions to prevent me from running away again; on the other hand, she treated me much better than before, asking me to do less housework, often giving me candy or biscuit or pocket money. Each day she locked the door and did not give me the key. When she went shopping, she asked me to go with her. I found I was unable to run away again. At the same time, I thought now that she had changed her attitude, I should forgive

A Painful Reminiscence of a Dignified Soul

her and not run away again. Anyway, having a home of one's own is much better than roaming on the street

One day I told my sister-in-law that I wanted to go to the refugee camp to thank that uncle. She did not agree. She was still afraid I would run away. I had to give up the idea. From then on, I quietly stayed at home, sometimes reading books, newspapers and sometimes helping to do house work or playing with my niece and nephew, waiting for the opening of the next school term.

My sister-in-law began to consult with her friends and neighbors which high school is running more properly or perfectly in Hong Kong. Which school's teachers are more knowledgeable and competent? Finally, she chose the Southern China High School for me and I agreed. She took me to go to the school to enroll my name in it. Then she bought me a new satchel and lots of pencils and notebooks and some other stationery and encouraged me to study hard. I was excited that a new life of mine will begin.

On September 1, 1938, the new school term began. I went to the Southern China High School jubilantly. I was in the junior first grade. I had mixed feelings. On the one hand I was proud to be a high school student; on the other hand, I was anxious and afraid I could not catch up with the lessons and was jeered by others. I was only ten years old and I had in fact jumped the sixth grade in primary school. I hadn't learned all the curriculum of that grade due to taking refuge during that period. But I had no route to retreat now. I could not go back to primary school to make up missed lessons. I had to brave all the hardships and march forward without hesitation. Nothing is difficult for one who sets his mind to it. I determined to make double efforts to meet the situation.

All the following year I concentrated my mind and strained every nerve to study lessons. In the class, I carefully listened to the teacher. While I met difficulties, I asked classmates for help or went to the library to find reference books to read. Once I ran to the school library to borrow books during the class break. When I ran back to the classroom, the class had already begun. I was late. According to the classroom discipline, I should stand to listen to lessons as a punishment. Students thought I should observe the rule, but the teacher forgave me, pointing to the many books in my hand with an air of appreciation and explaining to the students, "He was going to borrow books, not play. Spare the punishment." I sat down red-faced.

With my great effort, by the end of the first grade I passed all the tests and was promoted to the next grade. I was glad and had more confidence in myself.

Zhong Da

During summer vacation, my third elder brother Da Zheng came to Hong Kong to see us. After the Sino-Japan war broke out, he also took refuge with my fourth and fifth elder brothers to Guangdong Province. He worked at a high school in the countryside. My third elder brother wanted to find a job in Hong Kong and often went out to visit the organizations which were recruiting personnel. He also often went sightseeing in the city, watched films, visited the museum, and toured the parks. I always asked him to take me with him. I was glad to have such a good time.

When the summer vacation was coming to its end, he still could not find a job. He decided to return to his high school. I asked him to take me to his school. I still did not want to stay with my sister-in-law. He agreed. My fourth and fifth elder brother were left in Hong Kong, they wanted to go to Fuzhou to meet my eldest brother.

My brother's high school is in a small town named Baihou, which is located in the Northeast of Guangdong province. One day my third elder brother and I boarded a northbound ship to Shantou, a coastal city. The journey was smooth. After disembarking the ship in Shantou, we put up at a hotel. My brother bought a lot of nice candy and biscuits which were not available in Baihou. The next day, we took a bus to a town named Gaobi. From Gaobi to Baihou there is a distance of about fifteen miles. As no public transport goes to Baihou, we had to walk all the way there. I had never walked such a long distance and the entire road was rough and among the mountains or along the fields, so I found it very difficult. The journey took us six hours. When we finally arrived at the school, I was extremely exhausted.

The next morning my brother went to see the headmaster of the school to report for duty. After resting a couple of days, my brother introduced me to a young teacher who was in charge of my class. He was a local people and was very proud of his native place. He led me to tour the town and introduced the history and the general situation to me, "Beihou is a small town in a mountain area, yet it is one of the most famous cultural towns, for it has a thriving style of civilization and has emerged a large number of talented and important people. 'Bei百' in Chinese character means Hundred. 'Hou侯' in Chinese character is one of the titles of high-ranking officials in the history. So 'baihou' means it is a place which produces hundreds of great men. Baihou is also a very beautiful place. It has idyllic, enchanting scenery, surrounded by mountains and fields with a clean river flowing through the middle of the town, dividing it into two villages. It is really an admirable land away from the turmoil of the world. Our school is located by the south side of the river."

Our school was named Baihou High School. The main building of school was a two story one. There was an auditorium, a kitchen, and canteen on the first floor. The classrooms, the library, and the teacher's room were on the second floor. In front of our school was a wide space of paddy fields. Beyond the field was a stretch of mountains. On the right side of the school were the houses of inhabitants and a road leading to the downtown. On the left of the school were many vegetable patches of the school. Behind our school was a short gentle slope leading to the riverside. On the slope was a very old banyan tree. The tree was very beautiful. The banyan tree was a parasitic plant. It has aerial roots that can grow into thick woody trunks. As this banyan is very old, it has many trunks which connect directly or indirectly to the central trunk. It has developed outwards into a sort of forest covering a considerable area. It is a local famous scenic site. During the summer, a great many people enjoy the cool under it.

The first year I studied in school went smoothly. Though Baihou was a poor countryside, quite different from the prosperous Hong Kong, but my mind was sedate and happy. I was living and eating with my brother in harmony. My teachers were respectable and responsible, my classmates were simple and friendly, and I could catch up with my classmates in lessons. Many times, my Chinese teacher praised my compositions and pinned them to a board on the back wall of the classroom. Some classmates even suspected that my compositions were not written by myself but by my elder brother. I did not vindicate with them. In the countryside I hadn't anything to worry about; I merely strained my nerve to studies. I was satisfied with my life.

I loved Baihou more and more. Countryside has many strong points. In the morning, the first cock crow is sweet to the ear. The sight of the rising sun glinting on the pastures was pleasing to the eye. The air is fresh and clean, every morning I would go out of my room to take some deep breaths. After school, I often toured the narrow paths among the fields or climbed the mountain opposite our school. The mountain is green and beautiful and has a very attractive name: "the moon-shaped peak". There are also many interesting things to do. Sometimes I would catch butterflies or dragonflies to make insect specimens. Sometimes I would go to the paddy fields with my classmates to collect river snails.

Once a classmate and I climbed up a longan tree to steal our neighbor's longan. I wrapped them in a blue scarf (our scout scarf). The next morning, I found my scarf had a bitten hole from a mouse. I had to ask my brother buy a new scarf for me. My brother criticized me. I felt of the guilty of stealing the fruit. I admitted my fault and promised never to do a bad thing.

Just as I was accustomed to my new life, an unexpected thing happened in the next summer. My brother did not want to stay in the countryside forever. He planned to quit his job and went to Chongqing to seek a brighter future. Chongqing was the secondary capital of China during the war time. Since the original capital Nanjing was occupied by Japan, the government of the Nationalist Party moved there. He told me his plan. I regarded it as a good idea and I thought he would certainly carry me to go with him, for I was only a twelve-year-old juvenile. But he did not want to take me and leave me at the school. I was surprised and insisted that I should go with him.

He did not agree and explained, "Chongqing is a city in Sichuan province, very, very far away. Now is the war time, the journey is very dangerous. I am taking a great risk to go there. Maybe I will have to pass some areas occupied by Japan. Who can foretell the exact nature of the difficulties and perils which will confront me? I leave you here for your sake. Here is safe, you can continue your studies peacefully without any danger. If you follow me, any unexpected mishap could happen and your studies will be delayed. If I can safely reach Chongqing, I will often write letters to you. When the war is over, I'll come to take you."

I had no reason to object. I could not force him to take me and had to obey his arrangement, though I was still unhappy and afraid. I lamented my bad luck. One miserable thing came after another unexpected thing successively. My brother's leaving was quite a thing coming out of the blue, I hadn't any psychological preparation. My mind was all in a haze. I wondered how I could live alone as a child in a strange place.

After my brother left, I had to live in the student's dormitory as a boarder student. At that time our dormitory was an old deserted ancestral temple. There were still many ancestral memorial tablets in it. During the school time scores students sleep there, it didn't matter much. But when the winter vacation came, life was horrible for me, especially the first dozen nights. On the first day of winter vacation, every student returned to his own home. I had to sleep there alone. The huge building was empty and desolate. There wasn't a single sound; there wasn't a single soul except me. Even during the day time, I felt uneasy and afraid. When the evening was coming, I was trembling all over. I wanted to run away, but where could

A Painful Reminiscence of a Dignified Soul

I go? Going to the fields? Going to the mountains? The same terrible places in the deep night in winter. I was panic-stricken. My heart throbbed fiercely. Every nerve of my body strained tightly. I imagined that the ancient souls were still lingering in the temple, gazing at me, and ready choking me to death any time. As I found no place to hide, I hurriedly buried my whole body into the quilt. But there was no use. I was still shuddering with horror all the time. I tried hard to go into a sleep, for in sleep I would forget the fear, but I just couldn't sleep. In the deadly frightening state, I was trembling under the sheet the whole night until the first ray of the sunlight of the dawn rescued me out of the wood.

Except the problem of fright, making meals was another serious trouble. I had to buy food myself, carry water from a distant well, and use the most simple and crude cooking utensils. I had no kitchen; I had to cook my food in the courtyard of the temple. In the morning I lit a fire in a charcoal stove to cook porridge. After breakfast, I went downtown to buy food. Then I returned home to prepare lunch. In order to save time and labor I usually made much plethoric food at a time and ate the leftover as my next, third or fourth meal.

In short, my life at that time was very difficult and weary indeed.

Anyway, I gradually overcame all the hardship and adapted myself to the new conditions. I began to pay more attention to study and take part in school activities.

Our school had some of its own characteristics. The guiding principle of our school is the theory of Tao Xianzhi. Tao was a renowned Chinese educator and reformer. He studied at Teachers College, Columbia University in America. After he returned to China, he joined Nanjing High Normal School and then Nanjing National Central University. He promoted "Life education" and championed progressive education. He was regarded as a liberal, creative, and adaptive educator. He introduced the concept of practical education. He believes that education and its application should not be separate but fused together into one single unit. His way of teaching is not rigidly based on the concept of teacher talk in front while the students sit at the back listen. In China there is a popular catchphrase "知难行易", which implies that "once knowledge has been obtained, then action would be easy." Tao reversed it to "知易行难", which implies that "action will produce knowledge." He attaches great importance to practice and stresses that only through investigating things can acquire knowledge. To put his ideas into practice, he founded the Xiaozhuang Normal College in Nanjing to train teachers and educators. Our school's founder Yang Dezhao had a deep faith in Tao's educational theory and asked Tao to help our school to improve rural education. Tao agreed and sent part of the teachers and students of his college to our school to practice his educational theories, took our school as a closely attached school to his college.

In order to practice Tao's "Life Education", our school set a clear target: To cultivate the youth "who should have creative spirit, scientific brain, artistic interest, healthy body fitting for labor," promoting "Fuse teaching, learning and practicing together into one thing," and "wielding hand and brain at the same time". To realize the above-mentioned objects, our school not only taught us knowledge in the classroom but also kept us connected to the life and society. We had vegetable patches near our school and a farm in the mountain in which planted pineapples, bananas, and other fruits. Every Saturday afternoon we went out to take part in various kinds of social activities: plant trees on the barren mountains, propaganda the meaning and progression of the war of resistance against Japan, scrawl giant slogans on the walls, go to family members of active servicemen or of martyrs to express our sympathy and solicitude, and so on. We also had many extra-curricular activities, such as singing group, dancing group, painting group, wood cutting group, etc. And we often held all kinds of contests, such as dancing contests, oratorical contests, etc.

Once I took part in a singing contest, I nervously stepped on to the stage and sang a folk song from Europe titled "I Am Now Going to Battle in the Front":

> I am now going to the battle in the front,
> I am now going to the battle in the front
> My lover wants to go together with me,
> Oh. My lover wants to go together with me.
> It's impossible to go with me,
> I am now going to the battle in the front.
> I'll certainly come back to see you
> If I were not shot dead in the front.
> Each and every woman of our country
> Is counting on my protection.
> And that is the reason
> Why I am now going to the battle in the front.
> I am now going to the battle in the front.

A Painful Reminiscence of a Dignified Soul

> I am now going to the battle in the front.
> Hello! Hello! Hello!

With the end of my song, there was a paroxysm of laughter in the hall. I did not know what the matter was. Maybe I sang so badly that they scoffed at me. I felt ill-at-ease. As I went back to my seat, my classmates around me asked, "Who is your lover? What is her name?"

"You are so young; you already have a lover?"

Now I was conscious why they laughed. My face blushed and I anxiously argued. "Now is a time of war. I really want to grow up rapidly and go to the battle in the front. What is wrong with me?"

They laughed and no longer made fun of me.

I earned a prize for that song.

Our school even had a theatrical troupe composed of teachers and students. Each term it would present a play. One semester it performed a tragedy play titled *The Light, Light Day of March*, which was really touching on people indepth. The story goes like this:

On a light, light day of March, a village girl and her lover were wandering on the slope of a hill and the footpath by the small river where beautiful azaleas blossomed exuberantly. Singing a love song with her lover, she plucked a piece of azalea and stuck into her hair. On a light, light day of March next year, the girl alone wandered the same slope and the footpath, where the azalea withered and bloomed again. Thinking of her lover in the battlefield, she plucked a piece of bright red azalea. While singing the same love song she declared, "My dear lover, when you come back after winning the battle, I'll stick the azalea before your breast, no longer stick into my hair." On a light, light day of March the third year, the girl came to the same slope and the footpath quietly, where the azalea withered and bloomed again. She plucked a piece of azalea and returned home. She mournfully stuck the azalea on the military uniform of her deceased lover in the battle front to which she made three deep bows and pledged that she would keep him in her mind all her life, her crystal tears were dropping down the floor in torrent.

It was said that the play was written based on facts. The story was so moving and the performance of the players was so perfect that many audience members, including myself, were shedding tears too.

Sometimes our school would hold debate contests. Before each debate, the teacher divided the students in a class into two groups: the pros and cons. Then he would set a subject for debate, such as "Is it the chicken that first existed on the earth or the egg?" or "Is it the circumstance that creates a hero or it is the hero who creates the circumstance?" To prepare for the debate, the students would have to go to the library to collect materials and to wrack their brains to gather their evidence for the debate. Sometimes each group would rehearse a debate before the formal debate. All those questions are impossible to obtain a definite answer. But the teacher can make a judge which group wins the debate according to the criterion: which group raises more sufficient, forcible reasons. Through each debate students would gain more knowledge and enhance their oratorical ability, so every student was interested in taking part in the debate.

At that time the government was pushing "The New Life Movement". It advocated a life guided by four virtues: propriety, righteousness, honesty, and a sense of shame. We were taught "The Song of New Life Movement":

> Propriety,
> Righteousness,
> Honesty,
> And a sense of shame
> Are embodied in our lives of
> Food, clothing, shelter, and action.
> This is the spirit of the New Life Movement.
> Neatness, cleanliness,
> Simplicity, thrifty.
> Set an example with one's own conduct,
> Do unto others as you would have them do unto you.
> Transfer the atmosphere of society with the same spirit.
> Social order and law are correct,
> Enlightening education is brilliant.
> Rejuvenate our nation with new foundation.
> All the future things are given birth today.

To promote the New Life Movement, our teachers made many speeches, advising us not to spit everywhere, not to sneeze in public, to adopt good table manners

A Painful Reminiscence of a Dignified Soul

such as not making noises when eating, reject immoral entertainment in favor of artistic and athletic pursuits, oppose laziness, filthiness, negligence, carelessness, indolence, hedonism and conspicuous consumption. Don't gamble, smoke, and drink alcohol. Spiritual values transcend mere material riches. Have consideration for others and their rights, not only one's own comfort. Resurrect traditional Chinese morality: loyalty, benevolence, uprightness, faith, bravery, rectitude, righteousness, compassion, temperance, magnanimity.

All these teachings left a deep impression. Though I did not practice them well, I learnt what is right what is wrong at least. All the teachings I got in primary school and high school are soaked into my bone which guides my conduct in all the time of my life.

Our teachers were all knowledgeable and kind, teaching us with great enthusiasm and patience. I especially loved my geography teacher named Lo Qingzhen. He is a very famous woodcutter, a friend of Lu Xun—China's most famous writer. He drew a huge map of China on the whole back wall of the classroom to help students remember the shape of each province, the principal rivers, lakes, transportation lines, and the location of important cities. He is very humorous. When he used a chalk to draw maps on the blackboard, he usually turned his head back and closed his eyes to show off his skills. He and my brother were good friends. He presented several woodcutter pictures to my brother as a souvenir.

My classmates were also very friendly and cordial. They were all country inhabitants and possessed many of their characteristics: simplicity, honesty, and diligence. I especially admired a female classmate named Yang Qingguo. Her parents had gone to Singapore long ago. She was left in Baihou to keep company with her grandmother. Before Sino-Japan war, her parents always sent money home so her life was well off. After Japan occupied Singapore, her parents could not send money home and her life became very difficult. Her grandmother was very old, hadn't regular work, and only did some odd jobs occasionally. She had to do some odd jobs on Sunday to support the family. In the morning she often had to go to the mountain to collect ferns for fuel before going to school. Her life was really hard indeed. In spite of this, she still had a good academic record at school. I guessed she must have studied deep into the night every day.

The first communication between her and I proceeded when we cleaned the classroom. She asked me, "You do not speak the local dialect. You must come from another place. Where are you from?"

"I come from Zhenjiang, Jiangsu province."

"Jiangsu? Jiangsu is far away from here. Why did you come from a city to the countryside?"

"I was taking refuge here. The Japanese army occupied my city."

"Oh, you are very unfortunate. You must have suffered a lot. I hope you can accommodate yourself to this poor place."

"Thank you! I will and I like Baihou very much."

In fact, I loved her very much secretly. She was hardworking, genteel, and a beauty. But I did not want to court her right now. I was still young. I wanted to wait until I got some achievements such as being admitted to a college or having a nice job.

At that time, Baihou was within the East-River Chinese Soviet Area, a guerrilla area of the Communist Party in Guangdong Province. The headmaster of our school was an old party member named Lo Yiping. While the Central Red Army made the long march westwards, he remained in Baihou to do underground work. Because of this, we could hear or read some news or policies of the Communist Party. From that information we were taught that liberated area was an excellent place, its government was clean, efficient and democratic, and the people living there were free and happy. The Liberation Army was brave and conducted the war against Japan actively. We were also taught that the Nationalist Party led by Jiang Jieshi was rotten. It practiced dictatorship. Corruption was an abiding feature of its rule. Nepotism and bribery were rife among the bureaucracy. It was passive in the war of resistance against Japan and active in the suppression of Communist Party. We were told that Communist Party had a lofty ideal: To realize a society of communism, in which there were freedom and equality, its principle of distribution is "Taking from everyone according to his ability; To everyone according to his need." At that time, I was an ardent patriot and full of ideal. I anxiously wanted to build up a strong, prosperous China. I believed the words and the policies of the Communist Party and had a deep faith in its political advocacy. I thought of Mao Zedong highly and learned many of his words from *Liberation Daily* or *New China Daily* such as:

> "The key of promoting democratic politics is to end the governing of the country by one party. If this question was not solved, all the affairs of the country would certainly be monopolized in

the hands of one party. Hence people of ability and wisdom cannot be commended, excellent suggestions cannot be practiced."

"Only based on the freedom of speech, press, assembly, association and the voting of government democratically, the politics is powerful, competent."

"American people are good friend of Chinese people. The aim of our party is to overthrow the dictatorial reactionaries of The Nationalist Party, to establish a democratic system of American style, so that people can enjoy the benefit brought by democracy."

I appreciated and believed his words and had a deep personality cult of him, regarding him as the savior of China. Once I heard the news that the Eighth Route Army led by the Party won a great battle against Japan's army in the north China, which was praised as "the big battle of one hundred regiments". I so adored the bravery of the soldiers and the brilliant leadership of Mao Zedong that I sang the song "Ode of Yanan" with wet eyes. This was the first time I was moved to tears for worshiping Mao Zedong. I decided to join the Party in the future.

In the year of 1944, after the Japanese army occupied Hong Kong, the South China High School, in which I have pursued my first grade, moved to Meixian County, Guangdong province. The news excited many of my classmates, including myself. Meixian county is not far from Baihou. We were considering whether we should transfer from our school to the South China High School. After deliberate discussion, four classmates and I decided the transference for two reasons. First, we believed that the South China High School, which came from Hong Kong, must have better teachers and equipment. Second, we were in the fifth grade. One year later, we would graduate from high school and might want to attend a university and take the entrance examination. A better school might give us a greater benefit in our last year of high school.

Several days before the beginning of the South China High School, we went to Meixian county. We stayed in a hotel for the time being. The school had built some simple teaching buildings and office, but no student dormitories. We had to find our living place ourselves. I managed to rent a room in a house near the school.

After settling down, I went to the school to enter my name for it. We didn't need to take an examination for we were transferring school and had qualified transcript of our school.

At school, I got acquainted with many students and teachers who came from Hong Kong. I highly respect them. They were true patriots, sacrificing their cozy, comfortable life to an underdeveloped city. Among our talks, they showed their deep love of Hong Kong and their determination of regaining and re-creating a brighter Hong Kong in the future. They often sang a song titled "Goodbye Hong Kong" to express their feelings and aspirations. The song is so touching to the soul and so pleasing to the ears that I soon learned it from them and sang it together with them.

> Goodbye Hong Kong!
> You are the passage of the travelers,
> You are also the native land of China's fishermen.
> You are the Heaven of the pleasure-seeking persons,
> You are also the battlefield of the revolutionary fighters.
> Here brims with the haughty good wines,
> Here also overflows the blood plasma of the heroes.
> Here there are famous beauties who sell their soul.
> Here there are girls who give up their lives for the country.
> Behold!
> The invader's flame of war has burned throughout the Pacific Ocean.
> Don't yearn for the temporary comfort,
> And neglect the guard against the enemy.
> No matter the battlefield is in the east, west, north or south,
> No matter the skin color is white, brown or yellow,
> Everyone takes the gun and shoot bullets at our common enemy.
> With our hands we have established the Hong Kong of today,
> With our hands we'll create the Hong Kong of tomorrow.
> Goodbye Hong Kong!
> Goodbye Hong Kong!
> Goodbye Hong Kong!

At the school-opening ceremony, our headmaster made a very inspiring speech. He stressed that the moving of the school was not an easy thing, but they overcame

A Painful Reminiscence of a Dignified Soul

all the difficulties to complete the job. He also connected our study with the war, saying, "Now we are engaging in a great war of resistance against Japan. All the army officers and soldiers were fighting bravely on the frontline, shedding their blood and laid down their lives for our country. You are not going to the fighting yet; the classroom is your battlefield now. You must do your best to study and prepare for serving the country in the future. Otherwise you will be unworthy of our fighters in the front and our country." His words goaded us a great deal.

After class began, all the teachers and students concentrated on their work or studies. The teacher in charge of our class made a very strict demand upon us. He pointed out our inadequate effort at any time and helped us to improve it. We liked him, even though he was very stringent.

I strained every ounce of my nerve to studies. In the classroom I listened to the teachers carefully. At home I worked long hours and often went to bed after twelve o'clock. I knew one year later I had to find a job or enter a college and both businesses need real knowledge.

Though we were very busy, our old classmates from Baihou High School would get together occasionally having small talks, making jokes, exchanging views and experience, or helping someone solve his problems. One Saturday evening we met at a classmate's room. We talked about our desires after graduation. One wanted to study science in college, another chose to learn liberal arts, others planned to go to work. I said I hadn't made a decision and had to wait and see the situation of the war and my elder brother's opinion. Then we had a casual conversation.

Classmate Yang Peilou began to make fun of classmates Yang Zhongnan who had already got married, "You must have been yearning your wife desperately all the time, and cannot sleep well. Be careful! don't catch lovesickness"

There was a roar of laughter among us.

Zhongnan tapped Peilou's head and responded positively with a smile, "Of course, I always think of her and write letters to her, but it did not disturb my study and sleep." Then he sneered at Peilou and continued: "If you had a wife, you would certainly be mad and have lovesickness."

There was a roar of laughter again.

Peilou made no response and changed his object to me, "Do you have a courtship with somebody now?"

"Oh no, not yet."

"Then, do you have a lover in mind?"

Hesitated for a moment I answered, "No."

My reluctant answer betrayed me. He said again, "Don't keep a secret. We are all old friends for years. Do you still not trust us?"

I felt I had to confess, "Yes, I love a girl very much. But I did not tell her. I want to tell her later."

"Who is she?" He asked.

"Our classmate Yang Qingguo."

"Qinguo! You really have a great vision. She is indeed a very nice girl. Her father and my father are cousins. I know her very well. You must be more active. You must not wait."

"I think I am still young. I am only seventeen years old. I want to tell her until I have got some achievement. For instance, when I have entered a university or I have got an admirable job."

"You are wrong. In the countryside people usually get married early. Some people even get married at sixteen or fifteen years old. If you do not take action quickly, you might lose her. You see, Yang Zhongnan already got married and had a child now." He turned to look at Zhongnan again.

I thanked him for his advice and promised him to contact her soon. I began to consider my love affairs. I wanted to write a letter to Qingguo at once, but the schoolwork was pressing and I thought if the courtship held up my study and caused the failure of my graduation, she would despise me. In addition, she was still not graduated from school like us; she could not get married now, so I decided to delay the courtship and continued to concentrate in study.

The time was flying; our last term of high school was finally ended. After a whole year's hard work, all my classmates from Baihou and I passed the examination for graduation. Altogether there were about two hundred graduates in that year at our school. At that time, the photo studio didn't have the technology to take a group photo of so many people. For having a commemorative article to mark the occasion, the school collected a two-inch photo from every teacher and graduate. The photo studio put all the small photos and his (her) name together neatly and took a twelve-inch photo. Each of us bought a copy of the picture so as everyone of us was able to keep all the teachers and classmates in our memory. It was really a very valuable keepsake.

By the end of the school term, our school held a grand graduation ceremony in which our headmaster offered all the graduates congratulations on their success.

A Painful Reminiscence of a Dignified Soul

He praised our great effort with which we got today's honor. He hoped us to make greater still success in our new posts—the universities, working places, or the army. The representative of graduates made a thank you speech, in which he said: "Thank our school and all the teachers wholeheartedly. With your loving heart you cherished a great number of students, with your great patience you passed down your knowledge to us. Your painstaking work haven't done in vain, you have reaped a bumper harvest. You are the cradle of our dream, helping us to accomplish our present goal and to create our future. We pledge we will do our best to study or work for the benefit of our country and people in the coming days. we will never fall short of the expectation of our Alma Mater. Thanks."

After the graduation ceremony, our class held a farewell party in the afternoon. Our class captain said a few words first: "Graduation from high school is the kind of once-in-a-lifetime event —a milestone event, we must celebrate it joyously to our heart's content. We have studied and made merry together for a long time, helping and encouraging each other. It is our fate to be classmates at this school, we must treasure this fate. Even though we will part from each other, let us always remember and keep in contact with each other. Now let us begin our recreational program." A female classmate sang song first, then other classmates contributed their dances, comic dialogues, then we had a game of "Questions and Answers".

A student raised a question first. "What is your wish in the future?"

There were many answers: "I am going to learn engineering in a university." "My interest is to play films." "I want to be a teacher in the future." "I'll go to the front." and so on. I didn't answer the question for I could not control my destiny then.

Later, another classmate made a question: "Which color you like most? Which animal you like most?"

There were also many interesting answers. I made an answer too, "I like the color blue the most. The eternal, vast sky and sea are blue which gives people open, broad, tranquil, peaceful feelings, so I like it most. As to the animal, I like kangaroo most, for it has the most affectionate feelings for her babies. She will carry her babies in her pouch day and night until they can hop around on their own. No other mother can hold her baby in her bosom or arms all the time no matter how much she loves her baby."

A classmate laughed, "You can go to Australia to get a kangaroo and put your baby in her pouch."

I laughed too.

At the end of the party, we all stood up and roared out the "Song of Graduation" with great emotion.

> Schoolmates,
> All of us rise up!
> shoulder the responsibility of the rise and fall of the country.
> Listen!
> Our ears are full of the laments of the people.
> Behold!
> The territory of our country is lost day by day.
> We have to make a choice between capitulation and war.
> We'll die a martyr's death as the master.
> We do not want to be slaves but to skyrocket to eminency.
> We are fragrant peaches and plums today,
> We'll be pillars of our society tomorrow.
> We have a happy get-together under the same roof today,
> We'll raise huge waves of the self-rescue of the nation tomorrow.
> Huge waves, huge waves, swell higher and higher unceasingly.
> Schoolmates, Schoolmates,
> Take out your strength promptly,
> Shoulder the responsibility of the rise and fall of the country.

At that time, all of us had ambivalent emotions. On the one hand we were glad and proud of being graduated. On the other hand, we would soon be separated from each other and each one would go a different way. We all had deep feelings in our mind after having studied and lived together for years. It was natural that we loathed parting with each other. No one could predict whether we could meet again in the future. We exchanged photos and gifts with each other as souvenirs and left our blessings and emotional words in each other's autograph albums.

A couple of days later, all my old classmates of Baihou High School left Meixian County and returned to their homes.

Before leaving, classmate Yang Pei Lou came to my place again and asked me, "Have you contacted with Yang Qingguo? How is the thing going on?"

A Painful Reminiscence of a Dignified Soul

I apologized to him and said, "I still haven't contacted her. The study was really pressing. I was afraid I could not pass the graduation examination, so I did not write her. I am sorry I have abused your kindness."

"It doesn't matter. Certainly study is more important than courtship," Peilou answered.

I thanked him again and accompanied him to the door. I could not bear the parting and stared at him until his figure disappeared in the distance. I had no home to go; I had to continue staying in Meixian County. I felt sad, lonely, and pitied myself. Every night I slept with sorrow as my only company. I wanted to while away my time by reading books, but I could not concentrate my mind to the words. I had to put down the book. Most of the time I spent window-shopping along the street or visiting my new classmates whose homes were in downtown of Meixian County. Sometime I had talks with my landlady. She was friendly and often helped me to prepare meals or to wash and mend my clothes. At the same time, I was considering what I should do in the future. I wrote letters to my eldest brother, asking his opinion. When my mind recovered its normal state, I thought of Yang Qingguo and decided to write a letter to her. But I had never written a love letter. I did not know how to express my amorous feelings toward her and not lose my face and dignity. I had written the letter several times, but each time I read the draft, I was not satisfied with it and crumpled the paper into a ball and threw it to the wastepaper basket.

One day I suddenly received a letter and suddenly still it was a letter from Yang Qingguo. Is it really her letter? I wondered. How could she write a letter to me? It was really a strange thing! With a pit-a-pat heart I opened the letter carefully and read it anxiously.

Classmate Da Zhong:

How are you!

Last summer you left our school. You went to a big city to attend a better school to seek a greater future with a pleasant mind.

Last summer I also left our school. I could not afford to continue my study and I had to give up my dream with a miserable mind.

You have completed the study of high school and will stride to the bright broad road, entering a university or finding a nice job; I cannot finish the whole lessons of high school and have to teach in a primary school in the northern part of Beihou to keep my living. I will stay in a small village all my life, sniffing the dust of chalk everyday till the end of my life.

I felt despair, I felt depressed, I felt lonely. Especially in the evening, the sadness oppressed me all the more, as if I was a deserted creature by the world.

I found myself to be weak and useless and need help. I want to have someone who can support me, encourage me, and give me strength. I survey all my classmates and acquaintances to choose the right person, but I cannot find an ideal one. Suddenly I think of you. You are kind, gentle, generous, and intelligent. You come from a big city and have seen more of the world. I think you are just the person I need.

I risk my self-respect to write this letter to you. Would you like to be such a person? Would you like to help a poor outcast? If you like, I would be happy. Please give me a reply. If not, I respect your decision and I would not complain that you are disgracing me and you can just throw the letter into a wastepaper basket.

With best wishes,
Qingguo

Reading the letter, I felt both excited and sorry. Excited that she would have me to be her friend; sorry for her difficult conditions. I had thought she was still studying sixth-grade in Baihou High School like us. I never imagined she was already deprived of schooling. My heart got heavy for her misfortune. I fully understood her feelings and her need. I immediately took a pen and a white sheet of paper to write a reply letter. I wracked my brain for a long time but I could not find appropriate words to write. I gave up. I decided to go back to Baihou to meet her personally. It would be more proper and effective.

A couple of days later, I set out my journey to Beihou. I visited my best friend Yang Zhongnan first and stayed at his home. The next day, I went to visit Qingguo at her home. She was glad to see me and received me warmly. She provided me a seat and offered me a cup of tea. Then we began to chat. She asked me how I had been in South China High School and what I plan to do next. I briefly told her my

A Painful Reminiscence of a Dignified Soul

life and study in Meixian county. Then I expressed my great sorrow that she could not finish her curriculum of high school and asked her how was she getting along recently. She said she regretted at her fate and had to resign herself to leaving high school and getting a job in a primary school. She also complained that she had no experience in teaching and often encountered difficulties. At times, she wanted to quit the job and find another one. I encouraged her to continue her work. Teaching is a noble job and bears great responsibility. When the students grow up and get great achievements, they will always remember and thank their teachers. She agreed with my opinion. Finally, I talked about the letter. I thanked her for sending me a friendly letter and I also frankly confess that I have loved her deeply for a long time.

Quite unexpected to me, she seemed frightened by my word as if she was stricken by a thunderbolt out of the sky. Her mouth opened wide and asked, "Ah, what letter? I have never written a letter to you."

"You did not write the letter to me?" I was also greatly surprised.

"No, I haven't written a letter to you."

I was quite embarrassed. Is she denying her own letter or did she suspect that I was cooking up an excuse for courting her? To prove my innocence, I took out that letter from my pocket and presented it to her.

She read the letter and grew shy and said, "It was not written by me, indeed!"

Both of us did not know what to do, what to say. We kept silent for some time.

Finally, I said, "Sorry I have troubled you. I just want to justify one thing. The letter was not forged by me. Please believe me."

With a shameful face, I said goodbye to her. I took the letter back and walked out. She ushered me to the door.

I went back to Meixian county disappointedly, wondering who wrote the letter and why they forged it. I guessed it might be written by Yang Peilou. He had urged me to contact her soon, yet I had not taken action for a long time. Maybe he wrote the letter to force me to contact her right away. I also believed that Qingguo had no interest in me. If she loved me too, she could express her feelings at our meeting, for I had confessed my deep love of her. I had a deep sense of inferiority and lost all the confidence for my future. I was depressed.

Curiously, a few days later I received another letter from Qingguo. I laughed up my sleeve. Peilou or somebody else counterfeited her letter again? I read the letter promptly. Stunned by the fact unexpectedly, the content of the letter proved that it was really written by Qingguo herself. It reads:

Zhong Da

Classmate Da Zhong:

How are you?

I do not know who wrote that letter and why he or she wrote it. But all the things and my mentality the letter described are true. I guess the writer must be a person who knows me very well. Maybe he or she is one of my relatives.

But the letter did not tell all my things and feelings. I think I have to complement it. As my life is very difficult and I have an old grandmother, many of my relatives are very concerned with my situation. My uncle decided that I need someone to help me and asked me to get married soon. He recommended our schoolmate Xiao to be my husband. I do not like his figure and manner and do not agree with my uncle's idea. But my uncle insisted that Xiao is a good student and his family is rich. According to China's long tradition, the marriage of sons and daughters must be decided by parents, following the old idiom "obey the order of the parents and the proposal of a matchmaker". My parents are not here now so my uncle can act as my father. I cannot refuse his proposal and had to obey his will. I have already been betrothed to him now. My destiny is predetermined that I must lead a miserable life.

Thank you for your love of me. But the seed of love was not sowed earlier, if it was sowed in an appropriate time, it would already blossom or even bear fruit and now is not the time.

I am sorry I have to tell you the sad news.

With best wishes!
Qingguo

I read the letter over and over again with great anguish, regretting I did not sow the seed of love earlier. If I wrote to Qingguo at the very time Peilou urged me to contact her, I might be able to change the whole situation. Why I did not write then? And "now is not the time" as she said. I felt wretched and all on edge.

A Painful Reminiscence of a Dignified Soul

I contemplated what I should do now. I was in a dilemma. On the one hand, I wanted to encourage her to break the betrothal with Xiao because she disliked him. On the other hand, China has a moral maxim: "One must not seduce his friend's wife". Xiao was my schoolmate too and I knew him. I hesitated. The conflicting thought tortured me several days. Qingguo was such a tender, diligent, beautiful girl. She was considered to be the campus queen in our school. I loved her crazily. But ethics is also an extremely important thing, I should not disrupt the betrothal of my classmate. After repeated deliberation, I finally decided to restrain my feelings and bear the bitter pain of missing her. I wrote a letter to her. I told her I really regret not to sow the seed of love earlier and now is not the time. I have to abide by the tradition and have no other way to choose. I promised her that I will love and remember her and keep a pure friendship with her all my life.

Not long afterwards, I received her reply. She told me since breaking a betrothal is regarded as an immoral thing in public opinion, she was also afraid to be looked down as a woman without morality and had to submit to her unfortunate morality. She agreed with my idea and said she also loves me and will love me forever. After that, we exchanged several letters as devoted friends. I continued to stay in Meixian county alone with an extremely dismal mind, knowing not what to do next.

Fortunately, not long after that dreary period, good news came. In September of the year, Japan declared unconditional surrender. Our country finally won the war of resistance against Japan. I was extremely excited because I could go back to my native land soon and after the end of the war, good news of my family also came one after another. My eldest brother was demobilized and returned to Customs in Shanghai from Fujian Province. My second elder brother was demobilized and returned to the Bank of China in Shanghai from Guizhou province. My third elder brother was demobilized and returned to the Bank of Communication in Shanghai from Chongqing. My fourth elder brother, who had joined the army, fought against Japanese army and was wounded in Fujian Province, also returned to Shanghai and studied journalism in a school. My fifth elder brother got a job in an office dominated by my third elder brother's father-in-law in Nanjing, the capital of China.

I also got good news soon. My eldest brother asked me to go back to Shanghai at once. He suggested me to take a bus to Fuzhou first, then visit one of his old colleagues in the customs office and ask him to help me to go back to Shanghai.

I began to plan my journey. At that time, communication was very inconvenient. Between Meixian and Shanghai is a long distance and there was no public transportation. Being a seventeen-year-old student without any social experience and connections, I found the journey very difficult. I consulted with my classmates and neighbors where I could find a bus to go to Fuzhou. but they did not know either. Finally, a classmate's father made a proposal. He asked me to contact big companies. They might have trucks to carry wares to and fro between Meixian and Fuzhou. I found that was a good idea and I visited one company after another. Through painstaking effort ultimately, I was able to find a company whose manager told me they would deliver a truck with wares to Fuzhou in a few days. I begged them to bring me there. They hesitated at first but at last the driver agreed to take me after I paid him a decent wage. He appointed a date with me and told me his last name is Liu.

One day we started our arduous journey in a very early morning. The truck was fully loaded with goods. I was sitting in the driver's cab beside Liu. Soon after leaving the town, we entered the successive undulating mountains. The road was narrow and rough. It seemed very dangerous. Despite the ugly conditions, Liu drove very fast. I was afraid, fearing it would cause an accident.

I begged him shyly, "Driver Liu, would you please drive a little slowly?"

"If I drove slowly, we will reach Fuzhou by midnight. You need not be afraid. I have driven the truck over twenty years. It doesn't matter," he answered confidently.

I could do nothing about it. I had to bear the panic. I had my heart in my mouth all the time

A large part of the journey was in a mountain area. Midway, we passed a line of cliffs along a deep river. It was really a horrible sight. I was extremely nervous and dared not look down the river. Gradually, we drove down the mountain and entered into a plain village. I was relieved. But only a few minutes later another perilous thing happened. Suddenly the front right tire flew out of the truck. The driver applied the emergency brake immediately and I was thrown forward with a loud scream. The truck slid a little way and lay on the roadside slanted. I thought we were doomed and had to stay in the village tonight, but the driver was quite composed. He took some instruments and stepped down the truck. He used a hoisting jack to lift up the right side of the truck and then he dismounted a spare tire from the truck and installed it to the front axle of the truck. Having finished all the work, he restarted the truck unruffled. I admired his skill and self-possession.

A Painful Reminiscence of a Dignified Soul

Not long after the accident, our truck began to wind up another mountain area. The narrow road rollercoastered around the mountains. Looking down the deeper and deeper valley, I sighed with emotion; not feeling fear now, but feeling blessed. I marveled at how lucky I was. If the tire flew off of the truck three or five minutes earlier, I would already have drowned in the river and went to the Heaven. If the tire flew off of the truck three or five minutes later, I would have fallen dead in the deep valley and now I was still able to watch the dangerous, forbidding pass alive with a smile. Why the tire flew out right in the time when the truck was in a plain village? Is there really a God who protects me? I congratulated myself on the narrow escape. This is my second close call. Shall I certainly have a good fortune later in my life?

We arrived at Fuzhou in the evening. I gave the driver Liu a hearty thanks and said goodbye to him. I took a rickshaw to the home of my eldest brother's colleague. He was the assistant director of Fuzhou customs named Lin Zhengchang. Formerly he worked in Shanghai. Before Japan occupied Shanghai, he was transferred to Fuzhou.

Mr. Lin received me warmly and led me to his drawing room. His family had four members: he and his wife, a daughter, and a son. We had tea and chatted there. They had already had dinner. His wife went to the kitchen to prepare a dinner for me. Mr. Ling asked me how my journey was today. I told him the details and the accident. He was surprised and congratulated me on escaping the peril. He also complimented me on my courage and intelligence, saying, "You are so young, yet you arrange such an arduous journey well yourself, finding a truck from a company, risking a dangerous journey. You are a small hero!"

I thanked him and said, "I am not an able man. The work is not very difficult. A small job."

A few minutes later his wife came in and led me to the dining room to have dinner. After dinner, she took me to the guest room, wishing me a good rest and leaving the room. I went to bed at once and fell into a sound sleep immediately. I was really exhausted.

The next day I told Mr. Ling I wanted to continue my journey to Shanghai and solicited him to plan an itinerary for me. He promised to help me, but he thought I did not need to hurry and had to rest for a few days after a long, hard journey. I had no reason to refuse. I thanked him for his kindness.

A few days passed, yet he still made no mention of the plan. I was anxious and asked him when he could make the plan. He told me he had a new idea now, "If you travel by land, there is no long-distance bus to Shanghai directly, you have to change two or three buses in the middle way. It is not convenient. You are still young and traveling alone is very dangerous in case you got ill or you were to be bullied or swindled by someone during the journey, no one could help you. I will be demobilized and return to Shanghai in three months. We will take the journey by sea. It is safe. You can wait and stay here and then go back to Shanghai with us. What do you think?"

It was quite an unexpected thing. I was hesitated. On the one hand, I hoped to go back home soon, but what Mr. Lin said was truly right. A juvenile traveling alone is dangerous. They will also return to Shanghai soon. It is a good chance; I should make use of it, so I decided to accept his invitation and said, "I would like to go with you. Thank you very much. But I am afraid it will cause you too much trouble."

"Don't mention it. No trouble at all. It is at my own convenience. Your elder brother and I had been working together for many years. We are good friends. I have a duty to help you. During the three months, you can have a tour around the city. There are many beautiful parks, natural scenery, and ancient buildings in Fuzhou. You can visit them. You can enjoy the attractive landscape and enlarge your knowledge. In addition, you can play with my daughter and son. You will not feel monotonous and humdrum here."

I appreciated his suggestion and began to tour the city. First, I visited the "Jiangbin Park". The Chinese character "Jiangbin(江边)" means "beside the river". From the park we could watch the river sight. The park is very long and at different parts there is various landscapes. There are sixty-four amazing sculptures of diverse styles in the park. It is said that they were created by gifted artists from fourteen different countries and regions. I watched them carefully. There is a sightseeing path above the water. While I was leisurely walking along it, I felt quite agreeable.

Next, I went to the mountain Gu. The Chinese character "gu(鼓)" means "drum". There is a large rock on the mountaintop shaped like a drum, hence the name Mountain Gu. The evergreen mountain is a famous Buddhist scenic spot. There are five hundred inscriptions on the cliff face made by erudites about one thousand years ago. The scene is really astonishing. At the top of the mountain, I appreciated the panoramic view of the water and land with a relaxed mind.

Later, I paid a call to the "Three Lanes and Seven Alleys". It is a district of streets featuring a cluster of ancient residential buildings and is the largest well-preserved historical heritage site in China. Some of the buildings dates back to the Tang and Song dynasties almost one thousand years ago. Most of the buildings were built

A Painful Reminiscence of a Dignified Soul

in Ming and Qing dynasties. Because of this, the district is nicknamed "an architectural museum of the Ming and Qing dynasties". These houses were built by huge old bricks and carried seashell decorations. The ornaments, wood carvings, and stone carvings show the special features of the past. They were the homes of famous people of that time including politicians, military leaders, writers, and poets. Some of their descendants still reside there. It is said that there were altogether 268 ancient houses there, but only about half of them remain well-preserved.

What left the deepest impression on me was the visit of Lin Zexu Memorial Temple built in 1905. I had heard the name of Lin Zexu when I was very young, but did not know the details. From the visit, I learned more of him and was greatly educated by his character. I wrote "A few reflections after the visit of Lin Zexu Memorial Temple" in my diary in the evening. It reads as follows:

"Lin Zexu was born in Fuzhou in 1785. His home was in the famous district of 'The Three Lanes and Seven Alleys' As a child, he was already 'unusually brilliant'. He rose rapidly through his public services. He was a formidable officer known for his competence and high moral standards. He became Governor-General of Hunan and Hubei provinces, where he launched a suppression campaign against the trading of opium. Later Lin arrived in Guangdong Province to take measures that would eliminate the opium trade. With an imperial commission from the Daoguang Emperor he halted the illegal importation of opium by the British. He forfeited almost 1,200 ton of opium of western merchants and destroyed them all in public. He Wrote a memorial to Queen Victoria of Britain, urging her to end the opium trade. He argued that China was providing Britain with valuable commodities such as tea, porcelain, spices and silk, with Britain sending only 'poison' in return. He accused the 'barbarians' of coveting profit and lacking morality. The First Opium War between China and Britain started in 1839. As Lin made significant preparation for war against the possible British invasion. The British sailed north to attack Zhejiang and easily landed and occupied Dinghai. The authority of Zhejiang complained that Lin stirred up the trouble. Lin became a scapegoat for those losses, because his opposition to the opium trade was the primary catalyst for the war. Though the Daoguang Emperor had endorsed the hardline policies advocated by Lin, but as the hardline policies caused disastrous war, he then blamed Lin and exiled Lin to the remote region in Xinjiang Province as a punishment. Though Lin was banished he did not complain. On his way to the place of exile he wrote a poem:

"If only in the interest of the country
Give no thought of one's life and death.
How can one make advance or retreat
By the consideration of one's weal and woe."

Even in the remote area he still organized the people to develop the agricultural production, donating his money to build the canals to irrigate the fields, leading a poor life himself. The Qing government ultimately rehabilitated Lin and Built the 'Lin Zexu Memorial Hall' in 1905. He became a symbol of the fight against opium and was praised for his constant position on the 'high moral ground'. Even the English scholar praised and admired Lin: 'He was a fine scholar, a just and merciful official and a true patriot.'"

I admire and respect Lin's spirit greatly. He loved the country, loved the people, his love is sprinkled throughout his works. He exercises a watchful self-scrutiny, living an honest life. His character is adorned by the fortitude, rectitude, braveness and benevolence. He is a national hero, an example of all the people. I am determined to learn from him and do my best to become a man of his kind."

After I finished the tour in Fuzhou city, Mr. Lin suggested me to make a visit to Gulangyu. He introduced me to the general situation of the island. "The island is not far from Fuzhou. It is a small island facing the city of Xiamen, a famous trading port of China. Gulangyu is one of the most attractive national scenic spots due to its natural scenery and its cultural heritage. It has beautiful beaches, winding lanes and mountains, and it is an exceptional example of cultural fusion. There are a great many buildings of various different architectural styles there. After our country lost in the first opium war and signed the Treaty of Nanjing with Britain, Gulangyu was constituted an international settlement on Chinese soil. Thirteen countries, including Great Britain, France, Japan enjoyed extraterritorial privileges and built consulates, churches, hospitals, schools, police stations, museums, and apartments there. That is the reason why so many different architecture styles can be seen throughout the island.

I accepted his suggestion. One day I took a bus to Xiamen, then I rode on a ferry to Gulangyu. Gulangyu means "Drum Waves Island" in Chinese characters. The island got its name because of the sound generated by the ocean waves hitting the reefs was like beating a drum. After got off the ferry, I roamed the beach first. The beach inclined shallowly so that even the children could wade out one hundred

A Painful Reminiscence of a Dignified Soul

meters or more and still the water would be below their knees. The water was clear, the sand was clean, and the air was fresh. From here to look at the vast boundless sea made me feel cheerful and carefree.

Then I stepped on the narrow path. Gulangyu is a pedestrian-only island, where not only cars are banned, but also bicycles. The only vehicles permitted are electric government service vehicles and fire engines. The paths are comparatively quiet. Green leaves made shade everywhere. Pavilions and towers set each other off to advantage. There are thousands of well-preserved architectures of various styles on the island including ancient Chinese architecture, Western style buildings, a Pakistani mosque, and a Roman catholic church. People also call the island as "World Architecture Exhibition".

The most striking scene on the island is Sunlight Rock. Sunlight Rock refers to two huge rocks that lean on each other, with one horizontal and the other vertical. The vertical rock is the highest point on the island, towering up in the air. On the top of Sunlight Rock, there was a small platform from which we could view the whole of Gulangyu island, Xiamen, and many islands around the Gulangyu. It is the best observation point on the island. Sunlight Rock is also the symbol of Gulangyu because our national hero Zheng Chenggong, who recaptured Taiwan from the Netherlands, had stationed and trained his troops in the island.

There are many old and precious pianos on the island, like the gold-plating piano, the oldest upright piano, ancient hand-operation piano, etc. The most important and largest one is the giant pipe organ. The local residents said that their island had only about 20,000 people, but had 5,000 pianos. They called their island "The Island of Pianos" or "The Island of Music". To visit the island is just like browsing the development history of world pianos.

The visit to Gulangyu reminded me of the time when our country was bullied and humiliated by the colonial countries. But I also felt a bit relieved that it has brought up a prosperous and fascinated Gulangyu which attracts the people of the world.

Mr. Lin also told me Fuzhou had many local and special products, so I also toured the market. In the handicraft store and department stores I did see many excellent, local, special products such as cork sculptures, buffalo horn combs, shell carvings, Shoushan stone carvings, lacquerwares, bamboo handicrafts, etc. I liked the Shoushan stone very much. The stone is quarried out from Shoushan mountain in the suburbs of Fuzhou. It is a pure local product; no other places produce it. It has a soft, smooth surface and variegated colors and is an ideal material for carving. There were many wonderful sculptured Buddha statues, incense burners, and figurines in the store. I appreciated them but could not afford to buy the precious things. I only buy a small seal and engrave my name on it.

Another local special product I highly valued was the lacquerwares. Lacquerwares are extremely glossy and handsome. They are objects covered with lacquer. Lacquerwares include decorative screens, vases, tea services, small or large containers, tableware, a variety of small objects carried by people, and larger objects such as furniture painted with lacquer. Their surface is sometimes painted with pictures, inlaid with shell and other materials, or carved.

Once I visited a lacquerware store and the salesman told me, "Lacquerware is the unique product of Fuzhou. It is one of China's three great handcraft treasures, enjoying the equal fame with the cloisonné of Beijing and the porcelain of Jingdezhen. The lacquer arts had won sixteen gold medals in international fairs in Berlin, Paris, and other cities."

He also said that the technology of making lacquerware is very sophisticated. The first step is making a clay or wooden mold, then applying one layer after another of lacquer on it, and finally finish it with polishing, painting, and embellishing. Every product has been through twenty stages in the process. It will take at least fifty days or even one year to finish one piece. It is handicraft, no two pieces are the same size and image. He urged me to buy some. I liked them very much and was amazed by the artistic products, but I could not afford to buy the precious items and only bought a lacquer vase. I also bought two silk umbrellas, one is blue and the other is pink. They are very light and exquisite with beautiful pictures on it and are also Fuzhou special products.

Time was really flying. Before I knew it, three months had nearly passed. Mr. Lin reminded us to prepare for the journey. I was delighted because I would soon be back home and began to pack my luggage. Mr. Lin booked five tickets, one of which was for me. I wanted to pay him back the money. He smiled, patting my shoulder, and said, "You think I cannot afford the money?"

I also smiled shyly and answered, "Thank you then, Uncle Lin."

Before leaving, Mr. Lin took us all to a restaurant to have a farewell dinner. He ordered several special cuisines of Fuzhou, such as pipe-shaped shrimp, lichee meat, and sea clam. All of them are very delicious. Mr. Lin asked us to eat as much as we could, for after leaving Fuzhou we could not taste them again.

A Painful Reminiscence of a Dignified Soul

Mr. Lin asked me if I had ever taken a ride in a sea going steamship. I answered I hadn't. He told me many people who first take a ship ride get seasick. His family had also suffered from seasickness. He introduced some of their experience and lessons to me, "You should have a strong mental state, confidently believing 'I will not get a seasick'. Stay busy and keep your mind occupied so that you would not think of the question. Seasick is very contagious you should avoid other seasick people, never watch them. If you go to the deck, you had better stay in the middle of the ship because it is the place where the motion is least remarkable, not like the bow and stern. In our ordinary life, everything we see like the furniture and walls are still. When a ship is riding, you see everything is moving. Our brain cannot adjust to the environment, so we feel confused and nauseated. The only thing that does not move on a riding ship is the horizon. When you feel bad, you can keep your eyes gazing at the horizon. It will help you restore your internal equilibrium. Avoiding excessive foods and strong food odors and laying down quietly on you back can also help prevent seasickness."

A few days later, we took a taxi to the pier and boarded the ship. After crossing the gangway, we entered the cabin. Two rows of bunk beds pressed up against the walls. We spread our bedding on the bunk, sitting down for a rest and having some drinks. Then I went out to make a tour around the ship, in which there were a lounge, a small shop, a medical clinic, a restaurant, and a dining room. Inside cabins are small, located in the ship's interior, away from the exterior walls. Outside cabins have a porthole.

As the ship was prepared for the voyage, the sailors lifted the anchor. The siren sounded loudly and the water was churned to foam beneath the stern. The ship wavered slightly with a creak, left the pier slowly, and started its journey. Gradually the ship was riding to the deep sea. It was the first time I took a sea voyage, everything was fresh, strange, and curious to me, so I kept sitting on the bench, stretching my legs on the decks, and enjoying the wide scenery.

That morning, the sky was clear and the wind was light, moving and pausing gentle as if with emotion. The sea was perfectly calm like a peaceful lake and its soft murmurs were scarcely audible. The surface was barely a placid ripple. The humming of the waves were comforting and beguiled me. The expanse of blue water was clean and soft, subtle and gentle, extending in every direction. We could not tell where the blue seas ended and the blue skies began, we could only see they were met on a dark blue curve line—the horizon. The warm, briny, odorous air coming from the sea made me feel refreshed. The extensive sea gave rise to many fanciful thoughts to me. Compared with the vast sea, how small are the men and the ship. The ship seemed just like a child's toy in the world and man, a grain of sand on the beach. We must guard from overweening and puff out our chests in our life.

At noon we had a good lunch, the lobster was tender and delicious. In the afternoon we played cards in the cabin. A whole day on the sea was passed quite peacefully and pleasant. In the evening, we went to bed early and the soft wind seemed to hum an eerie lullaby, cradling us to sound sleep soon.

The next morning a strong wind was blowing and pushing the still waters to choppy, the ship tossed from side to side. Darkness prevailed as clouds thickened and the sunlight was blotted out. The rain-soaked deck, lightning was accompanied by peals of thunder. Huge waves rolled across the surface and slapped at the side of the iron-grey ship furiously. As the ship was riding up and down widely, my abdomen began to feel discomfort. Later, there came a bout of vomiting and severe nausea. Mrs. Lin took care of me kindly and went to the medical clinic to fetch some medicine for me. Gradually I felt better and fell asleep.

At last we arrived in Shanghai. After the ship anchored, we disembarked from the ship. The wharf was crowded with people who were waiting there to meet their relatives or friends. My eldest brother and an officer of Shanghai customs were among them. When they saw us, they rushed forward to meet us. We were all excited. My brother talked with Mr. Ling for a few minutes and thanked him immensely for his taking good care of me. I also expressed my gratitude to him for their help. Then we shook hands and said goodbye to each other at parting. Mr. Ling's family and the customs officer got on an office car and went their way. Holding hand in hand, my brother and I walked to a trolley stop and took a trolley to go home. My eldest brother and I had been separated for over seven years. He hadn't changed much, but I had become an adolescent from a child. Both of us felt especially affectionate. He made many inquiries about my life and the journey.

I lived in my eldest brother's home. At that time, as there were so many people returned to Shanghai, the housing problem was very serious. My brother shared a two-story apartment with a colleague. My brother occupied the second floor and the family of his colleague lived on the first floor. On the second floor there were two bedrooms. My brother and his wife made use of one room and their daughter and son lived in the other so there was no room for me. I had to live in the attic.

A Painful Reminiscence of a Dignified Soul

After living there for several months, I found it very uncomfortable. The attic was very low and I could not stand straight. The ladder was narrow and it was very dangerous climbing up and going down. Furthermore, my sister-in-law seemed unhappy for I loaded more of a burden on them economically and spiritually. My other brothers in Shanghai had the same or worse housing problems. They also could not provide me a living place. I felt melancholy. I was brooding and at a loss for what to do. Shall I still stay in the present place and hold my temper in spite of the discrimination of my sister-in-law or shall I leave the home as I had down in Hong Kong? The first choice was not consistent with my character, I have a great sense of self-respect and dignity. The second choice would hurt my brother's feelings and was not safe. I wobbled between the two choices for a long time. Finally, I decided I should keep patience for a while and at the same time try my best to find a job. If I got a job, I had a proper reason to leave my brother's home.

It was difficult to find a job in Shanghai. Shanghai is the biggest city in China, there are a great many knowledgeable and talented persons. In addition, there were so many new people pouring into the city. I was a mere high school graduate, had no working experience or specialty, and could not speak the Shanghai dialect, so my chances of getting work were very slim. Every day I read the advertisement in the newspaper. Wherever they need a clerk, a shop assistant, or a worker, I went there at once to apply for a job, but all my efforts failed. I was despondent and melancholy.

One day I noted that a film studio was recruiting actors and actresses. I was interested in watching films, but I knew I didn't have that talent to be an actor. Spurred by the anxiety of getting a job, I boosted my courage to enter my name there. At first, they gave us a written examination and an oral examination. I passed. The third time they asked us to show our performing talent. They presented us with different situations and asked us to respond to them with our feelings of anger, sorrow, or joy through our facial expressions or body gestures. I hadn't the talent and always showed unsuitable images. I was eliminated.

I continued to seek a job. After countless failures, I got a chance. The Bank of Communication recruited two kinds of office workers: senior clerks and junior clerks. The application qualifications for senior clerk were university graduates. The application qualifications for junior clerk were high school graduates. I took part in the examination for the junior clerk. Unexpectedly and fortunately, I was accepted. We were titled as the exercise pupil(练习生). I finally got a job in November 1946. I was overjoyed with the gain and felt extremely happy I would live on my own soon and no longer discriminated by my sister-in-law.

The bank could not provide the dormitory right away. I did not want to wait and moved from my attic to the office the first day I went to work, I slept on the desk of the office. I could not sleep well at the first night. I had mixed feelings, happy for having a job and living on my own effort and sad for being unable to continue my studies. I thought about some of my classmates who were now studying in universities. I admired and envied them. I also thought of Yang Qingguo. After Japan surrendered, Qingguo restored her connection with her parents and went to Singapore. Before leaving Baihou, she disengaged her betrothal with Xiao. I regretted that I had been trammeled by the stale ethics and hadn't asked her to disengage her betrothal earlier. I had made a great mistake. If I did the right thing in time, I would have an ideal lifelong companion and now I lost her. Lingering on the two miserable thought, I could not help but burst into tears in a torrent.

My work in the bank was not serving the customer behind the counter as a teller. I was assigned to work in the economic research department of the head office of the Bank of Communication. My job was typing or copying the reports or research papers. The work suited me for I could learn some economic knowledge and improve my English through reading and typing those articles. All the leaders and colleagues in my office were researchers. I was only a high school graduate, so I had a grave sense of inferiority. But they were nice and did not disparage me. When I made some mistakes in typing English research reports, they did not blame me but helped me to correct them.

While I was working in the bank, I took part in various kinds of social activities. I wanted to contact more people. As I was deeply persuaded by the communist propaganda in Baihou high school, I had a firm faith in communism. I was eager to find underground communists and participate in the Communist Party. The first activity I took part in was a course of lectures on literature and art set up by The Association of Literary and Art Workers of Shanghai. It was free. About two hundred people took part in it. It gave ten or more lectures by famous writers and artists. In that course I learned some knowledge and made many friends. After the end of the course, I formed a literature research group named "Spark Society", implying "a single spark can start a prairie fire". I invited seven or eight friends to join the society. We held a forum every two weeks discussing famous Chinese or foreign works. We had discussed *The True Story of Ah Q* by Lu Xun, *Camel Xi-*

A Painful Reminiscence of a Dignified Soul

angzi by Lao She, *How is the Steel being Tempered* by Nikolai Ostrovsky, etc. Each time, apart from the discussion of the literary works, we also talked about some social problems, in which I often expressed my belief in communism.

In summer 1947, the university began to recruit new students. I thought I should continue my study. I decided to enter a famous evening university in Shanghai, named The College of Industry and Commerce of China. I chose mechanical engineering as my major. I did not like bank work, I wanted to be an engineer in the future. Our class began on September 1st. From then on, I was really busy. I had to work during the day time, went to college in the evening, and did my homework or reviewed the day's lessons in the deep night.

When the winter vacation came, I attended a dance training class run by a dancer named Dai Ailian, the most famous dancer in China at that time. She taught the folk dances there. Folk dances were very popular in the liberated areas and promoted by the Communist Party. I thought I should learn them and through them to spread the faith in Communist Party among other people. At the dance training class, I recognized a classmate named Zhou Chaohai, who was working in Shanghai railway station. After some time, we became good friends and often exchanged our opinions on the situation of our country. We found that we shared many common ideologies and views and had deep confidence with each other.

One day he invited me to have a dinner at his home. I attended the feast and enjoyed a very nice meal. After dinner, he and I went into the living room where we had a heart-to-heart talk. He told me he and several schoolmates had set up an evening school for workers in 1944. At that time, Shanghai was still under the control of Japan. The life of the worker was extremely poor. A large part of them were illiterates. They decided to help them to learn reading and writing. The school was free without charging tuition from the students and the teachers were volunteers without salary. The name of the school was "Jiguang". This Chinese phrase means, "pool the wisdom of the masses and absorb all useful ideas". Though they were still high school students without teaching experience, they were earnest. One year later, Japan capitulated. The school enlarged and also invited several university students and middle school teachers to teach there. They not only taught knowledge but also gave talks on current events, disseminated democratic ideas, interpreted revolutionary principles, and taught progressive and revolutionary songs. They recommended progressive, revolutionary books and magazines to the students, like *Democracy*, *Mother*, *How is the Steel being Tempered*, *On Coalition Govern-*

ment, etc. and organized them to discuss the contents of the books and air their views. After introducing the situation of the school, Zhou asked me whether I would like to join them and teach in the night school. He said if I was interested in the job, he could introduce me to the school. I thanked him for his concern and promised to tell him my decision in a couple of days.

On my way home, I was extremely excited. I have been hoping to join Communist Party all the time and I finally found a chance today. Though Zhou did not mention a single word of the party, I was sure the evening school had the party's background. If I took the job there, they would certainly mobilize me to join the party sooner or later when they were satisfied with my expression and believed that I was qualified.

But I encountered a problem. I was now studying in an evening college. If I went to work in the workers evening school, I could not continue my studies in the evening college. I was on the horns of a dilemma. I eagerly wanted to learn more knowledge and I was also anxious to take part in the revolution, but I could not do the two things at the same time. I was deeply vexed. After two days of fierce mental conflict, I decided to take part in the revolution first for the following reason. Going to college is for my future, a thing for an individual; taking part in the revolution is for the country. Now we are engaging in a great liberation war, millions of soldiers are risking their lives fighting in the front. I must also do something to speed up the day of liberation. The party's underground work in Shanghai is also very important, it will help to decide the destiny of our nation. I can suspend my studies for a time and make up the whole delayed course in the future. With that decision, I told Zhou I was glad to be a voluntary teacher in the workers evening school.

One evening Zhou took me to the night school and introduced me to the schoolmaster who welcomed me and told me that as all the lessons in the school already had their teachers, he wanted me to teach folk dances after class, comment on current situations to the students, and take part in their discussion meetings. I agreed, recognizing that they did not need any new teacher in reality, they just want to recruit a revolutionary.

I had a great passion for the job. From then on most of my spare time were spent in the workers evening school. I regarded it as a serious revolutionary work. At school I made friends with the workers. They were simple, honest, and eager for learning knowledge. Each evening as soon as they finished their work, they

A Painful Reminiscence of a Dignified Soul

hurriedly came to school, disregarding their tiredness. Folk dance was not a compulsory course, but many students attended the course despite their fatigue.

The first folk dance I taught them was Yangge dance. Yangge means "rice-sprout songs". Yangge dance is a traditional folk dance originally performed in the open air in rural north China. Later it was converted into a symbol of communist art in Yanan and used as a tool to enlarge the party's influence and disseminate the party's ideas. At that time, I had a faith in Communist Party like crazy. I told the students that the Yangge dance was very popular in liberation areas, almost everyone can dance it. I encouraged them to learn it. The dance movement is very simple and easy to learn. It hasn't much artistry but contains great political meaning, so students liked it and danced it enthusiastically. Apart from dance I also taught them the progressive or revolutionary songs, like "Solidarity is Strength", "You are a Beacon", "The Sky of the Liberated Areas", etc. Once I taught them a folk-dance set to music. The music is titled "The Song of Youthfulness". Its movement was very beautiful and graceful and its music was sweet and pleasant to the ear. It was performed by two pair of girls, but male students also liked to dance it. The words of the song are:

> After setting down beneath the mountain
> The sun will rise splendidly again next morning.
> While withering mournfully this year
> Flowers will bloom vigorously again next year.
> A small beautiful bird flies away,
> Disappeared without any trace.
> My youth will never come back
> Just like the small flying away bird.
> My youth will never come back
> Just like the small flying away bird.
> After teaching the dance and song, I made a comment on it.

"While you learn this dance and song, you must grasp the essence of it. It stresses that unlike sun and flowers, once the youth is past, it will never come back. Youth is the prime time of a person's life. This period of time is not long, so while you know your youth will never come back, you must cherish and value your youth, you must make the most of it. Now our country is in a crisis, we need to think how can we help to solve the problem. Every person has a responsibility to his country. Do you think so?"

They agreed with my opinion and expressed they would do their best to make use of their youth to serve the country and the people.

I often had talks with the workers, even invited them to my dormitory or go to the park. During our talk, I would introduce to them some democratic and communist ideals and some situations of the liberated area, which I had heard in Baihou. We also talked about the current affairs, the corruption of the Nationalist Party, the rocketed prices, or their own problems and difficulties. I lent some progressive books or magazines to them, such as the magazines *Democracy*, *Extraction of Articles*, and *Information of the World* and the books like *Public Philosophy*, *Materialist Dialectics*, *Mother*, etc.

In order to extend the influence of the workers school, I also invited my friends in Spark Society to the school, trying to lead them to the revolutionary road. Because of various reasons, some friends declined my invitation politely, some went to the school occasionally, and only one friend was greatly interested in it and went to school together with me every time. She is a graduate of a normal school named Liu Fengqing. I was glad that I had attracted a person to the revolutionary road and I had a good company to go to school.

The evening school also connected its education with the revolutionary activities outside the school. For example, we organized the students to take part in the January 29th student movement in Tongji University and to participate in the May 4th Campfire Party in the Communication University. We also inspired the students to organize their co-workers to fight against the Black Union controlled by the Nationalist Party. In a factory, some students together with their co-workers even successfully overthrew the Black Union and established their own labor union. Whenever and wherever the reactionary Nationalist Party murdered the revolutionaries in Shanghai, our school would mobilize teachers and students to donate and deliver condolence to the family of the martyr. Once our school and other evening schools put on a performance. Our school performed two small self-written and self-directed dramas, *Blood and Flesh, The Elegy of Death*", and the dance "The song of youthfulness", and a Yangge opera *The Brother and the Sister reclaim Wasteland*". This opera was a kind of song-and-dance opera which reflected the life in the liberated areas and corresponded with communist policies. It was first performed in Yanan and Mao Zedong had watched it and highly praised it. The

A Painful Reminiscence of a Dignified Soul

other school also played many heart-stirring programs. Several hundred people watched the performance. They liked the content and form of the production. A few of the spectators were even moved to tears by some items.

Once the teachers and students of our school took part in a great patriotic demonstration organized by the underground party of Shanghai. Thousands of people, including workers, intellectuals, and local residents marched on the streets. We shouted the slogans repeat and repeat along the way: "Anti civil war!", "Anti-hunger!", "Practice democracy!", and so on. We also sang many songs such as the song, "Solidarity is Strength".

>Solidarity is strength,
>Solidarity is strength.
>The strength is iron,
>The strength is steel.
>It is more solid than iron,
>It is stronger than steel.
>Open fires at the fascist dictatorship.
>Destroy all the institutes of non-democracy.
>Send forth shining light with boundless radiance
>Towards brightness,
>Towards freedom,
>Towards new China.

And "The Song of Oddness":

There were few oddness in the past,
There are lots of oddness this year.
Wooden stool climbs up the wall,
Lampwick breaks the iron pot.
Lampwick breaks the iron pot.
Oddness is much. Oddness is much.
Oddness, Oddness, Oddness is much
Walking into the downtown this morning
I saw a dog biting a man.
They only allow the dog barking and barking,
But not permit people to speak with their mouth.

Zhong Da

When we reached the North Sichuan Road, a very busy street in the center of downtown, the garrison department of Shanghai sent mounted troops to assault the demonstration procession. When the horses ran into the procession, the marchers would escape, but the dispersed marchers would soon return to the procession, so the mounted troops could not stop the demonstration. Following the procession, there was a large police car on top of which a machine-gun was mounted. The muzzle of the gun aimed at the marchers but the policemen did not dare to spray gunfire. The demonstration was a great success, widely extending the influence of Communist Party and frightening the reactionary.

One evening I went to the evening school with Liu Fengqing. After the end of their class, I helped the students to rehearse a Yangge opera I taught them last time which they would perform in an evening party very soon. They performed it, but the effect was not good. A student forgot his lines several times. Another failed to express her feelings well and her movement was not right. I reminded them the words and corrected their expression and actions. Fengqing also helped them to improve their play. We rehearsed the Yangge opera again. The result was still not very good. I wanted to close the rehearse, but the students were in high spirits and asked to rehearse once more because they had to perform it in a couple of days. I agreed and helped them better their rehearsal. When we finished the rehearsal, it was already very late. The students' homes were near the school, it did not matter much. But Fengqing and I met great difficulties because there were already no bus and tram then. We had to walk back home and our homes were a great distance. It would take us almost an hour. Now we had a serious problem. At that time, Shanghai was a curfewed city. When we walked near Shanghai railway station, but about one third of the way through our journey, the curfew time started. What shall we do? Continue walking on? We would be arrested. Stay in the open street? It had the same danger. Thinking it over and over again, we had no other choice but to stay at a hotel. We immediately entered the Hailong Hotel nearby, registering a room as husband and wife relations.

It was an awkward situation. She was an unmarried woman; I was an unmarried man. We slept in one room on one bed. The trouble soon came. As the saying goes "Human beings are neither wood nor grass, how can they be free from emotion?" I was twenty-years old; she was nineteen. We were all at the period of adolescence, a period of having strong sexual desire. It was the first time I slept with a woman. On this occasion, I naturally had an immense sex impulse and had an urge to have sex with her. In addition, I was full of curiosity about sex. I eagerly wanted to taste it. I almost could not control myself. At this critical moment, my sexual desire fiercely struggled with ethics. I was considering a question: Am I going to marry her? If I decide to marry her that I have a sex with her before marriage doesn't matter much; if I do not want to marry her, that I have a sex with her now is a serious mistake. It will hurt her physically and be psychologically deadly. Shall I marry her or not? Fengqing is a pretty girl, kind, elegant, and good tempered. I admire her, love her. Yet she has a weakness, she is short. I am short too, only 165cm. If I marry her, our children would be short. They will suffer all their lives. I hesitate. Considering for a long time the benefits of our descendants, I finally decide that we should not get married and let her marry a tall person. After I made that decision, I thought I must not have sex with her and restricted my sex desire.

Restraint of sex impulses is easy to think and to say, but while a beautiful, attractive girl is asleep beside you, it is an extremely difficult job for a young man. All that time the natural sexual impulse always urged me to act. At the same time, my conscience always forced me to check my frenzy. The whole night I was in a drastically sexually excited state and could not sleep a blink. I suffered a great lot, but I was also proud of my will and due to the pure, clean relationship, we are able to remain constant, devoted friends all our lives.

After several months I of working in the evening school, one Sunday the headmaster of the school invited me to his home to have lunch. He was an office worker in the Electric Power Company of Shanghai named Zhang Shanji. After lunch, we had small talk first and then he had a serious talk with me.

He said, "You have been a voluntary teacher in our school for a long time. You worked hard and made great contributions to the school and the students. We thank you very much. You must have guessed that this school is led by the Communist Party. It indeed is. And the party has been observing your work and personality all the time. Now the party organization considered that you are already in conformity with the standard of the party and you are worthy to be a party member. The party wants to know now if you are willing to join the party. What do you think about the matter?"

I was excited. It was the day I had been longing for a long time. Now my wish came true. I replied, "I would like to join the party. Communist party is the vanguard of the proletariat. If I can work within the party, I believed I would do the revolution work more effectively. I urgently hope that China will be liberated as soon as possible."

"I am glad you would like to join the party. You are welcome. Now you should fill out an application form first." He went to his desk and took out an application form and handed it to me. "After you finish it, return it to me."

I thanked him for his concern and returned home.

Very soon, I filled in the application form and handed it back to Shanji. A few days later, he told me that the party organization had already granted my application. He congratulated me that I had been accepted by the party. He told me many party's disciplines and asked me to observe them strictly. He especially stressed the importance of keeping secrets of the party.

He also warned me, "We are doing underground work. A party member's identity is not open. You only know I am a communist and can contact with me only. Every party member has only a single-line link, so that if a communist was arrested and forced to tell the names of the communists to the Nationalist Party, he could only provide one name."

I understood that the rule was necessary and I also felt it very comical. I did not know whether Zhou Chaohai who introduced me to the school was a communist or not, yet I believed he certainly was. Later, I was asked to make an oath to the party in front of Zhang Shanji and the flag of the party. I pledged: "I'll make a lifelong commitment to the cause of communism. Put the party's interest above everything else, abide by the party disciplines, fear no difficulties and always work for the party, work as a role model for ordinary people, preserve the secret of the party, keep faith in the party. Be tenacious and never betray the party." After the pledge, I became a candidate member of the party formally.

One day a friend in my Spark Society named Zhang Hui came to see me. He told me that he had a friend, a professor in Daxia University. His name is Guo Mangxi. He is a member of the Democratic Party of the Workers and Peasants of China. He has enthusiastically promoted democratic ideals and opposed the corrupt Nationalist Party. Though he is not a communist, he has supported the Communist Party firmly and had taken part in the underground revolutionary work. He has helped to transport many youths to the liberated areas. He is also an enthusiastic writer and is now arranging to set up a publishing house to publish his works and his friends' works and revolutionary books. He named it Teacher and Friend Publishing House. As he is short of money, he wanted to find some collaborators.

A Painful Reminiscence of a Dignified Soul

Zhang Hui asked me whether I would like to cooperate with him. I regarded the professor's plan was very useful. We need more valuable and revolutionary publications. I decided to join his work. I did not have much property but I did save some money. I was thrifty and my salary from the bank was very favorable. A year has twelve months, but the bank pays us seventeen months' salary each year. Our bank pays us our salary on the first day of each month. If the prices of goods that month shoot up twenty percent, the bank will compensate the twenty percent money to us on the last day of that month. Due to the preferential treatment of the bank and my thrift, I accumulated some money in the two years and I wanted to spend them in the place of most worth.

I began to participate in the preparatory work of our publishing house soon. Professor Guo was a highly knowledgeable, good-tempered, honest scholar and we were getting along well with each other. I looked for our office and bought a lease authority of a room with 100 grams of gold in Qiujiang Road. The room was beside a high school and near the railway station. It was a favorable location. Unfortunately, not long after our work, a terrible tragedy occurred. Professor Guo was trapped by a special agent of the Nationalist Party and was killed cruelly in Zhabei Park together with six other revolutionaries. Their bodies were destroyed to such a degree that it was impossible to make out their identity. Only by a metal button Guo's wife was able to recognize Guo's body from the obscure corpses. This news greatly shocked me. I was very sad and exasperated and went to see Guo's wife, expressing my condolences and soliciting her to restrain her grief to stay in good health. I pledged to double my effort to avenge her husband's death.

In order to realize Guo's unfulfilled desire, I was determined to continue the work. Considering I was not a writer and scholar, I hadn't any works to publish and I didn't have the ability to arrange a publishing house, I decided not to set up a publishing house but a bookstore. Bookstores can also be used to spread revolutionary ideas. I named it The Daybreak Bookroom, alluding that our country will be liberated soon. I tried my best to search for and buy at wholesale the progressive and revolutionary books, such as *How is the steel being tempered*, *The History of U.S.S.R.*, *The Public Philosophy*, etc. and I sold them at cost. I also put a big advertisement on the famous *Impartiality Daily* (大公报) to solicit friends of the Daybreak Bookroom, trying to recruit more revolutionaries.

At that time, I was only enthusiastic in revolutionary work, but extremely lacked revolutionary experience and vigilance. The name of my bookstore itself and the books we sold exposed my background. Very soon my bookstore was headed by police and I did not know. Fortunately, Zhou Zhaohai, who worked at the railway station near my store, urgently told me that the party got the information that my bookroom had already been under surveillance by the police and instructed me to withdraw at once. I was alarmed and never went to the bookstore again. A few days later, when I visited my eldest brother, my sister-in-law told me that a stranger had come to her house and asked her where I am now living and she did not tell him. I knew I was in a dangerous situation. From then on, I changed my living place all the time.

One day, Fengqing came to my place, asking me to help her to solve a problem. She had a classmate, a bosom friend of hers, who sang very well and was recently enrolled by an art troupe of the army of the Nationalist Party. Now the troupe was preparing to retreat to Taiwan. Fengqing advised her friend not to follow them to Taiwan. All her parents and relatives also advised her not to go, but she insisted on going Taiwan, for she regarded it a great honor to be admitted by the troupe. Fengqing asked me to advise her not to go as an ultimate effort.

I laughed and said. "Her parents and bosom friend cannot prevent her from going, how can a stranger do that job? I haven't the ability."

Fengqing begged me to try again and again. Finally, urged by saving a young girl, I promised to try as a last resort.

A couple of days later, Fengqing carried her friend to my dormitory and introduced me to her. We exchanged a few words of greeting first, then I turned to our main topic, "I heard from Fengqing that you have been accepted by the Nationalist Party's army troupe. I congratulate you on your enrollment wholeheartedly. It is a golden opportunity. It is a highly great honor. I have heard that you will go to Taiwan soon. Is it true?"

"Yes, we will go to Taiwan in a few days," she answered.

"Why your troupe will go to Taiwan? Why will it not stay in Shanghai?"

She did not answer.

I continued, "They are escaping to Taiwan. They cannot stay in mainland any longer. The liberation army has already crossed the Yangtze River, occupied Nanjing—the capital of Nationalist Party, and will liberate all the country soon. The Nationalist Party will have a mere small island—Taiwan. If you go to Taiwan, you will have at most ten million person audience who will enjoy your songs. On the other hand, if you remain here, with your sweet voice and beautiful song, you

A Painful Reminiscence of a Dignified Soul

can similarly be accepted by the art troupe of the Communist Party after Shanghai is liberated. Then you can have five hundred million potential audience—fifty times as much as Taiwan's population. Don't you want to have a large audience? You are enrolled by Nationalist Party was a great honor, but an enrollment of Communist Party will be a greater still honor. Which choice will be better for your future?"

She kept silent for a long time, then answered my question. "What you say seems having some reason, I'll consider it. Thanks!"

I saw her not insisting on going Taiwan and continued my words, "In addition, if you go to Taiwan you will separate with your parents, relatives, and friends. Perhaps you can never see them again. Do you not remember them? Do you not feel sad? Your parents will certainly miss you deeply all the time and have great pain. You don't mind their suffering? In addition, you might never be able to see again your homeland, the place you were given birth, the school you have attended for years. Will you not ache with nostalgia? Your bosom friend Fengqing will think of you always, will you not suffer from yearning for her?"

She looked at Fengqing with a little flush on her face. Fengqing said she agreed with my opinion and advised her to think of it again. She thanked me again and promised to reconsider the matter.

I said. "Don't mention it. You're welcome. It is only my opinion, which might not be correct. You can make your own decision."

They said goodbye to me and left my home.

A couple of days later, Fengqing informed me that she decided not to go to Taiwan. I was glad I saved a girl at that time. But several years later, it became my greatest regret and guilt. She was persecuted cruelly for she had been enrolled by the army troupe of the Nationalist Party. I had not saved her but ruined her. If not for my fault she would have a peaceful, comfortable life in Taiwan.

In the spring of 1949, Shanghai was already on the eve of the liberation. The main underground work of the party was transferred to protect the facilities and factories from the damage by Nationalist Party and to make social investigation, collect intelligence, and draw community maps for the cooperation with the liberation army when they enter and govern Shanghai.

Our school was assigned the work of protecting the factory named the Cigarette Company of China" the biggest cigarette company in our country that owned more than two thousand workers and staffs. When the Liberation Army was close to Shanghai, we set up a team equipped with rifles and entered and garrisoned the factory. Broad masses of workers warmly welcomed us and enthusiastically helped us. Nobody dared to prevent us. We patrolled the factory day and night, kept watch on the leaders of the Black Union and the suspected persons. My job was making propaganda, explaining the party's policies and the disciplines to the workers, and editing and putting up wall newspaper.

The People's Liberation Army were pressing forward nearer and nearer to Shanghai. By the end of May 1949, one morning the Shanghai residents woke up and suddenly found that there were lots of soldiers lying along the roadside or under the roof of the houses. Their horses were tied to the trees. Obviously they were not Nationalist Party's army, for they were wearing nice military uniform. These soldiers only wore simple green army uniform and a cloth cap on which were still clung mud and leaves. The residents were instantly conscious that the Liberation Army already entered the city abruptly. They were shocked by the strict discipline of the army and immediately harbored good feelings toward them. They didn't disturb their sleep. When the soldiers got up, the residents warmly welcomed them, showed their respect to them, and provided water and food to them. The soldiers declined their offer politely. Shanghai was liberated and escaped great destruction. The underground party of Shanghai had played significant function to thwart the plan of destruction of the Nationalist Party. There were also no accidents that happened at the Cigarette Company of China in which we stationed.

On May 28th, 1949, the Shanghai municipal government was formally established and proclaimed that Shanghai was liberated on that day. Shortly afterwards, Shanghai held a Shanghai Metropolis Great Joint Parade of the Army and People. About one million people and the army took part in the parade. First to enter the city were the military vehicles which were preceded by army flag. The car thundered past slowly. Then the horses' hooves was heard, the mounted troops holding sabers passed. Then the soldiers went forward with great strength and vigor. From time to time they sang the song "The Marches of the People's Liberation Army":

> March forward, forward, forward!
> Our troops are marching toward the Sun,
> Step on the soil of our motherland,
> Bear the hope of Chinese nation.
> We are an unconquerable army.

A Painful Reminiscence of a Dignified Soul

We are the armed forces of the people.
....

Following the army were students, workers, residents, and other people. They were simmering with excitement. Some of them held flowers, colored flags, others beat drums and gongs or performed the Yangge waist-drum dance. More people sang revolutionary songs like "The Internationale":

> Arise, the damned of the earth!
> Arise, prisoners of starvation!
> Reason thunders in its volcano,
> This is the eruption of the end.
> Of the past let us make a clean slate.
> Enslaved massed, arise, arise!
> The world is about to change its foundations.
> We have been naughty, we shall be all!
> It is the final conflict,
> Let us unite together, and tomorrow
> The international working class
> Will be the human race!
> It is the final conflict,
> Let us unite together, and tomorrow
> The international working class
> Will be the human race!

They also shouted slogans like "Warmly celebrate the liberation of Shanghai", "Warmly welcome the Liberation Army of China", etc. Many paraders held great red flags and the great pictures of Chairman Mao and the Commander in Chief Zhu De. Among the parade there were also many decorated, colorful cars. The parade marched in a formidable array and lasted more than half a day. The spectators of the parade on both roadside stretched miles long, holding colorful flags, waving hands towards the paraders, or letting off firecrackers to celebrate the liberation of Shanghai. Banners and slogans stretched across the streets. Cheers resounded like rolls of thunder. The whole city was full of jubilation.

Zhong Da

At that time, I was a starry-eyed Mao's worshipper. Of course, I was a fanatic parader in the march. I was excited that our dangerous underground work had yielded triumphant results and felt a bit elated and proud that there was a share of my effort for the emancipation of Shanghai. I shouted slogans aloud till I had a sharp sore throat and lost my voice. Watching the grandeur and magnificent spectacles and the countless paraders and spectators full of excitement and emotion, my eyes could not but well up with tears. This was the second time I was moved to tears by venerating and thanking Mao Zedong.

After the liberation of Shanghai, our working team still stayed at the factory, waiting for the person sent by the government to take over the company.

One afternoon we were chatting in the hall of the factory after lunch. I was sitting in a deep armchair while some workers were playing with their rifles. Suddenly the telephone rang and a worker went there to receive it. He could not understand what the caller said for the caller was a foreigner speaking English. He called me to take the telephone. I got up from the armchair and went to the telephone. The caller wanted to contact a consulate but dialed a wrong number. I told him this is not the consulate and hung up the telephone. While I was talking on the telephone, a worker who was playing with his rifle let his gun go off by accident. The bullet went straight through the center of the back of the armchair on which I had sat. I was aghast by the shot and felt how fortunate I was. If not for the call, the bullet would have exactly pierced my heart. This was the third time I narrowly escaped the death. I thought I might really have a good luck in the future. But who knows it? Whether the Chinese proverb would come true depends on my fate, not on myself. I had to wait and see.

The Liberation Army continued to advance toward the southwest of China. They needed much more volunteers to work in the newly liberated areas. They started a big scale recruitment in Shanghai and set up an organization called The Southwest Working Group. At that time, I was eager to take part in the revolution, so I quit my job at the Bank of Communication and enrolled my name in The Southwest Working Group. My name was among the group on the newspaper.

But before The Southwest Working Group set out, I noticed another advertisement in the newspaper. The Youth Art Institute in Beijing recruited artists. I liked this work better, so I changed my mind and entered my name in the Art Institute. After the examination, they appreciated my dancing and enrolled me. The Youth Art Institute enrolled over eighty people altogether, including some very famous artists and graduates of the art institute. A few days later, we took a train to Beijing. Many of our friends and relatives flocked to the platform of the railway station to see us off. Fengqing also came. She gave me a white sweater she knitted herself as a gift. I accepted it with contradictory feelings. I was glad she gave me a gift but I also felt sorry, for I was not going to have a courtship with her. I thought I did not deserve the gift. The train started, we waved goodbye, and I stared at her till she out of my eyesight.

The train dragged on slowly for many railway tracks had been damaged during the war. Sometimes we had to stay at a place for hours, waiting for the rail ahead to be repaired. The train was crammed full and stuffy. Many passengers were so tired that they lay under the seats or on the baggage rack. To while away the tiresome time, several artists of our group contributed their beautiful songs or cracked jokes. Though we were tired and weary yet still gay. The arduous journey lasted over two days before we finally reached our destination.

We were warmly welcomed by the leaders of the Youth Art Institute at the Beijing railway station. They took us to the headquarters of the institute by bus. The institute is led by the Central Committee of Communist Youth League. It had no big campus, only owned three or four buildings which were former properties of Nationalist Party and were confiscated by Communist Party. The facilities were very simple. We had no beds. Twenty or thirty people slept on the floor in a big room. At that time the party practiced a supply system. It provided us with food, clothes, lodging, and one or two RMB for pocket money without salary. Compared with my former income, it was beyond description. But it was my own choice. I had no complaints.

The institute held a welcome party for us. The secretary of the Central Committee of Communist Youth League Feng Wenbing delivered a welcome speech. He praised our high revolutionary spirit and hoped us to contribute our talents to the development of Communist art and culture. I was recommended by the group members to be its representative to deliver a thank you speech. I felt I did not deserve it and refused. But they insisted, I had to obey. I made a brief speech, thanking the leaders of the Communist Youth League and the Youth Art Institute for their trust and concern, promising that we'll learn from our forerunners earnestly and do our best to serve the people and the Party.

Soon after we arrived in Beijing, the Founding Ceremony of the People's Republic of China was held on October 1st, 1949. On that day, the Tiananmen gate tower was decorated with big red lanterns and colorful banners. Tiananmen Square was filled with hundreds of thousands of cadres, workers, students, soldiers, and civilians. The members of our unit were sitting on the ground by the roadside near Tiananmen gate tower. It is an advantageous location for watching the celebration and the parade. When Chairman Mao and other leaders stepped on the Tiananmen Rostrum, the square resounded with cheers like rolls of thunder. Mao waved his hand to the crowd and walked back and forth across the length of the balcony, extending his blessing to everyone on the square. Peng Zhen, the mayor of Beijing, declared the opening of the celebration. A military band played the Chinese national anthem. Mao pushed the button by himself and the first five-star red flag was gradually raised in the square. In the meantime, the cannons fired twenty-eight times. Chairman Mao solemnly declared. "The Central People's Government of the People's Republic of China has been founded... The Chinese people have stood up". The resonant voice shook the whole square and the crowd went wild, waving their banners and shouting slogans supporting the Communist Party and Mao. The band kept playing "The East is Red", "The Internationale", and "The March of the People's Liberation Army". Then the large-scale military review and mass parade began. The army, navy, and air force troops marched first in full military dress, followed by tanks and cannons. In the wake of the soldiers was the procession of the cheering paraders. The procession was led by the Young Pioneers. They were followed by waves upon waves of workers, peasants, government employees, students, athletic group, literary and art groups and Beijing civilians. Thousands of cadres and workers were carrying huge red flags, giant portraits of Marx, Engels, Lenin, Stalin, Mao Zedong, Sun Yatsen, Zhu De, and large slogan placards: "Celebrate the founding of the People's Republic of China!", "Long live the People's Republic of China!", "Long live the Central People's Government", "Long live of the People's Liberation Army", "Long live Chairman Mao!". Some students and artists played waist drums or Yangge dance. Seeing the magnificent sight, I was so touched that tears welled up in my eyes again. This was the third time I worshiped Mao to tears. In the evening, all the major buildings in the city had been strung with white lights. As Mao and the other leaders reached the Tiananmen rostrum, the fireworks began. The colors of the shooting fireworks were splendid. Thousands upon thousands of colorfully dressed people were performing folk dances in the square. Numerous people held red lanterns and wandered along the streets. The whole city was immersed in an atmosphere of triumph.

A Painful Reminiscence of a Dignified Soul

The Youth Art Institute had three main parts: a drama troupe, an orchestra, and a dancing group. It owned a small theatre in which they performed plays. The first two dramas performed by the drama troupe were *How is the steel being tempered*, a Soviet Union play. *And The Ditch of Dragon's Moustache*, a play written by the famous writer Lao She. The play warmly praised the efficiency of the Communist Party that not long after the liberation of Beijing, the dirtiest ditch in the city was completely cleaned. The orchestra and dancing group often perform music and dance in the theatre or other places. The institute also had a mobile drama troupe. They stayed on a train called the culture train and toured around the country and gave performances wherever they arrived.

The institute also had a task to popularize the mass artistic activities. Our leader asked me to help high schools to set up drama troupes. At that time, most high schools in Beijing were former missionary schools, boy students and female students were separated. I chose four boys' high schools and four girls' schools, established four drama troupes by matching a boy high school with a girl high school, and then sent each troupe two actors of our institute to direct them to perform a drama.

After I stayed in Beijing for some time, my ideology gradually had some change. Before the founding of the People's Republic of China, I had always lived in the area controlled by Nationalist Party. All the things about the Communist Party and the Liberation area I had learned came from my hearing other's speeches and reading of materials. At that time, I had a nearly superstitious belief in the Communist Party and Mao Zedong. Every word Mao said, every action Mao took, I accepted as gospel, as absolute truth, and I believed that everything in the Liberation Area was right and perfect. But when I personally lived in the area controlled by the Communist Party, I could see the real situation of it. I begin to have some doubts and questions in my mind. I found many things I had learned were not true and not all the things happened in the new society were perfect. With the elapse of time, with my growth from a wide-eyed child to a full-fledged youth, I gradually learned to see the reverse as well as the obverse side of everything. I found not all the things the party and Mao Zedong and veteran communists said and did were right. They also have weakness, sometimes they may make mistakes.

For instance, the first play the Youth Art Institute performed was *How is the Steel being Tempered*. The leading male actor of the play was Jin Shan, the vice director of the Youth Art Institute. The leading actress was Zhang Ruifang, one of the most famous players. She was also Jin Shan's wife. The director of the play was Sun Weishi, an adopted daughter of premier Zhou Enlai and a graduate of Soviet Art Institute. During the period of their rehearsal, Jin Shan had a courtship with Sun Weishi and divorced his wife Zhang Ruifang. Jin Shan was a veteran communist, Sun Weishi was once Mao Zedong's interpreter. Their actions left me with a very bad impression. I hate the people who reject the old and crave for the new. (Sixteen years later I also had some sympathy for Sun Weishi, for she was cruelly persecuted to death by Mao Zedong's wife Jiang Qing during the Cultural Revolution. Jiang Qing hated Sun Weishi for Sun had once been Mao's favorite.)

Another instance, at that time the orchestra of the Youth Art Institute went to the Middle-South Sea, the office of the Central Committee of the Communist Party, to play the accompaniment for the dance of the leaders every weekend. I, as the head of the dance group, was eligible to follow the orchestra to go there, but I never went. The party always promoted folk dancing and opposed ballroom dancing. In response to the party's call, I taught the folk dances to the workers of the evening school in Shanghai. Now the party leader Mao was addicted to the ballroom dancing. I found it difficult to understand such a thing. After liberation, all ballrooms were prohibited throughout the country, but there is still a ballroom in Middle-South Sea, the one and the only ballroom in the People's Republic of China. All the offices, factories, schools, universities, etc. were forbidden to organize the dancing party. All the people were forbidden to dance a waltz or tango. But the proletariat leader and his girls can dance a waltz or tango in the office of the Party Central Committee. Isn't it a ridiculous, shameful thing? Who can explain the reasons? I was only a mere new candidate of communist, I had no right to forbid Mao to play the dance but I opposed it. I protested it through my action and never went to that ballroom. This was the first time I had suspicions about Mao and the party. Yet on the whole, I still believed the communist ideal at that time. Dancing, after all, is a trifling matter of everyday life, I still remained in my faith in the Communist Party and Chairman Mao.

In March 1950, the party launched a nationwide campaign to suppress counterrevolutionaries. The government issued a directive on elimination on bandits and establishment of revolutionary new order, ordered the public security department to list all the Nationalist Party members, and stressed that whoever was opposing the rule of Communist Party must be heavily suppressed and punished. Numerous former Nationalist Party members were forced to register and identify

A Painful Reminiscence of a Dignified Soul

themselves to the public security department. In the initial period, the provincial cadres were comparatively cautious, but their work was criticized for being too soft by Chairman Mao who called for harsher measures. In Oct. 1950 Mao issued a new directive titled the Double-ten Directive, initiating a large-scale suppression. Mao stressed "massive arrests, massive killings were extremely necessary... only when this thing is properly completed can our power be secure... Cases of execution should be publicized by the newspapers to inform the masses.... Many places don't dare to kill counterrevolutionaries on a grand scale with big publicity. This situation must be changed."

Afterwards, most sentencing and execution were carried in rallies and people were forced to attend the rally to watch the terror scene. Liu Shaoqi opposed it for it would have a bad influence in the masses. Mao insisted on his opinion that, "the power base of the former landlords and Nationalist Party officials had not been broken as a result of leniency and that further executions are a necessary step. If we are irresolute and tolerant to this evil, we will alienate the people" He issued an order after another berating the local official's leniency and urged them to kill more. On January 21, 1951, Mao sent a telegram to Shanghai: "In a big city like Shanghai, probably it will take one to two thousand executions during this year."

A day later, Mao told the leader of Guangdong Province. "It is very good that you have already killed more than 3,700. Another three to four thousand should be killed. The target for this year's executions may be eight or nine thousand."

Insensitive to human loss, he nonchalantly handed down killing quotas in accordance with populations in the campaign. Mao argued that "the hard-mouthed counterrevolutionaries counted for less than one percent of the population in all regions, and that roughly 0.1 percent of the population would have to be executed in order to get rid of the worst counter-revolutionary elements."

In reality, many provinces did not have enough counterrevolutionaries. To meet the quota, many people were arrested recklessly based on assumptions and many cases were decided without thorough examination. The charges were lack of concrete criteria and many people were executed simply because of association with the former Nationalist Party government. The mass executions paved the way for a subsequent series campaigns and led to the implementation of quotas in campaigns. According to a document of the Communist Party for inside circulation, more than two million counterrevolutionaries were killed or in custody, with 712,000 executed, 1.29 million imprisoned, and 1.2 million placed under surveillance and control. Usually the official statistics are lower than the real number. The actual number of the victims must be larger than the published one. Most of the executed were the former Nationalist Party personnel, then the former employees of western companies, intellectuals whose loyalty was suspected. Some of the accused counterrevolutionaries were falsely labeled because of local disputes and many local officials used the campaign to rid themselves of political rivals.

I was quite surprised and wondered why should so many former Nationalist Party personnel be persecuted or killed? If they took any action to oppose the new government, you could condemn them as counterrevolutionaries. If they did not commit any crime now, even though they had opposed Communist Party in the past, they should not be punished or killed. In the past, the Communist Party always propagandized that they would forgive people's past misdeeds. In the "Three main rules of discipline and eight points for attention" of the People's Liberation Army, there is also an item: "offering good treatment to the captives". Obviously, the party's actions in this campaign did not match its past words. I did not deem party's action was right. But despite my different opinions, I did not air my views. Otherwise I would certainly be criticized to have sympathy with the enemy.

On June 25, 1950 the North Korean People's Army crossed 38 degrees north latitude on the Korean Peninsula, which serves as the military demarcation line between North and South Korea and started the civil war. The North Korean Army soon occupied almost all the territory of South Korea. Then the United Nations Army led by United State of America landed the south Korea and repulsed the North Korea Army to North Korea. At the request of the leader of North Korea Kim Il-Sung General, China sent its volunteer forces to Korea on Oct. 19th 1950. I had some doubts about the correctness of sending the volunteer to North Korea because I knew it was the North Korean People's Army that invaded South Korea first. Should we support and help an invader? But as North Korea was a member of communist camp, I could not oppose our Party's decision.

After the founding of the new China, the whole government was clean and was appreciated and supported by the broad masses, but there were a few officials who first came to the big cities from the countryside and could not resist the temptation and became corrupt. They began to take bribes or embezzle public funds. They endowed favors on their families, relatives, or friends and often held extravagant banquets at the expense of the state. These affairs defamed the image of the Party and greatly hurt the national economy, which was short of funds for the reconstruction of the country. The Party was alerted and launched a Three Antis Campaign throughout the country in 1951. The three antis were corruption, waste, and bureaucracy. The targets of the Three Antis were corrupted Communist party members, the wide circles of bureaucratic officials, and the managers of factories and mines who had some wrongdoings. But in fact, every cadre was examined.

During the "Three Antis campaign", while many corrupt officers were exposed, many bribers were still uncovered. Most bribers were capitalists, the factory owners or the shopkeepers. So soon after the Three Antis Campaign was going on, the Party launched another Five Antis Campaign. The five targets were bribery, theft of state property, tax evasion, cheating on government contracts, and stealing state economic information. Through this campaign large numbers of capitalists, industrialists, and businessmen were found to commit one or more of those crimes or wrongdoings. They were punished by fines or being sent to prison. After the two campaigns, corruption was sharply reduced and governments of all levels were kept clean for a few years.

Needless to say, the aim of getting rid of all those crimes and wrongdoings is quite right. It can increase national revenues, curb corruption and raise working efficiency. I supported the two campaigns. Yet I did not like the method they practiced. in my opinion, all the work and try should be conducted through normal, legitimate, judicial process. But the campaigns proceeded with the form of large-scale mass movement. Worker's parade was held, loudspeakers were set up at streets, putting immense psychological pressure on individuals. Everyone must pass a test. Many party cadres, business leaders, factory owners, and capitalists were forced to undergo public denunciation sessions and were often humiliated and tortured. Many "activers" made a random guess or even fabricated facts and in many cases the leaders of the campaign did not make a strict, thorough investigation and made convictions lightly. Many confessions were false and made under great pressure. For example, a company owner originally over-confessed by claiming to have illegally obtained fifty million RMB. His employees continued to criticize the owner for greater crimes until he confessed to having obtained two billion RMB.

As he did in the former campaign, Mao also set quotas for the present ones, saying that "We must probably execute 10,000 to several tens of thousands of embezzlers nationwide before we can solve the problem." He justified his tough line in a broadcast: "We definitely have no benevolent policies towards the reactionaries or the counterrevolutionary activities of the reactionary classes. Our benevolent policy does not apply to such deed or such persons, who are outside the ranks of the people; it applies only to the people." During the campaign, many people were unjustly, falsely, or wrongly charged or sentenced. About 200,000 accused committed suicide and they had to kill themselves at home or jump from buildings to the street, because if their bodies could not be found, their families would be tortured about their whereabouts.

The Youth Art Institute also unfolded the Three Antis Campaign. All staff were examined, including myself. I had once been assigned to go to Shanghai to buy stage settings. Some people, who were usually eager to search for the counterrevolutionaries, claimed that I must have embezzle money and forced me to confess my guilt. I did not say much, just asked them make thorough investigation. All the account of the items I bought were very clear. They may have even gone to Shanghai to check the receipts. All their investigation proved my word up to the hilt. I passed the examination.

After the check of corruption, we began to examine waste and bureaucracy. Every cadres made a self-criticism: how they abused their position; how they alienated themselves off from the masses; how they infracted the rules. Many professed that they had used office telephone to make personal calls and used office letterhead paper to write their own letters. They promised that afterwards they would strictly separate public properties from private things and never use people's money for their own purpose. We not only made self-criticism but also criticized each other. I was very naive then. I once at a meeting face to face criticized the director of our institute, who was also the vice secretary of the Central Committee of the Youth league, that he had ridden a public car to visit North-Sea Park on a Sunday. Fortunately, I did not get revenge from him and he even patted my head after meeting and called me "little devil" - an endearing address to a young revolutionary. I highly respected him. He was a very enlightened communist. His name is Liao Chengzhi, the son of Liao Zhongkai, a close friend and assistant of Sun Yatsen. After Mao Zedong's death, Liao was recommended to be the Chairman of the PRC. But unfortunately, before the election of the People's Congress, Liao died of disease.

While the Party and the government were doing large scale work in the political and economic domain, they were also doing a lot of work in the ideological field. In September 1951, the party called for the intellectuals to reform their thought, demanded them to arm themselves with the thought of Marxism-Leninism and Mao Zedong thought, and throw away the vulgar perspectives of individualism, liberalism, and the thought of the reactionary bourgeoisie. The movement-imposed doctrines on the intellectuals, made ideological purges of them, and required them to remold themselves according to communist ideology and become new socialist men with new minds, new ideas, new emotions, new attitudes, and absolutely obey the lead of the Communist Party. Every Saturday afternoon a meeting for "thought examination" was held for all the intellectuals. At the meeting, everyone had both to criticize themselves for incorrect thoughts and be subjected to the criticism of others. Everyone was asked to "lay one's heart bare to the party", telling the party all one's social relations, innermost thoughts including the ugly, mistaken ideas without concealment. Everyone's detailed background was compiled into a file. The dossier was kept by the personnel management of one's unit. Any new report was written by one's boss and added into one's file. No one was allowed to read his own file.

This campaign was quite a new thing to me and many ideas were quite different from what I had learned in the past. In the past I learned "Don't talk about one's merits; Don't talk about another's weak point" and now we should criticize others in public. Many things which I deemed to be correct were now regarded as wrong. For example, if a man has an aspiration to become a great writer or scientist in the future, we praise him for having a lofty ideal, a determination, a strong will and now he would be criticized for he held individualism or individualistic heroism because the party and Mao always stress that everyone should regard himself as a screw of a machine, a tool of the party. Again, I always think everyone should be outspoken, call a spade a spade. But now such a person would be criticized for he held liberalism or violated the party's discipline. In my childhood and youth, I was taught that snitching on one person to someone else was a base behavior. If anyone has done something wrong, we should leave it to be corrected by himself by his senses, reasons and his conscience. Now the party promotes it, asking everyone to report to the party what he sees or hears of others. I was really confused. I could not judge what idea is wrong, what idea is right at that time. But even though I was in a puzzle, I refrained from telling others' things to the party, and I did deeply despite a certain "comrade", who enthusiastically monitored everyone's "wrongdoings", like a cormorant coolly scanning the fish, and reported them to the Party secretary almost every day. He might think he was close to the party. I did not think so. I believed he was just licking leader's boots for his promotion.

At the thought examination meetings, I learned many new derogatory titles of wrongdoings such as individualism, individualistic heroism, liberalism, covetousness for fame and position, petty bourgeois sentiment, absolute egalitarianism, lack of the sense of organization. etc. "The sense of organization" means one must have absolute faith in the Party organization, reporting to and depending on the party organization all your things. With so many derogatory titles, everyone could easily label oneself or others as wrongdoer or evildoer or class enemies at every meeting.

During the 'Thought Reform Campaign", I reported all my thoughts and history to the party in details And because I was still young and my history was simple, I passed the examination without much trouble. The only thing they suspect was I had set up the Literature Research Group "Spark Society". The Party sent a cadre to Shanghai to investigate. He found that all I had done were good things and the problem was passed. I was severely criticized for two main faults: First, "Lack of the sense of organization". I had few communications with the party organization, rarely reported my thoughts, and never informed others' "wrongdoing" or "wrong thoughts" to the party organization; Second, "don't attach importance to political studies". After the founding of the People's Republic of China, I thought our greatest political work had been done, the revolution had completed. The regular political work should be done only by political workers. All other people should concentrate their energy to do the work of their own field, so I spent most of my time in reading scholastic books and learning the Russian language. But the party asked us to study Marxism-Leninism, Mao Zedong, and the policies of the party every day. I was not accustomed to it. The Party demanded all intellectuals to be both "red and expert". Red means "perfect in politics" and "absolute obedience to the party". If an intellectual devoted himself single-mindedly to his professions and book learning and paid less attention to political study, they were denounced as "only expert without red" or "white". I was classified among the "white".

During the "Thought Reform Campaign", many school curriculums were restructured. Science and engineering adopted the Soviet models. Some social sciences like sociology and political science were regarded as "pseudo bourgeoisie science" and were abolished. Intellectuals who studied overseas were forced to confess to their role as "implementers of the imperialist cultural invasion". Writers and artists were organized to study Mao's speech "Talk at Yanan Forum on Literature and Arts" and were ordered that their works must serve politics and mainly describe and express the lives of workers, peasants, and soldiers. Many famous writers, philosophers, architects, and scientists proclaimed that they had made great mistakes in the past and felt guilt and remorse. For example, mathematician Hua Logeng, who had got the employment contract of tenured professor at Illinois University, abandoned the preferential treatment and returned to serve the native land, but was tormented almost to death by suicide. Shen Congwen, the master in literature and the professor of Beijing University, attempted to commit suicide but failed. He was removed from the job of professor and worked at the history museum to record and maintain the relics. Mao Yisheng, my cousin and the designer of the first great modern bridge in China, was forced to make a self-criticism. He said, "So far I had always been serving for the reactionary ruling class. I was an exploiter," "In fact, the construction project of the great bridge of the Qiantang Bridge were full of the blood and sweat of the working people, but only I got the fame for it," "I had the two special properties of the intellectuals: self-centered and self-important," "I had thirteen faults: individualism, liberalism, factionalism, heroism, bureaucratism..." Even this self-criticism did not satisfy the party. The newspaper *Light Daily* pointed out that he did not dig out his ideological root. He wrote another self-criticism, admitting that he had been chasing fame and position wholeheartedly for thirty years as one day. He was the tool utilized by the reactionaries of the Nationalist Party. Only by demeaning himself to such a degree was he able to go through the pass. The most famous writer Guo Moruo announced that all the poems, articles, and books he had written in the past were all bourgeoisie works and should all be burned up.

Mao put the intellectuals in the bourgeois camp, writing "Intellectuals are unstable, swinging in the wind. They read a lot of books, but they are ignorant of real life." The intellectuals were grilled by the thought reform week after week, month after month, forced to produce endless self-criticism. In short, the entire intellectuals were enfolded in a world of fear with a mind of depression. The traditional character of Chinese people has deteriorated into one of submission to order. Many people found that their character had more or less twisted. Those who had originally been talkative and optimistic now became taciturn and cunning.

By the end of 1951, the Ministry of Culture organized a visiting delegation to go to North Korea to convey sympathy and appreciation of the people to the volunteer army. Apart from an artistic troupe, the Ministry of Culture demanded each literature and art organization in Beijing to send a representative to the delegation.

Zhong Da

The Youth Art Institute designated me as the representative to join the delegation. The delegation had many famous actors of Beijing Opera, actors of the Local Opera, comic dialogue and musicians. The most famous dancer Dai Ailian also join the delegation. I believed that the voluntary army would surely be excited to see them. We first took a train to Shenyang, the capital of Liaoning Province. Then we went to Dandong, a city opposite to North Korea, separated by the Yalu River. There were thousands of soldiers who were sick, wounded, and the demobilized. We first visited the wounded and the sick in hospital. All of them looked pallid and haggard. Some were still groaning agonizingly on bed. This miserable sight reminded me how cruel the war was.

We held a great meeting to receive all the soldiers there. The delegation asked me to deliver a speech before the performance of the troupe. I highly thanked and appreciated them and wished them a happy and healthy life. According to the original plan, we should go to the front line in North Korea, but the authorities there informed us that they had difficulties to receive us, so we did not cross the Yalu river and returned to Beijing.

This tour was also redolent me of one of my former students in the evening school in Shanghai—a very pretty young girl with an attractive name 杜鹃, which means "azalea". She joined the people's liberation army after the liberation of Shanghai. During the Korean War, she was sent to the volunteer army. She fought bravely in Korea and unfortunately sacrificed her life there. Her slim, lively figure always lingered in my mind. Was it worth it for her death in that war? Should our country make such great sacrifice for the General Kim Il Sung of North Korea? I doubted it. I hated war.

Also in 1951, the North korea sent an military delegation to visit China accompanying them was a song and dance troupe. The government appointed the Youth Art Institute to arrange the reception work of the troupe and the institute assigned me to do the job. I formed a small reception team to arrange their board, lodging, and performance. They were warmly and carefully received. Through the interpreter I often had talks with them, asking them what they wanted and needed. We led them to visit some famous scenic sites of Beijing. We also introduced each other country's affairs and situations. They highly respect their leader Kim Il Sung and eagerly taught me to sing the song "Song of General Kim Il Sung". For politeness, I leant it honestly, perfectly, and often sang it to please them, though I do not know a single Korean word. We organized two performances for them at an open-air theatre in

A Painful Reminiscence of a Dignified Soul

Zhongshan Park for it had a seating capacity of five thousand people. Their performance was excellent. Their songs had a quick, lively rhythm. Their dance actions were bold and unconstrained. Most of the audience had never seen a foreign performance. They enjoyed and praised their art highly and often clapped their hands enthusiastically. The actors and actresses were joyous for their success.

During the period, we formed a nice relationship. After their performance in Beijing was finished, they went to other cities to give their performance. Before leaving, they all signed their name in my album. One of the singers named 朴仁锡 (Piao Renxi) even wrote a letter to me after they left Beijing. She was beautiful, sang very well, and was very friendly with me. I might have courted her if there wasn't the ban that a Chinese was not allowed to marry a foreigner at that time.

I was also very thrifty in spending public funds. The government appropriated 20,000 RMB at the disposal of the team, but I only spent a little more than 5,000 RMB and the guests were quite satisfied with my reception. On the contrary, the reception term of the military delegation had got 100,000 RMB budget and they used them all and asked for some additional budget. I criticized them to be too extravagant at the summing-up meeting.

In 1952, the Party organized many Central Land Reform Working Groups to take part in land reform. The Youth Art Institute sent me and a musician to join one of the working groups. Our working group was to go to Hunan Province. Our group was divided into six teams. I was in the sixth team. Our team had about thirty persons. All were intellectuals, including eight professors, one leading priest of Christianity, and one leading priest of Islam. The others were doctors and teaches. Our team leader was Cheng Minde, the director of the mathematics department of Beijing University. I was appointed to be the vice team leader. I was horrified. I was only twenty-four years old. Most team members were much older than I and were highly qualified intellectuals, how could I be a vice team leader? But I had to obey. The only reason for my appointment, I guessed, was because of my party membership. The party wanted me to display the function for the party. Not knowing how to do that job, I decided I just did the servant's work for the elders and let professor Cheng do all the leading work. Though our title was "land reform working group", I knew we need not do the actual work. In fact, we were sent to the countryside to transform ideology through observing the land reform.

We first took a train to Changsha, the capital of Hunan Province. The leaders of Hunan province gave us a warm welcome, providing us excellent board and lodging. The next day a leader of the province delivered a report to us on the situation of the land reform of the province. He said after two years of land reform, this work had basically completed, only last few villages were to be reformed this year. He also explained the policy of land reform. The provincial leader also took us to visit the Hunan University and the Xiangya Medical College. Xiangya and Xiehe hospital in Beijing are the most famous hospital built by America.

The next day we took a bus to Changde county. The leaders of Changde County also gave us a warm welcome. Then they sent us to a village named Xiaowupu. The village head arranged for us to live and eat with the peasants. I lived in the house of a middle peasant who had a son and a daughter-in law. His son was a militia. They were kind to me. There was already a local land reform working team there. They welcomed us. We will not work separated from them, but coordinated with them and was led by them. They first held a meeting with us, introducing the procedure of the land reform.

The leader of the working team told us, "First, we will hold a meeting of all the peasants in the village, proclaiming the beginning and the aim of the land reform. Then we will divide all the families into five categories: 1, Landlords who possess large lands and perform no manual labor; 2, Rich peasants who own land and work on it themselves while still hire other workers or rent some land to others; 3, Middle peasants who own land and work on it themselves without exploiting others; 4, Poor peasants who has very little land and farm implement and have to rent land from others; 5, laborers who occupy no land and have to live on meager wages or loans. After that we'll go deep among the masses, eat, live and labor together with the poor peasants, which we call taking the root on the masses. We'll encourage the poor peasants to rise up to struggle against the landlords, and asked them to link up and exchange information and ideas with each other. Then we'll hold 'Speak Bitterness Sessions', letting poor peasants accuse the landlords and hold the struggle meetings against the landlords; finally, we'll order the landlord to hand over their land and farm implements and movable properties, which will be distributed to the poor peasants and laborers."

One evening a local cadre led me to visit a poor peasant. He asked the whole family get together around an oil lamp, then he told the family, "There is good news for you. Thanks for the concern of Chairman Mao, the land reform will be launching very soon. Will you welcome it?"

"Of course, we welcome it," an old peasant answered.

A Painful Reminiscence of a Dignified Soul

The cadre asked him again, "Do you know why you are so poor?"

"It's my fate. It's predestined."

"No, it's not true. It's because you are being exploited by the landlord. You work hard year-round and then you have to hand over a large part of your crops to the landlord. On the other hand, they do not do any work but eat rich delicious food, wear silks, satins and woolly coats, live in splendid houses, and own servants and concubines. All those things they enjoy are grabbed from you. They overworked you and abused you. They often beat you, forced you to pay exorbitant rents, or jailed you for debt. That's why you peasants are so poor."

The peasant kept silent. He did not know how to reply.

In order to pursue him, the cadre used a story from a novel, "There was a landlord, who, in order to get the peasants to start working earlier, sneaked into his chicken coop and imitated the crow of a rooster in the wee hours of the morning. The sleeping cocks were awoken and started crowing too. Then the landlord knocked on the door of the peasants' lodgings and shouted, 'Get up, Get up! The cocks are crowing. Why you are still sleeping in bed? You lazy bones!' The peasants had neither a watch or a clock and had to drag themselves out to the field and started their long workday under the stars. You see, how wicked is the landlords! You had really lived in deep waters and burning fires of the old society. It was a hell for you poor peasants. Now you are liberated, you must rise up to knock down the landlords."

"Yes, yes, the landlords are really cruel," The peasant agreed reluctantly.

I did not say anything. The cadre was satisfied and we returned home.

The members of the Central Land Reform Group were not assigned to do any concrete work, just followed the local cadres to visit the peasants and took part in the meetings or struggle sessions. But I, as a member of Communist Party, was requested to do some job. Once I was asked to admonish a landlord to admit his guilt and act honestly. The landlord was a young man in twenties. He had a mother and a wife. I went to his home and advised him to confess his crimes sincerely and hand over his movable properties frankly. He promised to do what I advised him to do, but his mother made a request. She said, "You can label me as a landlord, but my son should not be labeled as a landlord. He should be categorized as the son of a landlord."

She explained that the young man's father died only a short time ago and he never received any rent. I could not answer her request and told her the question must be decided by the land reform working team. Later I did tell the team leader that if what the woman said is true, I agreed with her opinion. But the team still labeled the young man and his mother as landlords.

My other job was to lead a small team to arrest a landlord who lived in Changde county downtown. One evening I and six militias walked downtown. Each militant was equipped with a rifle. The landlord's house was in the main street of the downtown. Its front door was facing the street. Its back door was leading to the riverside. I asked two militias to guard the front door, two militias to guard the back door, I and two militias were going into the house to arrest the landlord. We knocked on the door. No answer. We knocked again and again. Still no answer. We kicked the door open and burst into the house. There was no creature inside. We searched every corner carefully but couldn't find any person. I judged that he must have escaped and we could not find where he hid. I decided to return to the village. After the land reform, I congratulated myself that I hadn't caught the landlord. If he did not escape, we arrested him, and later he was executed, I would be a murderer and I would regret all my life. He was a businessman then, even though he owned a great deal of land, there wasn't any warrant for his execution.

The first struggle session in our village was held on the threshing ground, which was surrounded by dilapidated huts with wooden framed window and gray roof tiles. The landlords were made to stand facing large crowds, waist bending, hands behind their backs. A heavy placard was hung on each landlord's neck that made them into an awkward position. Some poor peasants poured out their grievances and hates against the landlords. The crowds shouted slogans and brandished their fists or farm tools in the air. Among all the shouting a poor peasant rushed fiercely toward an old landlord, who was the main target to be struggled that day. The poor peasant forced the landlord kneel on the ground. Then he turned over to the peasants, waving a cane with blood clot on it and a white shirt stained with red blood and exclaimed, "Comrade, this shirt and cane are the proof of the guilt of the landlord. Once I borrowed some money from the landlord. Later he demanded me to repay the debt but I had no money. He used the cane beat me fiercely again and again, so that I was seriously wounded. How cruel is the landlord! Can we spare his terrible crime?"

"No! No! We can't spare the crime!"

"We must punish him severely."

"We must criticize and annihilate this criminal!" The peasants shouted in unison.

A Painful Reminiscence of a Dignified Soul

Among the roar of the crowd, the poor peasant smacked the left face of the landlord with his right hand and then slapped his right face with his left hand and repeated again and again.

"Whack! Whack!" the crowd shouted.

The incessant loud, angry bellowing terribly frightened the landlords. All the landlords admitted the crimes the peasants accused them. Yet, I noticed though many people yelled loudly, they hadn't any expression. Some lowered their heads and did not look at the scene. Some even seemed to loathe all the sight.

After a long time, relentless struggle, the leader of the session finally declared, "Today's meeting is a great success. We have heavily punctured the enemy's arrogance and highly boosted the people's morale. We will continue to condemn our enemies later and today's meeting is ended here."

Later there were many "struggle sessions", during which the landlords were subjected to interrogations, accusations, and harangues from the peasants who had previously been exploited or mistreated by the landlords. All peasants had to attend these sessions, which were always ended with acts of violence such as slapping, kicking, beating them with farm implements, hanging them up by their wrists or feet from the tree, or other tortures of more ghastly kinds. We from Beijing usually objected violence but local cadres considered it necessary. They argued that Mao's policy is "Violence is justified and necessary in land reform movement". They regarded that violence were legitimate acts for revenge by the downtrodden. They thought that in order to raise the peasants' consciousness, enticing them to participate in the land reform without the fear of repercussions from the restoration of the old regime, violence was unavoidable. Where there was no violence, local cadres were accused of "far too polite", "far too lenient" and was ordered to have no mercy to the landlords. The dissidents, who thought that the present method turned the traditional social system upside down and advocated "peaceful land reform" were fiercely criticized. They were even to be accused of obstructing the land reform. Being afraid of making mistakes, we kept silent without airing our views.

In fact, the poor peasants hadn't much interest in criticizing and accusing the landlords. They were eager to obtain the landlord's properties. They knew all of the landlord's land and farm implements which could not be hidden. What they did not know was the landlord's movable properties, money, gold, silver, pearls, jewels, etc. They were anxious to force landlords to hand over their moving properties and reveal the place where they hid them.

In a struggle meeting, the poor peasants asked a young widow landlord to tell them where she had hidden her treasures. The young widow said, "I haven't hidden any treasures, I haven't any more treasures, I have already handed over all my things."

The crowd shouted, "You are lying! You are lying! In the past you always wore jewels. You were always dressed richly. You must have hidden something. Tell us where you hid them."

Some peasants around her forced her to kneel down and slapped her face.

The young widow cried and pleaded, "I have handed over all my jewels and valuable things. I haven't left anything at home. Indeed!"

"You liar! You liar! Confess! confess quickly! Tell us where you hid your things," The peasants howled and slapped her face.

The young widow repeated and repeated again that she had left nothing at home. But the peasants did not believe her and whipped her with farm tools more and more fiercely. The young widow screamed loud and loud desperately. At last she could not bear the sharp pain and gave in. She led the peasants to her backyard, where they dug out some of her beautiful wedding suits, wedding ring, wedding bedding, and some cheap jewels. The poor peasants were satisfied and carried all the things away triumphantly, scolding the widow again for she had told lies and leaving her alone at home. All the things they grasped, it seemed to me, were not worth much money, but were very, very dear and precious to the widow. Losing a dear young husband was already a very unfortunate, painful thing for her, now the only mementos were also being grabbed away. What excruciating pain and sorrow would she feel? I didn't think the peasants should confiscate them, but I did not raise my opinion. I had to save my skin.

In another struggle meeting, the poor peasants whipped a landlord, asking him to reveal the hiding place. The landlord said he hadn't hidden anything. The poor peasants whipped him fiercely, yet the landlord insisted that he hadn't hidden anything. Two or three peasants discussed how to deal with the stubborn landlord. A peasant suggested that "We can use thorn to beat him. Thorn has many short prickles, which can hurt the fresh only and cannot hurt the bone. It cannot beat a man to death." They found it a good idea and went to the wild to pick rough shrubs. They wielded the thorns on the landlord's naked back. With each whipping, some prickly shoots stung into his flesh, the landlord uttered a heart-rending cry. The peasants whipped again and again and the heart-rending cry repeated again and again. yet the landlord still insisted that he hadn't hidden anything. The peasants could do nothing about it but escort the landlord back to the makeshift jail. I did not know whether the landlord really hadn't hidden anything or he had an extraordinarily strong will that he would rather bear the pain than reveal his hiding place.

We stayed in the village for three months. According to the original plan we should go back to Beijing, though the work of the land reform still hadn't completely finished then. Before leaving, our team held a summing-up meeting. in which everyone expressed that he(she) had got deep education of class struggle, but what one really felt, nobody would ever know. I myself was telling a lie too. I had a great doubt about the method of the land reform. Dividing the land to the poor peasants, I think, is right. Sun YatSen also promotes "equalize the land ownership". But it should take a peaceful procedure, the present method is barbarous.

The government of Changde county held a send-off gathering for us and our group leader thanked their care and help. Then we started our journey to return to Beijing.

From 1953 our country began to carry out the First Five-Year Plan. But the distribution of the budget, in my opinion, had some problems. For example, during the period of the First Five-Year Plan the spending on the military, plus arms-related industries took up sixty-one percent of the budget while spending on education, health, and culture combined was a miserable 8.2 percent. Even Stalin criticized our First Five-Year Plan: "This is a very unbalanced ratio. Even during wartime, we didn't have such high military expenses." In those days, China had little else to sell but food. We had to sell agricultural products to buy machines. China's arable land is relatively small and its population is the largest of the world. Our agricultural products were woefully inadequate at that time. We should not deprive people of food to export for buying weapons.

In Youth Art Institute I had often been assigned to do administrative work or so-called revolutionary work, like the land reform. I didn't like it. When I quit the evening university in Shanghai, I had a plan that after the revolutionary work had been completed, I should continue my study. I thought it was the time now, so I asked my leader to send me to Beijing University, but my application was declined. The secretary of our institute told me, "We still need you now, you should obey the need of the revolutionary work." I had to obey.

In 1954 the secretary told me, "The Youth Publishing House, also under the leadership of the Central Committee of the Youth League, needs editors now. We are going to transfer you to that unit, what do you think?" I said I still wanted to go to the university. The secretary said that the Publishing House needed editors urgently and that I should go there now. I had no reason to refuse and had to obey the decision.

The Youth Publishing House had four editorial departments: Department of Political and Ideological Education, Department of Literature, Department of Social Sciences, Department of Natural Sciences. It also published three magazines, titled respectively *The Countryside Youth*, *The High School Students*, and *The Traveler*. I was assigned to the editorial department of the magazine *The High School Students*. *The High School Students* had been a very old magazine established and edited by a very famous writer Ye Shengtao, which had helped to bring up many famous writers. It had originally been published by The Enlightenment Bookstore in Shanghai. After the liberation, The Enlightenment Bookstore was handed over to the Youth Publishing House, so the magazine *The High School Student* was published by the Youth Publishing House now. The editorial department of the magazine had nine people. The chief editor was Ye Zhishan, the son of Ye Shengtao who was the minister of the Ministry of Education now. Liu Zhong, a famous writer of children's readings, was the vice chief editor. My work was to edit articles of literature and ideological education. Sometimes I would go out to gather materials and wrote articles myself or translated articles from Soviet Union magazines and published them in our magazine.

Once I went to Baiyangdian village, Hebei Province to interview a police officer. They had captured a culprit with a very interesting, twisting process. The culprit's family had held a grand funeral rite, carrying the culprit's coffin to the wild and buried it under the earth. But the police suspected that he was really dead. Through a complicated reconnaissance and eavesdropping they finally caught him in a cave in his courtyard. I wrote the event and published it in the magazine. Many readers liked it and fed back that it was like a detective story.

In Baiyangdian village I also visited a few peasants. Two years ago, I had taken part in the land reform. I had witnessed that the poor peasants to be very glad that they got their own land. But this time I found the peasants seemed to be unhappy. They told me all the changes after the land reform. At first, they set up mutual aid teams. It was a simple form of helping each other which only involved the temporary sharing of labor and capital. Individual households remained the basic unit of ownership and production. But now the mutual aid teams were transferred to the cooperatives, in which their tools, draft animals, and labor were shared on a permanent basis. Every member of the cooperative got the same share. They said they did not like those changes. I did not exactly know which form of operation was better at that time, so I did not air my view. But I have some suspicion about the cooperatives because Soviet Union had built the collective farm and failed. I hoped we will not repeat the mistake.

In order to understand the high school student's life and thinking deeply, I wanted to do some voluntary work at a high school. My leader regarded it a good idea and approved my application. I had a friend working at the fifth girls' high school and I decided to go there. The school welcomed me and assigned me as a teacher in charge of a class of grade two. The headmaster Cao Yiweng told me that all the students of that class were those who failed to go up to the next grade. It was a disorderly class. Many of the students in that class were not only failed in academic performance but also were often late for school, did not observe public order, or even had undesirable conducts. She hoped me to find some way to improve the situation. I hadn't thought they would give me such a work. I replied that I would do my best to achieve her desire, but my ability was poor and I hadn't teaching experience. I hoped she did not hold too high of expectations of me.

I kept close contact with the students and regarded them as friends and family members. I did not loathe or despise them but respected them. I surveyed each student's problems and situations, helped her to overcome shortcomings, and develop merits. If they had practical difficulty, I helped them to solve it. I encouraged them to establish confidence. I visited their families, asking their parents to cooperate with the school to educate their children. I not only inculcated them with the reasons and truths but also set example for them. Once I went to class a little late because of the busy traffic, I apologized and made a bow to them for being late and asked to be excused. I made strict demands on them, but I criticized them less and praised them more. I believe that praise is a mental tonic.

At that time there was a very famous translated book from Soviet Union titled *The Story of Zoya and Shura* which enjoyed equal popularity with the book *How steel is being tempered.* Zoya and Shura were sister and brother. Under the careful education of their parents, they have cultivated many great personalities from their childhood, such as respect for their elders, the willingness to help others, diligence, active labor, the passion for life, wide interest. etc. In 1941, German fascists invaded the Soviet Union. Zoya, a high school grade three student, voluntarily joined the guerilla. One day she was arrested by the enemy when she burned the enemy's building. She suffered severe torture. When the German invaders forced her to report the secret of the guerilla, she did not leak any secrets. The enemy was infuriated by exasperation and hanged her. Her younger brother Shura joined the army to render service to his nation and avenge his elder sister's death. After training, he drove a tank to the front. He was brave and skillful in battle and established unusual merits repeatedly. Finally, he died a heroic death on the eve before the victory of Soviet Union. It was a real-life story. I presented each student a copy of that book, asking them to read it honestly and write a comment after reading and learn the character of Zoya and Shura. The book yielded a great influence.

Gradually, the class made some progress. Its name often appeared on the roll of honor. By the end of the school term, it was commended by the school as an advanced class. The headmaster asked me to make a speech to all the teachers of the school to introduce my experiences. I declined because I thought I had nothing to say. But she said my experience would be of some help to the school. I could not refuse again. I made the speech, telling them what I had done during that school term.

Before leaving the school, I arranged a last class meeting. I called it "Fifteen years afterwards" I asked the students to take that class meeting as a get-together of alumni. At that meeting, each student told what she had become fifteen years afterwards. I requested each student to give free rein to her imagination to design her future. It was a very interesting meeting. A student said she had become a scientist and showed a queer model of her invention before us. The next said she was a musician and sang a beautiful song. The third told us she had been awarded an advanced teacher and show off her certificate of merit. The fourth contributed a delicate dance. The fifth wore white clothes and declared she was a doctor. The sixth boasted she had become a weightlifter. She lifted a round bar-bell made of paper with her right arm and boasted that barbell was fifty kilograms, and so on.

The performances caused a lot of laughter and claps. All of us were very happy. At the end of the meeting I bade farewell to them and left them a last word: "One's fate is determined by oneself. You must make a definite answer to a question: Are you going to be one of great worth or one of worthless; one of somebody or one of nobody; one of the respected or one of the despised."

My work in the Youth Publishing House was an exhilarating experience, but this happy time was too short lived. In 1955, a campaign of eliminating the counterrevolutionary clique of Hu Feng and all hidden counterrevolutionary elements was launched. Hu Feng had been an old leftist. He was born into a worker's family.

A Painful Reminiscence of a Dignified Soul

He joined the communist Youth League in 1923. Soon after he was accepted by Tsinghua University, he discontinued schooling and returned to the countryside to participate in revolutionary movements. In 1928, he went to Japan, where he earned his living by writing political essays. As a result of his leftist activities, he was deported by the Japanese government. Upon his return, he joined the League of Leftist Writers Federation, which had been founded by Lu Xun, China's most famous writer. He considered himself to be a Marxist, but he opposed the Communist theory that literature had to reflect class struggle. He wrote many articles to express his resistance to the doctrinarism in communist literary circles. After the founding of the People's Republic of China Hu continued to express his opposition to the sterile literature policy of the Party, and he did not agree with Mao Zedong's "Talk on Literature and Art" in which literature and art were defined as political instruments and must mainly express the lives of the workers, peasants, and soldiers. He was criticized that his thought on literature and art was the capitalist, bourgeoisie, individualist literary thought. In 1954, Hu defended himself and submitted the "Report on Recent Years of Artistic Implementation", a three hundred thousand word report. This report offended Mao. At first Mao titled Hu Feng and his followers as an "anti-party clique". Later the term was changed to "counterrevolutionary clique". Hu was described as a double-dealing counterrevolutionary who put on a disguise to hide his true features. Who was different in word and deed and deceived us by his false appearance. Who coated with Marxism in his long-term anti-party and anti-people activities and cheated writers and readers. On this account, many counterrevolutionaries had wormed their way into our ranks. This time, he was no longer regarded as a "deviationist guilty of subjectivism, emotionalism and aestheticism, but as a counter revolutionary leader". Hu's views were regarded as protesting totalitarian control of intellectual and artistic activity, and his clique had connection with other counterrevolutionaries, so Hu is indeed the spokesman for all counterrevolutionary classes. Because of these reasons, this campaign's target was Hu's clique and all kinds of counterrevolutionaries. By the end of the campaign, Hu was deprived of all his posts and sentenced to fourteen years imprisonment. During the Cultural Revolution in 1969, he was sentenced into life imprisonment without appeal. He was heavily tortured and became mentally ill in prison. He was only rehabilitated and released in 1980.

After the campaign started, the Youth Publishing House set up a leading group of eliminating counterrevolutionaries. The head of the leading group was an old communist coming from the countryside. He was an ultra-leftist. He considered that there were three counterrevolutionaries in the editorial department of the magazine *The High School Students*. I, as a member of the party, was also delegated to take part in the investigation. One of the suspects was an editor named Wang Yanan. She was regarded as a counterrevolutionary for her elder sister "escaped" to Hong Kong before Liberation and Wang did not go with her. The head of the leading group decided that Wang must be left in China as a spy to contact with her elder sister. I, as an investigator of the case, began to search the evidence. I went to Wang's home and asked her why she did not go to Hong Kong together with her elder sister. She explained, "I have relatives in Hong Kong, my elder sister liked the life of Hong Kong so she moved there. She is not a member of Nationalist Party, nor a capitalist. She has her family with children. I have my family with two children. Both my elder sister and I had already gotten married for over ten years. We had few contacts with each other. I like editorial work and I have worked at the Enlightenment Bookstore for many years. I have deep feelings with my colleagues and the book store. I like the party and have confidence in the party, so I did not go to Hong Kong. My sister had her likings and I had my own ideas. We did not interfere in each other's affairs."

I also had single talks with her two children, a girl and a boy. All their talks were the same with their mother's word. I could not find any doubtful problems. I also visited many editors and workers of the former Enlightenment Bookstore. They all said the same thing as what Wang said and they never saw Wang had any abnormal behavior. They praised Wang for working hard and having a very open and frank disposition, saying whatever she has on her mind. I also made all efforts trying to find some questionable points of her, but I could not ferret any evidence to prove she was a spy. Based on all my investigation I reported to the leading group that I did not think Wang was a counterrevolutionary.

Another suspect was the editor of the natural science articles, whose name was Jiang Lihan. He was considered to be a counterrevolutionary and receive large sums of money from Nationalist Party for two reasons. First, Jiang was a member of the Youth League of the Three Principles of the People led by the Nationalist Party. Second, he had devised an explosion case. The fact of the explosion case was like this: Jiang had published a short article on our magazine. The title of the article was "How to make soda water by yourself". After that, we received a letter from a high school student. He complained that while he made the soda water according to the recipe of the article, the bottle was exploded and his skin was hurt. The group leader decided that Jiang was an active counterrevolutionary and reported the case to the higher authority and the *People's Daily* immediately carried an editorial on this case which warned the whole country how dangerous and cruel was the enemy, who wanted to kill our students through the explosions and called on the people to dig out more and more counterrevolutionaries. This case was quoted as the first example of the counterrevolutionary action during the campaign.

With the assignment on me, I carried out an in-depth investigation. I visited his home abruptly. There was a heap of junk in his rooms. His wife had no work and his children were dressed in rags. It did not seem to be a disguise for all the furniture and dresses and sheets were old things. Seeing such a situation, I thought he would not receive money from Nationalist Party. It is a fact that he was a member of the Youth League of the Three Principle of the People, but a being member of that Youth League before liberation was as common as being a member of Communist Youth League today. It was not an espionage agency. I could not regard a member of that Youth League was a spy without any evidence.

As for the accusation of being an "active counterrevolutionary" I also had a doubt. The magazine *The High School Students* had a large circulation of 300,000. There must be tens of thousands of students who had tried to make soda water during that summer, but only one student reported the explosion and according to the student's report, he did not use soda water bottle to make the soda water, he was using a small medicine bottle to make it and the bottle was exploded when he shook it and the explosion merely hurt the skin. The wall of medicine bottle was very, very thin at that time. That was the exact situation of that explosion. I thought if Jiang had a scheme to kill the students, the dose of his recipe must be much larger than that he wrote. Furthermore, if Jiang believed that his recipe was able to kill a man, then after his article was published, his aim was already achieved and thousands of students would be killed, he had to escape or hide at once. But he did not show any unusual expression and came to the office calmly till we received the student's letter. After all the careful analysis of the case, I believed that if Jiang should bear the responsibility of the accident, it was a fault of negligence, not a crime. There was no enough evidence to prove that Jiang must fall into the category of an "active counterrevolutionary". I reported my opinion to the leader of the campaign, I hated to cater to whatever the superior said, I must tell the truth.

Zhong Da

The third person who was considered to be a counterrevolutionary was an artistic editor named Huang Yinong. He designed a cover of the magazine to express our condolence over Stalin's death. The picture had a red background rimmed with black edges. The color red in China is used to celebrate joyous occasion while white shows sad things like the death of a person. The group leader decided that Huang, who used the red cover to celebrate Stalin's death, must be a counterrevolutionary. Huang explained that his design was just copying the pattern of the Soviet Union. All the workers of the Youth Publishing House had gone to the USSR Embassy to express our condolences over Stalin's death. All the decorations there had a red ground rimmed with black edges. I guessed that they must take red as a symbol of revolution and communism, so they used red to worship their lofty cause of communism and used the black rim as a symbol of their solemn and profound sadness for Stalin's death. Huang's explanation was true, so I did not think he was a counterrevolutionary. Even though the Soviet type of decoration was not in keeping with China's tradition, Huang's imitation of that type was a mistake, not an act of counterrevolution. In addition, the cover was approved by the Party group of the magazine, I admitted that I should bear part of the responsibility. All 300,000 copies of the magazine with a red cover were changed with a new white cover.

My opinion met serious criticism. The party committee even held a meeting of all the party members to denounce me. They could not call me a counterrevolutionary. My history was clean. I took part in the party when I was young. They gave me a title "shielding a counterrevolutionary". I did not agree. The three persons were neither my relatives nor my friends, we were mere colleagues known each other for a short time. Why should I shield them? But under the great pressure, if I insisted on my view, I would meet much more trouble, I admitted that I lacked the sense of class struggle. Soon afterwards, I was sent to the Party School of the Central Committee of the Party for brainwashing.

I was not depressed and did not regret the event. Since my childhood, I was taught that a man must be honest. I was practicing the principle, I was not catering for the leader's wrongdoing and I was not following the flow. I remained calm and peaceful and even a bit proud. I despised the group leader of the campaign, who could do nothing good but tried his best to ferret more and more "class enemies" so as to get political credit and gain rewards. Before the campaign, he ranked fifth on the list of the leaders. After the campaign, he ranked second on the list. I guessed he must be dissatisfied for he was unable to rise to

A Painful Reminiscence of a Dignified Soul

the top rank. The three "counterrevolutionaries" were subjected to all kinds of suffering, but finally were rehabilitated years later. Jiang Lihan, as his name was published in *People's Daily* and became well known, had to change a name to teach in a high school.

In China there is a proverb: "Blessings never come in pairs and misfortunes never come singly." This word was corroborated in my case. During that period, I was having a courtship with a girlfriend. She was a graduate of a normal school. She was a little more than an average height, pretty, and humorous. I loved her and obviously she loved me very much. On the weekends we often went to the park, museum, or cinema. We talked about everything, our livelihood, our interest, our ambitions, and our views about literature, art, and politics. We often played jokes on each other. She was a member of Communist Youth League. She admired me being a Communist. We were on good, intimate terms. To be frank, I told her all the things I had done in the campaign and the criticism and punishment I got. I expected she would understand and believe me, but she more believed the party. She told me she wanted to stop our courtship. I had a very strong sense of self-respect. I agreed at once. I was not angry with her. After so many years' ideological indoctrination, almost everyone took politics as the first important thing in his life. I understood her thinking and feelings.

There were also much bad news from my family during the campaign. My fourth elder brother Da Cheng was sent to the country to reform through labor. During the War of Resistance against Japan, Da Cheng joined the army to fight the enemy in Fujian Province. Once in a battle against Japanese army in Xianyou County, he was seriously wounded. He was sent to the hospital to cure the wound. After the restoration of his health, he was assigned to work at the local military service bureau. After the end of the war, he went to Shanghai to study at Shanghai Press College. After graduation, he got a job at the tax bureau of Shanghai. During the campaign of the eliminating counterrevolutionaries, the party of the tax bureau regarded the military service bureau as a reactionary organization and titled Da Chang as a historical counterrevolutionary and sent him to the countryside to labor there. A hero fighting against Japanese army suddenly became a criminal. He was not sent to the court, for his "crime" was minor, which did not merit the sentence. Yet a conviction by the court would be better. A formal sentence has a definite term. Without a formal sentence, his exile to the farm was effectively a life sentence. He labored at the farm for over twenty years. If not for Mao Zedong's death, he would have to labor there forever. He was rehabilitated in 1980 and resumed his work at the tax bureau of Shanghai.

My fifth elder brother Da Zhi suffered from the same treatment. After the end of the war, he returned to Shanghai from Fujian Province. He could not find a job in Shanghai. My third elder brother's father-in-law Zhang Xisan, a civilian major general(文职少将) of Nationalist Party's army, hired Da Zhi to do clerical work in his office in Nanjing. Zhi worked there for about two years. When Zhang Xisan was ordered to go to Taiwan and left Nanjing, Zhi found a job at a private bank named Guohua Bank in Wuxi Municipality. After Liberation, he strongly supported the party and was titled as an "activist" at the bank and was granted an interview to the mayor of Wuxi Municipality. Later, the party called the staff of the private bank to join the Bank of People. Zhi took the lead to quit his job at Guohua Bank and joined the Bank of People. He was transferred from Wuxi to Zhenjiang, his salary reduced from 130 RMB to a little more than 30 RMB. Later he was transferred from the Bank of People to the Government of Gaochun county. During the campaign, he was sent to a farm to reform through labor for he had worked in Nationalist Party's army. He also labored in a farm for over twenty years until he was rehabilitated in 1980. The unjust treatment of my case and the unearned punishment of my two elder brothers made me suspect the correctness of the party.

I went to the party school in the early Spring of 1956. Our school was on the suburb of Beijing. All the students were party members of the departments directly under the Central Committee of the Party. We lived in the school. Every Saturday afternoon, after school was over, the school's bus would carry us back to the downtown of Beijing and on Sunday afternoon it would take us back to school. The living regulations were very strict, like that of a military camp: The time of getting up, taking a nap, switching off the light, and going to bed were all strictly stipulated and everyone must observe it. Our curriculum included philosophy, political economy, the history of the development of society, and the history of the party. We were divided into many party groups. After each class, we would discuss it in the groups. I was assigned as the head of a party group. I did not want to take the job for I loved the idiom: "Happy is the man who is relieved of his official duties", but it was the party organization's order and I had to obey. There were ten people in my group, two were female. All of us were friendly, we were studying and working together with suppleness.

A Painful Reminiscence of a Dignified Soul

Our textbook of political economy was translated from a version of Soviet Union. Many views of it I didn't agree with. But at that time our party extremely worshiped the Soviet Union. The smallest criticism of Soviet Union was condemned. Though I am accustomed to speaking straightforwardly, taking the lessons from the campaign of eliminating counterrevolutionaries I had become cautious and rarely aired my view of opposition. But once I found a definition of poverty on that book was so ridiculous that I could not help but burst out my opposition in the discussion. That definition is like this: "There are two kinds of poverty: relative poverty and absolute poverty. The relative poverty means though the worker's living level may rise a little each year, but compared with rich people, whose living level rises much higher each year, the worker's life has become relatively poor. The absolute poverty means the worker's living level is lower each year than that of the past year. The American worker is in both relative poverty and absolute poverty." In western economic books there are also the terms of relative poverty and absolute poverty, but their definitions are quite different from that of the Soviet Union's book.

I raised a different viewpoint, "I agree the American worker's life is in relative poverty, but they are not in absolute poverty. According to the definition of absolute poverty in the textbook. American worker's life has become poorer and poorer, their living lever in 1956 was lower than their life in 1955; their life in 1955 was worse than their life in 1954… It is obvious not a fact. Everyone knows that almost every American family owns a car now. If their present life is worse than the past, then in the past each family should have two or three cars. Can it be a fact? We cannot say American workers are in absolute poverty."

My view was criticized but did not cause much trouble, for the leaders of the party school were relatively temperate. But this view was later reported to the Youth Publishing House by a classmate of mine and was constituted a crime.

In October 1956 there was a nationwide revolt in Hungary against the government and its policy. The revolt began with a student demonstration, which attracted a great many people. During the demonstration, a student was shot dead. The paraders wrapped his body in a flag and held above the heads of the crowd. As the news spread far and wide, the revolt erupted throughout the country and the government was overthrown. A new government was established and pledged to re-establish free elections. Then a large Soviet force invaded Budapest and other regions of Hungary and controlled the situation. I considered the armed intervention unnecessary. If the problem was solved through negotiation, it could avoid great sacrifice and avoid a bad name of intervention of other country's internal affairs for Soviet Union. The armed invasion greatly alienated the western Marxists, led to splits and considerable losses of membership for Communist Party, for many Western communists opposed the armed invasion. I agreed with their views. This opinion was also criticized but did not cause much trouble too.

My study in the party school did not make me progress. On the contrary, it made me regress. I became more and more distrustful of Mao Zedong and the party, whose actions were always not in keeping with their words and I had more and more doubts and suspicion about their ideologies and policies. For examples:

In the article "On New Democracy" Mao wrote: "The republic will confiscate the land of the landlords and distribute it to those peasants having little or no land, carry out Dr. Sun Yatsen's slogan of 'land to the tiller', turn the land over to the private ownership of the peasants. A rich peasant economy will be allowed in the rural areas." China completed the land reform by the end of 1952. The poor peasants had their own land, but only two years later their land was collectivized and not long after that was nationalized. Mao boasted that the peasants were glad and welcomed the change. Do you believe it? I had gone to the village Baiyangdian and I saw with my own eyes the peasants were unhappy. They complained secretly that their lands and implements were forfeited. All those who opposed the collectivization were seriously criticized or persecuted. In Mao's article "rich peasants are allowed in the rural areas", but during land reform rich peasants were categorized as the enemy of the people.

In the same article, Mao wrote: "In the new-democratic republic under the leadership of the proletariat, the state enterprises will be of a socialist character and will constitute the leading force in the whole national economy, but the republic will neither confiscate capitalist private property in general nor forbid the development of such capitalist production." The Common Program of the Chinese People's Political Consultative Conference also declared that "our economy includes five economical elements: state-owned economy; co-operative economy; private economy; the economy jointly operated by state and private capital; individual economy."

But In the early 1950s, the state already began a preliminary socialist transformation of capitalist industry. Commerce and agriculture instituted a state monopoly of the purchase and marketing of the products of private enterprises and the peasants. Between 1953 and 1956, It developed public-private partnership. They called it state-capitalism. Soon after that, the state-capitalism was transformed into socialism and all the property of the private enterprise were confiscated, including handicraft industry and the individual business. Obviously all the transformation of agriculture, capitalist industry and commerce were entirely violated what Mao had said in his article. It eliminated all the private ownership. The peasants lose their land, the capitalists lose their factories or stores, small shop owners lose their business. what was their fault? What was their crimes? Why should their properties be confiscated?

Take the case of my third elder brother's father-in-law Zhang Xisan as an example. As I mentioned before, he was a civilian major general of nationalist army. Before Nanjing was occupied by the Liberation Army, he was ordered by his superior to withdraw to Taiwan. He carried large number of precious telecommunications equipment to Guangzhou, preparing to take a ship to Taiwan. But after a second thought he decided to revolt from the nationalist party and surrender to Communist Party. He carried the telecommunication equipment to Chongqing and handed over all the equipment to the people's government. He did not receive any reward from the government and got no work. Since he had no income, he used all his little savings to open a very small candy shop to keep a living. He was in so difficult condition that sometimes he even begrudged giving a cake to his daughter. During the socialist transformation campaign in 1956, his small shop was confiscated. He had a wife and two young daughters in primary and high school. He was sixty years old and could not find a job. The whole family depended on his wife, who worked at a recycling center with a wage of 25 RMB per month. Was Mao's policy correct? He had betrayed his word completely.

Another example, Mao wrote in his article "On Coalition Government": "The honest way is immediately to proclaim the abolition of the Kuomintang one-party dictatorship, to establish a provisional central government composed of representatives of the Kuomintang, the Communist Party, the democratic league and people with no party affiliation.

"Some people are suspicious and think that once in power, the Communist Party will follow Russia's example and establish the dictatorship of the proletariat and a one-party system. Our answer is that a new-democratic state based on an alliance of the democratic classes is different in principle from a socialist state under the dictatorship of the proletariat. The proletariat, the peasantry, the intelligentsia and the other sections of the petty bourgeoisie undoubtedly constitute the basic forces determining China's fate.

"Once formed, this coalition government will in its turn provide full freedom for the people and so consolidate its own foundations. Only then will it be possible to hold free and unrestricted elections throughout the country... Freedom of speech, press, assembly, association, political conviction and religious belief and freedom of the person are the people's most important freedoms."

Mao firmly opposed Nationalist Party's one-party dictatorship and devoted to establish a democratic coalition government, but as soon as he seized the power, he established a one-party dictatorship. All the so-called Democratic Parties and the mass organizations or any other groups hadn't an equal standing with the Communist Party. All of them were led by the Communist Party and had to follow upon the heels of the party tightly. Mao Zedong promised people so many freedoms but once he seized the power, he denied people all those freedoms. Mao had broken all his words. Could we still trust him as a brilliant leader? Could we call the government a democratic one?

Again, one of our textbooks in the party school was "the history of the development of society," which taught us: "The development of society of the world was divided into five periods. The first was the slave society; the next was the feudal society; the third, the democratic society; the fourth will be the socialist society; and at last will enter the communist society. The development of society has to follow this sequence and cannot skip over any period. Before 1911 China was a semi-feudal society, it could not skip into socialist society directly, it has to undergo a period of democratic society."

Mao also wrote in his article "On New Democracy": "The Chinese revolution cannot avoid taking the two steps, first of New Democracy and then of socialism. Moreover, the first step will need quite a long time and cannot be accomplished overnight." "Our general program of New Democracy will remain unchanged throughout the stage of the bourgeois-democratic revolution, that is, for several decades."

As a historical period, slave society, feudal society, bourgeois-democratic society all lasted hundreds or thousands of years. Even if the New Democratic period needed not hundreds of years, it needed at least "several decades" as Mao defined. "Several decades" includes years from twenty to ninety. Let us take an average value, say five decades. Then the period of China's New Democracy should be at least about fifty years.

A Painful Reminiscence of a Dignified Soul

Our new democracy started after the founding of the PRC, Oct. 1, 1949. By the end of 1956, the party declared the socialist transformation had been basically accomplished. The declaration meant the period of new democracy had ended. Can the huge task of the third historical period be completed in mere seven years? Mao had entirely violated his words, violated the natural laws. In order to fulfill his ambitions, he threatened people to skip into socialist society at the expense of people's lives and properties and interests. Mao's betrayal of his words caused a great many mistakes and sacrifices, I no longer believed Mao and despised him now. Through the studies at the party school, I found my thinking became clearer and deeper.

In February 1956 in the twentieth Communist Party Congress of the Soviet Union, Khrushchev delivered a secret speech entitled "On the Cult of Personality and its Consequences" He denounced that Stalin fostered "cult of personality" for himself and perpetrated great crimes like the execution, torture and imprisonment of large number loyal party members on false charges and the practice of mass terror. It shook me to my roots. I pondered that question for a long time. All we had read and learned was that Stalin was a great leader and we respected him very much. Now the speech made all the thing upside-down. What was the actual state of affairs? After thinking it over and over again, I believed Khrushchev was telling the truth. He could not tell a lie for it was an extraordinarily dangerous thing for him to do that.

I also contemplated the situation of our country. As I mentioned before I was distressed about what Mao Zedong had done after the founding of the PRC. He forgot all the words he had promised and took a premature advance in every area of the country. He was just following Stalin's mistake. I welcomed Khrushchev's speech. Perhaps these bitter, penetrating lessons of Soviet Union would trigger Mao Zedong and the party's introspection, helped them to recognize their questions and correct their mistakes. I harbored a happy hope in mind.

Two months after Khrushchev's speech, Mao Zedong made a speech on April 28, 1956 in the enlarged meeting of the Political Bureau of the communist Party, among which he said: "Let a hundred flowers blossom in arts area and Let a hundred schools of thought contend in science area be our policy for flourishing arts and culture and developing sciences." I was happy to hear that word. I regarded it as a sign of the first effect of Khrushchev's speech.

In September, 1956, the eighth Party Congress was convened in Beijing. The congress "underscore the persistence of the system of democratic centralism and collective leadership, the opposition of personality cult, the development of the inner-party democracy, and the strengthening of the link between the party and the masses."

In November 1956 in the second plenary session of the eighth congress, Liu Shaoqi stressed to broaden the scope of socialist democracy, to restrain the leader's power, to strengthen the supervisor of leaders. Premier Zhou Enlai also said that referring to the lessons of Soviet Union's mistake, democracy must be enlarged and he criticized the tendency of rash advance in 1956.

On February 27, 1957, Mao made a speech "On the correct handling of the contradictions among the people" in which he said: "We are confronted with two types of social contradictions—those between ourselves and the enemy and those among the people. The two are totally different in nature. In our country, the contradiction between the working class and the national bourgeoisie comes under the category of contradictions among the people.

"There are still certain contradictions between this government and the people. These include the contradictions between the interests of the state and the interests of the collective on the one hand and the interests of the individual on the other, between democracy and centralism, between the leadership and the led, and the contradictions arising from the bureaucratic style of work of some of the state personnel in their relations with the masses. All these are also contradictions among the people.

"We in no way mean that coercive measures should be taken to settle ideological questions or questions involving the distinction between right and wrong among the people. All attempts to use administrative orders or coercive measures to settle ideological questions or questions of right and wrong are not only ineffective but harmful."

On March 12, 1957, Mao delivered a speech in the conference on publicity work He said: "Our country should take a policy of 'set free'. Let the people go their hold to air their views. Let them be bold enough to speak, to criticize." And he proclaimed "the party will launch a rectification campaign to criticize subjectivism, factionalism and bureaucratism."

All these talks and documents made me feel happy and excited. Gradually, I believed their words more and more. I began to hold a hope that after learning the lessons of Soviet Union, Mao Zedong and the party were really conscious of their mistakes and determined to correct them.

A Painful Reminiscence of a Dignified Soul

In the spring of 1957, my studies in the party school were finished. I returned to the Youth Publishing House and worked as an editor of the magazine *The High School Students* again.

The party and Mao continued to solicit people's criticism and determined to improve their work. On April 27, the central committee of the party issued "the instruction of the rectification campaign" and officially declared the launch of the campaign in the whole party. On April 30, Mao and other leaders invited and had talks with the heads of all the democratic party, Mao said "We had wanted to hold a rectification campaign for many years, but could not find the chance. Now we found it. At present the atmosphere of criticism was already formed. Let this atmosphere keep on continuously. We hope our party's style would be improved in real earnest through the criticism."

In response to the party and Mao's call, all the organizations of the party and government, the schools and universities, scientific research institutes, the art and culture organizations summoned meetings of different forms in succession, listening to opinions of the masses inside and outside the party, welcoming them to fire shots and air views fully. The broad masses of the people raised countless criticism and suggestions on the work and policies of the party and the government. Newspapers reported the critical speeches and views of the masses in their original state without any change or whitewash. In every organization, big character posters flooded on their walls. It was really a new and dynamic atmosphere indeed since the founding of the People's Republic of China.

Like all other units, many editors of our publishing house put forward their views or criticism of the party. But a large part of the staff still had wariness because the reminiscence of the terror of the former campaigns still remained in their minds. I also had two minds: On the one hand, I thought Mao might really recognized his fault and wanted to correct; on the other hand, I had already learnt that Mao always betrayed his word, I had to be careful. The party committee of our office called a meeting after another, repeatedly asking us to speak out freely. They cited Mao's quotations "People can criticize officials of all levers, to help the Party to overcome its mistakes or weakness" and "People can say whatever they want to say and say to the fullest for our country's future sake." More and more editors raised their writing brushes.

Yet I still not fully believe Mao. Waiting for a long time, finally I was touched by a Mao's word "Socialism requires 'people with lofty ideals and braveness'" and "People with lofty ideals and braveness(仁人志士) is a highly sounding, precious idiom of China." When I thought of the future of our country, I decided I must be such a man. I calculated that even if I would be persecuted again, even if my salary would be reduced, I need not fear. I was still single; I could not get others into trouble. I decided to speak out. I put up a big character poster on the wall and made a critical speech in a meeting. I was mollified that I had done something good for the people and the country. My main criticism was: "The eliminating counterrevolutionary campaign was erroneously extended. The party hastily made wrong convictions without exercising serious investigations and intensive researches. The party should practice democracy, letting people to tell the truth." I hoped people's opinions and criticisms would help the party to correct its mistakes and really practice democracy. I expected the party would soon begin the rectification rampaign to overcome the bureaucratism, factionalism, and subjectivism as it had proclaimed. But after so many criticisms and views were raised by people, we could not read any articles which criticized the "three -isms". On the contrary, we read more and more articles which criticized the contents of what the people formerly "spoke out freely and aired views fully."

In the middle of May, only a few days after Mao encouraged all the leaders of the Democratic Parties to make criticisms. On April 30, He wrote another article "The things are changing," giving the criticizers a title of rightists and accusing them to be furiously attacking the Party. He suddenly shifted the "Rectification Campaign" into an "Anti-Rightists Campaign". This change made me puzzled. Only a couple of months ago, Mao continuously said "we should handle the contradictions among the people correctly; to use administrative orders or coercive measures to settle ideological questions are harmful… Let a hundred flowers blossom. Let a hundred schools of thought contend." and he solicited people's criticism and views. Why now he said quite the opposite words. At first I guessed there might be two reasons. First, he was an ignoble person who had always gone back on his words, like all he had done after liberation. Second, he might originally have some enlightened ideas, but was opposed by most of the cadres coming from the countryside, he had to obey the majority of the party leaders and changed his word.

But later I discovered what Mao did was a real trap. I got some news. At the same time in February 1956, while Mao solicited criticisms from the people, he told the high-ranking cadres in a meeting that the rightists were starting a rampage, attacking the party and the socialist system. He wanted to uncover all those who

A Painful Reminiscence of a Dignified Soul

dared to oppose the party, and expose every possible potential dissident. He confided his scheme to the few special cronies: "We want to let them speak out. Let all those ox devils and snake demons curse us for a few months... How can we catch the snakes if we don't let them out of their lairs? We wanted those bastards to wriggle out and sing and fart, only in that way we can catch them... casting a long line to bait big fish... Inviting them speak out so that we could then use what they said as an excuse to victimize them".

From all those his words and acts, I recognized that Mao was indeed a base and shameless person who was good at carrying on schemes and intrigues. All the things that happened during the last four or five months were a mere premeditated intrigue of him. And his trap was extremely successful. Before we know it, we are up to our necks in the trap. Once the watergate was opened a fraction, a deluge of dissents dashed out. Millions of people were caught in Mao's snare. Over one night all those innocents, who spoke out and aired views, became the "enemies" of the people. Not "a hundred flowers blossom", but one flower blossoms and ninety-nine flowers are brutally snapped. The Anti Rightists Campaign like a violent storm at once started all over the country.

In Youth Publishing House a leading group of Anti-Rightist was soon established. The chief leader of the campaign was the same leader who had led the former "Campaign of Eliminating Counterrevolutionary". The party committee held a mobilization meeting, calling all the staff of the publishing house to report, expose, unmask, and denounce the suspicious rightists. Very soon the walls of the office building were full of big character posters once again, but the contents of the posters were quite the opposite of that of the posters put up one month ago. All the content of the former posters were now the evidence of the crimes of their writers. Criticism meetings were held every day in every department.

At the denouncement meetings, the accused was fiercely criticized. Most of the accusations were groundless. The active accusers, who wanted to get the leader's favor and reward, were swollen with arrogance, relentlessly denounced others, confounded right and wrong, elevated minor shortcomings to the level of principles, or just fabricated facts. Most people were forced to follow the general trend and make criticism on the accused to protect themselves. The accused were frustrated and exasperated. At first, they tried to argue for themselves. But the experience soon taught them the more argument about their innocence, the more they were deemed to stubbornly resist the campaign. They had to swallow any denouncement and insult in meek submission and made self-criticism. Regularly if one's first self-criticism was not deemed to be satisfactory, one had to make a second, third or more self-criticisms to get a pass. And at these denouncement meetings no one should support the accused. Everyone must know these unspoken rules. Otherwise, no one could tell what calamities might land upon him.

For example, on a meeting denouncing Peng Zigang, the chief-editor of the magazine *The Traveler*", Peng's colleague Zhou Shacheng, also an editor and an old communist, "jumped" out and said, "Before liberation, risking the danger of cutting head, Peng did not oppose the Party, how could she oppose the Party after liberation when her position was raised?" For this word, Zhou was expelled from the party and sent to the countryside to do manual labor with rightists too. Both Zhou and Peng were my devoted friends. Zhou told me he never regretted what he had done for Peng and Peng's son told me his mother thanked Zhou and remembered Zhou's word in her mind all her life.

Six kinds of punishment were being imposed on the rightist, depending on the seriousness of the "crime". The first was an indefinite jail sentence. The second, dismissal from employment to work under the supervision of the laboring people with the monthly salary of 16 RMB. The third, suspension of employment, great reduction of salary and demotion of grades in rank. The fourth, labor for one-year probation, after which some other punishment could be administered if warranted. The fifth, small reduction of salary and demotion of grades in rank. The sixth, label of rightist with no other punishment.

There were over ten editors were formally labeled as rightists, including four leaders: the general editor of the publishing house, Li Geng; the chief editor of the magazine *The Travelers*, Peng Zigang; the vice chief editor of the magazine *The High School Students*, Liu Zhong; the chief editor of the magazine *The Rural Youth*, Meng Qinyuan. What were their "crimes" and experiences and characters? I would relate briefly below.

Li Geng is a sober-minded scholar of great learning, always pondering things diligently and deeply, and regarded books as his life. He often goes about his work with the throttle full open. He joined Communist Youth League in 1934 and was one of the leaders of the underground student movement. He enrolled in the New Fourth Army in the early years of the 1940s, fighting the Japanese army in the north of Jiangsu Province. After the founding of the PRC, he was assigned to establish the Youth Publishing House and to be the general editor of it. He had edited and revised hundreds of good books during the past seven years. And suddenly he was labeled as the enemy of the people. His main "crimes" were: First, he criticized that the party could not accept any different ideas and regarded all different ideas as heresy. People who wore different opinions were often wrongly accused or tortured. Second, He was in favor of the restoration of the former private publishing house Enlightenment Bookstore. He was labeled as Ultra-Rightist and his salary was reduced from over 200 RMB to 30 RMB.

Peng Zhigang was the most famous female correspondent in the 1940s in China. She was a writer of keen intellect, has a pair of sharp eyes and a trenchant pen. She had written numerous attractive reports, which had original, unique views and cut into the ills and evils of the time accurately. She insisted that writing must be loyal to one's feelings, not simply submit to political demands. Her most distinguished character is candid and unrestrained; she can't keep anything to herself and wears her heart on her sleeve. She always beams a propitious smile like a never growing up child. She has a heart as warm as fire radiating power and light. She is affable to everyone and hasn't a mote of bureaucratic airs treating all the colleagues alike. She joined the Communist Party in 1938 and worked as an underground party member in Chongqing, the capital of China during the war of resistance against Japan.

Her main "crimes" were: First, she wrote a report "Mr. Mao Zedong is coming Chongqing", in which there was a word "Mao seems to be a scholar coming from the folk." This word was considered a vicious slander on the great leader. That article had created a great stir in the country and left a simple and honest impression of Mao in people's mind and now became an evidence of crime. Second, she said the monopoly of the purchase and marketing of the vegetables was not right. This idea was considered a wild attack on socialist system; Third, she was in favor of the restoration of the private publishing house, like the Enlightenment Bookstore and promoted to set up "magazines compiled by like fellows", not led by the party or government. Fourth, she disliked the endless political campaigns and hoped the party let people have more time to do their professional work. Her "crimes" became twisted, blown out of all proportion. Peng vindicated that her report did not depreciate Mao but praised him. She believed that Mao himself must have read her article and did not find fault of it, for when she met Mao in a feast, Mao first called her name and said "you are fatter than before". She also denied all the accusations and handed in her letter of resignation. She wanted to go back home as a housewife. She did not know that quitting her job was not allowed and she was already a criminal now. Once she attended a criticism session at the auditorium on the fourth floor of the *Beijing Daily*. During the session, one of the rightists jumped down from the flood to commit suicide. In spite of this, the session still went on in perfect order. She understood the cruelty of the campaign then. Afterwards, she no longer justified herself for whatever she had said and done. and Imitated other rightists' self-criticism she put many great negative labels on herself. She was labeled as Ultra-Rightist and her salary was reduced from over 200 RMB to 30 RMB.

Liu Zhong was a famous writer of children's books. He was one of the path breakers of China's children's literature. He had written about seventeen books for children. He joined the Communist Party in 1947 in Shanghai and then went to the liberated area in 1948. He was my direct leader in the magazine. Whenever I had problems or difficulties, he helped me to solve them earnestly. Honesty is a salient virtue in his character. He is gentle, urbane and debonair. He is amiable and easy to approach. He was painstaking with his work, polishing articles patiently, revising printer's proofs carefully. His main "crime" was he criticized that the party and cadres from the countryside had some discrimination against the intellectuals. After he was labeled a rightist his wife divorced him.

I was also labeled as a rightist. My main "crimes" were: First, I criticized that the party of the Youth Publishing House did not make serious investigation before categorizing people to counterrevolutionary so as to erroneously extend the scope of attack. Second, I had made "wrong" talks against the conduct and economic theory of the Soviet Union. My salary was reduced from 89 to 78 RMB. My rank of cadre was demoted one grade.

During the Anti-Rightist Campaign, at least 550,000 students, teachers, scientists, doctors, writers, artists, cadres, and other professionals fell prey in the trap. Many honest old party members, many innocent naive youths were become "the enemies of the people". In our sister unit *The Youth Daily*, there were seven leaders, six of them were labeled as rightists, the last one was labeled as right opportunist. In a university, a teacher was sentenced to three years in prison and worked in a wild mountainous area to build a road. His crime was a single remark: "China's reliance on the Soviet Union should not be 'absolute'." A university student, only eighteen years old, was labeled as a rightist, just because he had said "it was unfair that the leader of the college always sent students with revolutionary family back-

A Painful Reminiscence of a Dignified Soul

grounds to study abroad and the students' academic accomplishments were never taken into consideration."

Many officials used the campaign to settle personal scores. They purged talented people through the campaign, of whom they were jealous or with whom they did not get on well. Others acted out of sheer retaliation. An official took advantage of his position to travel many places for private pleasure. When he came back, he asked the accountant to reimburse him for the cost of the trip. The accountant turned him down, saying it was against the financial discipline. The leader harbored a deep resentment against him. When the campaign started, he found his chance of retaliation came. He declared that the accountant was from a capitalist family, nursed a great deal of grudges against the party and the socialist system, and thus labeled the accountant as a rightist. The accountant's downfall came from his naiveté in "politics" and his trust in the Party. Not only the single accountant was naive, all the victims of the campaign were naive. They did what the party told them to do and then became class enemies. And the evidence of their crime were their own words, the words "furiously attacking the Communist Party and socialist system."

A more absurd thing in the campaign was that Mao also set a quota of five percent as the number of rightists in every unit. It showed how evil-minded and foolish Mao was. I deemed him to be evil-minded because he wanted to smash so many intellectuals. I deemed him to be foolish in the extreme because a set quota would certainly omit many enemies he wanted to catch and wrongly catch many innocents as enemies. Suppose there was a unit which was controlled by Mao's enemy and in which eighty percent of the staff were Mao's enemies. Now the unit only needed to hand out five percent of Mao's enemies and the other seventy-five percent of Mao's enemies were missed. On the contrary, if there was a unit whose staff had been strictly examined and all of them were truly loyal to Mao. Now it had to hand out five percent of its staff as Mao's enemies, these five percent were definitely wrongly hurt.

The five percent quota caused many ridiculous things. During the Anti-Rightist Campaign, in many units, very few words and conducts of their staff could be considered to be anti-Communist Party or anti-socialist system. Where would the five percent rightists be found? The leaders of those units found it difficult to determine who should be rightists. They took different methods to round up the number to five percent. Some units drew lots to decide who should be labeled as rightists. These rightists were categorized the "lot-drawing rightists". Some units labeled those who never say anything as rightists. They were condemned they won't speak out their hatred openly. These rightists were categorized the "rightist who have poison but not released it". Some unit's leaders were kindhearted, who did not want to nail the label on anyone else and wrote his own name on the list to fulfill his duty. These rightists were categorized the "self-acknowledged rightists". Here were only a few examples. Curious and brutal things were countless.

The campaign caused many miserable things. Many rightists were persecuted to death or suicide. More died from malnutrition, illness, freezing cold, overwork and accidents when they labored in very bad conditions, such as in the "Great Northern Wilderness" in Heilongjiang Province, the extreme north territory of our country, where the temperature can be -38 degree C. The greatest negative consequence of the campaign was that it shut up all the mouths of the people, including the most senior officials. Nobody dared to complain or criticize Mao and the party, so that Mao could do whatever he pleased to do and planted seedlings of greater calamities in our country.

After the "Anti Rightist Campaign" I came to realize that Mao is a very cunning, low-down politician. In 1956, under the pressure of Khrushchev's speech and the circumstances of that time, he delivered some beautiful, enlightening speeches and articles, pretended to favor democracy and superficially agree Khrushchev's criticism of personality cult. In fact, he held a completely opposite idea with Khrushchev. He believed in Stalinism and was eager to keep and extend the personality cult of him. He hated Khrushchev and was afraid of the impact and effect of Khrushchev's secret speech. He knew that speech had aroused a serious domestic problem, threatening his power and position. For example, inspired by Khrushchev's speech many Chinese people heightened their sense of anti-personality-cult.

Many similar questions were raised among cadres and the intellectuals. They asked: "In the past, we eulogize Stalin, which was now considered to be a cult of personality. But we also composed and sing the song 'The east is red' to praise Mao. Is it also a cult of personality? Shall we still sing that song?"

"We shout 'Long Live Chairman Mao!' This is not appropriate because it is a feudalist practice. It is also a kind of personality cult, which disparages the power of the collective leadership of the party. Hanging the huge portrayal of Mao Zedong on the wall of Tiananmen gate tower, is it also a personality cult?" Some people even openly opposed the personality cult: "Do away with blind faith in a single person," "The country does not need an emperor." Mao hated those questions and did not want the Chinese people to oppose the cult of personality.

Another example is Mao was greatly annoyed with the Eighth Congress of the Party. Influenced by Khrushchev's speech, In the Eighth Congress, Liu Shaoqi and Deng Xiaoping no longer mentioned "Mao Zedong thought" in their reports. The resolution of the Eighth Congress also did not mention the "Mao Zedong thought." It was quite different from the resolution of the Seventh Congress of the Communist Party, which had clearly declared that "Mao Zedong Thought is the guiding principle of the party." The resolution also emphasized collective leadership, opposed personality cult, and pointed out "The principal contradiction of our country is no longer the contradiction between proletariat and bourgeoisie, but the contradiction between the requirement of the people for the rapid development of economy and culture and the present economy and culture cannot satisfy the requirement of the people." Premier Zhou also made a speech at the congress. He pointed out that all levels of government, fearing attacked for right deviationism, elevated high economic targets. He was sure those plans were impossibly fulfilled and that was a phenomenon of impetuosity and rash advance. He said, "It would be very dangerous to rush into projects that have no basis in reality". He opposed and corrected the rash advance and his view was embodied on the second five-year plan (1958-1962), approved by the Eighth National Party Congress.

Mao harbored a deep resentment against the two reports and Premier Zhou's speech and the resolution of the congress. But under the domestic and foreign situation of that time—not long after Khrushchev's speech and many people praised his report, he found it not convenient to criticize them. He kept silence temporarily.

While Mao hated Khrushchev's criticism on the personality cult of Stalin, fearing his fate would be the same as Stalin's. he was also pleased that he could get great advantage from Khrushchev's speech. Khrushchev's speech both gladdened and worried him. The challenge of Stalin's prestige would certainly threaten his prestige, for he was loyal to Stalinism and was the Stalin of China; But topping Stalin from his pedestal also opened a door of the opportunity to achieve his greatness. Khrushchev's criticism against Stalin gave rise to an ideological confusion and the split in the International Communist Movement. Mao had a wild ambition and believed that he could gain the support of all the communist parties which opposed Khrushchev's line and establish his own "center for world revolution".

He tried to split communist parties, to set up Maoist parties and launch Maoism all over the world and become the leader of the International Communist Movement. He looked down on Khrushchev. He regarded himself to be the same generation with Stalin and Khrushchev was a second generation. To replace the position of Khrushchev had long been Mao's dream. He had a confidence and envisaged a prospect: "Communist parties all over the world will not believe in Soviet but believe in us." He even dreamed that after usurping Khrushchev's position he would continue to vanquish capitalism and surpass the United States of America. He told his top echelon: "China will become powerful in eight years", and Khrushchev "will completely bankrupt."

After the end of the Anti-Rightist Campaign, a couple of rightists of our unit were sent to the labor camp in "Great Northern Wilderness", all the other rightists, including Li Geng, Peng Zigang, Liu Zhong and I, were sent to the countryside to do manual work in early 1958. There were also a few cadres to go with us to supervise our reform through labor. Our working place was Qi village of Anguo county. Anguo is located in the center of Hebei Province, about 200 kilometers south of Beijing. It is China's largest collecting and distributing center of Chinese medicine.

Qi village is not far from the county proper. We were instructed "to live with the peasants under the same roof, eat at the same table and labor together with the peasants." I was living in an old female peasant's home, she has three sons and two daughters. Her husband had passed away. Her three sons were working in the field, her two daughters were studying in primary school. They were all very kind and welcomed me. I did not despite farm work and did not regard the punishment as a shameful thing. In my mind, our food and clothes are coming from agriculture. In the past I ate and clad other's produce, now I'll eat and clothe my own produce, it is a glorious thing, so I worked hard and tried to learn all kinds of farm work. I think the peasants and I are equal and regard them as brothers and sisters. And since I had lost my mother when I was very young and now an old woman took good care of me, I was glad and called her mom. It was absolutely a natural unintentional revelation of my feelings, not making a show. We were getting along very well like a family. Very soon I acclimated myself to the new circumstances.

Apart from doing farm work we rightists had a meeting every week, in which we would report our work, examine our thoughts and make self-criticism and criticize each other. On these meetings one rightist often said how great crimes she had made, how shameful she had betrayed the party, how much progress she has made in ideology and often criticized other rightists for neglecting the reform of ideology. I look down upon her. She is just downgrading others in order to show her to be a highly remolded person. I never over blame myself and never demean myself to cater for the desire of the leader. Each meeting I made the same self-criticism: My ideology was lagged behind, still staying in the stage of old democracy, not reaching the level of socialism yet, so I was often received criticism that I always neglected ideological remolding. I was not angry, just found it laughable. And I never criticized others.

Not long after we worked in the village, one day one of our rightists Fan Mengran suddenly disappeared. Our leader mobilized us all to search for him everywhere in the village but we could not find him. We suspected that he might run away to go back to his home. A couple of days later, a villager came to report that he saw a corpse in a wild pond. We went there and identified him to be Fan. He committed suicide. Fan Mengran was an editor of the editorial department of literature works, a handicapped creature, around thirty years old. His main crime was that he had written a poster "Comments after reading the article 'The origin of the slander'". That article was written by a very famous ancient writer Hang Yu in Tang dynasty one thousand years ago. The main idea of that article is like this: "In ancient times, men of noble character scrutinize themselves very strict and in an all-round way, while they demand others little and are magnanimous. In present time, men of noble character are quite the opposite, they demand others boundlessly, extensively, comprehensively, but scrutinize themselves very little. The root cause of such thinking is sloth and jealousy. The slothful cannot improve themselves, and the jealous are afraid that others may excel. Then when success is achieved, slander is generated; When there is lofty virtue, defamation comes with it. Living in this kind of world, intellectuals find it really difficult to have a good name and a perfect morality. If the high-ranking officials with lofty ideal can keep principle in mind tightly, I say, the country would be governed more perfectly."

Fan Mengran put great premium on that article and thought our country's present state of affairs was just like what the article described. His view was considered as a fierce attack on the party and its leader. He got a heavy punishment. He was single, not married yet. He had often been unjustly criticized. He had physical defect and was still forced to do manual work. He must have felt desperate and could not bear the pain both psychologically and physically, so he decided to go to his final resting place. He was still very young, but he was not allowed to display his talents for the benefit of the country, he could not realize his dreams and deeds, it was really a pity. I was very sad and sympathized with him deeply, but I did not say anything. No one showed their sympathy in public, for suicide was regarded as a protest against the party.

Early in 1958 Mao initiated a campaign against the "four pests" - mosquitoes, flies, rats, and sparrows. Which was deemed as an overture for the nationwide mobilization of the Great Leap Forward. He succinctly put it: "The whole people, including five-year children, must be mobilized to eliminate the four pests" Contest was held among enterprises, government agencies, schools, etc. My landlord's children were asked by their teachers to take a fly swatter always in school or at home and were taught how to make a catapult and mousetrap. Whenever they flapped a fly, they collected it in a bottle for being counted by their teachers. Those who killed the most were named model students. They were each given a quota of a hundred dead flies a week. They made traps and shoot at birds. Some boy students climbed the trees to knock down sparrow nests, kill the nestlings and break eggs. Life-sized straw men stood everywhere to frighten the birds, students and other people chased the birds around, beat gongs and drums, bang pots and pans to scare the birds. All the voices and rackets kept the sparrows in flight finding no place to land until they fell down from the sky for exhaustion. In the cities, all the people were also mobilized to battle against the sparrows, including officials, scholars. Guo Moruo, the president of the Chinese Academy of Science at that time, wrote a very long poem titled "Swearing at the sparrow" published on "Beijing Evening Paper" The photo of Su Buqing, a famous mathematician, member of the Chinese Academy of Sciences, was published in the newspaper. He is beating the washbasin to shoo away sparrows.

Mao believed sparrows eat grain seeds and an official wrong data that "Each sparrow ate some 4.5 kilograms of grain annually" But according to the research of the specialists, sparrow is one link of bio-chain, its main food is pests of crops. During the campaign, it was said that at least eight million birds were killed. The extermination of sparrows led to an upset of the ecological balance and enabled population of locusts and other crop eating insects ballooned, Due to the absence of natural predators, bugs destroyed crops and caused a substantial reduction of grain output which exacerbated the great famine.

Without consulting scientists and making any scientific research Mao made such an absurd and harmful decision.

A Painful Reminiscence of a Dignified Soul

After the "Anti Rightist Campaign" Mao greatly enhanced his personality cult and nobody dared to air their true views and oppose him, he gradually revealed his true face. He publicly exposed his opposition of the Anti-Personality-Cult and the de-Stalinization campaign of Soviet Union. He argued that the general line of the International Communist Movement (ICM) had been correct during Stalin's tenure, that he was not just a Soviet Union leader, but a leader of a world-wide ICM, who could not be swept aside by Khrushchev. He told the Polish Communist Party that "Khrushchev's opposition to personality cult was without substance" He persisted that Stalin's line was correct and Khrushchev betrayed it.

Using his prestige Mao constantly encouraged and promoted his own personality cult. In an enlarged Political Bureau meeting he said "There are right and wrong two kinds of personality cult, we should insist on the right kind of personality cult, like the appropriate worship of proper objects such as the correct aspects of Marx, Engels, Lenin, and Stalin, Which we must worship, eternally worship, and it's terrible not to worship them. The truth lies in their hands, why shouldn't we worship them?" Mao maintained that Stalin's "merits outweighed his demerits, and castigated Khrushchev for tossing away the "daggers of Leninism and Stalinism", and tossing away these daggers would undermine Chinese socialism. He said "The member of a team must worship its team leader, failing to do so is wrong." "It was not appropriate to negate the personality cult in principle." He also warned other Chinese leaders that "In Soviet Union they (imply a criticism of Khrushchev) used to praise Stalin to the sky, but now they condemned him to hell. Some people in our country echo the cult of personality." His word was implying a criticism of Liu Shaoqi, Deng Xiaoping and other top-ranking leaders. And not long after that he retaliated what Liu and Deng had done at the Eighth Congress, Mao declared In the third plenary of the Eighth Congress: "There can be no doubt that the contradiction between proletariat and bourgeoisie, between the road of capitalism and the road of socialism are the principal contradiction of our country. The resolution of the Eighth Congress has one section, which writes the principal contradiction of our country is between an advanced social system and a backward productive force. This formulation is incorrect. The resolution of the Eighth Congress should return to the version of Seventh Congress's Resolution." A correct resolution was overthrown. A single party member can deny the resolution of the Party Congress. It is really a strange thing, which can only happen in China under Mao's rule.

In November 1957, Soviet Union celebrated the 40th anniversary of socialist revolution and convened the conference of the Communist Party. The conference was attended by leaders of sixty-four Communist Party, among which twelve of the communist parties were in power. Mao attended the meeting. He wanted to place himself in the summit as a leader equal to Khrushchev. At that conference Mao delivered a speech, in which he talked about the war and death with a gross language, flippant manner, and an indifference to human suffering: "The enemy would not fall down itself unless you hit it. Just as the dust would not run away itself unless you sweep it. What should we fear for nuclear war?" "There are 2.7 billion people in the world, even half of it were died, there are still half remained. China has six hundred million people, even half of it were died, there still are three hundred million there, but Imperialism would be razed to the ground and the whole world become socialist. After a few years there would be 2.7 billion people again." His word shocked and upset all the audience. Even the Stalinists were appalled. Only twelve years after the tragic Second World War, all the country and people of the world wanted to avoid war and raise living standards, now a mad man wanted a third world war, and a nuclear war, with the death of half the population of the world. At that meeting Mao also made a fallacy: "People say that poverty is bad, but in fact poverty is good. The poorer people are, the more revolutionary they are. It is dreadful to imagine a time when everyone will be rich… From a surplus of calories people will have two heads and four legs."

Khrushchev did not agree Mao's view, he believed "there was a real possibility of peaceful coexistence with the west." "No world war is needed for the triumph of socialist ideas throughout the world." "Only madmen and maniacs can now call for another world war." "millions of people might burn in the conflagration." He urged Mao to be conciliatory towards the west. "To avoid anything that could be exploited to start an armed conflict, to drive the world back into the cold war 'rut'". He promoted peaceful competition and he had the confidence of winning the race. In that year Soviet Union launched its first artificial satellite, leaving the United States of America behind. The news vibrated the whole world. At that meeting Khrushchev also proclaimed that Soviet Union will overtake United States of America economically in fifteen years. Following Khrushchev's proud word, Mao proclaimed that China will overtake Britain economically in fifteen years.

A Painful Reminiscence of a Dignified Soul

Mao believed his thought was the development of Marxism-Leninism. Soviet Union accorded his thought no such honor. Even Stalin hadn't said anything like this. Mao was vexed, questioning: "Did philosophy really reach its limits with Marx and Lenin?"

Mao knew that he lacked the economic and military muscle, if he wanted to defeat Khrushchev and achieved his goal, he had to have real strength, he must have more advanced weapons, more steel and other industrial and agricultural products

Mao also realized that if he wanted to achieve his goal, he must obtain the strength in short time. He knew man's life is limited. China has a common saying: "There are very rare person who can live till seventy". In 1950, at his first visit to Soviet Union, Mao made a speech to the students studying there, in which he said "The world is yours as well as ours. It is ours because we are in power now; But in the ultimate analysis, it is yours because we'll passed away early or later. I have a desire: If I could live fifteen years more I would be perfectly satisfied." he speculated he could still live fifteen years. he had to fulfill his plan within this time, otherwise he could not achieve his goal in his lifetime. He determined to hasten, force all the people to complete his goal and he had the confidence he would defeat Soviet Union and the United States of America in fifteen years.

Why Mao believed he could fulfill his plan in such a short time? I guessed he must be completely carried away by his success in the civil war. He calculated that he could defeat eight millions army of Nationalist Party in the civil war in three or four years and became the emperor of China; now he had six hundred million people absolutely at his disposal, and he could use every resource of the nation at will, why he could not realize communism and become the emperor of the world in ten to fifteen years? He did not know why he could defeat Guomindang in a few years. He thought it was because of his extraordinary talents. It was not the fact. It is because the people made all their efforts and sacrifices to realize a great ideal—to build a more prosperous, just, democratic country as Mao promised. Now he betrayed his words and forced people to do what they hated to do— to confiscate their land and properties, to do backbreaking labor day and night to realize his own private ambition, how could he be successful? He was just carried away by his flight of fancy. He could only damage the interests of the people and the country.

When Mao return to China from the Soviet Union, he immediately pushes on his plan crazily, frantically. In January 1958, Mao convened a meeting in Nanning,

Guangxi province. At that meeting he emphasized high speed again and again, and fiercely criticized the "Anti Rash Advance" promoted by Premier Zhou. He said, "Anti Rash Advance" disheartened the six hundred million people. It is a mistaken guiding principle." He also put forward an impracticable plan for the Great Leap Forward, forced the provincial chiefs to raise high targets. Two months later, he convened another meeting in Chengdu, Sichuan Province. He continued to criticize "Anti Rash Advance" and proclaimed that "the General Line of 'Go all out, aim at highest, and get greater, quicker, better and more economical results in building socialism' has already been formed." He forced the provincial chiefs to raise high targets again. One month later, he convened two more meetings still in Wuhan, Hubei Province and Guangzhou, Guangdong Province in succession. In these two meetings he executed the same task he had done in the former two meetings. He travelled north and south, east and west of the country, held four meetings within four months to push the great leap forward, trying to fulfill his plan and realize his ambition as soon as possible.

During those meetings Mao prodded, goaded, cajoled and forced the whole party into subjection to him, accusing the provincial leaders and the planners of economy to drag his feet and hold the country back. He whipped them into shape and pressed them out of their lethargy. He described the party leaders as "a bunch of zombies with a slave mentality." and criticized those who favored a more cautious tempo as "women with bound feet'. He argued that those who were against his insistence of "rapid advance" and preached caution were against Marxism, and therefore were rightists. He ordered to adjust the targets of agricultural and industrial output set by the Eighth Congress, highly raised the number of the target. He took direct managerial control of the economy. He also stressed that classes continued to exist even with the establishment of a socialist economic system. Workers and peasants belonged to the laboring class and were good. But the remnants of imperialism, feudalism, bureaucratic capitalism and the national bourgeoisie still existed and they would oppose the socialist transformation.

In order to foster his prestige and intensify his personality cult, Mao ordered Premier Zhou Englai to make self-criticism in front of dozens of provincial chiefs. He humiliated and abased Zhou in front of his subordinates and implied that Zhou was only fifty meters away from being a rightist. Zhou perceived the danger and made self-criticism: "opposing rash advance is a problem that caused directional mistake and error. It is a type of right-deviating conservative mentality. It is a policy of hindrance contrary to the chairman's policy of promotion. I take the chief responsibility for this erroneous opposition to rash advance." Mao was not satisfied with Zhou's self-criticism. Zhou submitted his resignation from his position, but his request was denied. Mao knew Zhou was a highly competent man, he needed to use Zhou's ability to serve his deed. Under Mao's pressure Zhou made a self-criticism again: "I take the main responsibility for submitting the report opposing rash advance, in effect dashing cold water on the upsurge among the masses. The result was not to promote but to hinder; not greater, faster, better, and more economical, but less, slower, shoddier, and more wasteful. That is the essence of the problem." Zhou still could not get a pass. He made the third time self-criticism: "I am one of the people most responsible for the opposition to rash advance and should therefore learn even more from this incident." "The historical experience of China's decades of revolution and construction proved that Chairman Mao is the representative of truth." Mao was satisfied and let Zhou pass. Mao used his enormous personal prestige to compel his top echelon and provincial chiefs to bow to whatever he said. He told them: "There has to be a personality cult. It is absolutely necessary."

Under Mao's pressure or for licking the boots of Chairman Mao, provincial chiefs and the heads of government departments put forward higher targets one after another. For example, Metallurgy Ministry head Wang Heshou set a steel production goals that it will reach 120 million tons by 1962. General Wang Zhen, who was in charge of agricultural reclamation in Xinjiang Autonomous Region, proclaimed that 300 million Mu(a Mu is one-sixth of an acre) of virgin land would be cultivated within ten years. Ke Qingshi, the party secretary of Shanghai Municipality, had a project of cultural revolution for the next fifteen years: "Everyone can read Marx's *Das Kapital* and is proficient in calculus. Flies, mosquitoes, bed bugs, rats, sparrows, and other pests are all long extinct and every work team has its own Li Bai, Lu Xun, and Nie Er (China's most famous poet, writer and composer) The ultimate construction of communism is not far away." Radical speech, thinking became the mainstream and the guiding force.

Elating by the high-sounding words of his Ministers and provincial chiefs, Mao lost his head. He repeated in every place that we must build up our strength quickly. "Speed is everything—the essence" "China should go its own way on the socialist road, China's path could outpace the Soviet Union much faster." "We will do the things Soviet Union completed in 40 years (1917-1957, from the October

Revolution to the twentieth party congress) within 13 years (1949-1962, from the founding of the PRC to the last year of the second five-year plan). He changed his demand each year, even each month. In November 1957, he proclaimed that China will overtake Britain economically in fifteen years. In February 1958, he said that our speed of production could be much fast, we could overtake Britain in ten years. On April 15, 1958 at the Wuhan meeting he said: "With the great leap forward, the speed for catching up Britain in industry, agriculture production can be faster than we had predicted". At the Guangzhou meeting he said: "With six hundred million people, with the accomplishment of Anti-rightists, each year we engage in fierce efforts four times, it is quite possible to catch up United States of America in fifteen years." On May 8, 1958 he said: "Dispelling feelings of inferiority, and stimulating a dauntless creative spirit of daring to think, daring to speak, and daring to act, which will definitely help in achieving our goal of surpassing England in seven years and overtaking the United States of America in another eight or ten years." On June 23, 1958 he declared that, "by 1962 we can produce 75-80 million tons of steel so we don't need five years to catch up with Britain, two or three years will do". He threw his country into a frenzy, "Battle hard for three years to change the face of China."

For beating Khrushchev, for the realization of his ambition of becoming the emperor of the world within his lifetime, he launched the great leap forward movement. He spelt out to the small cronies what he meant to do once the Great Leap Forward was completed: "Now the Pacific Ocean is not peaceful. It can only be peaceful when we take it over." He also told selected provincial chiefs: "In the future we will set up the world Control Committee, and make a plan to unify the world." In August 1958 He boasted: "In only ten to twenty years, the Soviet Union will be two times as rich as U.S. and we will be four times as rich as U.S." He declared to the atom bomb maker: "We are not only the political center of the world revolution, we must become the center of the world revolution militarily and technologically." He was confident he would be the greatest man in the world. Once he told the Australian Maoist leader Hill: "In my opinion, the world needs to be unified… In the past, many men, including the Mongols, the Romans, Alexander the Great, Napoleon, and the British Empire, wanted to unify the world. Today, both the United States and the Soviet Union want to unify the world. Hitler wanted to unify the world… But they all failed. It seems to me that the possibility of unifying the world has not disappeared… In my view, the world can be unified." Mao clearly felt that he was the man for the job. He thought that he owned the largest population in the world, which no other country could be compared; he could channel every resource of the nation into his movement; and he had already absolutely controlled the people and the country, he would certainly reach his goal.

He started the Great Leap Forward Movement.

Mao knows nothing of economics, knows nothing of science and technology, and knows nothing of the law of nature. He only knows the political trickery through repeated reading the book "The history of twenty-Four dynasties". He wanted to do the things which human beings could not reach, without any consideration of morality, without any consideration of shame, without any consideration of human life. He directed a most ridiculous, most cruel, most atrocious, most farcical play in world history. Its cost was tens of millions of lives, countless waste of resources, time and human labor.

Mao started his great leap forward from agriculture. He knew that only by greatly raising agricultural products first China can change from an agrarian society to an industrial society. Mao also knew China's productive forces were still very low and backward, impossible to rapidly increase agricultural products by the conventional practice, so he must take radical measures. For this reason, Mao devised an "Eight Characters Charter for Agriculture of Mao Zedong". The eight characters were soil, fertilizer, water, seed, close-planting, protection, tending, tool. Mao attached great importance to the Eight Characters Charter and had full confidence that if the peasants carried them out, the agricultural products would certainly soar up quickly. He called on the peasants of the country to fight a "people's war" in farming to "go all out, aim at the highest, and get greater, quicker, better and more economical results in building socialism" and put "Eight Characters Charter" into effect. All the newspapers and magazines gave wide publicity to the Eight Characters Charter. Only the People' Daily had published about 80 editorials on the Charter and praised it as a fundamental law of fully using the natural potential to guarantee successive high products. All the media also published the instructions, demands and measures of the Eight Characters Charter, which were ordered to be strictly followed. The main points stressed in the "Eight Characters character" were as follows:

> **Soil:** Soil was deemed to be the most important word of the eight character. The Charter demanded to make an overall survey,

planning and rational use of land, deep plowing and soil improvement. Deep plowing was especially emphasized. The leader of the program demanded the peasants to plow one to two meter deep of the soil and plow entire soil of the country so deep within two or three years. Some village leaders implemented the order earnestly and forced the peasants to dig down six or seven feet. At that time, I was laboring in the countryside. I didn't believe the practice. In my opinion, a reasonable deep plowing might be all right, for it made the soil softer and root could extend more easily, but plowing so much deep was obviously unscientific. The surface soil is fertile with humus while the deep barren soil hasn't any organic materials. Bringing the immature soil to the surface not only wasted the labor but also was detrimental to the surface fertile soil and greatly reduced the output. Most peasants had the same idea, but they had to plow deeper and deeper, for it was the order from above. Marshaled by local cadres, millions of peasants gathered in the fields and dug deep soil. Some enthusiastic cadres called the peasants to "fight a fierce battle", forced them to work day and night, or even worked successively for two or three days. Peasants were hamstrung by excessive work and all their energy was sapped. They knew their labor were all to no avail, but no one dared to complain. If one aired any different idea, he would be blamed as a conservative person or persecuted. I was taking part in the deep plowing and felt extremely tired too. I also kept silence for the same reason. I could not forget the lessons I got at the Anti-Rightists Campaign.

Close-planting: This word was regarded as the second most important word. The charter demanded close planting and intercropping so as to produce maximum possible output of crops per unit area. in the past the peasants usually sow twenty or thirty Jin (a Jin is 500 gram) of wheat as seeds in one Mu of the field, now their leaders ordered them to sow fifty or one hundred Jin of wheat as seeds in one Mu (a Mu is one-sixth of an acre) of the field. In some "advanced" county they even sowed two or three hundred Jin seeds in one Mu. For growing rice, the peasant greatly shortens the distance between the plants. In some villages they transplanted two or three million rice seedlings in one Mu of paddy field. With excessively close-planting, rice seedlings could not get adequate ventilation and sunlight, the seedling was as thin as a matchstick, and in some fields the grain produced was less than the seed grain that was sown.

Fertilizer: The Charter demanded to increasing the application of fertilizer and rational application of fertilizers. At that time there were very few chemical fertilizers in China, so the authority emphasized the peasant's home fertilizer and the native chemical fertilizer, such as the earth from walls, Kangs, and kitchen ranges. The cadres always set a very high quota of the fertilizer for the production team, demanding them apply 50,000 Jin or 100,000 jin of fertilizer on one Mu of the field. Some county leaders even demand the peasants to apply 200,000 to 300,000 Jin fertilizers on one Mu of field. The excrement and urine of the human beings and animals are limited, where can the peasants get so many fertilizers? Sometimes the peasants had to destroy their own kitchen ranges or part of their walls to scrape up enough fertilizer to meet the quota. In our village we practiced a fraud to fulfill the quota. I had also done the work of collection of fertilizer. Early in the morning I drove an ox-drawn cart to the field. I waved the whip in the air and snapped it crisply, and the cow broke into quick trot. With a spade I filled the cart full with the soil from the field, drove the cart back to my home and dumped the earth into the pigsty. I drove the cart to the field to carry more soil again and again, and dumped them into the pigsty again and again. Then I mixed the little pig dung with the huge soil, carried all the soil back to the field with the cart and stacked them in heaps for the examination of the inspectors. The same soil of the field was regarded as the fertilizer now for it contained a wisp of pig dung. Even the inspectors knew the fact too. We all did the absurd thing just for the report to the leadership. We all also knew our labor was completely a waste but we had no way to avoid it, we had to obey the orders, we had to satisfied Mao's desire.

Water: For the water conservation the Charter demanded construction of projects for irrigation and drainage. Every village was ordered to build reservoirs, canals, ditches, wells in a big scope. Even the mountain villages were ordered to dig wells where there were no underground waters. A model county Changan proclaimed that it would build 2,232 motor-pumped wells, 888 artificial wells, 200 irrigation canals and other facilities within the winter of 1958 and the spring of 1959. The cadre always kept peasants' nose to the grindstone.

Protection: The Charter demanded to prevent and control plant diseases and radically eliminate all the pests in a few years. All the governments mapped out their program. Some provinces and municipalities proclaimed that there already appeared counties without diseases and pests in paddy fields.

Tending: The Charter demanded to practice intensive cultivation and improve farming methods, promoting timely field cultivation, irrigation, application fertilizers, and meticulous care of crops throughout the growing period. The cadres always set high, irrational demands, forced the peasants do the neck breaking work in the field.

Seed: The Charter demanded the use of seed from high-yielding improved varieties. Superior seed strains should be created through strict scientific research. Now the peasants were pressed to use any methods to create good seeds. You can imagine what the result would happen.

Tool: The Charter demanded to improve old-style tools and develop new tools. The peasants were also pushed to device highly efficient instruments of production in short time.

The absurd orders came down one after another: to plow deep and plant close, to apply huge amount fertilizer which nowhere could be found and eliminate all pests in a definite time. The peasants were tired out by too much running around.

A Painful Reminiscence of a Dignified Soul

The basic reason for the preposterous things happened in the practicing Eight Characters Charter was the fierce pressure from above. Chairman Mao's word was the laws that had to be obeyed without failure. He pressed the provincial chiefs and Ministers to set high targets. These officials pressed their subordinates to carry out the high targets. Then their subordinates raised the quotas and pressed their subordinates to carry out the higher quotas. Officials raised the quota at each level till the production team leader. In addition, there were also opportunists who boasted they could create miracles in order to get their superior's favor.

Media also performed very bad functions. For example, without any check of facts, the People's Daily reported on Jan. 12 1958 that: "In Henan province, a 'Sputnik Co-operative' had produced 1.8 tons of wheat on one Mu of the field—more than ten times the nom." On Sep. 18th 1958 it published a headline news on the front page that "Peace Agricultural Cooperative in Henan province produced 7,320 Jin wheat per Mu." Some newspapers even boasted that "Jianguo Agricultural Cooperative in Hubei Province produced 36,956 Jin early rice per Mu"; "Red Flag Commune in Guangxi Province produced 130,434 middle rice per Mu". They also spread many absurd slogans. such as "Bitter struggle for three years will bring a thousand years of happiness". "How much big boldness you have, how much big products the earth produce!", "Politics in command!" "Changing China's face in three years!" They provided all the false news and big words every day.

At the same time, China's most famous scientist Qian Xuesen provided a "scientist foundation" for high yielding agricultural products. He wrote an article in Youth Daily on June 16th 1958, proving that it is possible that the output of rice and wheat can be raised to more than 40,000 Jin per Mu, the output of vegetables can be raised to more than 1.6 million Jin per Mu. He also wrote several similar articles on other magazines. Mao praised him; millions of people believed him for he was the top scientist in China. These articles caused very bad influence and great disaster at that time. I did not know why he wrote those articles; he was forced to do the thing or he was just echoing the great leap forward movement and following the trend. I did not want to blame him too much but I thought he should at least make an apology for this great mistake afterwards. Everyone must hold an account for one's actions. It was a great pity that he didn't make a single word of apology until his last day.

Under the great pressure from above and the far and wide false propaganda, a tendency of boasting was rampant everywhere. Exaggerated rhetoric became concrete demands. Impossible whimsy was supposed to be reality. Telling fake fantasies was commonplace and was raised to an incredible degree. "Sputnik fields" mushroomed.

In order to realize his selfish will-o-the-wisp dream Mao made the bold exhortation: "Conquer heaven and earth." "Capable women can make a meal without food." —a reversal of a pragmatic ancient Chinese proverb "No matter how capable, a woman cannot make a meal without food." inspired by Mao's words Local leaders competed with one another to see who could create the greatest deed. One brigade proclaimed they produced more than one million Jin sweet potatoes per Mu; the other collective announced they produced one hundred and twenty thousand Jin of wheat per Mu and ten thousand Jin peanuts were harvested per Mu. Rice grains the size of soybeans, soybeans like potatoes, sesame seeds rivaling corn kernels, Peanuts like sweet potatoes, sweet potatoes as big as watermelons. A pig put on flesh nineteen Jin per day; Hens laid ostrich-sized eggs. Some brigades used papier-mâché to make three feet long cucumbers, five Jin tomatoes, elephant-like pigs to cheat their leaders. One of the authority's and media's mission was to compose nonsense achievements. The whole nation slid into doublespeak. Word became divorced from reality, virtue and responsibility. Fanaticism overrode caution, ignorance triumphed over reason. Lies were told with easy because they would not be punished but be praised. Sensible cadres and common people did not like all those absurd words and things, but Chairman Mao appreciated them and encouraged them.

For example, Fan county, Shandong province, proclaimed that "within two years it would realize full industrialization and electrification, achieve grain yields of 10,000 kilos per Mu, build four to six universities and one academy of sciences, and realize the ideal of 'from each according to his ability and to each according to his need'", "For everyone who enters the new paradise, there is no need to pay for food, drink and clothing. There will be all kinds of fresh meat, four dishes per meal, fruit every day, and all kinds of clothes." Mao read Fan County's article at the central committee meeting in Zhengzhou on November 6th, and wrote a memo: "This is very interesting; it's poetic; but it also seems feasible." and distributed the article to central government leaders, heads of major regions and provincial party secretaries at the meeting.

Another example, the party committee of Xushui county, Hebei Province proclaimed: "Socialism will be more or less completed in the second five-year plan.

A Painful Reminiscence of a Dignified Soul

During the third five-year plan, we'll make the transition to communism in Xushui that will integrate industry, agriculture, the military, education, and commerce into a whole." Pleased by their high ideal and enthusiasm, Mao Zedong himself visited Xushui County in Autumn 1958. The county declared that there was a high-yielding wheat plot so closely planted that they could support a small boy staying on their top. This miracle was proved by a picture published on the newspaper. They said the yield from the plot was thirty thousand Jin per Mu, over ten times more of that from the most fertile land in the country. When local cadres boasted to Mao that they were going to produce ten times as much grain as before. Mao was delighted. He smiled broadly and responded: "When you produce more food than you could possibly eat, what are you going to do with all that food? It is not bad to have too much food. The state doesn't want it, you can keep plenty as your own reserve. You can eat five meals a day! You can cut your working hours by half. Now that you need not work full time, you can spend the other half time obtaining knowledge and enjoy in entertainment". This miracle had been repeatedly reported by all the media. Under the influence of Mao, most high-ranking officials and 930 prominent individuals from more than forty foreign countries, more than 3,000 units and some 320,000 people toured Xushui. Once the local carder explained to a Russian delegation how they had created such a miracle, the visitors did not say a single word. After they left the plot they privately talked to the Chinese official: What happened in Xushui is dangerous. During Stalin's campaign of collectivization, the same thing happened in our country, and severe starvation resulted." By mid-Oct. 1958 the fraud had been exposed. It was revealed that the high-yield miracle was a fabrication. According to the superior's order, peasants moved crops from several plots of land to that show plot. And many of those crops dies within a short time because of the late transplantation and the high density. Despite the fabrication, the creators of the miracle did not receive any punishment. The party still paid tribute to Xushui for its high enthusiasm and the rapid pace towards Communism. While the People's Daily declared that "We can produce as much food as we want." Mao even asserted publicly that "We must consider what to do with all this surplus food."

The victims of the exaggeration of agricultural products were the peasants, because rural areas were taxed on a percentage of their output. As the brigade had falsely claimed fantastic high yields, they had to pay much higher taxes and they could keep only a little of their true output and caused starvation.

Zhong Da

The village in which I labored was also forced to do all the absurd orders from above, but our village leaders were not similar to those "advanced villages", they did not court publicity, did not "Launch the Sputnik". They just asked the peasants to do their utmost to meet the target the superior demanded. They were also kind toward us coming from Beijing. They knew we were not used to manual labor yet, so they did not ask us to take part in the "fighting the fierce battle" at night or went far away to build the reservoir. We were just asked to perform the ordinary field work, like deep plowing the soil, close planting crops, gathering and spreading fertilizers, etc. The peasants had no stomach for work at all but were forced to do corvee at the behest of the cadre. They did not like the new methods of farming, especially the deep plowing and the close planting. Once a very old peasant, an old party member, told me his feelings for giving vent to his anger: "I have lived so long and I was a farmer all my life, but I have never seen or heard such nonsense way of farming." I consoled him and I said I highly respect him. The peasant had no enthusiasm in their work, for they worked for collectivity and received the same reward no matter how much work they had done. And as much work they had done were fruitless, they worked more but could not get more reward, or even get less reward than before. In addition, they were often overworked and had no energy to do house work, they were angry. They did not dare to complain but they would resort to the passive form of protest—slack in work. Sometimes, if no leader was present in the field, peasants would sit down and chat for half an hour before they started working. During their work, they were not exerting much of their strength. or stood still, leaning on their hoes resting for a while. When the regular break arrived, they would take out their pipes and smoke for a long time. They were very poor, some families even hadn't money to buy the necessary clothes. They were not allowed to leave the countryside to seek a job or beg in the city. They hadn't any hope or desire.

Once I asked a strong young peasant, "What is your highest expectation?"

He replied, "In my life if I can have a chance to visit West Lake in Hangzhou, I would die with satisfaction."

His answer made my heart cry with sadness. A round trip to Hangzhou was only a matter about 30 RMB and he was wondering whether he could have that chance in his entire life. What a tragedy it is! I wanted to help him to realize his dream, but I did not dare to do so because I was a "class enemy". I might be accused of corrupting a young peasant's mind or to stir up his hate against the Communist Party.

A Painful Reminiscence of a Dignified Soul

During the period of the Great Leap Forward, total output of grain was reduced year by year. In 1960, the total grain output was 287 billion jin, 103.1 billion jin less than 1957. The Great Leap Forward in agriculture, which had cost countless peasants' sweat, blood, and time, turned out to be a great jump back.

For promoting productivity in industry, Mao took steel as the key pillar. On August 16, 1958 he put forward a grand plan "surpass Britain and catch up with America" in the Politburo meeting at the town by Beidai River. He demanded the entire people to double the output of steel in one year, from 5.35 million tons in 1957 to 10.7 million tons in 1958; next year 27-30 million tons; with three years bitter fight reaching fifty million tons; In 1964, 150 million tons. He said, "At that time we'll surpass America and become number one in the world. Isn't it a good thing being number one in the world?" When he made this call, 1958 had passed almost eight months. At that time the output of steel was only three-million-plus tons. He wanted to produce seven million steel in the last four months, wasn't it an idea of a maniac? What made him seek high speed so eagerly like a madman? He dreamed to become an emperor of the world within the time of his life. Many intellectuals were aware of the folly of such a plan, but their experience during the Anti-Rightist Campaign taught them to keep silence. They were waiting to watch the farce.

Of course, Mao himself knew he had no advanced technology, he could not reach his goal through usual, conventional mode of production for manufacturing so much steels. To give full vent to his half-baked dream of turning China into first rate power rapidly, he, like raising his "Eight Characters Charter" in agriculture, ordered the whole people, without any knowledge of metallurgy, to establish small backyard furnaces to make steel. At that time steel was called the "supreme commander". "Steel was everything".

Answering to his order the campaign swept like a giant wildfire across china and affected every aspect of social life. All sorts of Inapt and completely ineffective furnaces, large and small, built of brick, stone or earth and fueled by wood or coal. were established in every office, school, factory and even hospital. All the people, including juvenile over age 12 were asked to take part in the great campaign. Personal sacrifices were demanded of everyone. The steel-making went on twenty-four hours a day, seven days a week, attended by old and young alike. sweating and exhausted. In every backyard furnace site of every unit, red flags fluttered, drums and gongs were struck, slogans such as "Long live the great leap forward!",

"Realization of communism in three years!", "10.7 million tons of steel this year!," "We are in an era: one day is equivalent twenty years.", "The whole people smelt the steel; The steel smelt the whole people." were placarded on walls or blared from loudspeakers. All the units were given a quota, they had to fulfill or over fulfill it to meet the wild target set by Chairman Mao.

Mao visited a backyard furnace in Hefei, Anhui province in September 1958, which was claimed to be manufacturing high quality steel. Mao praised it and regarded it as an example for the units all over the country.

In the countryside, millions of furnaces were made too. In many villages, clusters of hundreds of backyard furnaces stretched several square kilometers across a field or a hillside. Instead of doing farm work many male peasants had to build and tend to backyard furnaces During the harvest season, a lot of crops were rotted in the field for lack of the labors.

To supply the raw materials for making steel, peasants and workers went to the mountains to search iron mine and extract iron ore. Where iron ore was unavailable, they produced steel out of scrap metal. Useless woks, pans, pots, tools, and even bicycles were requisitioned from every household to supply the scrap for the furnaces. Pupils were sent to streets and every corner to search nails, wheels and any other scrap iron. It did seem ridiculous to melt scrap iron to produce iron, to destroy pots to make pots. In fact, most of the melted pots could not make pots again, because they contained too many impurities. To supply the fuel for making steel, people cut down trees from forests. Many mountains or hills near the furnace sites were denuded of trees, bringing immense disaster to the local environment. Wood like broken tables, chairs, bed planks, and other wood furniture were also requisitioned from every household, very often good furniture were taken over for use without any compensation.

The national steel making frenzy was whipped up, even more absurd and unrealistic than the fierce fighting in agriculture, an article published in *People's Daily* vividly described the fanatic scene of the movement. Its title was "The boiling day and night; night and day", in which there was a sentence like this: "A great army of millions of steel makers entered the barren mountains and wild ridges, awakened the countless hills from their sound sleep; in the perennially silent mountain valleys, demolition heroes ignited detonators and explosives to open the mine, the inexhaustible ores and coals poured out toward the furnaces like flowing water." Such instigating descriptions were full of that article.

A Painful Reminiscence of a Dignified Soul

During the movement, I myself also took part in the production of steel. It was a great project organized by the county. The work site was close to an iron mine. All the peasants of the county were divided into three groups: The villagers of the first group were responsible to extract iron ore from the mine and supply the ore; The villagers of the second group were responsible to cut down trees from the mountains, split the wood and supply the fuel; The villagers of the third group were responsible to build the clay furnaces and smelt the steel. The peasants of our village belonged to the third group.

One day in September we set out to the worksite. It was a great distance, we had to walk over fifty miles to get there within two days. Each of us, holding a spade in hand, proceeded in a long column, among which there were several carts loading utilities, implements and bedrolls. It was really a magnificent sight. On the first day I stood up to the arduous journey fairly well, but on the second day I was exhausted, trudging wearily, mechanically, dreamingly with aching and swollen legs. I even walked for some distance while I was really sleeping. I did not know how could I do that miracle thing. I speculated that the reason might be "while we sleep our brain does not completely rest, some part of which can still work, leading us to do things normally.". And I remembered a past fact: When I was in high school, a classmate did get up at midnight, open the door of the dormitory, walk a few seconds outside, then come back, shut the door, go to bed and sleep again. Next day the classmate, who had watched what he had done, asked him why he got out at midnight. He was surprised and said he completely did not know what he had done. It was a mere somnambulism. I thought I must have done the same thing. During that journey not only I was exhausted, many others had the same problem. A few of them even felt dizzy or delirious and had to rest for a while. An old peasant who sat on the top of the utility of a cart fell down dead while he slept.

Finally, we arrived at the worksite. It was a vast expanse of sweet potato fields covered with a green sea of the leaves. How beautiful a sight it is! But we immediately became the murderers of the great scene, cutting all the leaves out and building the clay furnaces. The sweet potatoes were far from ripe, very small, and could not be used as food. We worked throughout the night, lit by torches. When the dawn of the next day came, another marvelous spectacle emerged before our eyes: Just over one night, hundreds of clay furnaces neatly arranged conjured out of a vast expanse of the field—a sight that resembled the scene in the Arabian Nights. A miracle appeared with a pointed finger.

We put the ore in the furnaces and started the fire to smelt the steel. We took turns to attend the furnaces and stoke the fuel. We rested and slept on the ground. On average we could sleep only four or five hours a day. The ore supplier told us that the iron mine was not hidden inside the mountain, but a layer of iron ore uncovered on the ravine. Its thickness was only about an inch. According to the professional Its iron content was very low and its impurities were high, it was of no worth to exploit at all. But no one considered the question. The only thing we had to do was to fulfill the target the superior assigned us. Quality mattered nothing.

Several days later our steelmaking work was finished. The melted liquid iron and the dregs were mingled with each other. When they were cold, they formed lumps of slag, which were reported to the superior as steels.

Our target was triumphantly fulfilled. All our energies and all the materials were exchanged to a lot of useless things. I also felt great regret that a large number of sweet potato plants were destroyed. If waited till their harvest time, they would produce at least a whole year's worth of food for one thousand people. That meant more than one thousand peasants would not starve to death in the later famine.

Mao had visited modern steel works in Northeast area in January 1959, where he found out that high quality steel could only be produced in large scale factories using reliable fuel such as coke. However, he did not order a halt to the backyard furnaces so as not to dampen the revolutionary enthusiasm of the masses. The movement was only quietly abandoned much later by the end of 1959. To Mao, the success of the great leap forward was much more vital than the lives and properties of ordinary people. People's sufferings were completely not Mao's concern.

At last it was declared that 11.08 million tons of steel was produced by the end of 1958. So that the wild production targets of doubling the national output within one year was to be met. But the qualified steel was reported only eight million tons. Almost all the so-called steel that was produced by the backyard furnaces turned out to be completely useless lumps of slag. Only very little output consisted of low-quality lumps of pig iron which was of negligible economic worth and had to be refined into steel.

According to official estimates, 600,000 backyard furnaces were established, ninety million people took part in the production of steel, plus the people who directly or indirectly supported the movement, there were altogether over 100 million people, one sixth of the whole population of the country. They were ordered to put aside their normal work to take part in the marvelous steel producing movement, which made great destruction of ecological environment and great waste of material resources. The preposterous plan was doomed to failure. There are natural laws governing everything. You cannot help the rice shoots grow faster by pulling them upwards, which can only quicken their demise. All-out effort won't bring accelerated steel growth overnight

In 1958 The party authority in Xushui County proclaimed that they set up "people's commune" to transfer from socialism to communism. Mao appreciated the name: "This name, 'people's commune' is great! French workers created the Paris commune when they seized power. Our farmers have created the people's commune as a political and economic organization in the march toward communism." He wrote "The people's commune is great!" in a sheet of paper, which was published in the newspaper throughout the country. With his obsession by communism and with imposing totalitarian control of the people, Mao eagerly started the people's communist movement. People's Daily cited his word and declared: "In the near future, the People's commune of Xushui will bring its members to the most wonderful paradise in human history, to the days of 'from each according to his ability, to each according to his needs.'" The word "The people's commune is great!" was treated as an imperial edict by leaders of every level to transform cooperatives into gigantic people's communes, which would combine government and agricultural production together and became the foundation of Communist Party power in the country. The whole rural area of the country was in a frenzy, setting up people's commune following the example of Xushui. Within a year, 740 thousand agricultural cooperatives were amalgamated into twenty-seven thousand communes. Peasants' lives were controlled and collectivized. Salaries of cadres were abolished, all the necessities of life of the peasants were received equally from the Commune. Elated with his great deed Mao once flaunted: "Back in 1949, when our army crossed the Yangtze River, an American wrote a book titled 'China Strikes the World". Now, ten years later, with the creation of people's communes, China is going to shake the world again." And he predicted that the transition to communism require three to four, or possibly five to six years. All the leaders were speaking the same word which was Mao's word. What they really thought, no one would ever know. Anyone who opposed the people's commune would be labeled as counter-revolutionary and suffered from persecution.

While the people's communes were generally set up, in many villages, the peasants, who believed that communism meant the abomination of private ownership, started to ransack the local shops and robbed neighbor's' possessions. After the people's communes were set up, Mao began to think about establishing a free-food supply system. In the winter of 1958 Mao called for the organization of public mess halls in the rural people's communes. The media propagandized that the formation of mess halls fosters collective living habits, which leads to the development of communist consciousness, and can release women out of the household and into the effort of creating community dining rooms, nurseries, homes for the aged, etc. Mao regarded family as the social foundation of the private ownership system and a major impediment to communism. He said: "Families are the product of old age and every trace of old age will be eliminated in the future." "the family must be eliminated." He also advocated egalitarianism: "Some people say that equal distribution produces slackers. But how many slackers in the last twenty-years? I haven't seen more than a handful." In fact, the setting of the canteen was his another means to control the peasants and realize his ambition.

During the campaign of setting up the canteen, eating at home was banned. Peasants had to eat in the mess hall. In setting up the mess halls, kitchen utensils like woks, pots, pans, kettles, knives, spoons, basins, bowls, cups, plus chairs and tables were requisitioned. Grain supplies were centralized at the communal kitchen, along with firewood, livestock, and poultry. Even wild herbs were handed over to the canteen. Cadres and militia ransacked homes. Kindergartens, nurseries and facilities for the elderly were established with resources seized from families without compensation. Even small plots of land for personal use become collectively run in the process of merging the commune. No vegetables and livestock belong to individuals. Household stoves were dismantled, bricks and the other materials were used to build the mess hall. The Peasants went to the mess hall three times each day. They can eat at their heart's content. Some young peasants usually took three or four buns for a meal. Now they could have six or seven at one go. If someone threw away leftovers no one blamed him for it is public meal. As Mao had said and worried about "what to do with the extra food," villagers believed that the state had access to vast stores of food to supplement local supplies when they ran out. It caused a great waste. In the past, peasants used to be very thrifty, controlling their stomachs. Even in the bumper harvester year, they would keep enough reserve for meeting emergency. Each peasant's house had various pots and pans, in which were rice, corn, millet, peanuts, etc. kept for meeting natural calamities. Now all privately held food was requisitioned: grain bins emptied, pickle jars confiscated, and livestock turned over to the mess halls. During the land reform poor peasants confiscated landlords' possessions; in the commune, the confiscation extended to all the peasants. Canteen had robbed every morsel of grain the peasants had reserved for meeting hunger.

The canteen also caused many inconveniences. For example, peasant had no fuel and kettle to heat water for drinking. Bathing was also a question. Some sympathetic leaders allowed the patients to leave one stove to boil water and cook special meals for invalids and pregnant women. But even this concession was attacked by party die head as a vestige of privatism. Fuel is an absolute necessity of life in rural areas, especially in northern China, where people sleep on Kang. Kang is an elevated platform, which is heated by the byproduct of household cooking in the winter. Without private cooking the peasants had to sleep on a freezing Kang. Some peasants' homes were far from the mess hall. They had to walk long distances and spend a long time to have their three meals per day. In the mountain regions, people had to tramp over hill and dale for a bowl of gruel.

In the canteen, anyone who disobeyed the cadres could be deprived of food, and villagers were forced to surrender their very survival to their cadres. Cadres always took more than their share. They grip the handle of the rice ladle of the peasants. The masses complained: "Make friends with a canteen manager and you'll never want for buns and soup." "There are no limits on the stomachs of the kitchen staff and the rations of the team leaders and managers." Some team leaders and managers hire the prettiest girls as kitchen staff and mess around with them. A cadre used the extra grain rations to seduce and rape thirteen women.

During the process of communization, most peasants detested and loathed the commune and canteens but they did not dare to say. They had no interest in production for all the produce belongs to the state and the commune. They paid no attention to the collective properties. By the end of 1958, the shortage of food had appeared. In the spring of 1959, starvation became widespread. The popular criticism of the canteen grew bolder and many commune kitchens had to be closed for their food were running short. To respond the crying that the peasants lacked food, oil, and cloth Mao said: "Is there really no food, oil, or cloth at all... Well-to-do middle peasants like to hoard grain but don't like to surrender it; they want capitalism, so yowl the hardship of the peasants. When they yowl down there, some people at the prefectural, provincial, municipal, and central levers yowl, too, don't they? Whose standpoint is it? Is it the standpoint of worker class or the poor and lower-middle peasants, or the standpoint of the well-to-do middle peasants?"

Mao's words sealed the lip of all the cadres. Mao also wrote a letter to provincial leaders on Feb. 22, 1959, in which he indicated his belief that the food shortages had not been caused by crop failure but rather by a conspiracy: peasants were hiding grain, so he ordered to launch an anti-hiding campaign to "educate the peasants". A month later at a Communist Party meeting in Shanghai (from March 25 to April 1), Mao again told top party leaders "to be relentless" toward the peasants and to procure "a third" of the total crop produced. "This is not ruthless, it is realistic... If you don't go above a third, people won't rebel... We had to feed the cities and satisfy foreign clients." In Mao's eyes, the need of foreign clients is more important than the life of Chinese people.

Yet, different voices and criticism about the great leap forward, commune and mess hall came more and more. Under the pressure of so many problems and difficulties, Mao was obliged to share part of his power to Liu Shaoqi and resigned his position as Chairman of the People's Republic of China, leaving the awful mess to be settled by Liu. And the People's Congress elected Liu as the Chairman of the PRC.

In an effort to overcome the difficulties, discuss the problems during the Great Leap Forward and correct the left-deviationist tendencies, the Central Committee of the Party decided to hold a conference in Lu Mountain in Jiangxi province.

Before the conference, in order to encourage the attendees to speak the truth frankly and boldly, Mao asked all cadres to learn "the spirit of Hai Rui". Hai Rui was a famous honest and upright official of the Ming dynasty. He had once submitted an appeal to the emperor, in which he exposed the malpractices and corruption of officialdom and the evils of the ruling class; put forward reformatory suggestions; and hoped the emperor to accept his opinion and correct all the faults. The emperor was angry and ordered his subject to arrest him at once lest he escape. His subject told the emperor that "He would not escape. He was a very famous foolish official. He had already bought a coffin for himself and bid goodbye forever with his wife. He knew he would be executed after offending the emperor." Hearing this word, the emperor hesitated and read Hai Rui's appeal several times and did not kill Hai Rui. Mao also wrote a letter in "communication within the Party", goading cadres to tell the truth. To show his sincerity Mao even gave a copy of "The Biography of Hai Rui" to Marshal Peng Dehuai, the Minister of National Defense.

A Painful Reminiscence of a Dignified Soul

On July 2, 1959 the Lu Mountain Conference was convened. During the first few days of the meeting, attendees freely aired their views on the problems of the great leap forward. Marshal Peng Dehuai expressed his opinions bluntly: "The grain yield figures provided by the commune were higher than the reality." "Setting the figure of 10.7 million tons of steel in a year is a little hotheaded." "We started on the people's communes a bit too early. We didn't carry out trials. If we had tested the method for a year before launching it, that would have been better." "No one pays any attention these days to collective decision by the party committees, instead, one man makes the decisions." He regarded "prematurely offering free meals" and "advocating eating to one's heart's content" as "a kind of leftist inclination".

The Vice Minister of Foreign Affairs Zhang Wentian pointed out: "Some people equate the rationing system and communal kitchens with socialism and communism, and if they do not practice the rationing system is insufficiently progressive and if they do not run the communal kitchens is not socialist. In fact, these are a different matter altogether and fall into different categories. Socialism does not necessarily employ methods such as rationing and communal kitchens."

And many other delegates, such as Huang Kecheng, the general chief of staff of the people's liberation Army, Zhou Xiaozhou, the first secretary of the party of Hunan province, also openly raised their opinions.

Later Peng also wrote a letter to Mao. In his letter, he first affirmed that "The accomplishments of the 1958 great leap forward are absolutely undeniable." he also affirmed that "The 1958 rural communization movement was of enormous significance." Yet at the same time he pointed out that "The capital construction projects of 1958 now look to have been a bit too numerous and carried out a bit too hastily." "The bourgeois climate of exaggeration and petty bourgeois fanaticism easily leads to leftist error." "Political commandism cannot replace the laws of economics, and even less can it replace concrete measures in economic work."

Though all those opinions were correct and their talks were the fact, and Peng's letter was rather moderate, yet Mao still could not tolerate. He criticized those speeches: "The trend toward pessimism is an extremely evil trend that corrupts the party and the people; it violated the will of the proletariat and the impoverished peasants, and also violates Marxism-Leninism." He even accused some criticism was "deliberately sabotaging the dictatorship of the proletariat and splitting the Communist Party."

Mao revealed his true scheme. He asked his subjects to learn from Hai Rui just for "enticing snakes out of their holes," as he had played in the Anti-Rightist Campaign in 1957. Since Liu Shaoqi, Deng Xiaoping no longer referred Mao Zedong Thought as the leading line of the party and opposed personality cult, Mao had a deep hatred towards them and suspected their loyalty. He wanted to know the true thought of all the high-ranking leaders and test their loyalty and faithfulness through the Conference. Now he accomplished his purpose.

Mao circulated Peng's letter to all the attendees and pressed them to criticize Peng and other opponents. In Its original plan the Conference was to correct the leftist tendencies and mistakes in the great leap forward, but Mao turned over its direction and had the Conference pass a resolution, which labeled Peng Dehuai, Zhang Wentian, Huang Kecheng and Zhou Xiaozhou as "a right-deviating opportunist anti-party clique" with Peng as the leader. They were charged for savagely attacking the party's general line, the great leap forward, the people's communes, the leadership of the central committee of the party and comrade Mao Zedong. Peng was charged as a conspirator and was dismissed from his post as the Minister of National Defense

Peng was a staunch and upright commander, who kept never becoming corrupt and never mincing his words over the wrong things. Even in 1940s in Yanan he opposed to chant "Long live Chairman Mao", to sing the Mao anthem, "The east is red", and to establish the deification of Mao. All these talks were killed off by the Rectification Campaign launched by Mao and Mao set out to tarnish Peng's credit and reputation and to unnerve him. After the founding of PRC, he continues talked about Mao's corrupt lifestyle: the luxurious villas all over China and the procurement of pretty girls as "selecting imperial concubines". In the early 1958 Mao wanted to build an absolutely gigantic strike force—no fewer than 200-300 nuclear submarines and decided to squeeze out far greater quantities of food to pay for the huge amount of hardware to Russia. Peng sent Mao a cable, advising him to reduce food collection and noticing him that many children died in the kindergarten and many old men died in the Happiness Court. He got no response. And Mao expressed his view: "Yes, a few children die in the kindergarten, a few old men die in the Happiness Court…… If there is no death, human beings can't exist. From Confucius to now, it would be disastrous if people didn't die." Mao had always hated Peng to death. He finally purged Peng in the Lu mountain Conference and later tortured Peng to death during the Cultural Revolution.

A Painful Reminiscence of a Dignified Soul

Mao was extremely narrow minded and cruel; at the Lu mountain Conference he even criticized his close secretary Tian Jiaying severely and almost included him in the "anti-party clique". Tian served Mao as secretary for 18 years. At first, he respected and loved Mao very much, treating Mao as his father and teacher. He was honest, bookish and naive and deeply concerned about his country and his people. Once Mao had teased his young secretary, saying that after Tian died, on his tombstone should be engraved the word "Here lies a man whose passion was for books." Afterwards Tian found some of Mao's ideas were not correct and had different views with Mao. As he loved Mao he was worried about Mao's future and often made plain-spoken admonition to Mao. He had advised Mao: "You can rule the country, you should not rule your close assistants"; "Don't leave anything to be condemned after you pass away"; "If you listen no criticism, others would find it hard to give advice." During the Great Leap Forward he had many opposite views: "When advanced cooperatives were introduced, the peasants complained that we were going too fast. Now we were trying to adopt a still higher form of organization, the people's commune. They were economically unsound." "We cannot ignore our low level of agricultural production or disregard the need to feed and clothe our hundreds of millions of people. It is absurd to think we can march into a communist society by dragging a naked and starving population along with us." "The plan for the great leap forward, trying to use people's commune to walk the road from socialism to communism, from poverty to abundance, was grandiose utopian." Mao asked Tian how he comment the play "The dismissal of Hai Rui" written by the historian Wu Han. Tian responded "There was no problem about the play; the condemnation of the play was a literary verdict, a campaign to warn the intellectuals." even though Mao regarded the play was an anti-party work. During the Lu Mountain Conference Tian advised Mao "To be close to worthy subjects; keep away from mean men". Mao replied: "Listening to your tone, you are a worthy subject at least, and Peng Dehuai, …, … are worthy subjects too. Is Wu Han a worthy subject also?". All Tian's words were for Mao's good, but Mao took Tian as his enemy. In the Cultural Revolution later, Tian was ordered to be suspended from work and make self-examination. He was exasperated. He did not make any self-examination for he was sure he hadn't made any mistakes. He told his friend:

"Lin Zexu's poem is my motto:

> If only in the interest of the country
> Give no thought of one's life and death.
> How can one make advance or retreat
> By the consideration of one's weal and woe.

I'll keep to the truth to the last time, to the stop of my respiration. I'll never betray my soul; I'll never succumb to suppression."

He knew the party would hold a meeting to condemn him soon. He was unwilling to be insulted by those shameless people. Leaving a last word "A true scholar would rather die than be humiliated" he hung himself in Mao's library. He demonstrated his opposition by taking his own life. He died when he was only 44 years old.

After the Lu Mountain Conference Mao launched a nationwide campaign against right deviation. In this campaign over ten thousand people were labeled as right deviating opportunists, and lives of tens of thousands of their relations were jeopardized. Anyone who had different opinion or resisted the orders from the superiors were hounded down. Mao continued to carry out his wrong line, lost no chance to laud the great leap forward. He persisted: "The relationship between our achievement and our shortcomings is, as we usually say, the relationship between nine fingers and one finger. Some people suspect or deny the 1958 great leap forward, and suspect of the advantages of the people's communes, this viewpoint is obviously completely wrong." "No matter how many problems we have, in the final analysis it does not amount to more than one finger out of ten." "To think that a campaign of such a momentous nature could have been launched without making a single mistake was an error. To doubt the great leap forward was an error, and to stand by and watch from a critical distance was an error." Under that atmosphere his erroneous policies and directives were intensified, many wrong or evil practices revived; exaggerations, promotion of communism were widely spread. An already profound trouble became worse and worse.

Though the situation was in a complete mess, Mao was still proud that he made a great accomplishment and arrogant that China was advanced toward communism much faster than Soviet Union ideologically, politically. Khrushchev regarded the Great Leap Forward and the cult of personality of Mao were emulating Stalin and Stalinist policies. The ideological disagreement about the Great Leap Forward seriously worsened the relations between China and Soviet Union. Mao criticized Khrushchev's concept of "peaceful coexistence" and "peaceful transition" and saw Khrushchev's rapprochement with the West as a renegade of the socialist revolution. He chose the ninetieth anniversary of Lenin's birth in Apr. 1960 as a chance to publish a manifesto entitled "Long live Leninism", which said that "advocating a peaceful road to socialism is unacceptable, is revisionism; and that if the communists were to take power they would have to resort to violence." Khrushchev deemed the ideological radicalism of the PRC destabilized the politics of peaceful coexistence with the West. He criticized Mao: "You want to dominate everyone, you want to dominate the world.", He became skeptical of Mao's mental health, fearing Mao's confrontational behavior might provoke a nuclear war between the U.S. and the Sino-Soviet alliance. At an international meeting of communist and workers parties in Bucharest in 1960, Mao and Khrushchev argued and each attacked the other's interpretation of Marxist doctrine as the incorrect road to world socialism. Mao argued that Khrushchev's greater emphasis upon material easiness would make the people ideologically soft and unrevolutionary; Khrushchev replied, "If we could promise the people nothing, except revolution, they would scratch their heads and say 'Isn't it better to have good goulash?'" When Soviet denounced the People's Socialist Republic of Albania and its leader Enver Hoxha, who had refused to abandon Stalinism and had aligned with the PRC. and stopped Russian aid to Albania. Hoxha said to his people: "Even if we have to eat the roots of grass to live, we won't take anything from Russia." Mao immediately send food to his only brother country. By the end of 1960 the split was manifested as open criticism. When Khrushchev and Peng Zhen openly argued at the congress of the Romanian Communist Party. Khrushchev insulted Mao as "a nationalist, an adventurer, and a deviationist" Peng Zhen called Khrushchev a Marxist revisionist whose regime of the USSR showed him to be a "patriarchal, arbitrary and tyrannical" ruler. In 1961, Mao started a propaganda campaign against Khrushchev and waged a tit-for-tat struggle against modern revisionism. He formally denounced Khrushchev as "Revisionist traitors". Khrushchev further responded to Mao's criticism by withdrawing some 1,400 technicians from the PRC, which led to cancellation of some 200 scientific joint projects.

In 1960 the situation of the countryside became very severe. The food shortages, reduction of production, increasing of edema, and death of hunger emerged in large scale all over the country. More and more officials and peasants got bolder to voice their criticism and urgently demanded that the communes be disbanded.

Finally, the harsh reality forced Mao to make some concession. But he did not admit his fault and shifted the disaster onto his subjects. He instructed officials to correct the unhealthy things, proclaiming: "In the next few months we must resolutely and thoroughly correct the extreme errors of the communist wind, the exaggeration wind, the coercive commands wind, the cadre privilege wind, the chaotic directives wind relating to production. With an emphasis on redressing the communist wind, we also redress the other four unhealthy tendencies. One good method is for each provincial party committee to carry out a comprehensive and thorough investigation of one commune with serious errors to gain a clear idea of the situation……". In fact, all the source of the five wind is himself. He should correct his evil idea, not to order his subjects to make a so called a comprehensive and thorough investigation. And if his subjects made a thorough investigation, they would find the real source was Mao's order and instruction.

To alleviate the situation the Central Party Committee first restored the practice of allocating plot of land for household use and allow commune members to raise their own livestock and poultry. Grain rations are to be distributed to households and individuals. Villagers can eat at his own home or eat at the communal kitchen and hand over their rations to the kitchen. Later it revised the former requirement that every production team must operate a communal kitchen and allowed the commune members themselves to decide whether they operate a communal kitchen or not. When the peasants had the freedom, the communal kitchen throughout the country were disbanded at once. But all these instructions and measures came too late, the commune already had little food or no food. An unprecedented famine in world history was inevitably happened during a period of normal climate with no wars or epidemics.

The famine was spreading throughout the countryside. The first symptom of famine was edema. The edema patients had deep hollows under their eyes, almost transparent swollen face and limbs. When you press it with a finger, the place you pressed would form a deep indentation. When you released the press, the indentation remained. Edema and hepatitis were epidemic, both of which were effects of the exhaustion of the food supplies. Many families crushed corn cobs into powder and mixed with a little corn flour to make buns. An even cruder kind of bun was made by mixing crushed rice husks and corn cobs together with a small amount of ground corn. Elm flowers, willow leaves and dandelion were also their dishes. Such rough, unpalatable fare were taken as treasures for they could save lives. Many people could not walk steadily and didn't have the energy to work.

When the famine went on worse and worse, every living or growing creature was consumed. After every goose, dog, and cat had been killed and consumed, all the trees had been stripped bare of their bark and leaves. in many countries there were no food at all, people ate anything that could fill their empty stomachs—weeds, grass, shoe soles, insects, rats, decayed fruit and vegetables. They forage for food everywhere, picking any green plant and put it in their mouth, not caring whether or not it might be poisonous. They dug up and ate worms such as earthworm, that could be found in the soil. In some places, earth eating had become prevalent and had caused a number of health problems, including severe constipation. Many peasants were so extremely emaciated that they shrank to mere heaps of skin and bones, and eventually fell dead of starvation. Between the line of living and dying, few people even chose to eat human flesh. Often the acts of cannibalism were carried out on the corpses of the dead, but murder also took place. A peasant one day burst into the police and threw himself on the floor, screaming that he had committed a terrible crime and begging to be punished. Eventually it came out that he had killed his own baby and eaten it. In one case, an official heard about a teenage girl whose parents had died of hunger. Near death, she killed her four-year-old brother and ate him. Filled with pity and a sense of helplessness, the official finally arrested the girl, reasoning that at least in jail she might get something to eat. A couple had abducted and murdered a number of babies and sold them as rabbit meat at high prices. The couple were executed, but it was widely known that baby killing did go on at that time.

In the past when there was a famine, sufferers could flee from famine anywhere. During this time the villagers could not leave their village. An "urgent Communiqué" of the Central Committee declared that anyone who leaves rural areas is a vagrant. Local officials enforced the travel ban brutally, beating lots of peasants to death. Police blocked refugees from leaving villages. Those who tried to escape the famine were rounded up, died of starvation in detention centers. The peasants could only stay home and await death.

In Xinyang county, Henan Province, more than a million people—one in eight—are wiped out by starvation and brutality. In barely nine months, more than 12,000 people—a third of the inhabitants—die in a single commune. Thirteen children beg officials for food and are dragged deep into the mountains, where they die from exposure and starvation. Forty-four of a village's 45 inhabitants die; the last remaining resident, a woman in her 50s goes insane.

When Mao heard about the Xinyang incident, he acted delusional, declaring that the landlords had retaken control and wrecked the disaster. Several thousand local officials were accused to be responsible for failing to follow Beijing's orders and were arrested and beaten and hundreds were killed. In fact, they had been forced to follow his orders: "Communism is good, to carry out the communism in the countryside."

Unlike any previous famines in China, this one covered the entire country. Famines are usually caused by plague of insects, like locusts or bad weather, flood or drought, they are always occurred in part areas. This famine is a man-made disaster caused by the order of the central government, so no area can escape. The government blamed the famine on exceptionally severe natural disasters and the Soviet Union demand of repayment from China. It was a sheer lie.

Despite the famine were widespread in the countryside, Mao continued to export grain. He was determined to keep his face and convince the outside world of the success of his Great Leap Forward. He refused foreign aid. When the Japanese Minister of Foreign affairs told his Chinese counterpart Chen Yi of an offer of 100,000 tons of wheat to be shipped out of public view, he was rebuffed. John F Kennedy also said "We have had no indication from the Chinese Communists that they would welcome any offer of food", for he was aware that the Chinese were still exporting food to Africa and Cuba during the famine.

The death toll of the famine was estimated by many home and foreign reporters and scholars with different methods. Two of them estimated over twenty million, three estimated over forty million, eight estimated over thirty million. All the estimations are horrible. I don't mind which estimation is closer to the exact number of deaths. I think even a single man died of hunger due to another's error, the man who caused the death is a criminal. Yet the party and the government have never investigated and affixed the responsibility of the person who caused the unprecedented great famine.

In October 1959, the Party decided to remove the label of rightists for those who were remolded appropriately. As a trial, each unit was allowed to remove only one righter's label. The cadres and rightists of our unit began to discuss whose label should be removed this time. At the meeting each rightist should related his(her) own self-evaluation and made comments on others. One female rightist

A Painful Reminiscence of a Dignified Soul

believed she would be chosen because she often said she had made great progress ideologically. I did not hold any hope for I remained the same as the past, having no changes. I was often criticized to neglect the ideological remodeling. A few weeks later, quite out of my expectation, our leader declared that I was chosen to be the first label removed rightist. I did not know the reason. I guessed maybe because I was listed in the fifth category of rightists, the "crime" I had made was lighter than others'; or because my relationship with the peasants was rather good and my labor was generally praised, someone commended that I was laboring as a 'small tiger'. Anyway, my rightist label was removed. I was pleased.

Before the rural new year of 1960, we were called to go back to Beijing. I had double feelings; glad for returning home, sad for leaving the place where I stayed for two years. I suddenly felt I was deeply attached to Qi village. I wandered the places I favored again and again: the murmuring stream fringed by the untrammeled wildflowers and weeds, the pine trees on the top of the hill against the vast expanse of the sky, trying to keep them forever in mind. I had long intimate talk with my landlord and visited several peasants who were friendly to me, thanking them for their care and said goodbye to them.

After I returned to Beijing, I found the famine not only paralyzed the countryside, the cities also suffered extreme shortages of food. Even in the capital, the monthly grain ration was cut several kilograms, some of it was supplied with corn flour. Fresh vegetables rations were reduced to less than two hundred grams a day. At dawn, there were long queues outside every food store, whose limited supplies quickly sold out sometimes and left shoppers go back home with empty hands. Cakes, nuts, candies, canned goods, fruit, etc. vanished from the shelves of the shops. Buying any food needed coupons: grain coupons, cooking oil coupons, meat coupons, egg coupons, bean curd coupon, sugar coupon, salt coupons, cotton coupons, cloth coupons, and many more. Each person got half-pound of meat, half a dozen eggs, one hundred grams of cooking oil per month. Malnutrition was rampant. Survival became everyone's overriding concern.

Unable to solve the catastrophe the government called for tightening belts and "striking a balance between work and rest". It meant reducing people's workloads and political obligation to minimize calorie expenditure. In Nov. 1960 Central Government launched a nationwide movement to collect and manufacture food substitutes or alternative food. Newspapers and many organizations, such as Chinese Academy of Sciences, Entomology Research Institute, suggested many methods to make substitutes. Many families steamed rice twice: they cooked rice, then adding water and cooked again to increase its volume. The government also disseminated the method, telling the double-cooking rice increased its nutritional content. In fact, the additional cooking destroys vitamins, making this rice less nutritious. Many people grew chlorella in human urine at home. They stopped going to the toilet and peed into spittoon instead, then dropped the chlorella seeds in it. The seeds grew into something looking like green fish roe in a couple of days. Then people scooped them out of the urine, washed and cooked them with rice. The food was truly disgusting to eat, but it contains rich protein and did reduce the swelling. Many residents planted things in their backyard. They began to learn planting, weeding, fertilizing and watering. The most challenging job was to collect human waste. The stinky smell often caused nausea, but they had to bear it. Some young people pounded their leather shoes and leather belts with rocks to soften them. They cooked them and ate them. They had to chew the leather for long time. When it was soft enough, they swallowed it.

Some people and the army went to the Mongolian highlands to catch gazelles. The population of gazelles had declined enormously and at some places they disappeared at all. It was a disaster for the ecology protection.

During the time of hardship Premier Zhou suggested that the central committee set an example by "eating vegetarian". Mao announced to party members that he would "share weal and woe with the nation" and give up eating meat. In fact, all he did was to eat fish instead. Nor did he refrain from all meat. His doctor told him the cholesterol content of pork is higher than beef and mutton and his staff and chef drew up a comprehensive set of western-style menu made up of beef, mutton and vegetable dishes for him, so his claim of refraining from meat was a mere farce.

After Mao brought about economic chaos, he left Liu to salvage the situation. Facing the crisis, Liu and other important leaders adopted further measures to improve the straitened situation. They took a policy of "adjustment, consolidation, replenishment and enhancement" to the national economy. In order to bring the famine to a halt, they instituted the policy "Three freedoms and one contract" in the countryside(that means giving more freedom to peasants to plant their own crops; further opening of free markets; more responsibilities of enterprises for their own profits and losses; and assignment of output to households), and let peasants lease some land. Liu rehabilitated all the right deviating opportunists labeled after

A Painful Reminiscence of a Dignified Soul

Lu mountain Conference except Peng Dehuai. He and his like-minded colleagues gradually got the economy back into shape. When Liu solved the problem, Mao blamed Liu betrayal his ideals and often put the brakes on liberal measures. The lack of ideological unity limited the effectiveness of reform. Sometimes Liu disagreed Mao's position. In Aug. 1961 Mao once again to fix the high food extraction figures, Liu pressed him to set them lower to prevent the famine. Deng Xiaoping supported Liu's work and defended Liu's practices by quoting an old saying: "It doesn't matter whether it's a yellow cat or a black cat, as long as it catches mice."

According to the Party Charter of the CCP, a Party Congress is to be convinced every five years. The Ninth Congress should be convinced in Sep. 1961. As his policies were widely opposed, Mao was afraid he would be dismissed through the vote of the Congress, He despised the Charter of the Party and ordered to convene a conference that would not have voting powers, thus averting the threat of being removed by the Congress.

In Jan. 10 1962 a five-level cadre conference was convened with 7,000 participants. Mao's aim of calling this conference was to use the meeting to spur on his officials to further enhance his policies. But Liu Shaoqi delivered a speech which had a different opinion to Mao's keynote text. He said: "Originally we believed that in these few years we would have a great leap forward in agriculture and industry. We didn't leap forward, however, but actually fell significantly backward, resulting in a big saddle shape. Agricultural output, far from rising in 1959, 1960 and 1961, dropped, not a little, but tremendously." "People do not have enough food, clothes or other essentials." Liu pointed out that the straitened circumstances arose from work errors. He said: "Man-made disasters strike the whole country. We must remember the lessons." He dismissed the official explanation for the calamities, saying there was "no serious bad weather" "When I went to Hunan, the peasants said it was three-part natural disaster and seven parts man-made disaster. If you don't acknowledge this, people won't accept it." He also proposed a "seven-three ratio" of accomplishments to errors to replace Mao's "Nine fingers and one finger". "In a portion of places, the shortcomings and errors comprise more than three parts. In some places the shortcomings and errors outnumber accomplishments. If we fundamentally refuse to acknowledge that there have been shortcomings and errors, or claim they're just minor issues and try to beat around the bush or cover things up, and don't practically, realistically, and thoroughly acknowledge our past and existing fallings, then no summing up of the experience can be carried out, and bad cannot be turned to good." Liu also said: "The Three Red Banners are experiment, and whether they're correct requires testing them in practice... Some problems cannot be seen so clearly at present, but after five or ten years, we can summarize the experience, and at that time go a step further in reaching a conclusion."

Liu himself knew the danger of having different ideas with Mao, but he decided that as a leading member of the state he had to prevent more people starved to death, he had to utter the plight of the Chinese people.

Liu's speech brought a torrential response from his audience. Seeing the Chairman of the State admitted the fault, many local-level cadres could hardly wait to tell the truth. They complained that they had been under tremendous pressure throughout the Great Leap forward. They were pushed to set ever higher and more impossible production targets and they had to lie and cheated when the target was impossible to meet. The 7,000 cadres conference became the most liberal meeting since the founding of the PRC.

Mao had not expected Liu could speak different opinions so boldly. Mao regarded "The Three Red Banners" as an elaborate design and a great success, but Liu said it was but a policy to be tested in practice. Mao decided that Great Leap Forward had achieved an overwhelming accomplishment, but Liu denied it. Mao was furious and complained: "He is not using the class standpoint." "He is not addressing the question of whether we are going the capitalist road or the socialist road." But under the atmosphere of the Conference and Liu had taken many measures to alleviate starvation and motivate productivity, Mao could not criticize Liu openly. He had to keep his temper and pretend there were no differences between him and Liu and Liu's supporters. But since then he nurtured a violent hatred against Liu. From the 7,000 cadres meeting he was convinced that Liu was not loyal to him and prepared to revenge in the future.

After I returned to the Youth Publishing House, my work has changed. Before I was settled down the village, I edited articles of literature and ideological cultivation in the magazine High School Students. Now the leader considered that I could not be trusted in politics and asked me to edit books of popular science. I like the change. I had been expelled from the party two years ago. And though my rightist label was removed, we remained the "label removed rightist". I no longer like politics and regard it a dirty game and try to steer clear of it as far as possible. If I was still assigned to edit articles of ideological cultivation, I had to propaganda

A Painful Reminiscence of a Dignified Soul

Mao's ideology. I hated to do that. My new job can help me increase knowledge. When I edit a book, I had to read a lot of reference books and magazines related to the subject of the book. It will widely extend my vision and knowledge. Isn't it a very interesting work?

I worked hard at the Publishing House and I edited some popular science books such as "The vast new fields sciences open", "An answer to the children who fancy flying to the stars", "The science in schoolboy's satchel", "Green leaves and red flowers" " The story of buoyant force" and so on. They were warmly welcomed by the children. Some were awarded a prize and some were reprinted even now.

Due to my "bad political background" I suffered many setbacks in love affairs. In 1954, because I was criticized during the Eliminate Counter-revolutionary Campaign, a nice lover betrayed me as I had mentioned above. When I was In the Party School in 1957, a female classmate introduced a girl friend to me, but soon after that I was labeled a rightist, our connection stopped. During the period in the countryside, we were not allowed to court. A rightist who was concerned with my love affairs once had a talk with me: "You are already thirty years old; you should consider this affair now. You cannot court here but you can recognize someone here. Then after you go back to Beijing you can contact her. The peasant, in whose home I live, has a daughter, who is very simple, honest, diligent and pretty. If you agree with my idea, I can ask her father's opinion." I have never looked down village girl. They are simple and pure. Their educational level is low, but I can help her or send her to school. I agreed his idea. But even countrymen are afraid of political consequences. Her father declined politely. After I came back Beijing, two or three friends introduced girlfriend to me. Some girl refused to contact me; some girl I was not going to meet. I wanted to wait till I met an ideal girl. My marriage was delayed.

In 1962, my third elder sister-in-law suggested to marry her younger sister to me. I know that girl, whose name is Zhang Runshu, pet name Xingqi. I had seen her at my third elder brother's home in Shanghai in 1948. At that time, she was only ten years old and I had taught her revolutionary songs and folk dances. At present she was already a fourth-grade student at Chongqing Medical College. She is honest, outgoing and pretty. I agreed with pleasure. Both her parents and Runshu herself agreed too. They understand me well, don't mind I am a label removed rightist. A difficult problem of mine was suddenly solved so smoothly. I was very delighted and invited her to Beijing during Summer vocation.

Zhong Da

In the afternoon of Aug. 7, 1962, she arrived in Beijing, I went to the railway station to meet her. Separated for 14 years, what would we feel at the moment when we met again? I wondered. I waited impatiently. Finally, the real time came. A great tidal wave of people came rolling out of the gate of the station. My eyes kept traveling right and left, frantically searching for her among the crowd. Suddenly I found her and waved my hand widely to her. Very soon she saw me too. She ran out of the throng toward me with a smile and I ran to meet her too with a pit-a-pat heart. We grasped hands tightly, exchanging a few warm greetings with each other. She didn't put on any cosmetics and wore simple blue clothes. Her countenance was benign. I liked her plain, natural decoration and manner. She did not take many things, just a satchel on her back and a hand bag. I wanted to take over her satchel but she declined my help politely. My office was not far away, only two stops of the tram. we decided to walk there. Strolling slowly hand in hand along a main street, I introduced something about Beijing to her. The weather was very hot, we entered a cold drink store and bought a small refrigerated melon. We cut it in the middle and each had a half. While we were eating, she told me her experience on the train. At that time the train was very slow. It took her two days from Chongqing to Beijing. The compartments of the train were crammed and stuffy, she could not sleep at all. She was rather tired yet still excited. After we arrived at my office, I led her to a female dormitory in which our office already arranged berth for her. I did not talk with her any more for I knew she had been exhausted after the arduous journey, I asked her to sleep first and I would wake her up to have dinner later. Then I said goodbye to her and went back to my dormitory which was not far from hers.

We had a very happy time. I led her to visit almost all the famous Beijing's sights: the Palace Museum, the Summer Palace, the Temple of Heaven, North-Sea Park (the former Imperial Winter Palace), etc. One night I talked with her on the top of the city wall till the wee hours. It seemed we had endless words to communicate. She told me many things about her study and her family. Her academic performances were good, but the life of her family was very miserable. After her father's small candy shop was confiscated in 1956, the whole family had to depend on her mother's tiny wage. Her mother was working at a recycling center, handling the waste papers, a very dirty job. She was already over sixty years old, each day after work she was exhausted. Furthermore, her father was labeled as a historical counterrevolutionary, being under surveillance and control all the time. He was angry, but could not appeal for justice. Her younger sister was at a high school. After hearing her words, I was very exasperated. The Communist Party was too unfair to her father. He believed Communist party, betrayed the Nationalist Party, handed over many precious things to the government. According to principle, he should be praised and awarded a prize, but he was regarded as people's enemy. It is utterly beyond reason. If he went to Taiwan, his life, as a major general in the Army, would be very comfortable. I consoled her and related all the details of my experience in the past several years. I told her I had deeply worshipped Mao ten years ago, but now I saw his true face. He is utterly shameless, speaks all the nicest things while doing all the vilest things. His conduct is always variant with his word. He has no sense of justice and gratitude and always returns kindness with enmity, having wronged and persecuted millions of former revolutionaries and honest intellectuals. I also encouraged her to be strong-willed, never stoop to difficulties, and don't mind the discrimination of others. I promised to help her father economically immediately.

We also discussed when should we get married. She was already on fourth grade, one year more she would graduate from Chongqing Medical college. At first, we prepared to get married after she graduated. Later we found that there was a policy that year: On the work of job assignment upon graduation, the authority should give consideration to the married students so that the couple can stay together. For this reason, we decided to get married right now, hoping she could be assigned to a job in Beijing. We applied for a marriage certificate from civil administration office. My office allotted to me a little two-by-three-meter room, which formerly was a storeroom with no window and no space to move around after placing a bed, a small table and a chair. We didn't mind that. The office had no spare room. They managed to vacate a store room for us was already a great concern.

We got married on August 22th. At that time the wedding ceremony was very simple. I invited my leader as the witness of our marriage. I prepared a lot of fruit, candies and cakes to entertain the guests. The wedding ceremony was held in the backyard of our office in front of my wedding room. No seat, all stood there. All the guests were my colleagues and friends without any of my family members and relatives. A few guests made some short speeches, blessing on our marriage and my wife and I thanked all the guests for their presence and concern. They asked us to sing songs. I did not sing. My wife sang some Chinese and Soviet songs. All the wedding was simple, plain, but warm, lively and solemn.

Zhong Da

My wife left Beijing on August 28th. I saw her off on the platform of the train station. The happy time was short-lived and the painful time facing us would be very long. The Chinese proverb "The greatest sorrow is to say goodbye upon leaving and say adieu upon dying." is true indeed. Leaving one's beloved is indeed the most sorrow of the sorrows. Both of us had an aching heart. We stayed on the platform till the starting time of the train was near, we reluctantly made the last handshake, said the last word "goodbye", and separated with each other. I watched her getting on the train sadly. After she took her seat, she stretched her hand out of window to me. I rushed there and raised my hand to grip hers. The two arms like a bridge linked two regions and the bridge would soon break. The whistle sounded and the guard drove us leave the train, my wife and I had to let off our hands. The train started, we stared at each other with red eyes until she disappeared from the sight. I returned home alone, suddenly a couple became a single.

According to the regulation of the government, the couple who live in different places have 12 days family leave to get together each year. In January 1963 I took the leave to Chongqing to see my wife. Her family lived in a small room under the stairs with no window. Even in the daytime, the lamp had to be open. When I went there, her family let me and my wife live in that room, her parents and younger sister stayed at their friend's home. Though it was in Winter vacation, my wife was not free, for she had a graduation fieldwork in a hospital to practice what they had been taught in class. The hospital for her clinical practicing is on the other side of the Yangtze river. She had to get up very early each day to get there by a ferry and always came back late, so we had a few times to get together. In order to have more time to stay with her I usually accompanied her to take the ferry to the other side of the Yangtze, then on the sand beach I hugged a goodbye with her and stared her running up a steep flight of steps to her hospital. Though I had a leave of twelve days, she had only one Sunday to accompany me to tour the city and to taste the special cuisine of Chongqing in a restaurant. We also went to the theater and cinema two or three time in the evening.

I had much contact with her parents. Her father was tall, kind, poised with a woebegone face. His eyes had deep-grown crow's-feet at the corners. Her mother was a thin, good-natured, demure woman. Her brows were knitted in a frown. They were both in a bad mood. Their youngest daughter was a lovely, charming girl. She was only sixteen-years-old, always wearing an innocent smile. Several times I invited them to go to the restaurant and cinema. They were always politely de-

A Painful Reminiscence of a Dignified Soul

clining, but I insisted and they had to accept my invitation. I always ordered the most delicious dishes for them. I knew they never went to the restaurant.

I spent a lot of time to console them. I said: "I know you are in a situation of adversity. You are wrongly labeled as a historical counterrevolutionary and your life is difficult. But you need not be sad or dismal. Sadness and worry do nothing good for changing the adversity, only hurt your body and mind. you should have a broad mind, a quiet mind, a happy mind to deal with your situation. Let those slanders say what they please. you need not be ashamed, for you have done nothing wrong. You are innocent; they are criminals. you should not be distressed about your adverse condition. on the contrary you must respond to it with cheer, forbearance and self-assurance." I also introduced my own experience to them: "I had been labeled a rightist, an enemy of the people, but I had not worried a mite in my mind. I hadn't made any mistake, but spoken the truth. I was proud of my act. I had done all things with good conscience. And that good conscience bore me up through the dark time and the filthy society. I always kept my mind in peace and happiness." Finally, I encouraged them to bear the present difficulties bravely and patiently and always harbored a hope: eventually the situation will be changed someday. They agreed with my idea and promised to try their best to do that. I asked them to take good care with each other. I gave them some money. They declined my offer politely, but I persisted in giving them and told them it was my duty. Finally, they received it.

I also asked her youngest sister to lead me to visit Chongqing's scenic sites. She accompanied me to visit the "Mr. Bai's Mansion", which was used as a Sino-American Cooperation Institute during the war of resistance against Japan. After the war it served as a jail which had locked up many famous communists. She also took me to watch the "Merit Record Tablet for the Memory of the Victory of the War". It was highly magnificent. I advised her to study hard and take good care of her parents. I bought some candy and a big colored balloon to her, who liked the balloon very much and thanked me.

The happiness and excitement were a brief duration, I had to leave my wife and her family by the end of the leave. She had no time to see me off at the railway station. Instead her mother accompanied me to go there. My mother-in-law and I knew each other fifteen years ago and had a deep affection between us. At the parting both of us felt very sad. She said she was already very old and afraid she would never see me again. Her words deeply touched me. I said: "Don't mind that. You are still very healthy. I will come to see you each year." When I boarded the train, her eyes welled tears on her haggard face. She was nailed on the platform until my waving hand disappeared from her eyes. My heart was throbbing with pain. It was a mother's tear. That tear was embedded in my memory forever.

After I returned to Beijing, I wrote a letter to my wife, telling her I had returned to Beijing safe and sound.

"Dear Runshu:

"I have been back to Beijing safely. Please rest assured!

"The journey is really tired, bored and weary, quite unlike the journey I went to Chongqing. On that trip I was happy, full of hope. What was waiting for me would be a smiley face, sweet talks, agreeable sightseeing and a pleasure of meeting your parents and younger sister. Though tired yet still spirited, ignoring all the unpleasant things. The return trip was completely different. The familial images disappeared, the warm voices silenced, all things seemed lost. My heart was filled with sadness, chilliness, melancholy and despondency. The stuffy compartment, the passenger's gossips made me sick. I became fidgeted and my mind was all in a maze. It was really an awful experience.

"Now I resumed my work, very busy. But I still cannot concentrate my mind at work right now. I have always been thinking of you, always remembering the time we spent on the city wall; we rowed the small boat on the lake of park; we hugged on the sand beach of the Yangtze River. I am longing to see you and embrace you all the time, but it is impossible. we are now separated thousands of miles away from each other. I can only heave a disconsolate sigh.

"Half a year later, you'll graduate from college. I hope you will be assigned a job in Beijing, then we will be able to live together.

"I know you will be very busy in your last semester, please take good care of both your studies and your health. Don't worry about me, I can arrange my things well. I have been living alone since I was only twelve years old.

"Please give my kindest regards to your parents and your younger sister!
Zhong"

Very soon I received her reply. She told me she also missed me very much, she was glad to marry me for I am her desired, ideal companion. She still remembered every single detail of our wedding day, and regard that day to be pure, splendor and elated, which changed our life. She was afraid that I must have great difficulties to be living alone and asked me to take good, nutritious food to keep fit.

A Painful Reminiscence of a Dignified Soul

During the following seven or eight months both she and I were anxiously waiting for the decision of her job assignment, a day which will decide the fate of our life.

The day finally came. By the end of August, I received a letter from her. It was really a bolt out of the blue. She was not assigned a job in Beijing. I was thunderstruck numb. There is a policy that all the married students should be assigned to a place where their spouse is, why she was not assigned a job in Beijing? I must deliver a protest, I think.

My wife told me she was writing the letter with tears. The policy of assignment of the graduates has changed this year. It no longer gives consideration to the married graduate. She was not only sad that she was not assigned to Beijing, she was also exasperated that the assignment was very unfair. Her academic achievement was excellent that she should be assigned to a fine place, but she was assigned to a worst place—the farthest, secluded county named Youyang, a southern border of Sichuan Province with Guizhou Province. The reason was her bad political background. Before graduation every graduate should be subjected to a thorough investigation. She honestly told her examiner that she had been married to me, a label removed rightist. Her honest report became a stigma on her, plus her father being a historical counter-revolutionary, her destiny was sealed. She was angry, dismal and frustrated for such an unreasonable and relentless decision. She tried hard to keep calm but was unable to do so. She was plagued by insomnia, always thinking of the gloomy future and the suffering of our separation. She wanted to protest, but she knew it was of no use at all and perhaps It would cause more trouble. She even desired to commit suicide but loathed to leave me alone in the cold world, so she did not do that. She hoped me not to be too despondent.

I could not express how I felt when I read her letter. I was tormented by mixed feelings: misery, compassion, irritation and hatred. It was beyond all description. I was just brooding and brooding, kissing the letter again and again, for there remained her tears and scent. After thinking of the situation for a long time, I decided that while she was so desperate, I should not tell her my real feelings to add her worries, I must encourage her so as to release her agony. I began to write a letter to her.

"Dear Runshu:

I am glad to receive your letter though it conveyed bad news.
I quite understand your feelings, but I love to see your smile not tears. Tears and dispirit mend nothing. What is needed is courage and resolution, letting hope over fear, letting optimism

over pessimism. Harboring a lofty ideal in mind: go to the hospital affectionately. When more and more patients' illnesses are cured by you, you will feel happier and happier. As for the political discrimination you need not consider it at all. Let those mean people do evil, you just plume yourself on your virtue. Separation is only a temporary thing; you will eventually be transferred to my place early or later. Now is already September, only three or four months later I can take my next year's family leave to go to your new place to see you. It will be a very exciting moment. There is a very famous, beautiful ancient poem written by a Tang Dynasty poet Qing Guan.

······ ······

'The tender feelings soft as water,
The ecstatic moment elapsed as a dream,
How can one bear the grief of parting
On the bridge made of magpies?
If the two hearts are tightly united forever,
What is the need of staying together
Day after day, night after night?'

Our two hearts are tightly united, let us not hurt ourselves too much by the temporal parting, Let us encourage and alleviate each other! Be calm! Be happy! Be confident!
Take good care of yourself!

Zhong

After finishing the letter, I felt better myself. I mustn't be depressed too. I went to bed sedately.

All those days I have been contemplating how terrible our social system is. We have been deprived all our rights. If in any other countries, or in the old China before "liberation", I could at least quit my job and go to her place or she quitted her job and came to my place. But in new China it is impossible. Quitting your job means you do not obey the assignment of the government and can never get another job. Moving is also out of the question. Every person was a registered permanent residence in a place, if you want to move to another place you have to get a certificate of public security organ, but the public security organ will not give you the certificate unless your unit approve your movement. In addition, all the necessities of life, like rice, oil, cloth, etc. are supplied by coupon and the coupon you can only get from the local government. Even if you want to give up your registered permanent residence, flee to another place, you cannot keep living there for you cannot get the local coupons. I think we are not citizens but slaves, and we cannot complain, otherwise we will be labeled counterrevolutionaries.

I am anxious waiting for the coming of 1964, I want to use the family leave to go to see her on the first day of that year.

After the 7,000 cadres conference Liu and other pragmatic leaders adopted further measures to adjust the policies, the situation of our country had become better. Productivity was recovered, agriculture products went up, starvation stopped. The national economy began to take an all-round favorable turn, the government raised some wages of workers and cadres in 1963. My salary was not raised for I was a label moved rightist.

Though the situation of our country was improved, Mao hadn't any appreciation or gratitude to Liu and his followers' work and achievements. On the contrary, he always had a negative view and criticized many policies and measures they had taken. He perceived the central committee under Liu's leadership to be departing further from his line in economic, political, domestic and foreign policies. Mao regarded all they had done were restoration of capitalism. In a summer afternoon in July 1962, Liu came to Mao to report that Chen Yun and Tian Jiaying wanted to present him their views about land distribution. Mao released his resentment that had been built and stored up for a long time and exploded with anger: "The Three Red Banners have been refuted; the land has been divided up again. What have you done to resist this? What is going to happen after I'm dead?" Liu was also angry and blurted out: "So many people have died of hunger. History will record the role you and I play in the starvation. and the cannibalism will be written in the books." The two men had many arguments. Liu believed that the past policies had been disastrous, and had to be discarded. Mao persisted to push forward the realization of communist ideals through class struggle. The relation between them became worsened and the tension in their relationship seeped through to their outward behavior.

With the failure of his "Great Leap Forward" Mao realized that catching up and exceeding Soviet Union and America economically was but a dream, he never mentioned those words again. He also recognized that he could not become the leader of the world communist movement ideologically, politically, for after so many years' effort and endeavor he only won one Brother-Party, the Communist Party of Albania. The only problem left for him now was how to keep the position of China's emperor, lest he would be overthrown by his opponents and criticized by China's Khrushchev after his death.

Since Liu Shaoqi described the famine as a man-made disaster and denied his ideology and policies, Mao considered and discerned that Liu was his opponent and enemy. He decided and planned to eliminate Liu.

Mao is an evil and sly dictator, he knew he must carry out his schemes in the dark, unnoticed and step by step. He must make full preparations, creating, cheating and whip up public opinion against Liu's ideologies and policies; enhancing his own personality cult; striking the smaller "devils" first, then the bigger ones. He did not touch Liu right away and carefully concealed his strategy, ensnaring his enemies with trappers. Though Liu was his main target, Liu had no inkling of what was landing on him.

When the starvation was stopped. Mao started clearing the ground for his goal. The most powerful weapon Mao could wield against Liu was class struggle. He is the representative and leader of the proletariat, of the worker and peasant class; His opponents' standing is capitalist class. What are the crimes of Liu? All the things Liu has done. Mao has a famous quote: "Whatever the enemies support we must oppose; whatever the enemies oppose we must support." So everything Liu and his followers practice and promote is wrong, is a crime.

In Sep. 1962 in the Tenth Plenum of the Eighth CCP Central Committee, Mao criticized the "three winds" (Wind of Gloom; wing of individual farming and wind of reversing verdicts) and declared: "there are class enemies and anti-communist ideology in anytime, at anyplace." "Throughout the entire history of the proletarian revolution and proletarian dictatorship, and in the entire historical period of the transition from capitalism to communism, which may last several decades or longer, there exists a class struggle between the proletarian and bourgeois classes and a struggle between the two roads of socialism and capitalism……This class struggle is complex, tortuous, varying, intense and sometimes fierce. It's unavoidable that this class struggle should be reflected within the party." He also said:

A Painful Reminiscence of a Dignified Soul

"The Party itself had become a haven for capitalists. Members of the bourgeoisie were right in the party ranks. China was facing a danger of capitalist restoration that relentless class struggle had to be fought." Obvious his words were warning Liu and his followers though he did not mention their names.

In 1962 at the Science and Technology Conference, Chen Yi, the minister of foreign affairs said: "China needs intellectuals, needs scientists. For all these years, they have been unfairly treated. They should be restored to the position they deserve." At the same meeting, Premier Zhou said: "In socialist China most of the intellectuals and scientists could be counted as members of the laboring class and therefore friends of socialism, and he argued that "To destroy superstition (of scientists) does not mean to destroy science. In fact, destroying superstition rely on scientists." Mao, who was always hostile to intellectuals, refuted and criticized: "Who makes history? The workers and peasants, the laboring people, or someone else?" He determined that "it is the workers and peasants, not the scientists and intellectuals who made history." He rebutted the opinion of Chen Yi and Zhou, saying, "The party has not yet properly educated intellectuals. The bourgeois spirit hangs like a ghost over their heads. They are vacillating."

In May 1963, Mao said that, "at present, there appeared a grave, sharp class struggle in Chinese society. Capitalism and feudalism were attacking furiously."

In July the same year, he repeated that "In the ideological front, there were problems in all the areas of education, theory, science, literature and art, newspaper, magazine, publication, broadcast, health and sports."

In Dec. Mao criticized the Department of Literature and Art: "We have established a socialist foundation in our economy, but the superstructure—literature and art—has not changed so much. Dead people are still in control of literature and the art… Even party members are enthusiastically promoting feudal and capitalist art but ignoring socialist art. This is absurd." He blamed: "All the books in the store are 'well-known', 'foreign' and 'ancient'" "All forms of art—operas, theatre, folk arts(including ballad-singing, traditional storytelling and comics), music, the fine arts, dance, cinema, poetry and literature were 'feudal or capitalist' and 'very murky'. They were all 'poisonous weeds'". He ordered to send artists to the countryside to reform thought: "Throw singers, poets, playwrights, and writers out of the cities." "Drive the whole lot of them down to the villages. No food for those who don't go". He was going to crackdown on his opponents and to exile writers and artists. What Mao had in mind was a completely lifeless society, devoid of civilization, deprived of representation of human nature and human feelings. He wanted the entire people with no knowledge and sensibilities and to absolutely obey his orders and instructions.

While Mao criticized those opponents, he also steadily fueled his personality cult. Eulogies of Mao and homage to Mao increasingly dominated textbooks, publications, radios, newspapers and every sphere that affected people's minds, captured everyone's eyes and ears. Mao himself indoctrinated the population with a diary of a dead soldier called Lei Feng and launched a campaign "learn from Lei Feng". He created Lei as a role model for all the people. The essence of Lei Feng was his "boundless love and devotion to Mao". Almost on every page of his diary there was a pledge like: "I must study Mao's works, heed Mao's works, follow Mao's instructions, and be a good soldier of Mao's" In his diary Lei recorded how he was inspired by Mao to do good deeds, and swore that he was ready to "go up mountains of knives and down into seas of flames" and to "have my body smashed to powder and my bones crushed to smithereens" for Chairman Mao. Lei highly advocated hatred. He wrote a poem "The Four Seasons", in which he expressed how he would treat the "enemy":

"Like spring, I treat my comrades warmly,

Like summer, I am full of ardor for my revolutionary work.

I eliminate my individualism as an autumn gale sweeps away fallen leaves,

And to class enemies, I am cruel and ruthless like harsh winter."

What Mao intended to do was obviously to enhance his personality cult, to exhort all the people to have "boundless love and devotion to Chairman Mao" like Lei Feng. Many people suspected whether the so called "Lei Feng's diary" was true or not.

On Feb. 9 and 29 1964 Mao met with two leaders of foreign Communist Party. During their talk Mao criticized the International Liaison Department of the Central Committee. Its head Wang Jiaxiang had advanced suggestions in 1962: "1, Conciliation was desirable and it was unnecessary to overthrow imperialism to realize worldwide peaceful coexistence; 2, China should avoid an open rupture in Sino-soviet relation and should consolidate the Sino-soviet alliance; 3, China should adopt a relatively appeasing attitude toward the American imperialists and should no longer sent troops abroad at another country's request; 4,......, 5,......" He also believed that armed conflict was not the only means of achieving national independence; China should not encourage the people of other countries to rise up in revolution and should not interfere the internal affairs of other countries. Mao regarded that policy was an "attempt to appease US-led imperialism, Soviet-led revisionism, and reactionaries in all countries, to minimize the support to national liberation struggles and revolutionary movements." He abbreviated the opposing views as "three appeasements and one minimum".

In the same month, Mao criticized the Ministry of Agriculture, which promoted that the peasants should have a plot of land for personal needs; there should be free markets; the peasant should assume sole responsibility for his profits or losses; the production team should contract with each household for production quotas. He abbreviated it the "three freedoms and one contract"; And he criticized the Department of United Front Work, which did not mention the class struggle. He summarized: "'the three appeasements and one minimum' was their foreign program; 'the three freedom and one contract' was their domestic program. These people, including some members of the central committee, secretary of secretariat, vice premier, pursued the revisionism. There were more in the departments of the government and provinces. Their aim was to dismiss the socialist agricultural collective economy and to bring down the socialist system." Mao's words reflected that he firmly believed China already existed revisionists in the central committee of the party though he did not name Liu Shaoqi.

In June, 1964, Mao directly attacked against the All China Federation of Literature and Art: "For the last fifteen years, the organizations and magazines under its control basically had not been carrying out the party's policy and in recent few years had fallen to the edge of revisionism. They acted like overlords, shying away from close contact with the workers, peasants, and soldiers. They don't reflect the socialist revolution. They're moving in the direction of revisionism. If these organizations are not thoroughly reformed, one day they will become like the Hungarian Petofi Club." At the same time Mao launched a rectification movement in literary and art circles. During the movement many famous writers and artists were denounced and some leaders of the Ministry of Culture were dismissed.

Mao's Rectification Movement in Cultural and Art Circle was met with much criticism. Deng Xiaoping made a speech at the meeting of the Secretariat of the Central Committee of the Party, criticizing the messy condemnation against the writers and artists. He said: "Many people do not dare to write articles now. The Xinhua News Agency only received two articles per day. On the stages of the theatre are only appeared soldiers and fighting. This play was allowed to play, that play was not allowed to play. Those "revolutionists" want to seek names by criticizing others, to grind others under foot for their personal advancement. We must put an immediate stop to this state." His words were true and right, but conflicting to Mao's ideas and to no avail. Deng became Mao's number two enemy.

In order to hunt more "witches" Mao set up a Cultural Revolution Team in July 1964 and assigned Peng Zheng, the mayor of Beijing Municipality, as the leader of the Five Person Team. Another leader of the team was Lu Dingyi, the minister of the Ministry of Publicity of the Party Central Committee. Peng Zheng and Lu Dingyi often had opponent views, why Mao let them to lead the team? It was his scheme. He was sure they would make greater mistake, then he could punish them severely, He always trapped people in this way, just as he had done in the Anti-Rightist campaign and Lu Mountain Conference. He lured people to say or do something, then used their own words or conduct as evidence of their crimes.

On Sep. 11 1964, according to Mao's instruction, the State Council issued a notice, which pointed out: "Universities of Liberal Arts were gravely divorced from reality, the influence of capitalist and revisionist ideology were widespread. The students may become the successors of the capitalism and there was the danger of 'peaceful evolution'. Those colleges should be moved to the countryside or to be affiliated to the factory and take the work-study or farm-study program."

Mao also criticized that the Ministry of Public Health did not serve the people, only served the bureaucrats. Ironically, there was a host of doctors and nurses serve a single man, the emperor. Why he did not send them to serve the poor people in the countryside?

On Dec. 5 1964, Mao believed that a large part of the management and operation of industry were already changed into capitalist mode. In short, Mao regarded all the opponents and pragmatists were capitalists or revisionists, he intended to use class struggle to discard all the deadwood.

On Dec 12, 1964, Mao put forward a new concept "the leaders who take the capitalist road" He accused that those leaders were practicing revisionism and becoming capitalists sucking the blood of the workers. He declared that there already appeared a bureaucratic-capitalist class in China, that class and the class of workers were two sharply opposite classes. He also pointed out that those leaders were not only existing in the local organization but also existing in the Central Committee of the party. They were the targets of class struggle and the targets of revolution. He blamed that there were two independent kingdoms in Beijing: The Secretariat of the Central Committee of the Party led by Deng Xiaoping and the State Planning Commission led by Li Fuchun. Now Mao's sword already directly pointed to Liu's closest followers.

In the early days of 1964, I took my second family leave to see my wife. formerly I only knew her working place is far away. It is an abstract concept. I did not know how arduous is the journey. Now I experienced the exact hardships. I took two days train from Beijing to Chongqing, then rode a steamship down the Yangtze River to a county called Fuling. On the Fourth Day I took a boat upstream the Wu River toward the next county called Wulong. The boat was moving very slow. In places where the stream of water was swift, the boatmen had to go ashore to tow the boat up. The journey lasted two days. On the sixth day I took a bus to the fourth county called Pengshui. On the seventh day I took another bus to Youyang county—my destination. During the seven days' journey, when I was on the train and boat, I could not sleep; whenever I arrived at a new county, I had to find a hotel to stay and search for the bus station or the steamboat company to buy a ticket in a quite strange place, I had no time to rest at all. In addition, it was winter time, I often had to suffer the bitter cold in the open air. You can imagine how much exhausted I must be. When I finally arrived at Youyang, I rested on a bench for a while, then I found a public telephone booth. I made a call to the hospital asking the telephone operator to tell my wife that I already arrived to the bus station. My wife knew I would come on that day but could not know what time I would arrive, so she was unable to receive me at the bus station. After my wife got my news, she rushed to the bus station and I hurried up to greet her with a tight handshake. Though having been tired out I was exultant, and my wife was smiling from ear to ear. She took over my knapsack and held my hand to walk to her hospital.

At hospital we were welcomed by three or four her close colleagues. They congratulated her on getting together with her husband coming from Beijing. We thanked them for their concern. After a few compliments they left, letting me have a rest. While I lay in bed my wife went to prepare the dinner, an excellent meal: Black bone chicken, pork braised in brown sauce. etc. Both she and I do not drink wine, but for celebrating the union she bought a bottle of beer. The last course was sesame stuffed dumplings made of glutinous rice flour. She told me her mood was greatly improved, she like her work. Most of her patients were peasants, she treated them warmly and patiently. And she felt that the warm treatment the poorer peasants received, the more gratitude they showed. She perceived it as the greatest reward. I praised her to do the right and glory thing. We had a very happy night.

But the next day I did not feel well. The long period of exhaustion finally got me. I came down with a headache and high fever. I lay in bed the whole day and took some medicine. I recovered in two or three days. My wife was very busy; during the day time she treated the patients, at night she had to take part in the political study. Only in Saturday evening and on Sunday she could accompany me. I toured the town alone, which was very small and did not take me much time. Most of the time I read books at home. I also visited a local high school to solicit the opinions of the students on the magazine "High school students". The headmaster of the school warmly received me and organized a forum for me with the students. He also asked me to make a speech to the students. I did not want to talk about politics and ideology, I introduced the recent development of science and technology to the audience.

On the only Sunday during my leave, my wife took me to visit the scenic spot of the town—a big cave. The cave was rather dark. We took steps forward and stared with all our eyes. A level gallery let to a large cavern hollowed out of the mountain and dimly lit by slits contrived in the roof. It was deadly quiet, there were no other visitors at that time. There were some stalagmites in it and many limestones on the ground. I picked up a couple of small stones as a souvenir. We walked around the cavern for a while and went out. This was the one and the only day she was able to accompany me to tour the town.

Soon the parting day was coming, she helped me to pack the knapsack and gave me a beautiful blue woolen sweater as a gift, which cost her one third monthly pay. Both of us had a heavy heart and did not know what to say. She was worried if I can stand up the seven days journey again. I promised her that as soon as I arrived in Beijing, I would send her a telegraph. Then we set off for the bus station, hand in hand, my heart was so full that I did not say a word. She was silent too. Before I boarded the bus, we finally exchanged the same words: "You are alone, be careful, take good care of yourself!" I kissed her goodbye and got on the bus. When the bus started, I saw tears trailed down her eyes. My heart was broken.

On the return journey I contemplated one thing: how stupid, how deficiency of human nature the party leaders were. The time of the trip plus the family leave is almost one month, a waste of my working time. The government had to pay my salary and all the expenses of the journey. It is a sheer squander of manpower and the money of the government. And the foolish policy caused great suffering of millions of separated couples. What is good for this policy? On the other hand, apart from his wife, Mao Zedong always forced or lured women or girls to accompany him, but not allowed a couple to live together. Was it right? Was it just? I wanted to protest but I knew the only result would be my being criticized or persecuted that I deny the interest of the party. I had to keep silent, and all the millions of separated couples must keep silent. It is really a tragedy.

After returning to Beijing I decided not to think of those unhappy things, just concentrated my mind at work. My work does not involve politics and can help the youth to increase knowledge, from which I can earn some pleasure.

A few months later my wife told me she was pregnant. I was both happy and worried. I advised her not to overwork herself lest it cause a miscarriage. Later I suggested her to come to Beijing to give birth to the baby so that I could take care of her. She had the same idea. When the date of childbirth was near, she applied for maternity leave to go to Beijing, but the party secretary of the hospital did not approve her application. Having known the refusal a fierce anger overtook me; it seeped upward through my veins up to my head. It was quite an absurd thing. A 56 days maternity leave is China's legal leave. She uses her own legal leave to come to Beijing, the leader has what right not to allow her leaving the hospital for Beijing? She protested but to no avail. She could not leave Youyang county without the hospital's certificate. I went to Ministry of Civil Affairs to sue the hospital, but they said they should not interfere local affairs. We had no way to protect our rights. I did not know the exact reason why the secretary refused her application. why he was so heartless and senseless. I guessed he must nurse a jealousy against my wife: She has a chance to go to Beijing, the capital of our country; he, the leader of the hospital, hasn't the chance to look at the prosperous, splendid city, so he must not let her go.

This event made me furious and instigated me making a deep thought. What kind of a society we were living in? Not a socialist society, not a feudal society, it can only be categorized a slave society. But this slave society is different from the old slave societies in the history. It is a special slave society. In all the old slave societies there were many, many slave owners. The slaves were the properties of their owners and were forced to obey their owners. In China's slave society, there is only one slave owner, who is Mao Zedong, all officials and people are his slaves. But the officials have a double status; they are slaves as well as slave owners. The premier, minister, party secretary of the province are Mao's slaves, but they are also the slave owners of all their subordinates. The party secretary of the county is the slave of the party secretary of the province, but he is also the slave owner of all his subordinates. On the analogy of this pattern, all the party secretary in a unit are half slave and half slave-owners. Only the common people are pure slaves. A mere hospital party secretary could absolutely control the lives of all the staff of the hospital. This pattern of society is Mao's invention. He called it the "one party dictatorship". Every party leading cadre can be a dictator though he is the slave of his superior. Mao boasted it the most advanced, most civilized society.

My wife could not help but stay alone in the hospital, without a single family member or relative nearby. She felt nervous and afraid, for there were people died at giving birth to a baby, what would be her fate? I had the same fear. Though I knew the percentage of that incident was very low, there was still a possibility. In case the unfortunate thing happened, what should I do? Even I went to her place immediately I might not be able to see her again. Her body might be cremated already. I would lose my dearest forever; I would never see her smile and hear her voice again. Could I bear it? Or should I follow her to accompany her? I was troubled by those thought.

The day of her giving birth was nearer and nearer, and I became more and more anxious. In addition, the Mid-Autumn Festival (the eighth month 15 by the lunar calendar) was coming, which is a day for celebrating the reunion of the family. On that night, every family would get together, watch the moon and eat Moon cake. China has an idiom "Fine festival makes people miss his kin doubly." I longed for a reunion passionately but I could not. I felt miserable.

To alleviate my craving for seeing my wife I wrote a letter to her:

Dear Runshu:

How are you. The expected date of confinement is near, how do you feel? I am sorry I cannot accompany you and help you. You must take good care of yourself, having additional nutrients and a good rest. I pray to Heaven that everything will go on smoothly, safely.

The Mid-Autumn Festival is coming, but we cannot get together. I think of a unique way for us to enjoy that festival: On that night, we both look at the full moon from eight o'clock pm. In that way our eyesight will meet on the moon and link us together. Let us appreciate the moon and eat moon cake at the same time.

A Painful Reminiscence of a Dignified Soul

This special form of reunion will make us feel closer and happier. Do you agree with my idea?

I read a collection of Japanese ancient poem recently. I like it very much. I want to share some of it with you. It is called "Haiku poem (俳句诗)", which is the shortest poetry in the world. It consists of only three sentences with seventeen syllables. The first and the third sentence each has five syllables, the second sentence has seven syllables. It uses many metaphors and comparisons. I do not know Japanese, what I read is its English version. The poems are concise and evoke all sorts of my feelings. Here are a few examples:

> "Take me with you,
> Fly free from servitude.
> My kite."

This poem expresses the poet's longing for freedom. It also expresses my longings.

> "If I were the emperor
> Of a deserted island.
> It would be nice!"

The poet is feeling miserable and would prefer to be alone. In our society everyone is afraid and tell lies., so I also would like to be alone.

> "Watching the cormorant fishing boats,
> In time,
> I was full of sorrow."

After catching a fish, the cormorant is unable to swallow their prey and are forced to regurgitate their hard-won object. In our country, the peasants have to contribute too much of their crops to the government. So many peasants were starved to death.

> "Like the morning glory,
> How fleeting is my life.
> Today... and then...?"

The poet uses the morning glory, which flowers at dawn and fades by noon, to represent the fleeting of life. I have the same feelings. I have wasted so much time to do revolution and I am already near forties. What can I do in the future in this awful society?

> "My hunter of dragonflies,
> How far
> Would he have strayed today?"

This is one of the most famous 俳句诗 in Japan. The note of the poem reads: "The poet's life is very miserable, married at nineteen, widowed at twenty-seven and lost her only son next year. The deep sorrowful feelings led her to compose this great work." I have the similar miserable feeling. How far I would stray in my life?

> Do you like these poems?
> Don't forget to look at the moon on the night of the Festival night.
>
> With best wishes!
> Zhong

Afterwards she told me that night she did sit alone on a bench in the garden of her hospital with some moon cake. The surroundings were deadly silent, the air was cold, she felt both melancholy and delighted: Sad for she was lonely like a pity bird locked in a cage; pleased for she was reunited with me under the same moon. At eight o'clock, she began to keep staring at the moon, envisaging my image in her eyes. She nibbled moon cake slowly which was the symbol of reunion. She recalled many past things between us and felt as if we were near and close. From time to time she touched her big belly, caressing the baby inside, which is our crystal and future. She was nailed there until midnight, finally kissed the moon a goodbye with me, reluctantly returned to her bedroom. She said she will remember that meaningful night forever.

I was deeply moved by her love and felt great pity with her conditions, I wrote back to her that I had exactly the same feelings and thoughts at that night. I told her while I stared at the bright moon and nibbled moon cake, I remembered

A Painful Reminiscence of a Dignified Soul

a grievous song, which was the theme song of the famous American film Gone with the Wind I learnt in Shanghai in 1946. Facing the moon, I sang the song again and again:

> Regretted too late I know you today,
> And we have to part from each other today.
> Water is flowing in twisty stream,
> Flowers are falling like rain.
> It is harder still to expect to live together till white hair.
> Let white rock be the proof,
> Let the bright moon be the witness,
> My heart had given to you long ago.
> Wish us remember each other forever
> Even in the remotest corners of the world.
> Our loving heart will never remove.

All those days I was anxious about her safety. I asked her to send me an urgent telegraph immediately if there was any emergency.

Fortunately, in November 1964 I got the good news that she gave birth to a pretty girl safely. I was in an ecstasy of delight. The baby's weight was about six pounds. My wife's body was fine and she had hired a nanny to take care of her and her child. Now all my worry was released.

Half a year later, my wife took her family leave to Beijing with our baby. This time her leader dared not to violate the stipulation set by the government. I was wildly glad to see my daughter. Her skin was white, eyes bright, very lovable. She recognized and clung to her mother only. The first time I embraced her in my arms, she was afraid and cried. Only when her mother touched her body by her, she felt safe and stop cry. Once my wife and I went to a nearby cinema. Since cinema allowed no baby in, we left our sleeping baby on bed and asked a neighbor to take care of her. Not long after we left, the baby woke and found that woman was not her mother and cried loudly. No matter how that woman coaxed her, gave her toys or fed her milk, she kept crying wildly. That woman was afraid, fearing her long crying hurt her body, and asked another woman to go to the cinema to call us back. The cinema made a broadcast during the show: "Please Da Zhong go back home at once, there is an emergency." We ran back. Once my wife encircled the baby with her arms, she stopped crying. We were deep sorry we let our dear baby suffer so long a time.

During her family leave I had only one chance to go out with them for sightseeing. We went to the Summer Palace on a Sunday. We toured the park and took a bath in the Kunming Lake. The baby was not afraid of the water and like it, patting the water with her tiny palm. We also had a nice meal there.

Twelve days passed quickly; our happy days were soon ended. My wife started another arduous journey with a knapsack and a about fifteen-pound baby. I felt pity for her and sad for parting with them, but there was nothing I could do. I could only bemoan we were living in an age without human nature.

After Mao declared that there are capitalist roaders in the Central Committee and purged or criticized some central leaders in 1964, he went a step further to stress the class struggle in 1965. In order to stimulate people to purge his opponents relentlessly, fiercely, he asserted that there is only class nature and there isn't human nature. Every cadre was given three pamphlet "Anti Human Nature 反人性", "Anti Human feelings 反人情", "Anti Humanitarianism 反人道主义" as political study materials. We studied and discussed Mao's instructions and party's policies every Saturday afternoon. Everything was deemed to be political; every small thing was exaggerated to be grave event. Some authorities even said that all books were tools of class struggle. During that period of time people usually did not express any different ideas. I also hardly aired any opposite views. But the assertion that all books are tools of class struggle is too ridiculous. Even Stalin had said that language has not class nature. I could not bear to keep silent and I did not want to oppose that opinion openly. I Just raised a question: "How to use mathematical books as an instrument to wage class struggle?" No one answered my question, nor anyone criticized me, there was only a long silence. Fortunately, there was no dogmatist in our editorial department, otherwise I would get another accusation.

I found things had become more and more absurd. All human beings are born with emotions, like joy, sadness, anger, fear, surprise, disgust, compassion, etc. They are human nature, they are feelings of humankind, they are transcending classes. Now they are all opposed, denied. Humanism is a system of thought, offering people a source of morality and ethics based on reason, rational thinking and humanity. Humanism stresses the importance of caring for and respecting human beings and individual's dignity and worth. Now it was deemed an evil ideology. Criticizing human nature and humanism is abandoning all the morality and

A Painful Reminiscence of a Dignified Soul

eliminating the affection, love and trust among people. Mao said there is only class nature, then there is only proletarian class nature and capitalist class nature. Since these two-class nature are opposite, the relations between the people of the two classes will remain only hatred, enmity and struggle. Practicing Mao's theory, the whole world would certainly become relentless, barbarous. The heaven and earth are really turning upside down.

One day I read a report from the newspaper that Zhou Yang, the Minister of Ministry of Culture, was being criticized. One of his "mistakes" was he sent 60 RMB monthly to his father who had been labeled a landlord. The criticizer blamed that Zhou Yang, who sent money to a class enemy to keep him leading an extravagant life, is gravely bereft class stand. After reading that criticism I was frightened, for I was sending my father-in-law 30 RMB every month. Zhou Yang, as a high-level communist official, was still being criticized in public, I was a label removed rightist and my father-in-law was a historical counterrevolutionary. if my action was discovered what consequence would land on me? I was encountered a great difficulty. If I continued to send the money I would be denounced and punished; if I stopped sending the money my father-in-law's life would be difficult. I was in a dilemma, wobbling between the two ideas: sending or stop sending. After wrestling my brain for a long time, I decided to stop the remittent temporarily. My mother-in-law was still working though the wage was low, and their daughter already had work, they could ask their daughter for help. Having made the decision, I wrote a letter to my father-in-law. I told him the trouble I had met and I stressed that the stop of sending money was temporary, whenever the situation changed, I would resume the remittent and I asked his excuse.

Quite unexpected, several days later I got my father-in-law's replay. He told me the bad news: On that day when the postman sent my letter to him, a policeman happened to be at his home. After he read the letter, the policeman asked him to hand over the letter to him. The policeman read the letter and criticized him seriously and forfeited the letter.

Not long after that, the party secretary of the Youth Publishing House called me to his office. He told me they had received the letter I sent to my father-in-law from the Public Security department of Chongqing Metropolis. He said my mistake was severe and the party would hold a criticizing meeting for me.

Hearing his words, my mind was in a complete confusion: Why my fate was so bad: at the time when my father-in-law received the letter, the policeman was just in his home; What was the right of the policeman to forfeit the letter: why the policeman hasn't the slightest human nature and sent the letter back to my office? Why should such a simple letter between home constitute a crime? What punishment would the Youth Publishing House put on me? I was in distress, but I also warned myself that I mustn't lose my spirit and stoop to difficulties, I must brace myself for the worst sentence.

At the criticizing meeting I was denounced of all faults by a few leftists. Most colleagues kept silent. I made no refutation. At the end of the meeting the party secretary declared that I was no longer fit to stay in Beijing and transferred me to my wife's place. I was exiled to a small town in the remote mountain area.

I had no other choice I had to obey the decision. Sending money to parents is a crime. It is really an unprecedented and unrivalled preposterous event throughout the world in history. I was sad not merely for my own fate, but for the general degradation of virtue. Under the one-party dictatorship, under the cruel class struggle, it seemed all human nature, manners, feelings, bravery, pity, compassion, justice, reasoning were all lost. A policeman would find it a happy thing to make others suffering. I made no mistake and my work was commonly praised, and most colleagues were friendly with me. But the dogmatists decided I must be severely punished because I was a "Class enemy". I knew most of my colleagues did not agree with the decision, but they dared not to say anything. I understood their situation. I did not complain. I myself did not dare to make any protest. We all knew all different words were to no avail.

I love Beijing, where I had lived for nearly twenty years, which left me many precious memories. Before leaving I went back to some memorable place again, such as the city wall where I had a long talk with my wife at midnight; the Kuenming Lake in Summer Palace, where I had taken part in a competition of swimming. etc. I also bid farewell to some great friends. first, I went to see Peng Zhigang who had become my devoted friend and dear elder sister when we labored in the village. She felt sorry that I had to leave Beijing. She and I understood the society and reality fairly well. I did not need to make any explanation or complaint. Before I left her home, she grasped my hand tightly and wished me have a good journey. We promised to keep in contact always. And later she had once asked her son to come to Sichuan province to see me.

Then I visited He Chongfan, who was my classmate and bosom friend in Baihou High School and now worked in the Chinese Academy of sciences. He was a patriot. Near the end of the war of resistance against Japan, the government drafted well-educated people into the "Youth Army", which was equipped with American weapons. He joined the "Youth Army" and once went to the front in Burma territory. After demobilized from the army he studied chemistry in Zhongshan University. In the Chinese Academy of Sciences, he was also denounced for having been a soldier of the "Youth Army". But as he is an expert of natural science, he is not labeled a history counterrevolutionary. I told him I was exiled to a remote mountain area, maybe I could never see him again. Both of us felt great pain at heart. We just encouraged each other not to succumb to the dark reality and believed the one-party dictatorship would eventually be eliminated. We had a heart-to-heart talk and then said goodbye with a heavy heart.

Of course, I also said goodbye to many other friends and colleagues. They all sympathized with me and encouraged me to keep high spirits always and not stoop before difficulties. I was proud that I had some faithful friends.

I turned over my work to another editor and prepared my journey. I went to the Public Security Bureau to apply for the certificate of transferring my residence registration. This is a new thing in new China. Before the so-called liberation, anyone had the freedom of migration. I had moved from Zhenjiang to Hong Kong, to Baihou, Maixian and Shanghai without anyone's approval. Now if anyone wants to move to another place, he has to have a certificate. And this practice was called the "incomparable superiority" of communist China. I regret I had risked my life to fight for the realization of the communist China. But it was too late. I do not regret my former conduct, my conduct was for building a free, prosperous China which Mao promised. My sorrow was Mao's betrayal of his word. Now I was suffering from the dictatorship. I could not act in my own way. I had to be controlled by others.

I sold or discarded all the things I did not want to carry with me. bought a train ticket to Chongqing and left Beijing. No send-off meeting was held, for I was sent into exile.

A two days' train trip brought me to Chongqing. I went to visit my parents-in-law. They were glad to see me but also felt sorry that I was sent down due to their bad family background. I alleviated them that it was not their fault, they need not be sorry.

Two days later I took a ship to Fuling County.

I did not go on with the trip to Youyang. It was too far away a place. I did not want to go there. In Fuling there was a Sub provincial Administration of Sichuan

Province. Youyang county was under its jurisdiction, it had the power to change my residence registration. I went to the Organization Department of the Administration, appealing its head to let me stay at Fuling. I said I had worked as an editor in Beijing for a long time and I was afraid there was no suitable work for me at the small, remote town Youyang. The head asked me many questions and examined my file. Then he told me they would discuss the question and let me know the result later. I thanked him and left. I was pleased that he did not refuse my request point-blank, and his attitude was mild. There appeared a gleam of hope.

I stayed at a hotel waiting for the decision. Fuling is not a big city but it is well known in the country for its delicious preserved vegetable called "zha cai 榨菜" - hot pickled mustard tuber, which was even sold well in many foreign countries. And the city is by the Yangtze River, traffic is convenient, far better than remote Youyang county.

A couple of days later, the head of the Organization Department told me that considering I was a senior editor, there might not be a suitable work for me in Youyang county, so they decided to let me stay at Fuling, and he promised me they would transfer my wife from Youyang to Fuling later. With great satisfaction I gave him a hearty thanks. He reached out his hand for a handshake with me, I waved his hand up and down warmly and then left his office.

I was very delighted and contented, for staying at Fuling my wife and I could often go to Chongqing to visit and help her parents.

Shortly after the talk with the head of the organization department, I was assigned to work at Fuling Senior High School as an English teacher. I accepted the job and immediately went to the school to report for duty.

The school is in a small town named Lidu, which is also by the side of the Yangtze River. Our school is located on a mountain area surrounded by fields. The landscape is beautiful and the air is fresh. It is an ideal secluded place for study without the racket of the downtown. All the teachers and students had board and lodging at school. Most students were coming from peasant families. I liked my new work though I lost my old editor job. Communicating with young people is an exhilarating experience, I had a personal feeling at the fifth female high school in Beijing twelve years ago.

I began my new work soon. There were seven teachers in the "Foreign Language Teaching and Research Section". Three of them taught Russian language; the other four taught English. I began to learn the teaching methods from those experienced teachers. They welcomed me and we became friends very quickly. I prepared lessons carefully before giving lessons. Apart from teaching English in the classroom I often talked and played with students. Sometimes they would come to my room to have a chat with me or take remedial courses or make up missed lessons. We were not only teachers and students, but also friends.

Not long after my work was settled, my wife was transferred to Fuling. She was assigned a job at a Health Center in Lidu downtown. We were extremely delighted that we were reunited and had a family now. She was much emaciated. Having to work and bring up a baby alone, she must have been very busy and exhausted. My daughter was very cute, just a dainty bird of a child. She could already toddle a little and spoke a few simple words. She no longer remembered me, when I held her in my arms she still refused and struggled to break away from me. It was very funny. As there is a certain distance between my wife's health center and my school and there was a long flight of stairs of hundreds of steps to climb up the hill, we stayed on our own dormitory. Every weekend I went to her place.

Unfortunately, my peaceful life did not last long, very soon another huge storm swept across the country and I was persecuted again.

In 1965 Mao hastened his steps to eliminate his opponents. He dismissed the leader of the Ministry of Culture, the Director of the General Office of the Central Committee of the Party, the chief of the general staff of the People's Liberation Army and many others. In October of that year He asked the first party secretaries of the provinces: "What will you do if the Central Committee of the Party pursued the revisionism?" then he encouraged them: "If the Central Committee of the Party pursued revisionism you can rise up rebel."

By the end of that year, urged by Mao's wife and trusts, a writer named Yao Wenyuan wrote an article "the Comment of the play 'Dismissal of Hai Rue'" This article opened the prologue to the great cultural revolution. Mao finally unleashed his lethal attack on Liu and his confederate.

On February 7 1966, The Five Persons Cultural Revolutionary Team led by Peng Zheng submitted a Report to the party central committee. The report tried to make some proper restrictions on the "left" tendency on the academic discussion. It pointed out that "the discussion should persist in seeking truth from facts; all people are equal in the eyes of truth; should convince people by reasoning, not make an arbitrary decision or use power to coerce others like the scholar-tyrants do." As Mao expected Peng Zheng and Lu Dingyi were falling into his trap. Mao fiercely attacked Peng Zheng and other leaders of the central committee of the Party. Mao and his accomplice, his wife Jiang Qing, Kang Sheng and others, secretly worked out stratagem against his enemy in shanghai, calling the local officials and people to rebel.

In May 1966 Mao canceled Peng's Report, labeling it an anti-party program. He dismissed their official position and established a new Cultural Revolution Leading Team, which was under the leadership of the Standing Committee of the Political Bureau. Here hid the same sinister plot of Mao. He let Liu Shaoqi lead the cultural revolution, just as he had let Peng Zheng lead the "Cultural Revolution Team" before. He waited Liu to make greater "mistakes" and then use his "mistakes" to punish him.

In May 16, 1966, the People's Daily published the "The Notification of May 16" written by Mao's followers, which heralded the launch of the Cultural Revolution. It declared: "There was Khrushchev next to Chairman Mao." "Trust the masses, rely on them and respect their initiative, Cast out fear. Don't be afraid of disturbances. Mao has often told us that revolution can't be so very defined, so gentle, so temperate, kind, courteous, restrained and magnanimous." It called people to arm themselves to join a bigger undertaking, to fight the revisionism, to carry out the proletarian revolution to the end, to protect Chairman Mao; to purge undesirable influences from abroad and from China's past: capitalism from the west, communist revisionism from Soviet Union and feudalism from ancient China. In Mao's view all the culture, education, politics of ancient and modern, Chinese and foreign are wrong and reactionary.

After "The Notification of May 16" was published and Mao had stirred things up, Mao left Beijing again. "Let others stay busy with politics. We are going to take a rest." This was Mao's familiar strategy, allowing the snakes, his enemies, to come out of their holes. With his withdrawn, his enemies would show their hands, making it easier for him to strike them down. He stayed in Hangzhou for a while, away from political affairs pretended. The local authorities organized dancing parties for him almost every day. He enjoyed his life there and continued to stimulate the rebellion. By mid-June he went to his native village of Shaoshan. After staying there ten days he moved to Wuhan. He enjoyed the upheaval which was spreading quickly.

while he and his men roamed about big cities to incite a rebellion against his enemy, Mao plotted his strategy. He understood the real situation well: Liu Shaoqi was the President of the People's republic of China; he had a great many loyal followers in Beijing and provinces. To vanquish him and his group was not an easy job. Mao knew he could not crush Liu through the organization of the Party or the government. He needed his own advance guards and shock troops. Who would be his fighters? Mao and Kang Sheng found their main vanguards were in the high schools. They decided to recruit the most reliable supporters from China's 13 million high school students. They also had a good prospect of winning college students. They were juveniles, teenagers and people in their early twenties. They were brought up under red flags, indoctrinated with proletarian ideology, the personality cult of him, the militant mode of class struggle and trusted to be the successor and founder of communism. They were naive, simple, unsophisticated, courageous and apt to act rashly. They were endowed with the qualities of seeking for excitement, adventure, fulfillment and dedication. Mao was confident that he could easily cheat, utilize and manipulate them. Mao also regard workers, peasants and soldiers his perfect tools for they were ill-educated and credulous. He determined to leap over the party and state and go straight to those who revered him. He said "We have to depend on them to start a rebellion, a revolution. Otherwise, we may not be able to overthrow those demons and monsters."

In June Mao decided to suspend all classes and have students devote themselves full-time to the Cultural Revolution. Lessons of knowledge halted and students read and discussed Mao's comments on the educational system: "There must be a revolution in education. The phenomenon of bourgeois intellectuals ruling our schools can no longer be tolerated." Of course, this is only a pretext. The real aim of Mao is to eliminate his enemy. What he called the cultural revolution was in fact a political revolution, a coup d'état of the Party and the government controlled by Liu and his followers.

At the same time, Mao reorganized the leading group of the cultural revolution, which was composed of his wife Jiang Qing and his four devoted flatterers without a single former high-ranking leader, and he invested his wife with discretionary power so that he could do whatever he liked. The group called the students to be unwaveringly loyal to Mao, to hate class enemies fanatically. Under the new cabal, the cult of Mao was escalated to a fever pitch. Mao's face dominated the front page of People's Daily, which also ran a column of his quotations every day. The propaganda was splashed in outsize characters on the front page of all the newspapers, and declaimed in strident voices on the radio, carried by loudspeakers, creating an atmosphere of war time. More copies of Mao's selected works were printed than China's inhabitants. The Little Red Book had to be carried and brandished on all public occasions and its quotations were recited.

To spur the students and workers to rebel. Mao assumed a Marxist guise to bluff, ensnare them; to use the beautiful, sound rhetoric to cheat, mislead them and to breed resentment against his opponents. While he toured outside Beijing, he call on them "to overthrow the authority of the capitalist roaders", "to completely turn Heaven and Earth on their heads", "to destroy an old world and create a new one", "to be a hero to satisfy oneself for a lofty cause". "Rebellion is justified", "Great chaos will lead to great order" and so on.

Mao's words triggered the enthusiasm of millions of the youth and the leftists, who were zealous to realize the cause Mao promoted. At the same time, easy fame and power exerted a peculiar fascination on a great many people who were ambitious, vain, arrogant, conceited. They rose up to make the revolution.

In Beijing in many universities and high schools, students and teachers wrote big character posters to attack the party committee of their school and attack the party committee of Beijing municipality. One big character poster written by a teacher of Beijing University named Nie Yuanzhi was greatly praised by Mao. In order to use all the media to pump up more blind followers Mao ordered that Nie's big character poster to be broadcasted all over the country. The People's Daily published an editorial, calling the masses to rise up to sweep away all the monsters and demons. All these calls and propagandas caused great chaos in Beijing and a few other cities. Some students shouted: "We will be relentless! We will be brutal!" "We will strike you (Mao's enemies) to the ground and trample you!" "We will dig out hidden enemies, shed our blood, and sacrifice our lives for the final victory of the Cultural Revolution". The seeds of hate that Mao had sown were ready for reaping. Scores of teachers and cadres of the school were dragged in front of crowds and tortured. Their faces were blackened with inks and dunces' hats were put on their heads. They were forced to kneel; some were beaten up.

In Beijing University alone, the rebels ferreted out over forty cadres, teachers, students for struggling and beating, including the Party Secretary and the president of the school. Take an example, one of the most prominent theorists, Feng Ding, member of the standing committee of the Chinese People's Political Consultative Conference, vice president and the chairman of the philosophy department at Beijing University, was persecuted. He had joined the Party in 1926. and written many famous books, like "The commonplace truth", "The Communist view of Life" which had formerly been required reading for the younger generation. He was now being harshly attacked for promoting peaceful coexistence, peaceful competition, peaceful transition; opposing personality cult; denying the existence of class and class struggle in socialist society; selling the capitalist persuasion of fame and fortune, replacing the revolutionary dialectics with his philosophy viewpoint of subjective idealism, he was labeled as a revisionist and betrayer of Marxism. All his debates had been met with deaf ears or forbidden at all. Instead he had been fiercely beaten and humiliated again and again. Unable to bear the harsh, cruel persecution, he tried to kill himself three times by swallowing a large overdose of sleeping pills, but fortunately his son, who was very devoted and daring, saved him each time.

In order to alleviate the chaos, Liu Shaoqi decided to send Working Team to the universities and high schools to lead the Cultural Revolution. The working team in Beijing University stipulated some regulations and successfully checked the random struggle and beating to a certain degree. Liu transmitted the experience of working team to the whole country and recommended that the method taken by the working team to be correct, all the units could act accordingly.

Seeing his time was ripe for action Mao returned to Beijing from Wuhan on July 18th. A week later he told the secretaries of secretariat and the "New Cultural Revolution Leading Team" that "the working team played a bad function, hampering the development of the movement. We do not need working team, let the revolutionary teachers and students carry out the revolution themselves." On July 29th the new party committee of Beijing municipality declared to dismantle all the working teams. Shortly afterwards Mao further denounced that "sending working team was a mistake of direction and line. In fact, it is standing on the capitalist class standpoint to oppose proletarian revolution."

On August 5 Mao wrote "Bombard the headquarters—a big character poster of mine", in which he denounced that "During the more than fifty days since early June of sending down the working team, some leading comrades, from central committee to the local party organizations, stood on the reactionary capitalist standpoint, exercised the capitalist dictatorship to stamp out the vigorous great proletarian cultural revolution." Apparently, the poster was directed against Liu Shaoqi. And upon Mao's proposal, the central committee reorganized the central leading group, listing Lin Biao, Minister of National Defense, on second place as Mao's successor and downing Liu Shaoqi from second place to eighth place. On August

8 a "Decision on the Great Proletarian Cultural Revolution" was published, which prescribed: "At present time our goal is to defeat the people in power who are walking on the capitalist road, criticize the academic authorities, criticize ideology of capitalist class and all the exploiting class." "The revolutionary direction of the revolutionary youth and juvenile is always correct." At the same time Mao wrote a letter to the students of the high school affiliated to Qinghua University who had formed a rebel organization called the "red guards". He warmly supported their revolutionary action and said he will warmly support all the people who took the same revolutionary action whether in Beijing or in the whole country.

After Mao put up his poster, he declared at a post-plenum work conference of central leaders: "Beijing is too civilized! I would say there is not a great deal of disorder and that the number of hooligans (red guard) is very small. Now is not the time to interfere." Mao's endorsement of students' right to rebel had removed such restraints on violence as the work team had imposed. A "red terror" spread rapidly throughout the campuses of colleges and middle schools of the capital and a few big cities. Various of Mao's remarks indicated that Mao craved a measure of catalytic terror to jump-start the CR. He had no scruples about the taking of human life. In a conversation with trusties Mao went so far as to suggest that the sign of a true revolutionary was precisely his intense desire to kill. He further commented: "This man Hitler was even more ferocious. The more ferocious the better, don't you think? The more people you kill, the more revolutionary you are." Mao needed violence.

The first person who was beaten and tortured to death by the students in the Cultural Revolution was Li Jingyi, the vice secretary of the party committee of Nanjing Normal University. Her husband Wu Tianshi was the head of the Department of Education of Jiangsu Province. As Wu was the top leader in the educational circle, so Wu and Li were listed the first people to be criticized and struggled. Wu had appealed to the party secretary of Jiangsu Province that he and his wife were willing to admit their mistakes, correct their fault and burn all their works, but all to no avail. The party secretary told them he had no right to change the order from Beijing. Wu and Li were labeled the "representative of the feudal-capitalist educational line" "reactionary academic authority" and were denounced again and again. In the evening of August 3, 1966, the students of Nanjing Normal University assaulted their home, tugged them out to the campus of Nanjing Normal University. A group of cadres and teachers were pulled to the stage to criticize. Some stu-

A Painful Reminiscence of a Dignified Soul

dents poured the black ink onto the bodies of the "reactionary gang". They took turns humiliated their captives and then beating them with whatever was handy. Someone slammed a garbage can on LiJingyi's head. Barely conscious, the couple was pulled off the stage and paraded through the Nanjing streets. Somewhere along the way, both fainted from pain and exhaustion. The students then dragged the two across the ragged pavement, which was very hot, tearing the flesh from their legs, and their whole body were badly mangled. Li Jingyi, fifty-three, died on the street, her neck broken by the yoke. Several students peeled off from the group and dumped her corpse back at her home.

The students returned Wu Tianshi to the stage, which faced a hall where Wu had lectured on classical Chinese literature and education. Someone tied him with hemp rope on the ladder to exhibit to the public. Then they punched him, jumped on him and fractured both of his legs. Despite the torture, Wu insisted that he had never opposed socialism or the Communist Party. "What kind of person are you?" The students fired back at him. "I am Chinese," he replied, prompting them to intensify the torture. He was in a stupor for two days and died in the hospital on August fifth, he was fifty-six. His autopsy report lists six broken bones, a brain hemorrhage, and massive trauma to his internal organs. His two youngest sons living with him, aged fourteen and twelve, were forced to denounce him too; self-protection demanded they renounce their parents. And they had been commanded to acknowledge that their mother died of high blood pressure and their father of chronic hepatitis. Their parent's death magnified their reserve and saddled them with an inferiority complex.

Wu joined the Communist Party in 1943, having made many contributions to the revolution. He had been jailed by Nationalist Party for writing many radical articles. He was a famous educator. His book "Talks on the study spirit and study method of our ancient scholars" had great influence among students.

Two days after Li Jingyi's death, in Beijing the first person was beaten to death by the students. Her name was Bian Zhongyun, the party branch secretary and the headmistress of a girl school. The school was considered to be the best school in the capital, packed with high officials' children, including the children of Mao, Liu and Deng Xiaoping. On Aug 5 1966, the girls determined to rid the school of bourgeois elements. They accused five of the school administrators of having formed a "black Gang". They splashed them with ink, forced them to kneel and hit them with nail-spiked clubs. Bian was accused to pursue the capitalist educational line. cultivate successors of revisionism, oppose socialism and Chairman Mao and so on. They spat on her face, filled her mouth with soil, tied her hands behind her back and beat her black and blue. They ordered her to carry heavy bricks back and forth stumblingly. After two or three hours beating and torture, she lost consciousness at 5 pm. They dumped her into a garbage cart. A vice headmistress reminded the girls: "Bian is nearly dying, you need to send her to the hospital." The girls paid no heed to her word. Only after the school revolutionary team asked for instructions from Beijing municipal party committee, they sent Bian to the hospital. But at that time Bian's body was already stiff for long time. Traditionally, Chinese teenage girls are usually quiet, genteel, shy, mild and compassionate. They would bow reverently at their teachers. Now the girls suddenly became capable of unimaginable cruelty, buckling ferociously their teachers who had imparted them so much knowledge. What caused this change? The pure innocent girls were indoctrinated, poisoned and demoralized by their "great leader" who was the real murder of Bian Zhongyun. Those girls were also victims, their souls were distorted by the reality.

The death of Li, Wu and Bian marked the first murders of the cultural revolution in China, the state-sanctioned murder and state-enforced dishonorable behavior. The first killing in the capital and Nanjing were informed to Mao Zedong. He did not instruct to stop the terrible thing, which meant he expected such things carrying on and extending to a larger scale.

The bad news came thick and fast and each more terrible than the last.

Fu Lei was another victim, who was one of the most famous, prolific, refined great translators in China. He was trained in literature and the arts in Paris in his youth. He translated almost all the novels by Honore de Balzac and the novel Jean-Christophe by Romain Rolland and tales of Voltaire. His works totaled up to five million words. On August thirtieth 1966 midnight the Red Guards from Shanghai Conservatory of Music intruded his home to search for evidence of crime. They shouted "Down with the rightist Fu Lei!". Fu Lei told them his label of rightist was already removed. The students yelled "Your label was removed by the capitalist roaders in power, you are jackals from the same lair. If you do not capitulate, we will wipe you out. They blamed him to lead a capitalist life, the evidence of which was he smoked with a pipe, drank coffee, used western tableware including a table knife and play a piano to while away time. While they denounced him, they always slapped or beat him. They accused him to be the

A Painful Reminiscence of a Dignified Soul

father of the traitor Fu Cong, his son, who won a prize of piano competition in Poland, which was a revisionist country, the Soviet Union's accomplice. They read his son's letter to find the evidence of his illicit relations with a foreign country, but they found nothing wrong and as they were reading the sentence "The individuals of Poland were feeling at a loss, you do not need to feel at a loss. Great Chairman Mao's radiance lights up your road, you must not fall short of his leadership.", they did not know what to do and then reluctantly left his house. Next morning another group of Red Guards came to search and confiscate. They dug the ground of their garden and pried up all the floorboards but could not find anything they expected to get. On Sep. 2 Fu and his wife were dragged in front of their front door and forced to wear high dunce caps and stand on long benches to be criticized and slandered. Posters stating "Crush Fu Lei" and "Fu Lei must admit his guilt humbly." were pasted on the walls of his residence. For a lifelong time, Fu Lei believes that human character is above anything else, he cannot tolerate such injury to his spirit and bodies. After four daytimes and three nights torture. Fu decided to leave this world behind and asked his wife to take care of their sons, but his wife Zhu Meifu refused to stay alone and said: If you are determined to go to another world, I'll go with you together." After she cleaned her house the last time, they put 53.30 RMB in a letter as the fee of their cremation. They hung themselves from the ceiling to protest the dictatorship of the Communist Party and the torture and humiliation they suffered.

The most striking news I heard at that time was the death of Lao She, with whom I had some contacts. When I was at the Youth Artistic Institute, he often went to our Institute to watch and direct the rehearsal of his play <Dragon Beard Ditch> and we had a few talks. Later when I worked in Youth Publishing House, I had gone to his home inviting him to write articles for our magazine. I had intimate feelings to him. The unfortunate accident made me feel very sad and painful, his image appeared in my mind again and again.

Lao She is a very famous author of humorous, satirical novels and short stories. His novels "Xiangzi the Camel" (English translation names it "rickshaws"), "Four Generations under One Roof" were translated into many languages. An unauthorized and bowdlerized English translation, titled <Rickshaw Boy> became a bestseller in the United States. During the Sino-Japanese War Lao She was the head of the "All China Anti-Japanese Writers Federation". In 1946-47 He traveled to the United States on a cultural grant, lecturing and overseeing the translation of several of his novels. He was then the president of the Federation of Literature and Art Circles of China.

At the outset of the Cultural Revolution, In the afternoon of August 23rd 1966 he and other thirty or so famous writers and artists were trucked to an old Temple of Confucius. Large placards were hung on their backs, labeling them as "Reactionary academic authority" "cow demon and snake spirit". They were criticized, kicked and beat with the buckles of leather belts. Being the most famous writer and renowned as the "people's artist", Lao She was thoroughly beaten, blood streaming down his face and breast. Then He was carried to the Federation of Literary and Art Circles, where many Red Guards were already waiting for him. They imposed many fabricated crimes on him, accused him taking US dollars from America Imperialism. His matter-of-fact answers brought him more severe beatings in return. A female Red Guard lashed him with a belt fiercely. Lao She had an unyielding character and threw the placard on her head. Beating Red Guard was a crime of counter-revolutionary. He was titled "active counterrevolutionary" and sent to the police. It was said because premier Zhou's interference his wife was able to take him home in the early hours on August 24. At home she had to use cotton moistened with warm water to peel off his undershirt stuck to the flesh with congealed blood.

Early that morning, his wife had to go to the office, leaving him to rest at home. He decided to go out. Before walking away, he called his four-year-old granddaughter come out, embracing her in his arms and saying: "Little Yue, say goodbye to your grandfather!". This was the last word he said in his life. Then he trudged to the Peace Lake northwest of the city. Sitting alone there quietly he contemplated a whole day until late at night, according to the witness of an old man. Next morning the passersby noticed his floating body and reported to the police. The body was retrieved from the water and sent to the crematorium and was cremated the right day. His wife was so sad that she wanted to commit suicide and follow her husband right away, but some kind students dissuaded her from doing that, telling her "If you are going now, who will right the wrong later." Only by this simple word she got the courage to live on.

What Lao She contemplated the whole day, nobody would ever know. But everyone can guess he must have recollected his whole life: his childhood, his youth, his prime time and his aging period. He must also have thought of the glory, the sorrow, the sweets, the bitterness of his life. He loves his wife, his granddaughter and he wants to live on; but he has his dignity and majesty, he is already sixty-seven-year old and humiliated by teenagers. He could not bear the insult and humiliation and determined to leave her lovers and the evil world. In short, the white day time of Aug. 24, 1966 must be the most painful hours in his whole life.

Mao was not content with the chaos and violence in Beijing and a few big cities, he craved to spread violence throughout the country in no time. Mao told the Central Cultural Revolution Group: "One of the reasons the Soviet Union had discarded Leninism was that too few people ever saw Lenin in person." Mao proposed "The large number of China's younger generation should be given the opportunity to see the older generation of revolutionary leaders in person." In fact, he wanted his vanguards to see himself. Learning from the former emperors, Mao usually shrouded himself in mystery. He appeared few and remote, beyond human approach, so making his emperor countenance very precious. He believed If he bestowed his followers a favor of having a look of "the appearance of the emperor", they must feel it a great glory. In order to make best use of the youth and juvenile, he decided to invite all the revolutionary youth to Beijing to meet him and to learn the experience of Beijing's rebels and spread the violence throughout the country. He ordered all the governments, schools and transportation facilities to give the Red Guards and all the revolutionary rebels free trips, free board and free lodging throughout the country. In his struggle against the opposition, cost, means, morality, safety of lives was of no concern to Mao.

Very soon millions of young revolutionaries, including many primary school students, flocked into Beijing. They could take train and bus and ship without charge, they could be provided free lodge and meal by offices or schools in any town, and they had free admission to parks and recreational places. This caused a great chaos of transportation and social orders. The trains were overloaded. A train compartment designed to hold a hundred passengers now held one or two times that number. Sometimes the lavatories and door steps were full of people. Exit and entry to such compartments were possible only through the windows. Some students climbed up the train roof and lay on it. Many of those on top of the train fell off while asleep. All the classrooms of the school and the auditoriums of the offices turned into receptions. The furniture was piled up to make room for the mats used as bedding of the students. The local teachers, students and staffs of offices were busy to receive them and prepare food for them. As if all the money and labor force of the train stations, bus stations, offices, universities, High and primary schools were belonged to Mao Zedong who can spend and use them for the students' free trips at his will.

The greatest catastrophe of the free travelling of the students and rebels was the epidemic of disease. With the free travelling of students, a host of bacteria and viruses disseminated freely. Of the many diseases that thrived in the overcrowded, unhygienic conditions, meningitis was the most lethal. It was spread through coughing and sneezing. Lack of ventilation in crowded trains and dormitories helped its spreading. The disease first appeared in Beijing. Then it was carried to all cities along railway routes. Most hospitals did not have enough drugs to treat the disease. The United State offered medical help, but China did not respond to save face. The shortages of antibiotics were so severe that the government had to turn to pharmaceutical companies of Europe and Asia, purchasing several hundred metric tons of medicine. Control Centers were established to coordinate national efforts to prevent and treat the disease. But it was too late. By the time the situation had been brought under control, more than 160,000 people had died.

A student of fourteen-year-old boasted to me: He and three companies started from Chongqing to Beijing, having a glorious look at Chairman Mao and learning experience from Beijing's rebels, then went to Shanghai to visit universities; to pay homage to the sacred place of the revolution "Jinggang Mountain" in Jiangxi province; to view Mao's birthplace "Shaoshan" in Hunan province: to tour the big city Wuhan in Hubei province; and finally to return to home. He said they were not tourists, their trip was not for fun and comfort, they were soldiers going out to a war against an old world. He made one-month free travel without paying a single money. Yes, they were gratified by the generosity of Mao, they did not recognize they were used by him as his assailants or murderers.

Mao achieved his expectation, he held eight huge rallies on the Tiananmen gate tower from August 18 to the end of November of 1966 to receive more than 11 million revolutionary teachers and students from all parts of the country. He earned tens of millions more of devoted flatterers and blinded champions, which greatly enhanced his power and prestige and personality curt.

The first rally was held on August 18, thirteen days after the first killing in Beijing. Shortly after sunrise, Chairman Mao, clad in a grass-green People's Liberation Army uniform with a red star emblem on the cap, walked over the Goldwater Bridge beneath Tiananmen, smiling and waving to the crowds, shaking hands and moving among the people for a while. Then he returned to the bridge, pro-

A Painful Reminiscence of a Dignified Soul

ceeded toward the Tiananmen. At 7:30 A.M. the celebratory mass meeting began. To the songs of "The East is Red" Mao appeared atop Tiananmen. The chairman of the meeting Chen Boda lauded Mao with three accolades: "Great Leader, Great teacher, and Great helmsman." Then Lin Biao added "a Great commander." From then on, the Four Greats were used in every reference to Mao. Mao inspected the over one million youths and juveniles from the top of Tiananmen, waving to the masses. The red guards and other revolutionaries craned their necks, waving little red books and searching for Mao's figure with their eyes. A young girl from the school, in which Bian Zhongyun was beaten to death, presented Mao with an "Red Guard" armband and wore it round his sleeve.

Mao asked, "What is your name?"

She answered "Song Binbin (彬彬) ".

"What character is the Binbin?" "The character that means gentle and courteous." Mao said disapprovingly, "That name is not good. Yaowu (要武) would be better." Yaowu means militant and violent. With the armband on his arm, Mao thus acknowledged silently that he had become the red commander in chief of the red guards and firmly supported what they had done.

During all the other seven gigantic rallies, Mao waved to his admirers in the Tiananmen square from the top of Tiananmen, or in a convertible cruising through the Eternal Peace Boulevard. A red guard armband was prominently displayed on his left arm. Millions of revolutionary youth from all over the country were greeted and blessed by Mao. He declared the cultural revolution is a revolution that touches everyone's innermost being and purifies people's thinking. He praised the Reds' actions were very good and encouraged them take more militant actions and promised to support them. He also instructed all the people of the country to support them. Lin Biao, Mao's lieutenant, told the masses in Tiananmen: "Red Guard fighters: The direction of your battles has always been correct. Chairman Mao and the central committee support you! You have soundly, heartily battered the capitalist roaders, the reactionary bourgeois authorities, the bloodsuckers and parasites. Your revolutionary actions have shaken the entire society. You have achieved glorious results, you have done the right things and you have done marvelously!" At those receptions Mao called on the Red Guards to "destroy the Four Olds and cultivate the Four News. The Four Olds were: the old ideas, the old cultures, the old habits, the old customs." He did not mention what the so-called Four News were. They emphasized that the capitalists still plot to use Four Olds to corrupt the masses, subjugate the hearts of the people to accomplish their goal of restoring their rule.

For supporting the students Mao issued explicit orders to the army and police on the 21 and 22, August, saying that they must "absolutely not intervene" against the youngsters. In responding to the question from his subordinates "What if the red guard kill people?", the national police chief Xie Fuzhi said: "If people are beaten to death...it's none of our business...Don't bind yourselves by the rules set in the past... If you detain those who beat people to death...you are making a big mistake."

Mao used all the media to whip up people's hatred toward the so-called people's enemy.

After the first reception the Red Guards spread terror all over China and people were afraid of them. A wave of beating and torture swept the country. Violence, brutality, tragedy became commonplace everywhere.

Smashing the Four Old resulted an unprecedented damage to the nation's culture and civilization. It was disparaging to all traditions, Chinese and foreign, that were different from Mao's ideology. The red guards, proud with their own importance, marched along the streets, declaring "We are critics of the old world. We are creators of the new world." "We will use our iron brooms to sweep away all the foul things of the capitalist class." They gave orders to the restaurants, barber shops, tailor shops, photo studios and bookstores what they can serve what they must not. They made speeches, distributed pamphlets, and put out posters on the streets to announce their prohibition. They commanded that women must wear bangs and cut their hair to ear level and men must not have ducktail haircuts. Pointed boots, high-heeled shoes, narrow bottom trousers were forbidden to wear. A couple of days after their commands were published, they carried out their rules in the streets. They stopped passers-by whose appearance was unacceptable and humiliate them by shaving their hair, cutting bottom of the trouser leg, or cutting off their high shoe heels. etc. Nobody dared to resist them for opposing red guards was deemed opposing revolution.

They destroyed the street signs and names of shops, restaurants, schools, factories and hospitals with feudal, capitalist, and revisionist "decadent flavor", and replaced them with new revolutionary names. Beijing's widest street, the Eternal Peace Boulevard was renamed East-Is-Red Boulevard. Beijing Union Hospital, which was established by the Rockefeller foundation in 1921, became Anti Impe-

A Painful Reminiscence of a Dignified Soul

rialism Hospital. The East Everpeace Street, where there were many foreign embassies, was changed as Anti Imperialism Street. Tongren (meaning benevolence for all) hospital became worker-peasant-soldier hospital. The Yangwei Road in front of the Soviet Embassy was changed to Anti-revisionism road. Red guards surged into the renowned roast-duck restaurant Quanjude (meaning with all moralities). Pressed by the red guards, the workers of the restaurant smashed the seventy-year-old sign board of the Quanjude and replaced it with the newly painted sign board "Beijing roast duck restaurant". As "red" signifies revolution and "left" signifies progress, Red Guards decided to change the existing traffic regulations and insisted on red traffic light as the "go" sign and people should walk along the left side of the road, not the right side. Red Guards posted themselves at intersections and beside police officers redirected traffic this way. This action created chaos and caused countless accidents. Finally, premier Zhou explained to the red guards that such traffic regulations were followed the world over and that it had been proven scientifically that red light got people's attention. The question of traffic lights was thus solved. Many Red Guards changed their given names to Weidong 卫东 meaning defending Mao Zedong, Zhihong 志红 meaning determined to be Red Jige 继革 meaning continuing revolution.

Red Guards also went everywhere to raid churches, temples, palaces, ancient tombs, statues, pagodas, city walls, and historic sites, causing irretrievable damage. In Beijing, nearly all churches, temples and mosques were invaded or occupied by the red guards, who regarded religion as spiritual opium against people's mind. The Xishiku Church was raided by red guards. They destroy statues of Jesus and Mary with hammers and clubs. The figure of the crucified Christ laid headless among the broken statues. The typical Maoist slogan "Eradicate Religion" was hung on the building. An elderly Chinese priest was forced to kneel on the floor. In this painful state he was subjected to ridicule and commanded to renounce his religious belief. He refused. The Reds threatened to bury him alive if he did not apostatize. They smashed Buddhist temples, forced monks to betray their beliefs, defaced wall paintings of Buddhist gods, covering them with a coat of red paint, then painted portrait of Mao on top. Many Chinese temples were desecrated as schools or warehouses. The historic Confucian Homestead, Confucian Temple, and Confucian cemetery was attacked and vandalized by a team of Reds from Beijing Normal University led by Tan Houlan. The corpse of the 76th generation Duke Yansheng was removed from its grave and hung naked from a tree in front of the palace. During the raid more than 1,000 tombs and stone tablets were destroyed or damaged, and more than 1,700 volumes of ancient books and 900 scrolls of calligraphy and painting were set afire. The Reds also wanted to smash the Imperial Palace, but the Premier Zhou shut the Palace and sent army to prevent the entry of the Reds, so the most precious cultural heritage was preserved. Also by Premier Zhou's intervention, the Potala Palace in Lhasa Tibet was fortunately preserved.

The more common and terrible thing was they raided people's houses. The Red Guards took to the streets, giving full vent to their fanaticism. In the name of Smashing the Four Old with the license issued by Mao they destroyed their antiques, tore up paintings and works of calligraphy. Bonfires were lit to consume precious books. Many families' long kept genealogy books were burned to ashes. If there was a phoenix or a dragon carved on their bedstead or furniture, they would hack it off, because those images were considered "feudal". They destroyed their gardens, broke their goldfish bowls and bird cages. They taught them with Mao's word on raising flowers and nurturing birds: "Keeping flowers in pots and vases was a vestige of the old society and that only feudal scholar, officials and capitalist class would have the leisure to enjoy such arrangement." "Socialism had already arrived more than a decade before, and yet flower culture continued and thrived more than ever. All this had to be changed now." They instructed them to plant vegetables in their gardens. They overturned mattresses, peered inside fireplaces, sifted through the contents of the shelves and cabinets and confiscated gold, silver and jewelry. Some victim's houses were shared by others and they were squeezed into one or two rooms. A few victims were driven out of their houses and were carried to makeshift torture chambers.

The Prominent writers, artists, scholars, athletes and other top professionals, who had been respected and revered in the past, were now categorically condemned as "reactionary bourgeois authorities". They were usually tortured, humiliated and even beaten to death. In the long history who has seen such a cruel thing? Throughout the world which country has undergone such a sad tragedy? None. If Mark Twain, Ernest Hemingway, Charles Spencer Chaplin, Shirley Temple Black, or Muhammad Ali were persecuted or beaten to death by a dictator, what American people would think and feel of the catastrophe?

There are no accurate statistics about the number of victims in Beijing, but one internal party document report that in late August more than a hundred people were killed in every day; on August 26, 126 people died at the hands of red guards; the following day, 228; the day after, 184; on 29, 200. According to a conservative estimate, by late Sep. as the first wave of violence abated, at least 1,770 people had lost their lives, not including those massacred in the outskirts of the capital. And according to an official report, in August and September, the homes of 33,695 families in Beijing were looted, In Shanghai, 84,222 homes were looted. yielding 32,500 kilograms of gold; 450,000 kilograms of gold and silver jewelry; U.S.$ 3,340,000; other foreign currency worth $ 3,300,,000; 2,400,000 silver coins; cash, deposits, and bonds worth 3.7 billion yuan; 150,000 kilograms of pearl and jade objects; along with large quantities of commercial goods and other property, as well as priceless antiques, ancient paintings and books, which were all confiscated as "ill-gotten wealth of the exploiting classes" and went into the state coffers.

As our school is far from Beijing and in the countryside, the cultural revolution started a little later. At first stage, some enthusiastic students and teachers were just answered Mao's call to criticize the reactionary capitalist educational line. They wrote big character posters and held meetings to criticize the party branch secretary, the headmaster of the school, teachers who attached great importance to knowledge learning and teachers with bad background, including I. The following were some of their criticism and accusation:

"The Party secretary and the headmaster have always been pursuing a reactionary capitalist educational line. They advocated that 'the intellectual education is the first important thing', They said 'if you possess knowledge you will get along all right everywhere. It is an iron rice bowl which cannot be broken. Knowledge is a private thing in your own head which others cannot steal.' They encouraged us to become specialists, engineers. They introduced to us the old maxim '学而优则仕' meaning 'successful learning makes an official', implying that knowledge studying is the ladder for climbing up."

"They used the desire for personal fame and gain to injure our mind. They are the demons to kill without spilling blood."

"They used examination and test to torture us, a small test in each month; a middle test in the third month; and a final examination by the end of the school term. Mark, grade become student's very life; Examination becomes effective method teaches to control the students. Chairman Mao said: "We do not need examination. Why should we take examinations?" we must carry out his instruction and stop all the examinations."

"The student XXX committed suicide for failing in the entry examination to Beijing University. She was killed by the capitalist educational line. "

"The study is too tough, the homework is too much, and a large part of students have gotten nearsighted. We must correct the present situation."

"There are too few Chairman Mao's works in our teaching material and our textbook does not mention the Class struggle."

"We must reform the education from stem to stern."

"Chairman Mao teaches us that we should not only learn culture, we should also learn industry, learn agriculture and learn military affairs. We should go to the factory, the countryside and the army to learn from the workers, the peasants and the soldiers."

They ordered us to profess our mistakes and crimes we had done in the past, and expose other people's guilt to them. We were under severe suppression and born heavy weights in our minds.

Above all my worries about the political problem, I met a family trouble, too. My wife was discriminated at her hospital because of my bad background and her father's bad background. Her father was now being tortured and forced to sweep the street every day despite he was already seventy years old. Fearing his daughter to be criticized and persecuted he wrote a letter to Runshu, suggesting her to divorce me. My wife was in a dilemma. On the one hand she loves me; on the other hand, her circumstance was bad. She might be condemned without drawing a demarcation of class line with me and our daughter would be discriminated. A heavy weight was borne down on her and she did not know what to do. She showed her father's letter to me, inviting my opinion. I had the same dilemma. A conflicting emotion was fighting fiercely in my mind. I was not willing and could not bear to lose my beloved wife so dear to me; Yet I was also not willing to see her suffered because of my bad background. I could not tell my opinion right away and said I'll consider it.

I hesitated about the question for several days and could not sleep well. The images of my wife, a lovable, tender, considerate, diligent woman. always kept lingering around my brain. She had always calmed me when I was in anger; she had always comfort me when I was in depression; she had always served me with the tea and the best meals; she had never let me carry heavy burdens. Sundays, days of rest for most people, were her busiest day. She rose at the crack of dawn, swept the room, clean everything, prepared meals. After lunch, she did the weakly family laundry, sitting on a small stool and scrubbing the clothes on a washboard in a big washbowl. In winter the icy water turned her palms fresh red. Sometimes I wanted to help her to do some housework, but she always refused and asked me to do my own reading. Now I might lose such a nice, lovely company. I felt melancholy and depressing.

After several days' contemplation I finally decided to agree with her father's opinion. I made up my mind to bear the suffering myself and let her avoid the suffering.

I told her my opinion and asked her to write an application for divorce to the party secretary of her unit. She kept silent and went to the window, standing there still with a hand caressing the flower pot on the windowsill. She was staring at the distance and seemed to be meditating deeply. I was perplexed and uneasy. Was my opinion offending her? Was she complaining me heartless, abandoning her? I crept toward her, wanting to say something with her. yet I was afraid of enraging her. I stood by her silently for some time. At last I ventured to put a hand on the back of her palm, fearing she would whisk away my hand but she did not and still stood there stoically, motionlessly. She was not angry with me. At once a warm current of pleasure and gratitude flooded all over my body. Both of us had a complicated and conflicting feelings, which could not be expressed by words. We remained speechless. Silence conveyed our innermost thoughts and emotions: loving and parting, hot and cold, bitterness and sweetness, displeasure and gratification, helplessness and hopefulness.

After a long time of silence, I made a further explanation for my opinion. "I love you deeply, but I cannot bear the scene you are being persecuted and our child is being spat. Divorce is a better way for you and our child. I will never get married. If the situation is changed someday, we can get remarried again."

She still kept silent.

I added, "It is only my opinion. You can make the final decision." At last, with tears in her eyes she promised to consider the question again and went back to her home.

A few days later, Runshu came to my room and told me that for our daughter's sake she agreed with my opinion and had already handed over her application for divorce and her leader approved it. She said we had to go to the Civil Administration Department together to go through the procedure of divorce someday. Then she began to pack her things in my place silently. After finishing the packing, she carried her suitcase and said: "I am leaving. Take good care of yourself!" Hot tears streamed down both of our faces at the same time. I looked around my room, wanting to find something to give her as a souvenir and said:

"You carry away the radio with you. You can use it to white away your time." The radio was the most valuable thing in our home then.

"No. Leave it here. you need it. It is important to you." I no longer persisted in my offer, because the radio has shortwave, from which I often eavesdrop VOA and BBC, and that is the only source of true news I can get. She knew my habit of listening to the radio at midnight.

I Saw her off at the school gate and kept staring at her until her figure and weeping out of my sight. I went back to my room, which suddenly became, after her long-time presence in it, strangely empty and tranquil as a cellar. Parting from one's dearest person is really a sore beyond any description. I felt marooned on an isolated, deserted island. Having no mood to do anything I sobbed into my quilt.

The Cultural Revolution went on deeper and deeper, violence gradually appeared in our school too. The first brutal struggle meeting was denouncing the party branch secretary of our school.

On that struggle meeting, about a dozen teachers were herded on to the platform in the auditorium. I was among them. Our heads were covered with dunce caps—the tall pyramid shape paper caps. On our backs were hung from the neck's placards, on which our names were written in black with a red cross over it. Our heads were forced to bent low and our arms were held behind the backs. The secretary of the party, now a capitalist roader, was forced to kneel on a long, narrow bench. It was hard to keep a balance there and soon he swayed and fell onto the floor, cutting his forehead on the corner of the bench. He was forced to kneel on the bench again, blood seeping through his forehead and congealed on his face. One Red guard after another trooped on to the platform to accuse how he pursued the capitalist education line, and how he mentally, physically injured them. Then they asked him to admit his crimes. He said in the past he was only carried out the party's education line and did not know that was wrong. One red guard shouted out "That was not the party's education line that is Liu Shaoqi's capitalist education line. You and Liu Shaoqi are the same capitalist roaders. You still dare deny." And he slapped the secretary on the face, who fell from the bench again. And other red guard gave him more hits. The secretary yelled: "I am guilty, I am guilty, I'll repair my guilt. Please excuse me." The denunciation and beating went on for about one hour, the leader of the rebel declared the end of the meeting.

A Painful Reminiscence of a Dignified Soul

After the meeting, we were forced to parade through the streets to ridicule us in public. The secretary of the party led the parade, holding a small gong in his left hand and a small stick in his right hand. Between every short interval he had to strike the small gong with the stick and professed: "I am a cow devil and snake spirit. I have pursued the reactionary capitalist education line. I have hurt the students. I have committed a crime for which I deserve the punishment of ten thousand times of death…" It was a really funny spectacle. All the watchers on the street could not help but burst a laughter, yet also felt pity for him. At the parade I was burning with shame at first. Being humiliated in public is really a serious nerve-racking. I wanted to leave the parade, but after considering the serious consequences and remembering the Chinese proverb "Lack of forbearance in a trivial matter will spoil the whole", I did not leave. On the contrary, I thought why should I feel ashamed, I have done nothing wrong. Then I thrusted my breast proudly and strutted with my feet throughout the whole path.

After we paraded back to school, the leader of the red guard ordered us to write a deep self-criticism.

Next day I began to write my self-criticism. It was not a very difficult job for me. I had written many self-criticisms, and my self-criticism was always the same: "My ideology is lagging behind, still staying in the old democracy period, not advancing to the socialist period, so my speech and actions are always wrong. I failed to catch up with the new era……." I had never wronged myself as "I am a reactionary", "I am a criminal deserving the death penalty", "I thank the revolutionaries for saving me". Of course, all my self-criticisms were criticized not to be profound, but they could do nothing for they were unable to find any my concrete crimes.

The red guards made many other violent struggle meetings. They were all utterly unjustifiable and brutal. I had no interest to mention them.

One afternoon it was my turn to be denounced. Some "criminals" were accompanied me in the struggling. The hair of a female accused was half shaved and the other half was left uncut, a sign of humiliation known as "Sun-Moon Head" I was forced to stand in a "Jet-Plane style"—bent double at the waist, the head pulled back by their hand, the arms forced up high behind the back. Every criticizer and investigator were solemn and stern. I remained composure, I had made full psychological preparation for any rude treatment. One revolutionary teacher asked me:

"You rightists are always pursuing Liu Shaoqi's revisionary line, what mistakes have you made during all these years?"

"I just edited books and taught English, I hadn't done anything else. After I was labeled a rightist, I had made efforts to correct my mistakes and I was removed the label in the earliest groups in 1960. ......"

"That was the capitalist roader to remove your labels. It was invalid. You are still rightists." A red guard interrupted me. And I continued:

"After I returned Youth Publishing House, I edited scientist books, which were approved to be published by the authority and which had nothing to do with politics. When I came to this school, I just taught English, I haven't talked any negative political or ideological affairs to students and anyone else. Is English a capitalist or revisionist language?"

"You did worship capitalism, you did worship English. You had told me 'Thanks for the English language which saved your life'" a revolutionary teacher shouted, whom I had told the story of receiving a foreigner's call when I was in the cigarettes manufacturer in Shanghai.

"It's only a small talk, not praise west language." I argued.

"But it reflected your mental condition. It is a faith of capitalism." He insisted and many other attendants yelled the similar words. I did not protest and remained silent.

Suddenly another student asked:

"Why did you carry a recorder here. You want to connect with the Nationalist Party?"

Recorder in rural area was a rare thing at that time.

I explained: "Recorder is not a radio transmitter, it cannot send or receive any information from the Nationalist Party."

The student found no words to say.

Then an investigator questioned me:

"Which girl student you are seducing?"

I was quite surprised and answered firmly:

"No. I haven't seduced any girl student."

She produced out a slip of paper and said: "Evidence is here!" Then she read the slip:

Dear Teacher Da:

Thank you for giving me many most useful teachings and facilitating me to make great progress this term. You are leaving now and I feel very sad. I beg you to grant me two requests:

A Painful Reminiscence of a Dignified Soul

First, let me lie on your breast a moment; Second, Take a photo together with me as a permanent commemoration. Would you agree with me? Please give me an answer soon.

Your child, Sun Yizi

Then she asked me again: "Can you deny that? Which girl student wrote the slip to you?"

I felt strange. It is indeed a slip of mine, which I placed in between a book. How did it go to her hand? Sometimes students came to my room to take remedial lessons and often browsed my books. I guess it must be that a student discovered it and handed it over to her. Then I replied:

"I won't deny that. But that is not the girl student here to write. You can compare the handwriting on the slip with that of all the girl students I teach now. The fact is like this: Twelve years ago, I had once taught at the Fifth Female School in Beijing. Before I leave that school, a twelve-year-old girl wrote that slip to me and I had answered her: 'Thank you very much for your appreciation, but very sorry, I cannot grant your first request, for it is not fit to our country's tradition; but I can take a picture with you.' In fact, I didn't even take the picture with her, because very few people own a camera and I could not borrow one. I have always felt sorry for I haven't fulfilled my promise. The slip has her name there, you can go to Beijing to investigate it. It is a very easy job to find out the truth.

They looked at each other trying to find the right word to say, but they couldn't. then the red guard presiding the meeting said; "We'll make an investigation of that. Now you can profess what wrong you have done when you did the underground work in Shanghai. Have you ever been arrested by Nationalist Party? If you have, do you divulge party's secret or sell out other communists?

"I haven't done any such things there. All I had done were revolutionary work, I had never been arrested by Nationalist Party."

"We cannot just listen to you. We'll make a thorough investigation. List all the names of your comrades, friends, relatives in Shanghai to us, and their address. We'll send people there to check the fact. If we find you hide something, you will be seriously punished."

"All right. I'll provide the list to you."

The denunciation meeting continued, but they could only shout some slogans and threatened me to confess my guilty but could not raise any my fault. I was a newcomer to this school, not longer than one year; I had very few communications with others; and I didn't have any personal enemies here. They could not find any pretext to beat me, so I had a narrow escape from the physical hurt.

Finally, the leader of the meeting said, "We'll make a thorough investigation of your affairs. If you remember your fault or crime later, you must report them to us immediately." The meeting was ended there."

During the cultural revolution the former Shanghai underground party leader Liu Changsheng, his leader Liu Lingyi, the party secretary of All-China Federation of Trade Union and the ultimate underground leader Liu Shaoqi, the president of the state, had all been declared to be class enemies. The surname of the three person is the same—Liu. So the rebels called them "The Three Liu" and deemed that the whole underground party was the heaven of Liu family, and all the underground party members were suspected and subjected to investigation.

Later they did send two red guards to Shanghai to investigate my problem. They loved to do such a job, for it is in fact a free trip with public fund. Shanghai is the biggest city in China, they had a keen desire to have a look. My friends told me that they received the red guards' visit and told them all the revolutionary work I had done in Shanghai. As the red guards could not find any my fault, they never denounced me again.

I was a little relieved and I thought of my family things. Though my wife and I agreed to divorce each other, we were still not divorced legally. she had promised to make an appointment with me to go to the civil administration department to proceed the procedure of our divorce, but for a long time she did not contact me. I felt strange and I went to visit her on a Sunday afternoon.

She received me tenderly and I asked her why she still hadn't made the appointment. She said she was reconsidering our decision all the time. Her situation seemed not very severe recently. The rebel's main targets are the capitalist roaders now, they no longer pay much time to people who had bad family background. In her health center there were two doctors having bad background. One is my wife; the other is an old military doctor of the Nationalist Party. But as their medical skills were commonly considered to be better than others. Many patients, including the local cadres and the rebels, liked to seek their treatment, they especially like my wife's cure for her service attitude was very good. By dint of hard work she had gained the appreciation of the patients. As she hadn't great political pressure now, she didn't want to divorce me. Listening to her words I was greatly delighted. I formerly agreed to divorce her just because I wished to reduce her suffering. Now that her situation had turned to better, of course I was glad to remain our marriage relationship. I thanked her again and again for her love and magnanimity. She said it did not deserve to mention it. I gave her a warm hug and carried her and our daughter to a restaurant to have a delectable meal.

The cultural revolution pressed on and the situation became more and more complicated. The number of red guards and other rebels swiftly increased, there were ninety million red guards at the highest period, and they gradually divided into two factions. Though both factions declared that they were rebel factions and pledged to safeguard Chairman Mao, they had diametrically opposite ideas. People generally called them respectively the "conservative faction" and "radical rebel faction"

The main point of view of the conservative faction was that capitalist roaders still haven't occupied the ruling status of the whole party, not all the authorities of the party were capitalist roaders, so we should not make a complete overturn of the present establishment. They usually believed that the party secretary of their organization was a revolutionary one not a revisionist, who should not be overthrown. If they were attacked, they must protect them. Most members of the conservative faction were party members, Communist Youth League members and their followers. Most early red guards were in this faction. They first answered Mao's call to carry out the educational revolution denouncing and torturing the school leaders and professors and teachers. Later Mao revealed his true aim and declared "the main target of the Cultural Revolution was capitalist roaders." Suddenly almost all the earliest red guards' parents became revisionists or capitalist roaders, the class enemies, and their children became the "black" with bad background. Song Renqiong, the father of Song Bingbing who had tied the red guard armband on Mao's arm, was also titled a capitalist roader. The members of the conservative faction usually regarded themselves to be orthodox and pure and tended to protect the old party secretaries in their units, This faction blamed the opposite faction for attacking the wrong target whom they protected and proclaimed that there were many capitalist roaders and other class enemies in the opposite group, who wanted to restore capitalism.

The main point of view of the radical faction was that the capitalist roaders had already forged a privileged class, controlling the party and the present establishment, they must destroy them thoroughly. They took all the former high echelons and all their former oppressors were the targets of the cultural revolution. They believed that the class relationship had greatly changed, who were the leftists or rightists; who were the revolutionary or the reactionary must be differentiated anew. Their main members were millions of Mao's blind followers, the juveniles, youths, workers and some sufferers and victims of the former political campaigns. They were supported by Mao and his trusties, like his wife Jiang Qing, Kang Sheng, etc.

Both factions were in the name of Mao Zedong thought and Cultural Revolution, they divided on the question "who were the true 'capitalist roaders' inside the party?" They jostled for power and fought each other, manipulating the campaign to pursue their own goals.

Almost every unit had the two factions. At the beginning the two factions usually argued with each other in words, always selecting quotations from the works of Mao Zedong, Marx and Engels, which were favorable to its argument. Then being heated with passions they started fighting. Later the factions with same view began to establish ties with each other, the scales of fighting were enlarged. Finally, every city had two united organizations of the opposite factions. In Shanghai they were named "Red Guard Team" and "General Headquarters of the Workers". In Chongqing they were named "815" and "Carry the Rebel to the end", etc.

The violent fighting escalated rapidly. At first, they only used clubs, Iron bars, daggers, stones or bricks as their weapons, later they used rifles, light and heavy machine-guns, and even tanks, anti-aircraft guns, naval vessels. It was actually a civil war. During the fighting they killed workers, classmates, colleagues, teenagers, young mothers, even their family members of each other's opposite faction. In short, the victims were all their own fellow countryman, all their brothers and sisters. What was the worth of the fighting? It was of no worth at all. All the young fighters were just utilized by the emperor who wanted to eliminate all his opponents.

The first large scale violent fighting was originated from Shanghai. The "Red Guard Team", which was mainly composed of workers and boasted it owned one hundred thousand model workers, protected Cheng Peixiang, the first party secretary of the party committee of Shanghai. The opposite rebel faction "General Headquarters of the Workers" led by Wang Hongwen, which boasted to have one million

A Painful Reminiscence of a Dignified Soul

rebels, wanted to overthrow the Party Committee of Shanghai Municipality. This faction was supported by the "Small Leading Team of the Cultural Revolution" led by Mme. Mao.

At about two o'clock midnight of Jan. 6, 1967 the "General Headquarter of the Workers" assaulted the Party Committee of Shanghai in Kangping Road and fought with the "Red Guard Team", Which defended the office there. The fighting went on until six o'clock in the morning. At last all the twenty thousand "Red Guard Team" fighters capitulated and they were ordered to leave the office. The formal Party Committee of Shanghai was overthrown and very soon a revolutionary committee was founded to lead the biggest city in China.

Mao was immensely excited. He highly praised the action: "This is a class overthrowing another class. This is a great revolution." He had determined that the present established party and government organizations led by Liu Shaoqi must be destroyed. Now the rebel faction "General Headquarter of the Workers" first successfully seized power from his enemy, Mao's desire was initially realized. He greatly rewarded the rebels. The rebel leader Wang Hongwen was catapulted from a common worker to one of the top leaders of the country overnight.

After the so called "January Windstorm" the rebels of all the provinces and the cities subsequently tried hard to seize power by force, an all-round violent fighting between the two factions drastically escalated and the entire country was in a complete chaos.

In February 1967 several marshals and vice premiers criticized the chaotic phenomenon of the cultural revolution, which was denounced by the "Small Leading Team of the cultural Revolution" and which Mao called "a February Adverse Current". Some marshals were denounced by the red guards. Mao established himself as the omnipotence, purging anyone who suspected or opposed him. Even the most senior officials who hesitated to follow his direction were removed their posts immediately. In April, Mao openly expressed his ultimate enemy. Liu Shaoqi was publicly denounced by the "Small Leading Team of the Cultural Revolution".

After Mao's criticism, Liu had made a self-criticism on Oct. 23 1966, not only he admitted he had committed mistakes during the cultural revolution, but also criticized his mistake in 1962 and 1964, and analyzed the reasons for his mistakes, saying "First… Second… Third… Fourth… and the fundamental mistake was that I had not learned properly and grasped firmly Mao Zedong thought. And I did not ask advice from or report to Chairman Mao often enough." The self-criticism meant that Liu was willing to capitulate. Even in a war if the army of one country was willing to capitulate, the army of the opposite country should accept peacefully. But Mao never accepted any capitulation, he would be satisfied with nothing but his enemy's death.

In July 1967 Liu was first tortured at a denunciation meeting. He was marched onto the stage, where he was forced to maintain the jet airplane position and beaten by red guards. He was repeated pelted with copies of the quotations; his answers were drowned out by nonstop shouting of slogans. His face was swollen and his legs had been injured. His official residence was searched and the red guards plastered his walls with anti-Liu placards. His wife was also beaten and humiliated. After he was marched back to his office, he was filled with indignant fury. Summoning his confidential secretary and clutching a copy of the Constitution of the People's Republic of China, he protested: "I am the president of the People's Republic of China. You can do whatever you wish with my person, but I must defend the dignity of the president of the country. Who dismissed me as president? If you want to try me, you still have to proceed with the national people's Congress. What you are doing is humiliating the country. I am myself a citizen; why am I not allowed to speak? The Constitution guarantee that the personal rights of any individual cannot be infringed. Those who break the Constitution must incur the stern judgments of the law." Liu was kept in solitary detention. He was separated with his wife and children. At the parting time Wang Guangmei said: "Let Heaven collapse and earth sink down! Let this be the end!"

Liu said: "It looks as if it really is goodbye this time!" He just couldn't stop his tears falling.

Liu had never packed things for Wang in his life, now he folded her clothes neatly. In the last few minutes, the two sat gazing at each other. Then Liu who rarely cracked a joke said:

"This is like waiting for a sedan-chair to come and carry you off (to be married). Both made a bitter smile.

This was indeed their last parting. Afterwards even when Liu fell ill or in jail, Wang was not allowed to watch him.

After Liu was publicly criticized Deng Xiaoping was also denounced and dismissed from all his posts. Almost all the top leading official were renounced by Mao and he seized all the levers of power into his hand.

Encouraged by the victory of radical rebels of Shanghai and under the incitement and support of Chairman Mao and the "Small Leading Team of the Cultural

Revolution", the morale of the radical rebels all over the country was highly boosted. They vigorously strengthened the criticism and denunciation against the authorities of the capitalist roaders and seized the power. The fighting was escalating rapidly. It was estimated that one million guns were in the hands of civilians, causing heavy casualties.

To enhance the forces of the radical rebels, Mao ordered the Liberation Army firmly support the left revolutionary masses. But there were difficulties for the army to carry out his order. In every region and organizations there were rival factional rebel groups. All of them called themselves revolutionary rebel groups and all pledged to be loyal to Mao and all used Mao's quotations to meet their pleas and aims. As there was no clear, precise definition and criterion of "the left", so the army officials found it difficult to distinguish which was the real "the left", and usually tended to support the more moderate groups. Some army units even handed out weapons to the faction they decided to be "the left". Then the opposite faction raided arsenals to seize weapons for themselves. Thus, made the situation complicated. For instance. There was a famous incident known as "July twentieth" happened in Wuhan municipality, Hubei Province. The leaders of the military region of Hubei province considered as "the left" the local largest rebel group titled "million bold warriors" which had one million and two hundred thousand members. They supported it and suppressed its rival rebel group "workers' general headquarters". But the "Small Leading Team of the Cultural Revolution" regarded "million bold warriors" as a conservative group and sent one of its members Wang Li to go to Wuhan to settle the problem. On July twentieth many wrathful soldiers and rebels of the "million bold warriors" seized Wang Li and beat him and paraded him on the street, and even wanted to kill him. Finally, the Central Authority managed to rescue Wang Li. The leaders of the military region of Hubei province were severely punished and the rebel group "million bold warriors" was disbanded. Later, Wang Li, who had flattered Mao and was selected by Mao as the member of the "Small Leading Team of the Cultural Revolution", was also arrested by the order of Mao. Wang Li was chosen as a scapegoat of the chaos. This was Mao's customary tactics. During the "suppress counter-revolutionaries campaign" he forced and set quotas to local officials to kill more people. Then when people complained the over-killing, he blamed the local officials deviated the policy. During the "Great leap forward" campaign, he ordered and forced the officials and peasants to produce imaginary extra-high quantity of products, and then he blamed them to sweep the trend of boasting.

Facing the fact that it was difficult to determine which rebel group was really loyal to him, Mao had to give up the order to support "the left", abandoning his effort to identify factions as Left or Conservative, and called for all groups to unite. But the young rebels carried on fighting, each group claimed itself the revolutionary one and the rival was conservative.

In our school there were also two opposite factions. Some rebels even invited me to take part in their faction. They encouraged me: "You had been labeled as rightist, and those who framed you are now capitalist roaders. You must rise up to down with them." I declined politely and thanked them. I had seen through Mao's evil nature after so many campaigns. I clearly knew it was Mao who should be responsible for my suffering, because the anti-rightist campaign was launched by Mao. The executors of that campaign merely carried out Mao's orders, whom I did not want to denounce. I decided to stand outside the fighting. And I believed that the young people of both factions were but the tools of Mao or his enemies— behind and beyond them there must be manipulators who were really supporting or opposing Mao.

The opposite faction of our school not only fought each other within our school, they also took part in the fighting in the downtown of Fuling County. Since I did not take part in the faction, I could not relate the details of their fighting. There was only one thing a student told me, which etched deeply in my mind and made me feel very sad. Two third-grade girl students A and B were intimate friends but they had different views and took part in the different factions. In one battle, student A's faction assaulted a big building in the downtown, which was the stronghold of student B's faction. As student A charged from second floor to the third floor, she stretched out her long spear ready to thrust any enemy. In the middle of the stair she met student B. Thinking she is her close friend, student A hesitated without thrusting her spear into B's body. Just as that moment student B pierced her spear into A's body. As this piercing happened to go into the heart, student A died incurable. Later it was said that student B committed suicide because she repented and could not bear the prick of her conscience. I did not know whether the word was true or not. Nevertheless, no matter the victim was one girl or two, this was an unprecedented tragedy, which forced me into deep thought: From where the hatred of these young girls came from? Who was the breeder of the hatred? The breeder ought to be worshipped or punished?

Through one year's fierce fighting. by the end of 1967 almost all the old established institutions of the party and the government were overthrown and the new revolutionary committees of every organization were set up. According to Mao's instruction, all the new revolutionary committee should be composed of three parts: 1, the liberation army; 2, the remaining cadres who were not regarded as capitalist roaders; 3, the new rebels.

The cost of the one-year violent fighting was extremely heavy. According to the revelation of an authoritative archive, there were 57,227 violent fights involving more than ten persons; There were 9790 violent fights with a toll of over one hundred people; There were 227,300 people who declared their kin was dead. And these numbers were generally regarded as much lower than the actual numbers

Yet though the old party and state institutions were overthrown and the new revolutionary committee were established, the two opposite groups still remained, and the conflicts and struggles between them were still continuing openly or on the sly. The mini-war dragged on between the two groups.

In 1968, as the continuing violent fighting was going higher and became more harmful, Mao ordered that all weapons must be returned, but those who had acquired them were reluctant or refused to give them back to the army. The society was in a great chaos and the production was seriously interrupted. Despite a series of persuasions and commands from the central authority and chairman Mao, the fighting was still not stopped. One of the most stubborn rebel leaders was Tsinghua University's rebel faction leader Kuai Dafu, whom Mao had used to torture Liu Shaoqi and his wife. He thought he was the most leftist and ignored repeated orders to stop fighting, confident that he was carrying out Mao's earlier directive and determined to destroy his conservative opponents in the university. Finally, Mao decided to get him to toe the line personally. On July 27 1968 he dispatched 40,000 unarmed workers to Tsinghua university to disarm Kuai's group. Not knowing that the order came from Mao, Kuai resisted and his group killed five workers and wounded more than 700. Next day Mao called a meeting, summoning Kuai and other principal red guard leaders of universities to the Great Hall. Despite this red-carpet treatment, the rebels had been summoned to hear the death sentence of their movement. where Mao told them that it was his order to disarm Kuai's faction. He warned Kuai and the other leaders that they could each rely only 200 or 300 core supporters, whereas he could send in 30,000 workers, not to mention the number of troops under Lin Biao. if they went on fighting, the army would eliminate them. Kuai admitted his mistake and signed a record of the message, which was made public.

In the early years of the cultural revolution, by making use of the students and the juveniles who were still physically and mentally weak, Mao destroyed countless officialdom, including the president of the state Liu Shaoqi, and an equal number of the most famous and talented scholars, writers, artists, athletes, etc. and overthrew all the former authorities and established new revolutionary committees dominated by him.

After Mao had achieved his goal, he found the students having no use value anymore and decided to abandon them. As the idiom described: "When all birds are shot, the bow will be set aside; After all the cunning rabbits are killed, the hound is cooked." he kicked students out after their service is no longer needed. All student organizations were disbanded. The title red guard was finished, and the glorious days of red guard were ended after August 1968.

Then where should all the students be placed? As all the schools were closed for years and the situations of factories were deteriorating, Mao knew no working place could be found for the millions of students who graduated from high school or university and turned loose on the street seething with unrest, he decided to exiled the students from the cities to the countryside. He issued a directive that "The educated youth should go to the countryside and receive re-education from the peasants. It is absolutely necessary." "We should persuade cadres and others in the cities to send their children who graduated from middle schools and universities to the villages. Let's have a mobilization, all people in the countryside should welcome them." According to the Notification regarding work assignment for university graduates in 1968: "In general, graduates must become ordinary peasants or ordinary workers. A majority must become ordinary peasants...." University graduates were sent down to farm and factory. Kuai was sent to a plant is Ningxi, a very poor, backward region. On December 22th, 1968, Mao issued an instruction, ordered all the educated youth across China to "put politics in command, fight selfishness and repudiate revisionism, put the public interest first, submit to the needs of the state and go to the countryside and factories and mines, where the conditions are the hardest." Then all the graduates of the high school of i966, 1967 and 1968 years, whether they were willing or unwilling, went "up to the mountains and down to the villages." Those teenage students, who had paraded their prowess and instructed the high-ranking officials, professors, writers, were now become the small pupils of illiterate peasants.

According to an official statistic, during the twelve-year period 1967-1979, the number of rusticated "educated youth" totaled 16,470,000.

A Painful Reminiscence of a Dignified Soul

As the new revolutionary committees were composed of two groups, there would inevitably be different ideas and attitudes among them. On the political view and attitude of the new cadres and the masses, they could roughly divide into two parts. The first part was those who rose to power and high position during the cultural revolution and their followers, their political view was more radical, they were supported by Mao and his wife's clique; The second part was the former experienced party and government officials and their followers, including premier Zhou Enlai, marshal Ye Jianying. their political view was more reasonable and milder. The struggle between the two groups was continued and very complicated, because they all proclaimed they were observing Mao's revolutionary line and there was not a clear line of distinction between the "pros of Mao and cultural revolution" and the "cons of Mao and cultural revolution" The situation of the whole country was still a great mess and chaos.

Since the start of Cultural Revolution, everything was abnormal. The white in the past is black now; the black in the past is white now. What is right yesterday becomes wrong today; what is wrong yesterday becomes right today. A revolutionary today becomes a reactionary the next day, a reactionary today becomes a revolutionary the next day. Students were pitted against teachers, children again parents, wives against husbands. Neighbors spied on neighbors. Workers snooped on their mates. Everyone was forced to report on one's dearest. China was turned into a country of snitches. The stool pigeon became a hero of the revolution. The lunatic men were hailed as vanguards. Falsehood are flying and getting more and more absurd with every passing day.

People's life was busy. There were endless meetings to learn Mao's works and criticize class enemies and every institution kept a makeshift prison. Not only the famous scholars, writers were persecuted, many of the artists and athletes were tortured. The table tennis player Rong Guotuan, who had won the first Olympic medal for China, was persecuted to death. Yan Huizhu, the most female performer of Beijing opera, committed suicide, leaving her last word "I do not know what wrong I have made" Yan Fengying, the most female performer of a local opera, was killed. And after her death her belly was cut open to search a radio transmitter.

Mao had an intensely obstinate hate against the intellectual, for intellectual had knowledge, not easily blindly toeing his line. He believed "The more knowledgeable, the more reactionary." After he exiled the graduates to the countryside, he issued a directive that all cadres should be sent to the countryside group by group to facilitate their remodeling. As the directive was issued on May 7th, so the place the cadres lived and did manual labor were called "May 7 Cadre School". The schools were usually set up in the remote rural areas.

After fighting was stopped students were ordered to go back to school to "resume classes for making revolution" But they could not learn the traditional lessons, for the old textbooks, teaching methods and teachers had all been criticized, and no teachers and students knew what to do. The revolutionary committee emphasized to learn Mao Zedong Thought and politics and current affairs, to stick closely to functional subjects or to teach the ways of production. Math class consisted of figuring how much wheat could be harvested on one Mu of field; physics consisted of studying tractors, electric motors, water pumps; chemistry involved a daylong trek to a brewery; and how to grow rice and vegetables and how to run a machine, etc. no longer paying attention to the rudimentary knowledge. All these measures made both teachers and students feel wonder and sick, but no one dared to oppose them.

People's life was monotonous. There was no way to relax. Almost all the books, plays, operas, songs of the past, both home or foreign, were regarded feudalistic, capitalist or revisionist. For entertainment there were only Mao Zedong thought propaganda teams, which produce the songs praising Chairman Mao or the militant dance waving the little red book. On all the stages of China, only eight model Beijing opera created by Mao's wife Jiang Qing were performed. In cultural area it was really a poor, bleak, desolate and shabby desert.

The personality cult of Mao reached its climax. The central authority promoted the "three loyalties and four boundless loves": loyalty to Chairman Mao, to Mao Zedong thought, to Chairman Mao's proletarian revolutionary line; boundless love for Chairman Mao, for the Communist Party, for Mao Zedong thought, and for Chairman Mao's proletarian revolutionary line. Anyone who showed the least disrespect to Mao was seriously punished. A teacher once said: "We worship Mao like saying prayers to God." He was charged as a counterrevolutionary. removed from his teaching position and sent to the rural area. In addition, graphic or photographic images of Mao were considered to be sacred that any damage of them was deemed an act of crime. A student of only twelve-year-old knocked off part of Mao's statue by accident, he was labeled a counterrevolutionary and was denounced by the whole school.

Loyalty to Mao became the paramount virtue. Everyone's daily life was permeated with ritualistic practices of a religious nature. Mao was regarded as a demi-

A Painful Reminiscence of a Dignified Soul

god. At all offices, factories, schools, the day typically began with "requesting his instructions in the morning". Everyone lined up before the portrait of Mao and waved the little red books, wishing Mao three times longevity, and then reported to him what he was going to do and found a quotation from the little red book to encourage or resolve his work that day, such as " Set a resolution, fear no sacrifice, surmount all difficulties to win victory." At the end of the day people gathered again in front of Mao's portrait to report what work they had accomplished during the day and what problems they had met and solved by studying his works. This ritual was known as "asking instruction in the morning, reporting in the evening". During these ritual service people must hold Mao's little red book over their heart indicating their absolute loyalty and boundless love for Mao.

Grotesque forms of worshipping Mao had been commonplace. When you made a telephone, the operator would say "serve the people," and you would have to answer "wholeheartedly". If you were unable to reply the appropriate word, you would be asked to study Mao's works earnestly. Once I entered a grocery store, a shop assistant murmured "When sailing the seas, we need a helmsman" and paused and looked at me. I did not know what her action meant. Thinking for a while, I came to realize that she wanted me to complete the sentence. I answered: "When making revolution we need Mao Zedong Thought." Such exchanges had become a standard greeting.

Another way of showing loyalty to Mao was to wear a Mao badge on one's chest. The making, collecting, and trading of Mao badges became a national pastime. Badges varied in size from as small as a penny coin to as large as a plate. Badges were made of metal, glass, wood, or plastic in all kinds of designs. While the country was on the verge of economic collapse, the production of Mao badges escalated. According to premier Zhou as he was speaking of economic planning in March 1969 and deploring the wasteful use of aluminum in producing larger and larger badges, some 2.2 billion badges had been produced. Huge beige concrete statue of Chairman Mao stood everywhere with his right hand raised accepting the adulation of the masses. All the resources were used to serve the whim of Mao.

All the people, young and old, graceful and awkward alike, were forced to do the "loyalty dance" The basic steps of the dance was Yangge. The dance involved a movement of stretching one's hands from one's breast toward the portrayal of Mao or the sky. The loyalty dance is ugly, distasteful, disgusting. And while you dance you also have to sing the song "Beloved Chairman Mao":

Zhong Da

"Beloved chairman Mao,
You are the red Sun in our hearts.
How many bosom words we want to tell you,
How many warm songs we want to sing to you.
Hundreds of millions of red hearts are towards Beijing,
Hundreds of millions of smiling faces greet the Red Sun.
Wish you venerable old man boundless longevity!"

When a new instruction from Mao came, a loyalty dance parade was held. To see those old women with bound feet wriggling and twisting unsteadily all the way, you could not help but burst your sides with laughter and felt pity and sorry for them because they were forced to do what they would not like to do.

Mao made the whole people give a single allegiance to he himself—the people's esteemed and beloved father and savior.

All those odd, peculiar, ridiculous, and absurd things made me sick to death. I was angry and exasperated with the situation. I was a teacher I should impart my knowledge to students in classroom, but now I had to be denounced and instructed by students and other rebels in the auditorium, or study Mao's works and instructions, or do manual works. In political studies I had to speak the same idea that was deemed to be right currently. In the past if I had some different ideas, I could at least shut my mouth, but now if you kept silence, you would be regarded to make mute protest to the revolution and that was dangerous. I had been wronged for many times and had been hurt during the anti-rightist campaign. But at those time it was only a verbal slander; and now it is a violent, barbarous assault, no arguing, no reasoning, no vindicating at all. If a single dirty word would hurt a person, how much more would all these insults and physical hurting cause? Everyone was pretending, everyone was intimidated and everyone was wearing a mask, including I myself. I loathed to be living in this vast sea of torturers and liars. The whole world faded before my eyes. I couldn't bear it and wanted to escape out of the terrible circumstances, but how could I do it? where was the safe place, the peaceful place?

I contemplated these questions day and night. I often could not sleep throughout the night. I thought my life was now so utterly wretched that I would well wish to drop down dead. But that meant I was a coward and I hesitated; I wanted to protest the absurd cultural revolution, but I knew there was no use of it and I would

A Painful Reminiscence of a Dignified Soul

suffer greater tortures; I thought of going on a hunger strike, but the relentless leaders would pay no attention to you, they would delight to see the demons died of hunger to save grain; I intended to act like the brave heroes to criticize Mao openly, but I hadn't enough courage; I meditated a suicide like Fu Lai and Lao She, but what is the worth of it? They were blamed "to commit suicide to escape punishment", "to get deserved punishment". I regarded their death was a tragedy, a waste of valuable life; I wanted to live in seclusion amidst mountains and rivers with white clouds and birds as my company, but where can I live and how can I get food? I desired to flee to Burma or other foreign countries to ask for political asylum. but how could I cross the borders? I am a good swimmer. I can go to Yunnan Province and jump into a river flowing to the neighboring country at night. But if the river has a tall waterfall I would be tossed to death. And What would happen if the foreign government might not take refugee and repatriate me back? It is too adventurous. Brooding and brooding, it seemed there were not any way out of such ugly and ridiculous situation. I had to endure all the sufferings.

By the end of 1968, suddenly I got a disease. At first, I thought I was just catching a cold with a runny nose and cough. I didn't care about it much and believed my body could self-repair it. Later It gradually got worse. I went to the school infirmary to take some medication. But the medicines were not effective and my disease became heavier. I coughed up yellow mucus, sometimes mingled with blood. My breathing was shallow and fast. My chest was in pain when I coughed or breathed. I suffered from a high fever, sometimes as high as 40 centigrade degrees. I stayed in bed for three or four days. The school infirmary personnel concluded that I had got a Pneumonia. As my disease was very severe, the leader of the revolution committee of the school ordered two capitalist-roaders to carry me to the health center on a stretcher.

I was glad to be sent to the health center, for my wife was working and living there. My wife made a thorough examination of my disease, confirmed the diagnosis of the infirmary and wrote out a prescription. Then she went to the pharmacy to take the medicine and served me with them.

With good medications, with comfortable circumstances, with my wife's tender care, my disease was gradually cured and my health began to be recuperated day after day.

I enjoyed this period of time, for though I suffered from the disease, I did not have to attend the struggle meetings, to falsely praise Chairman Mao's great instructions, to violate my conscience to tell lies. But with the disease being cured my happy time would be ended and I had to go back to school again. I became worried and unhappy.

I really did not want to live that kind of vile, shameful life, I contemplated to find out a way to escape that life. I pondered over the question day and night. One day, I suddenly gained enlightenment from my disease: It was my pneumonia that bestowed the happy time on me; As long as I had a disease, I would have a happy time. What I needed was but a disease. Though I had no real illness, I could make a fake illness. I decided to make fake sickness. I knew it was not an easy job. In my mind I still had a clear sad remembrance: A rightist named Wu Xiaowu (pen name Xiao Yemu), a famous writer and our colleague, was really ill and could not go to the field. But the leader considered Wu was making a fake disease and forced him to go to work. Not long afterwards Wu was died of overwork. If my leader considered I had no disease and forced me to go back to school, then all my endeavor to make a fake illness was in vain. The question was how could I make a fake disease which others would believe to be a true one.

One day an idea struck me: I could take a fast. In the past, I had once thought of going on a hunger strike to protest the persecution, later I gave up the idea because I realized that an open hunger strike had no use. The persecutors had no human nature at all. Now I could make a secret fast to make my body weaker and weaker till I was looked as a real patient. This seemed like a good idea. But I knew hunger had a great pang, A long period of hunger would be an unbearable thing. I had experienced a severe hunger in Hong Kong when I was ten-year-old, could I endure it again? I wondered. I hesitated. I could not make a decision for a long time.

I consulted with my wife. She disagreed with the idea decisively. She said she was a doctor. She had seen many peasants who had suffered from hunger. The empty stomach would cause excruciating pain. You could not bear it. I argued that I knew hunger would cause great pain. It is a physical, fresh pain; but our present undignified, slavish life also causes great pain, a mental, psychological pain, which is much more painful than the physical pain, so I still want to take a fast. She did not continue the argument. knowing I had a very strong self-respect and attached more importance to spiritual life than to physical life. She found it hard to make a right choice. She kept silence. Finally, she suggested we make a deeper consideration and discussed the question later. I agreed to take a second thought.

A Painful Reminiscence of a Dignified Soul

A few days later she told me she still opposed me to make a fake disease through a fast, for even the school believed me to be really ill and gave me sick leaves. which could not last long and I still had to go back to school early or later. It was not worth to undergo that suffering. I smiled. I had also considered the same question and had thought out a solution.

I said, "I took part in revolution early, I want to find out if I am eligible to get an early retirement due to disease" In my wife's health center there was a nurse named Sun Shuyun, whose husband was working at the Organization Department of the party of Fuling County. I wanted to ask him about the retirement regulations of the cadres. If my working experience is in conformity with the regulations, I might be able to get an early retirement, then I can dodge the preposterous life forever. My wife also deemed it a good idea and promised me to ask the nurse's husband about that regulations when he came home to meet his wife at the weekend. The nurse's bed room was opposite our bed room and she was a good friend of my wife and me.

A week later my wife got the information of the retirement regulations of the cadres, in which there is a provision: "A cadre who has taken part in the revolutionary work for more than twenty years, he can retire ahead of time if he was serious ill and cannot continue to work." I was delighted. I took part in the revolution in 1948, and now is 1969. I have already worked more than twenty years, if I had a serious disease, I was eligible for applying a retire early. Now the only question left for me was to get a "serious disease" and I was confident I could create a "fake serious disease". I made the decision. My wife still hesitated. She had no heart to see my suffering. I pursued her to have a hard heart for a short time. I convinced her: "I would rather suffer physical pain than suffer mental pain; I would rather suffer the acute pain for a short time than suffer the continuous mental pain for another twenty years. If I went back to live the inhumane life, you would see my miserable face all the time; If I retired and became a free man, you would see my smiley face forever. Which face would you choose to see?" She made no replay. Then shaking her head slightly, she grumbled: "If you have made a determination, do what you liked. I had no right to interfere your decision." Our conversation ended.

Next day I began my fast, having no food the whole day but a couple of water. Though feeling a little hungry at night, I found nothing different from usual days. I was pleased and proud, for I had bravely started a great battle against the evil great cultural revolution. Four or five days passed I began to experience levels of pain I had never experienced before. My abdominal muscles were cramped and twisted severely. I endured the pain quietly, not wanting my wife to be affected. But she knew the fact and made a suggestion. She pursued me not to fast completely, but to take a few foods each day, so that my body could become weaker gradually, not precipitated. In that way I could reach the same goal with lighter pain. I accepted her advice. From then on, I took a bowl of rice and a few vegetables every day, no any meat. In order to make my body to be emaciated quickly, after each meal I also took some Epsom Salt to produce a diarrhea, making my food excrete out my stomach rapidly.

In order to get sick leaves continuously I had to have sick notes written by a doctor. In order to prove I had serious illness I had to provide medical certificates, such as X-ray examination, stool examination. In the health center I stayed, there was no such medical apparatus and instruments. I had to go to the county hospital to take the examinations and get the certificates. In order to make the result of my test to be positive, each time before I went to the hospital to take the X-ray test, I ate a great many very hot peppers to excite my stomach and intestines to change form. My tongue, throat and stomach felt as hot as catching a fire by the pepper. It was really a great torture, but I had to endure it. As I expected, each X-ray test showed my stomach and intestines had problems.

Each time I took a urine test or a stool examination in the hospital, I would go to the toilet to take a sample. I shut the door safely, then I took out a needle and pricked it into the tip of a finger, squeezed the blood into the excrement and urine, and used a stick to mix them together, so each report of the examination was a certificate that I had stomach and kidney problems. My wife had a medical college classmate who was working at the county hospital. I always visited her and she always prescribed what I asked of her and gave me a sick-leave note proving I had serious illness.

In order to make my fake sickness look realistic indeed, I often took some medicine and vitamin B that would tinge skin with yellow color. Gradually my whole body became as yellow as ripe banana.

Then I decided to take another radical step: pull all my teeth out, so that I would look as old as an over sixty-year-old man. In the past I had extracted two or three teeth because of periodontitis. Pretending I had infected with periodontitis again and suffered great pain, I asked a dentist to pull my teeth out. The dentist persuaded me not to extract them, But I insisted on taking them out, feigning that my teeth was so painful that I could not bear it. The dentist had to do as I asked of him. Then each time one tooth was extracted out and I bore a fit of great pang. Gradually all my teeth disappeared and my mouth became sunken deep.

With the fast going on I encountered fierce and fierce suffering. Skins were terribly cracked, mouth dry, saliva thick, lips and tongue swelled, mucous membranes broke because tissues lacking moisture. My breathing became short and rapid. I have throbbing headaches, drifting into a hazy delirium. Anemia often gives me spell of dizzy. Every muscle and every joint in my body ached. Arms and legs often cramped. The most unbearable pain was the stomach ache. It was acting as if catching fire twisting and contracting unceasingly or like a thousand nails turning in it. At such times I always press my two hands on the stomach tightly, trying to stop its movement. I became weaker and weaker. Getting dressed was difficult. I felt pain when buttoning a blouse, tying a shoe. Lifting a light thing hurt my arms and shoulders. Sometimes when I bent down to pick up something I dropped. I always had severe fatigue. All my energy was sapped and drained.

My wife couldn't bear to see my suffering and persuaded me to stop the fast. In fact, even I myself had considered to stop it, for the suffering was indeed too excruciating. Yet I was also unwilling to resign myself to defeat. My mind was racing back and forth between fast and non-fast. I was long vacillating and struggling between cowardliness and bravery. abandoning and persistence, retreating and advancing. Finally, I felt ashamed for lack of strong will. I decided I must grit my teeth and hang on; I must endeavor to make a bad situation into a good one, to turn tragedy into triumph; I mustn't fall short of success for lack of a final effort. I mustered up the determination to stick fast to the time I achieved my goal. I told my wife, though I was suffering physically I was very happy and excited mentally. I was able to stay outside the sphere of all the ongoing campaign. I did not have to take part in the great 'cultural destruction"; I did not have to bow before Mao's portrait and skip the loyal dance; and I did not have to say any words or take any actions against my conscience. There were no people had this sort of freedom I enjoyed now. I also consoled her that though I looked very ill, no organs of my body, such as lung, liver, kidney or brain, were really hurt. My health could be recovered and revived very soon after I retired. I gave her a salute with a funny smile asking her to support my effort and begged her to excuse me for causing her so much suffering and trouble. She wagged her head slowly with a bitter smile. She could not bear to see my painful figure, but she also did not want to destroy my plan. she was unable to give me a definite reply. She could only keep silent.

My determination encouraged me to go beyond what I should have originally been able to do. I bore all the suffering for one year or two, my health became heavily deteriorated. I was so weak that I often felt dizzy, and unable to stand. My body weight was reduced from 70 kilogram to 55 kilograms. The color of my body turned gray and yellow. Now I was really looked as a patient having a serious illness. I was only forty-three-year-old, but everyone assumed me an over sixty-year-old man. My friendly colleagues showed great sympathy on me. The school rebel cadres, who regularly came to examine my health situation, saw my condition was worse each time than the last. They could not but give me the sick leave. No one suspected I was fake ill now. I reckoned that it was the appropriate time to submit a retirement application.

I went to the county hospital and asked my wife's classmate to write out a certificate for me. Seeing my appearance become so haggard, without hesitation she wrote a certificate proving that my health was unfit to continue to work. She also prescribed some medicine and healthcare products for me. I conveyed my wife's regards to her and she asked me to convey her regards to my wife. I gave her a hearty thanks and said goodbye to her and returned home happily.

I sent the certificate to the school revolution committee and applied my early retirement. They said that they would discuss and consider it.

Now I was peacefully waiting for the decision from the school. I had confidence that they would approve my application, because I was a new teacher at the school, no one had any personal grudges with me, they would not deliberately disapprove of my application. I began to resume my regular, normal life again, having three meals per day, not too much, not too little; having a relaxing, agreeable sleep every night with a tranquil mind, without any worries or sorrows. I planned to restore my health slowly, keeping a patient's ugly appearance for a certain span of time, lest my recovered good appearance betray my fake illness. My wife was also relieved a great deal.

A couple of months afterwards I received a reply from the school. They granted my permission of early retirement and sent my application to the Organization Department of the Communist Party of Fuling County for approval.

I was glad and had greater confidence for my retirement. As I mentioned before, a nurse's husband was working at the Organization Department of Fuling

County, who had witnessed my deteriorating health for a couple of years. He was friendly with me and I believed he would certainly put in some good words for me.

As I expected, my early retirement was finally approved in early 1972. I was excited and thrilled. The Communist Party was clever, cruel and cunning, yet it was cheated by me. I had successfully escaped the fantastic, ridiculous life of the cultural revolution for two or three years. And I would not live that kind of life forever. The only loss of the early retirement was the decrease of the income. I would be paid only 80 percent of my salary later. I didn't care about that at all. Though poorer, but happier.

Finally, my singleness of aim and my strong will and resolution won the day. I transformed physical suffering into spiritual triumph. I savored the sweet taste of the triumph heartily. All my frustration, distress seeped out of my mind like wisps that floated into the sky, as if I have been released into the sea where fish can swim at will, or into the heaven where birds can soar freely.

During my "sick period", the Cultural Revolution had been continuing. Mao launched one campaign after another, Innumerable cruel and ridiculous things happened during those periods. China was thrown into great chaos.

After the faction fighting eventually abated, Mao triumphantly convened the Ninth Party Congress in 1969. Among the 279 new members of the Central Committee of the party, only 53 members of the Central Committee of the Eighth Party Congress were retained. This fact meant that more than two hundred former high ranking cadres were purged or imprisoned or killed, and most of the new leaders were ferocious rebel leaders and Mao's flatterers who hadn't any experience of government administration, such as the common worker Wang Hongwen and the political writer Yao Wenyuan who became the top leaders of the country over night. At that congress Lin Biao was written in the party constitution as "Mao Zedong's close comrade-in-arms and successor."

In the meantime, the Party Congress claimed that "there is ample evidence to prove that Liu Shaoqi, the leading capitalist-roader wielding power within the party, was a traitor, spy, and renegade hiding in the party, a running dog of evil imperialism, modern revisionism, and the nationalist reactionaries." The meeting decided unanimously to permanently expel Liu Shaoqi from the party, to dismiss him from all work within and without the party, and to continue to liquidate seditious crimes of Liu Shaoqi and his cohorts. When Liu heard of the permanent expulsion he was exasperated. His blood pressure reached 260/130, his body temperature rose to 40 degrees Centigrade. His disease was rapidly deteriorated. He could not get out of bed and nobody would help him wash nor use the toilet. He was covered with bedsores. While he was struggling between life and death, Mao showed no sign of relenting. After suffering all the tortures bodily, mentally his heart stopped beating on Nov. 12, 1971. He left this world alone without a single family member, relative, friend by his side and without leaving a single word. And his death was kept secret from his family and the people for a long time. His crematory certificate stated that his name was Liu Weihuang; occupation: None.

Maybe Mao was conscious of the fact that people were discontent with the cultural revolution, he tried to distract people's attention. Another ludicrous thing was trumped up by Mao. In August 1969 he suddenly called to prepare to fight a war, to eliminate any enemies resolutely, thoroughly and clearly. He repeated and repeated the importance of mental and material preparation of the war among the government and the people, asking the people to strengthen unity, eliminate factionalism and fight against common enemy corporately. Military expenditure increased greatly, intensely influencing the proper development of the economy and the living standard of the people. He also demanded all levels of revolutionary committee to set up air defense group and asked all the people to dig air-raid shelters. He put forward a strategic move of "Three Lines of Defense", Urban inhabitants and materials were dispersed to the country. All the high-ranking veteran cadres in Beijing were asked to evacuate to other places before October twentieth 1969.

Against which country Mao wanted to start a war? Which country was going to invade China? There was no such a country in the world. Mao just wanted to divert public attention, wasting people's labor and money to prepare an illusionary war and having no time and energy to challenge his power.

In January 1970 Mao launched a campaign of "One strike and three opposition" striking those who opposed the cultural revolution and all the counterrevolutionary activities, opposing corruption and embezzlement; opposing speculation and profiteering; opposing extravagance and waste. The campaign wronged millions of people.

In March 1970 Mao launched a campaign to check up the conspiratorial activities of the "516 counterrevolutionary group" Originally "516 group" was a small Red Guard organization. "516" is the abbreviation of "May sixteenth", a day on which the party declared the start of the cultural revolution. Later there appeared

A Painful Reminiscence of a Dignified Soul

many rebels who disobeyed orders or refused to recognize the authority of the new revolutionary committee, all of them then were regarded as members of the "516 counterrevolution group" Including students who had travelled to Beijing, red guards who had denounced party officials, rebels who had participated in power seizures. During this campaign almost 10 million rebels were suspected and condemned, of whom more than three million were wrongly regarded as members of the "516 counterrevolutionary group" and were arrested. Many of them were tortured to death.

Accompanied with the struggle between men and men, Mao also carried out a series of transformation. He expressed many absurd ideas and took many ridiculous actions, such as in the education reform, he said:

"Isn't absurd to establish agricultural university in cities, All the agricultural universities should be removed to the countryside."

"It isn't necessary to learn medical science after graduating from high school. A graduate of primary school learning three years medical education is enough. Had the two most famous ancient Chinese doctor Hua Tuo and Li Shizheng entered high school?" After a very short period of training. hundreds of thousands of students settled down in the countryside worked as doctors. They were being called "barefoot doctors" and caused many accidents and improper deaths.

Following Mao's instructions, On October 26th 1969, Ministry of Education started the educational reformation. All the universities governed by the central government in Beijing, including Beijing University and Tsinghua University, were forced to move down to other places and governed by local authorities or factories or mines. Part of Beijing University selected a muddy stretch of reclaimed land near the Poyang Lake in Jiangxi Province. The number of the institution of higher learning of the country was reduced from 434 to 328.

According to Mao's instruction "Do not need any examinations. What is the use for examination? It is good not to take a single examination. Abolish all the examinations." In June 1970 Qinghua University and Beijing University were approved to enroll new students from workers, peasants and soldiers. The entrance examination system was abolished. The university students were recommended by the masses, approved by the leaders of their units. Their mission was entering universities, governing universities, and transforming universities with Mao Zedong Thought.

"Workers Propaganda Teams" were sent to school, their duty was to "end the monopoly of school by bourgeois intellectuals" and to "break their dominance of the schools" These educational transformations stirred tremendous chaos in university and high school. Many students enter the university through the back door or their parents' influence. The educational level of the university students was quite different, some were primary school graduates, some were junior high school graduates, some were senior high school graduates, so that the professors could find no way to teach them.

Mao also made many fallacies. He said: "We have eight hundred million people, how can we make it without class struggle against each other?" Here he made the amount of the population as the criterion of the struggle, then what is the dividing line of the number for the struggle? Suppose this number is one hundred million, then any country, whose population is over one hundred million, must have class struggle; and any country, whose population is less than one hundred million, will have no class struggle. Isn't it a laughing stock?

In Sep. 1971 suddenly there was a hearsay that Lin Biao was a traitor, deserting his country. No one can believe such a thing and many suspected that the word is a rumor churned by Mao's enemies. Lin Biao was authorized by the emperor Mao himself as his close comrade-in-arms and successor on the Resolution of the Party Congress only two years ago, how could he betray Mao? Yet, ironically it is the fact. People's daily soon reported that Lin Biao and his family fled his country and died in a crashed down plane in the country of Mongolia, and a full-scale campaign of "criticizing Lin Biao," was spread out throughout the country. It is really a farce. But under Mao's rule such a farce "Today, a man; Next day, a ghost" was an institution. Niu Shaoqi had also been authorized by Mao himself as his successor in his book, yet he was eventually being denounced as "a traitor, spy and renegade hidden within the party" and was fiercely denounced and persecuted to death by Mao.

During the "criticizing Lin Biao" campaign. Lin was blamed to stage a counterrevolutionary coup. When his conspiracy was exposed, he and his family hastily took a plane to flee for their lives. They wanted to seek refuge with the revisionist Soviet Union. He was also accused to collude with four high ranking military officers to form a capitalist headquarters and he failed to fulfill an assassination of Chairman Mao. Since Lin Biao kept a horizontal scroll of calligraphy of a Confucian aphorism "Exercise self-restraint and return to rites" on his wall he was regarded to be worshiping Confucius and restraint himself for the time being and waiting for the chance to restore capitalism in China.

A Painful Reminiscence of a Dignified Soul

Mao had a sophistry that "class struggle was the sole motivating force of history." According to Mao, in order to make history progress, there must wage class struggle—man fighting against man, community fighting against community. As there is no end to history, so there is no end to class struggle and no end to have enemies. He demanded all the people and the party that "Class struggle must be always kept in mind, year in and year out, month in and month out, day in and day out" In order to create enemies he launched one campaign after another. More absurd, in each campaign Mao set a quota of the number of the enemy. Usually he set 5% number of the whole group. Each campaign he had to create a new 5% number of the enemy, for the old enemy had already become the "dead tiger" After ten campaign he would have 50% number of the enemy among the people. No wonder there were so many sufferers, victims in his rule.

Painfully witnessing all those cruel, ridiculous things I felt heartrending misery and sympathy for those tens of millions of victims; I was also happy I had escaped all of those cruel and preposterous campaigns. I stayed at home leisurely, peacefully.

After I retired, housework became my major job. My wife was very busy. As she was the most welcomed doctor by the public at the health center, many patients would wait a long time to get her treatment, so she had to treat more patients than other doctors. In addition, my family grew larger. We had another daughter in 1967 and had a third daughter in 1969. I also teach my eldest daughter English when she first entered the primary school. We had a very happy family life now. My wife was very considerate and tender. My daughters were all very cute and pretty, their faces were always wreathed in smiles which made me feel warm and delighted.

But I was not resigned to the status quo. I must consider our future, especially our children's future. After I was exiled from Beijing to the countryside, we became registered rural residence. According to Mao's policy, rural residents could almost never be able to move to the cities. He even forced millions of city youth to the countryside. If I kept staying hermitage permanently, my daughters would be rural residents all their lives. I did not like that prospect for them. I must try all means to leave the countryside and return to the city. I contemplated the question day and night.

One day I had an idea: Since I already retired, I might be allowed to return to Shanghai I lived before liberation, or to my native city ZhenJiang. If I returned and resumed an urban resident, I could request to transfer my family to my place.

I had four elder brothers and many friends and several comrade-in-arms of the underground work in Shanghai, they might be able to help me to achieve my goal. I planned to go back to Shanghai.

I discussed my ideas with my wife. She hesitated. We had suffered great pain of separation for years. It was not easy for us to be reunited, if we separated again, when could we be reunited once again? In fact, I myself did not like to separate too, but I thought I could go to Shanghai to have a try. If I was successful, so much the better; If not, I could come back. Both of us considered the question long, finally we decided to separate for the time being for the sake of our daughters' future.

I decided to take my eldest daughter to go to Shanghai with me for lightening my wife's burden and teaching her English continuously. My wife agreed and I bought two steamship tickets to Shanghai.

One day in the early Spring of 1972 I and my eldest daughter boarded on the ship. My wife and the other two daughters saw us off at the wharf by the side of the Yangtze River. We had mixed feelings. On the one hand we could not bear the parting; on the other hand, we pinned some hope on this trip.

The water of the Yangtze flow smoothly, but when our ship reached the Three Gorges area the torrent run fast. The mountains on both sides of the three gorges stretch more than 200 miles. The cliffs on both sides appear to have been cut by knives. The overlapping rocks make up layers of barriers that shield against sky and sunshine so that the sun can only be seen as noon and the moon will merely show at midnight. The elegant peaks of the lofty mountains and the grotesque structures, the lush flourish trees standing erectly in the cloudy air and the luxuriant grasses compose the scenery beyond any expression. I raised up my head to appreciate what's above and looked down to see the shadows of rocks and woods reflected in the clean water. I felt quite gleeful. We can often hear monkeys howling at both sides of the river, and with their brisk cry our boat ran swiftly like a galloping horse passed the Three Gorges. Then the Yangtze grows wider gradually and the water flows quietly. The whole journey took us six days, we finally reached our destination.

When I arrived in Shanghai, I first visited my eldest brother and stayed at his home. We were all excited for we hadn't met each other for more than ten years. During my stay there we had a long chat. We hadn't told each other our lives for many years, for we did not dare to write our story in a letter. The party organizations often open class enemy's letters. If they found we complained the party, we would get great trouble. Now that we were face to face, we revealed our true situation. To my great surprise and deep sorrow, I found my eldest brother was in an utterly awkward predicament. A few years ago, he was transferred from Shanghai customs to Shenzhen customs. At that time Shenzhen was a very poor fishing village. He was not accustomed to living there and often fell ill. his wife and two children were still in Shanghai. After working there for a couple of years, his health became worse. He was already near sixty-year-old, and when he fell ill nobody took care of him, he decided to apply a resignation. But at that time resigning one's job was deemed betraying revolution. Instead of approving his resignation he was expelled from the customs. He had worked at customs for more than thirty years and now hadn't either salaries or pensions. He had no money for food and medical treatment. He could only keep survival on his two children's support. His daughter was a teacher of a primary school, had two children; His son was working at the factory of steam turbine, had three children. Their salaries were low and their family burden were heavy, they could not provide sufficient money for their parents so my brother's life was very difficult. He wanted to get a job. He was a talented, knowledgeable person, conversant with Chinese and English and could do many forms of work. But he could not get a job for no units were allowed to hire an expelled person. An expelled person was categorized as bad element.

Later I visited my second elder brother. He had worked at the Bank of China for over thirty years. But not long ago, he was suddenly transferred to the Grain Bureau of the city. It was really putting a square peg in a round hole. He thought it must be because that the cadre of the organization department want to replace this golden job by his man. My third elder brother had worked at the Head Office of the Bank of Communication. After liberation the Head Office moved to Beijing, my brother did not want to go to Beijing and found a job at a factory. The other two elder brothers, as I mentioned before, were still laboring in the countryside as prisoners to reform through labor. Of us six brothers, after liberation, three became the enemies of the people, one was expelled, two lost their good job. We were all office workers, none of us was a capitalist or landlord. If we the common people suffered so much, how much worse had the landlords or capitalists suffered. Should a country create so many so-called class enemies? Though two of my elder brothers and I were all rehabilitated later, but what can redeem and recompense the mental and physical suffering of over twenty years we had undergone.

When I found my brother could not help me to achieve my goal, I began to visit my friends and the former comrade-in-arms at the JiGuang workers evening school. I first visited Zhou Chaohai who introduced me to the school. That school was founded by five persons: Wu Muliang, Zhang Shanji, Duanmu Qun, Peng Qiming and Zhou Chaohai. According to Zhou, the first three of them had already passed away because of being persecuted. His word surprised me greatly. Zhang Shanji had recommended me to the Party. He had worked at the Shanghai Electric Generating Plant and made great contributions to the revolution, how should he be persecuted to death by the party. His death caused me extreme grief and deep meditation. So many former revolutionaries, including the President of the State Liu Shaoqing, the marshal Peng Dehuai, Lin Biao and He Long, were labeled "counterrevolutionaries" after the founding of the People's Republic of China. Had they really committed great faults or had been wronged? Should we call Mao Zedong a great, brilliant leader or the most heinous, wicked criminal.

I told Zhou my situations and asked him: I was a Shanghai resident before liberation, should I return to Shanghai according to the party's policy? He said there isn't such a policy, and because Shanghai is too crowded it is very difficult to get a Shanghai registered residence. Then I asked him if he could help me to get a registered resident or get a job here. He said he would like to help me but he hasn't much power. He is doing propaganda work at a university. He promised he would try his best to help me. If there is any chance in the future, he would let me know. I thanked him, bid farewell to him and went back home.

Then I visited another founder of the evening school Peng Qiming. I told him my story and asked him to help me to move back to Shanghai. He showed great sympathy for me and said he was quite willing to help me but he is working at the Department of Sea transportation, he didn't have enough power to do that job. but he also promised if there would be any chance to help me in the future, he would inform me. I understood his situation and feelings. I thanked him profusely and said goodbye to him.

I went to see another evening school teacher named Dai Zhenyuan. He had worked in a famous newspaper before liberation. After that he was transferred to the Propaganda Department of the party of Huangpu District of Shanghai. That was a good job. But unfortunately, he was also persecuted and was sent back to his native village in the suburb of Shanghai. As he and I were fellow sufferers with mutual sympathy, we had intimate talk. I told him all my true story and my desire

A Painful Reminiscence of a Dignified Soul

now and asked him whether he could give me any help. He said: "the population control of Shanghai is very strict. It is very difficult for anyone to move in Shanghai, unless you have close relation with the person in power. When I was in the Propaganda Department, I knew some people in power. But now I was demoted to a villager. Who would still recognize me?" He seemed to be eager to help me but was not in a position to do that. He asked me to excuse him for being unable to help me. I replied with a smile: "Excuse what? You haven't done nothing wrong. I should thank you for your warm heart. I was a rightist; I quite know the ways of the world. 'Hot tea cools down when the person leaves the table'" He made a bitter smile and asked me to stay for lunch. I agreed. During the lunch he was still thinking about my problems. Suddenly he asked me a question: "Moving back to Shanghai is extremely difficult; would you like to return to a city not very far from Shanghai?" With my positive response he told me that he has a relative who is the military command in Yangzhou city, maybe he could help me to transfer there. I was very glad with his suggestion. Yangzhou is a city just on the opposite side of the Yangtze River of my native city Zhenjiang. I deemed it a good place. He wrote a letter of introduction to me.

    I took a trip to Yangzhou to visit Dai's relative. His office was strictly guarded and his house had a fierce dog. It seemed he had a great power there. With that letter he received me. I told him my situation and desire. He had some dialogues with me and asked me many questions. He considered my request for a while and then said, if I were still a cadre, he might be able to find an organization to receive me, but I had already retired and no unit can receive a retiree, so he was unable to help me. I was disappointed, I did not know whether he was not going to help me or he didn't have enough power to help me. Anyway, I had nothing more to do, I thanked him deeply and said goodbye to him.

    I went back to Shanghai and consulted with my elder brothers and friends. All of them concluded that I was definitely unable to return to Shanghai. I was disappointed and intended to go back to Fuling. My eldest brother disagreed with my idea and suggested that I could go back to my native city Zhenjiang and apply to return my own home. I said I had no place to live. He replied: "I still kept the title deed for our house. I did not know who had occupied it. You could ask them to move out. And we still had some relatives there, you can ask for their help." I considered it a good idea and agreed. He wrote two letters to our relatives and told me their addresses because I did not know them. I left my native land when I was only nine-year-old.

Zhong Da

A few days later I and my daughter left Shanghai for Zhenjiang. I first visited an uncle's grandson Da Zhuying. He was ten years older than I, but as my family generation was higher than his, he had to call me uncle. We had never seen each other before, yet he received me extremely warm. I stayed at his home temporarily. Then I went to my family's old house, which had long been occupied by a stranger named Tang Ruming, who had a wife and two sons. He was the manager of a hotel. I asked him to move out for I had the title deed for the house and had the right to do that. He said he had no place to move. I demanded him to leave again and again but he just ignored my demand and insistently refused to move out. He had wide connections with local officials I could not force him to obey my words.

My house had a courtyard and three living rooms. One living room is beside the courtyard. between the other two living room is a hall, which is used as a sitting room and kitchen. Tang and his wife lived in one living room; his two sons lived in the room beside the courtyard. The third room was a deserted one because it was badly dilapidated. The window was broken, the wooden floor was rotten, part of the wall had fallen down. As I could not drive them out. I decided to live in the ruined room. I hired several workers to repair all the damaged parts. After their work was finished, I decorated it a bit and bought some simple furniture and household articles and moved in from my grandnephew home.

Now I had a home in Zhenjiang and my wife had a home in Fuling, east and west, more than two thousand kilometers apart. Each of us shared the untold bitterness and sadness of the human being. The only thing that can comfort us a bit is that we still have the family leave: each year my wife can come to Zhenjiang to see me or I go to Fuling to see her. We determined that we would never give up until we reach our goal—transferring my wife and daughters from the countryside to the city.

After I settled down, I went to the Civil Affairs Bureau of the city to apply for permission of transferring my registered residence from Fuling County to Zhenjiang city. They received my written application and promised to consider it.

I waited at home, confident that they would approve it, for it was quite reasonable that a retired person returned to his own home.

About a month later I received their reply. They said that if I were a single, I could move back to Zhenjiang, but I had a family in Fuling, I should stay with my family, so they could not approve my application.

I was exasperated. Why a citizen didn't have the right and freedom to go back to his own home? I protested, but to no avail. They said it was the policy they must

A Painful Reminiscence of a Dignified Soul

observe it. If I was divorced, I was a single they would approve my application of returning home.

I wrote to my wife the result. She was also very angry. But she added a word in her letter: "Now that they said if we were divorced, they would give you a registered resident in Zhenjiang, then let us make a fake divorce."

I did not think it a good idea, for if we divorced, I have no right to apply for their transfer, I did not take her suggestion. I decided to find some other way to get the status of local registered residence.

I asked Zhuying and other relatives to help me solve the problem. I also often went to the library, museum, parks, trying to make as many new friends as possible. I hoped I could find someone who had enough power or abilities to help me to get the registered residence in Zhenjiang.

Very soon more than one year had passed. Though I had exerted my best endeavor, my thing was still not straightened out. My mind was very intricate and complex. When would I achieve my goal? Should I go back to Fuling or still stay in Zhenjiang? Could I appeal to a higher level of government for my local registered resident? I hated the present political system. All my six brothers moved into Shanghai freely after the war against Japan. We did not need to ask anyone's approval and no one forbade our movement. Now I could not return to my native land legally. What the world had become!

Despite my great distress I also had some joyful things to enjoy however. In the first place I was a free man now. I did not need to attend the absurd political studies and the cruel class struggles like other miserable people; I was now living a clean and peaceful life. I could do anything I please and I could go anywhere I like. Very few people had such a privilege in the chaotic situation of the cultural revolution. I was proud and elated myself and felt pitiful and compassionate for all those sufferers and victims. I congratulated myself on having taken that difficult and painful decision years before—to take the fake sick. For my freedom I had paid a great deal price. But all the terrible twinges and bitterness I had suffered proved quite worth all they cost me. "All is well that ends well".

Next, I was now living in my native land, a place where I was born, where I was taking the first breath of the air, where my eyes were catching the first glimpse of the sunlight, I love the place and have a deep feeling with it. Sometimes I called my relatives, sometimes I revisited the fields formerly owned by my father and dropped in on the home of the peasant who had tilled our fields. I still remembered the peasant's name: Lu Da and his son Lu Hu. Lu Da already died, Lu Hu received me warmly, did not regard my family as a landlord who had exploited him. when I was a pupil I often went to our field. It is a very beautiful place. At the end of our field is a slope of a hill which is facing the Yangtze river. On the hill there were a few mulberry trees. When the mulberries were ripe, I often went there to pick them. My parents' tomb was also on the slope of the hill. Once while I played there and was intoxicated by the scene, I even embraced a dream: When I grow old, I would build a small house on the top of the hill. Then I could breathe fresh air every day, watching the waves of the grand Yangtze in front of the house and enjoying the wide sweep of green fields behind the house. How nice was that prospect! Of course, the dream could never be realized, the land was state-owned now. Though my father and eldest brother had been the landowner and the peasant were the tenant, their relationship was very friendly. When the peasant had good harvest, our family accepted some rent; when the harvest was bad, we charged him nothing. And after 1937 we left Zhenjiang, we never collected any rent from him.

I also went to my parents' tomb to pay my tribute at the Clean and Clear Festival each year—a day of traditional observances in commemoration of the dead. My father and his wife were buried in the same grave. They rested there together happily, quietly. But Unfortunately, the peaceful days were disturbed by the government. One day our former tenant Lu Hu came to my house. He told me that the government noticed him that my parents grave must be moved to another place for the use of public construction. If we did not move it before the definite day, the government would root it out with bulldozers. I was very angry. That land was ours formerly, my parents would like to rest on their own land forever. The government had what right to confiscate our land? But we had to obey the order. Protest was useless. I contacted with all my brothers, asking for their opinion. Since the expense of moving the grave was rather high and our income were all very low, so some of them were hesitated. I insisted that we must move it, we must not let our parents' corpse be destroyed by the government. Finally, we decided to move it, I and other four brothers would share the cost equally. My eldest brother was exempt the expense for he had no income at all. Lu Hu helped me to hire several laborers to move the grave. Before the day of moving I went to the grave to make the last memorial service at their own land. I put a bunch of flowers and some sacrificial articles before their tomb. I kowtowed three times and then prostrated on the ground to breath the aroma of the damp soil, trying to sniff some of their scent. Then I stood up and walked round the tomb, scattering the petals of the flower on the ground and delivered some tribute of praise to them. This is a sacred land of my family but we could no longer keep it now. Waving my hand unceasingly, murmuring bye, bye continuously, I reluctantly parted my dear land.

Next day several workers came to the slope. They dug out the earth of the grave, opened the coffins, put the bones of each coffin in each earthen jar, sealed the opening of the jar, and then carried the jars to a barren mountain and buried them together in a new grave. I watched the whole process with heavy mind, but I also felt a little thankful that I had fulfilled a great obligation—to help my parents move to a new home. If I did not return to my native land, we did not know the government's notice, my parents' tomb would be uprooted by bulldozers.

Another thing that pleased me was that I had closer contact with my brothers, especially with my eldest brother. I often went to Shanghai to see him. I had an intimate feeling with him and was deeply attached to him, for he had fostered most of my childhood life. He was a man of true and honest conviction and had a broad, tolerant, easy-going habit of mind. He was expelled for nothing wrong, just because he wanted to resign to reunite with his family. He had worked in customhouse for over thirty years but could not get a single cent of his pension. It was an extremely unreasonable, cruel treatment. Yet he dealt with it coolly, bore the ill treatment and kept composed and quiet. He had a granddaughter working as a nurse in a hospital. When there was an old critically ill inpatient who needed to hire a person to watch his situation and inform the doctor in time in an emergency at night, my eldest brother would take that job. He would stay all night there awake to earn a very small sum of money. An over sixty-year-old man had to do such a bitter job for another old man. How pitiful it is! How unjust it is!

He also often wrote letters to me, giving me advice or introducing me some aphorisms, such as "Eloquence is silver, silence is gold." "Don't senselessly talk upon the shortcomings of others; don't recklessly presume on one's own good." "Meet the rich and powerful and give a sycophantic face, the most shameful; meet the poor and humble and assume a superior air, the most contemptible wretched." In each letter he wrote to me, he impressed two seals on the end of the letter. One seal is carved his name, the other is carved a word "But only try to have a clear conscience no regret to my mind". This word is the second part of an idiom "How can it be possible that everything is as one wishes, but only try to have a clear conscience no regret to my mind." (岂能尽如人意，但求无

愧我心) I cherish those words and always keep them in mind. His temperament influenced me a great deal.

After Lin Biao's death the confrontation between Jiang Qing and the premier Zhou became clearer and acuter. While Zhou and other pragmatic cadres tried to take some mild, reasonable policies or practice, Jiang and her clique denounced them to spur the right-deviating policy and to reverse the Cultural Revolution. Jiang wanted to bring down all the veteran cadres except their lackeys and puppets. Zhou emphasized "The veteran cadres are the valuable wealth of the Party. We must strictly distinguish between the two different types of contradictions." Zhou wanted to rectify the political and economic work, restore social order, oppose the rampancy of anarchism. Jiang widely engaged factionalist activities.

Mao was the backstage boss of Jiang Qing, but he had to make certain balance between the two groups. He always kindled the animosity of one group against another. Today he praised this group and criticized the opposite group; the next day he praised the opposite group and criticized the other. He was calculating, erratic and whimsical, and always change his words and policies. He made use of the opposition of the two groups to keep his absolute leading position.

In 1972 Zhou was diagnosed to have cancer in the bladder. The doctors reported to Mao and requested an immediate surgery for Zhou, stressing that the cancer was at an early stage and a prompt operation could cure it. But Mao ordered: "First: keep it secret, and don't tell the premier and his wife. Second: no examination. Third: no surgery." Though Zhou was ill and under attack, he continued to work hard for the sake of the fate of the country and its hundreds of millions of people. Sometimes he worked on his sickbed or while receiving blood transfusions.

As premier Zhou was working with illness, he needed strong helpers and he recommended Deng Xiaoping as a candidate. In order to keep the work of government going on effectively, Mao rehabilitated Deng Xiaoping and assigned him to be the vice premier in March 1973.

After Deng resumed his work, he and premier Zhou strived hard to bring order out of chaos and criticize the ultra-Left trend and anarchism. The Jiang clique always obstructed and criticized what they did. Zhou promoted production, Jiang criticized him to suppress revolution with production; The government exported some products to foreign countries, Jiang clique criticized the exporters to be traitor to China; The government imported some products from foreign countries, Jiang clique criticized the importers to worship foreign things and toady to foreign powers; Zhou endeavored to improve the quality of education. Jiang used some incidents to negate Zhou's rectification of errors. For instance, a student named Zhang Tiesheng handed a blank paper at the college entrance examination, on which he wrote a big zero and the word "To make revolution, one need not answer above questions." to protest the examination system. Jiang praised him as the "hero of blank paper" and published the event throughout the country. Later, a fifteen-year-old girl named Zhang Yuqin, who was indoctrinated by Jiang's educational policy and copied Zhang Tiesheng's action, handed in a blank paper in an English test, and wrote on the backside of the paper: "I am a Chinese, why should I learn a foreign language? Even though I do not learn 'ABCDE' I can still receive the baton of revolution and bury imperialism, revisionism, and counterrevolutionaries." Afterwards, she was criticized by the school and she committed suicide. This is a tragedy, which is obviously caused by cultural revolution, but Jiang seized the incident to make a big fuss over the event. She published the story in People's Daily and all other medias and proclaimed: "Zhang Yuqin is a victim of the revisionist line in the field of education and the event further proves that examinations are wrong", arbitrarily criticizing the education line practiced by premier Zhou and condemning the restoration of examination to be a comeback of capitalism.

In Oct. 1973, Jiang developed a movement of "fighting back against the activities of the resurging of the right-deviation", searching for the representatives of the restoration of capitalism. In Jan. 1974, Jiang edited an article "Lin Biao and the doctrine of Confucius and Mencius" and proclaimed that the revisionism is still the main danger, attacking Zhou and his followers without mentioning their names. Mao approved the publication of Jiang's statement of condemnation. Then the movement of the "criticizing Lin Biao and Confucius" was carried out throughout the country. A mass political struggle was developing in all spheres.

Mao's reason for criticizing Confucius, I guessed, might be twofold: In the first place, he has always been negating and disdaining Confucius. He has repeatedly criticized Confucianism and the ideas of exalting Confucianism and opposing the Legalist school in the course of Chinese revolution. He has regarded Confucius's ideology is opposite to his own and a danger to his rule. Confucianism attacks China's first emperor Qin Shi Huang who had buried four hundred scholars. Mao is the modern Qin Shi Huang and Marxist, he had to criticize Confucius. In the second place, though Liu Shaoqi and his followers were eliminated, there were still many pragmatic cadres in the new revolutionary committees, including premier Zhou and Deng Xiaoping. By criticizing Confucius, he could obliquely criticize those conservatives.

On the plea of criticizing Confucius, Jiang Qing exaggerated Zhou's "fault" to the maximum, condemning he is going back to the capitalist road. A Jiang Qing's accomplice even shouted "The campaign of criticizing Lin Biao and Confucius" was the second cultural revolution".

I respect Confucius and believe his thought is right. I was angry with the Criticizing Confucius Campaign. In order to refute their fallacies, I began to make a deeper study about Confucius's thoughts and got a clearer understanding.

Confucius gives the first priority to the cultivation of the morality of men. He believes "The cultivation of the person is the root of everything else." He takes moral cultivation as a criterion for measuring the value of human life. "The superior man thinks always of virtue; the common man thinks of comfort." "The mind of the superior man is conversant with righteousness; the mind of the mean man is conversant with gain." He writes: "Moral force is like the pole-star, which remains its place while all the lesser stars pay homage to it." He deems "Knowledge, benevolence, and braveness the three qualities are the highest extended virtue of the universal." The Confucians regards "Benevolence, righteousness, propriety, knowledge, faithfulness are the five constant virtues." and believe "Benevolence, righteousness, propriety, knowledge and faithfulness are not infused into us from without. We are naturally furnished with them." Confucians inculcated a profound distaste for material gains, the self-serving mentality, and all profit-seeking activities. They sought to perfect the very nature of men by stimulating its good potentials and suppressing its evil instincts. "When the love of dominance, boasting, resentment, and covetousness are repressed, this may be deemed perfect virtue."

Confucius emphasizes self-introspection, self-revelation, and self-improvement. He considers that "Pursuing self-cultivation and realizing the 'Doctrine of the Mean(中庸)' are the fundamental principles for disciplining people's lives and safeguarding the social order." Here "Doctrine of the Mean" means "being without inclination to either side, synthesizing all different opinions but don't support any one of them, hold and adopt the opinion which is not extreme." "Managing anything must conform the propriety, no excess than the requisite nor less than the need, and do not go against the normal practice." "All things develop together without jeopardizing each other. All codes function together without conflicting with each other." This idea is a little similar to Hegel's word "Truth is found neither in the thesis, but in an emergent synthesis which reconciles the two." "Life at its best is a creative synthesis of opposites in fruitful harmony."

Mencius, the second important apostle of Confucianism, writes "When Heaven is about to down great responsibility upon a man, it invariably first makes his mind and intention taste of bitterness; gives toil to his sinews and bones; exposes his body to hunger; subjects him to extreme poverty; and frustrates and wreaks havoc upon whatever actions he takes and does; it motivates his mind and leads endurance to his nature and makes him increasingly capable of what he formerly could not do."

Confucius emphasizes cultivation of men not simply for the sake of cultivation of men only. He considers that cultivation of men is the basis for doing other things perfect. He writes "Things being investigated, knowledge became complete. Their knowledge being complete, their thoughts were sincere; Their thoughts were sincere, their hearts were then rectified. Their hearts being rectified, their persons were cultivated. Their persons being cultivated, their families were regulated, their families being regulated their states were rightly governed. Their states being rightly governed, the whole world was made tranquil and happy." The final result of the cultivation of persons is the basis to regulate the family, to govern the state rightly, to make the world tranquil and happy. Confucius sees all the knowledge are coming from the investigation of things, and he recommends "Seeking truth from facts", which shows that he shares some idea of materialism. He believes "A man must perfect himself first, then he is able to perfect others, to perfect society." Confucians promote "people should struggle for truth, sacrifice their lives for their country." "Lay down one's life for a just cause" "Love kin and then cherish mankind; cherish mankind and then treasure all things.", "Foster my elderly and extend to foster other's elderly; nurse my infant and extend to nurse other's infants." They believe that the love is starting from the individual, family, then develop and evolve to the mankind and society and nation and considers that human being does not live for oneself only but also live for mankind and society and the country.

Confucius's political thought is based upon his ethical thought. He believes that "The ruler should govern his state by virtue." the government should rule through propriety and morality, and not by using bribery, force and coercion. He thinks "If you lead the people by virtue and the rites, then they will govern themselves, discipline themselves, and they will have a sense of shame, and moreover will become good." "The ruler should Love what the people love, hate what the people hate" "By gaining the people, the kingdom is gained, and if losing the people, the kingdom is lost." "When one by force subdues men, they do not submit to him in heart; When one subdues men by virtue, in their heart's core they are pleased, and sincerely submit." Confucius highly values the position and role of human beings and holds that "Populace being fundamental" "in a state the people are the most important element; the affair of state is the next; the ruler is the slightest". "Every Man has a responsibility for the fate of his country." He is against despotic and disdains for the use of brutal force. He says: "The decisive factor of a ruler's political success was the degree of the people's support. Only one who wins the support of his subjects can be a successful monarch, and one who loses the hearts of his subjects is a 'mere fellow' who should be killed by all of his people.", "A monarch who is harmful to his country should be replaced." "An oppressive government is more terrible than tiger." From his words we can see, though he advocates that people should respect and obey there monarch, he has never said that people must respect and obey all kinds of monarch and he holds the view that the monarch who is cruel or losing people's heart should be overthrown or killed by the people like the emperor Ji and Zhou (Ji and Zhou were two cruel tyrants of ancient China) Confucius maintains "A prince who breaks the law must be punished like an ordinary person." Confucius's words show he has some democratic thoughts.

In the "Book of Rites" compiled by Confucius there is a notion of the "Great Harmony"(大同).According to it, "The society in Great Harmony was ruled by the public, where the people chose men of virtue and ability, and valued trust and harmony. People did not only love their own parents and children, but also secured the living of the elderly until their ends, let the adults be of use to the society, and helped the young grow. Those who were widowed, orphaned, childless, handicapped and diseased were all taken care of. Men took their responsibilities and women had their homes. People disliked seeing resources being wasted but did not seek to possess them; they wanted exert their strength but did not do it for their own benefit. Therefore, selfish thoughts were dismissed, people refrained from stealing and robbery, and the outer doors remained open." Confucius advocates this ideal society where the government is ruled by the public, the leaders are the men of virtue and ability chosen by the people, which shows that Confucius has the idea of democratic election. He advocates the society where all the old and young, all the widowed, orphaned, childless, handicapped and diseased are all taken care of, which shows that he also has an idea of social security system, part of socialism.

Confucius is also a great educator. He devoted his whole life to education and bred thousands of brilliant disciples. He exhorts to adopt different methods of teaching in light of the various dispositions of students, to "Modify one's way of teaching to suit the aptitude and ability of each student." He advocates that every man is equal, "In education there should be no distinction of classes." Whether a student is rich or poor, they should be teaching without discrimination. He offered many disciples of humble origin the chance to acquire knowledge. He emphasizes to study for the sake of application, saying "They who know the truth are not equal to those who love it; and they who love it are not equal to those who practice it in earnest."

From my studies I firmly believe Confucius was a great thinker who has made great contributions to the culture and characteristics of China. A lot of his ideas are universal and timeless.

I also noticed how the Jiang Qing clique criticized Confucius. I found their criticisms were all fallacies and farces. For instance, they wrote:

"Confucius and Mencius dished up a reactionary program for restoring the slave system. Confucius said: 'Once self-restraint and restoration of the rites are achieved, all under heaven will submit to benevolence,' that is, all under heaven will submit to its rule."

This word meant that all the countries in the world would be in a slave system if they practiced rites and submitted to benevolence. Is this word right or wrong? Let every primary school student answer it. But Mao Zedong did practice the other way of the word; he has firmly opposed all the rites and benevolence and promoted cruelty, mercilessness and lawlessness.

Another instance, the Jiang clique said:

"Confucius and Mencius praised 'virtue, benevolence and righteousness' and 'loyalty and forbearance' and 'those who rule by virtue will thrive; those who rule by force will perish.' Lin Biao viciously used Confucian language to attack revolutionary violence and the dictatorship of the proletariat."

This word meant that "virtue, benevolence, righteousness, loyalty and forbearance are all bad moralities, and "those who rule by virtue will perish; those who rule by force will thrive" Would you agree with those ideas?

There were still many fallacies during the campaign of criticizing Confucius. I haven't the interest to mention more of them here.

I wanted to write an article to refute their fallacies, but I knew there was no use and the newspaper would not publish it. To vent my rage and despite I wrote a letter to the People's Daily to jeer them.

Dear editor:

You have done a very beautiful work during the Campaign of Criticizing Confucius, but I think your criticisms are still not deep enough. Here I cite more his vicious words to supplement your criticism. please publish them:

Confucius promotes "benevolence, righteousness, propriety, Knowledge and faithfulness." It is completely wrong. We must promote "cold-heartedness, wickedness, rudeness, ignorance and disloyalty.

Confucius praises "Gravity, generosity, sincerity, earnestness, and kindness," as five essences of behavior. It is quite absurd. We should praise "frivolity, stinginess, hypocrisy, half-heartedness and cruelty.

Confucius extols "benign, kind, courteous, temperate and tolerant" It is totally erroneous. We should laud "malicious, cruel, rude, extreme, bigoted."

All categories of Confucianism exhort such virtues as frugality, loyalty, honesty, temperateness, refrainment, magnanimity, and compassion for the poor, the weak. They are not right. We should exhort such virtues as waste, perfidy, deception, extremeness, indulgent, grudge and indifference for the poor, the weak.

Confucius says "The feeling of commiseration is essential to man; that the feeling of shame is essential to man; that the feeling of modesty and complaisance is essential to man and that the feeling of right and wrong is essential to man. without those feelings deserve not a human being." He is talking nonsense. We must correct it and confirm that without those feelings is a perfect human being.

Confucius believes that "In a high situation, he does not treat his inferiors with contempt. In a low situation, he does not court the favor of his superiors." On the contrary, the superiors must contemn their inferiors and the inferiors must bootlick their superiors'

A Painful Reminiscence of a Dignified Soul

Confucius maintains "The ruler should love what people love, hate what people hate." that is reactionary. Our Leader, like Mao Zedong, must hate what people love, love what people hate.

There are still many fallacies in Confucius' writings

If we observe Confucius's preaches our country must be ruined; if we act in a diametrically opposite way our country must be the first-rate country in the world.

Your reader a common people

I also send People's Daily an article, citing three poems from the book <Poems Classics> to blame those base, cruel oppressors. <Poems Classics> is one of the Five Classics compiled by Confucius and the important textbook of his teachings. It is the collection of the ancient poems in China, dating back to the eleventh century BC to the six century BC. Its content includes the war, the grief of women, the love and passion of the youth, the complains of the oppression or ill-treatments, and sarcasm etc. It is the oldest extant book of lyric poetry in world literature, so it has status in Chinese and world cultural history owing to its rich content and high achievement in ideology and art.

Look At The Rat

Look at the rat, the rat has a skin.
Yet some people have no manners.
A man has no manners,
What is he going to do, that he does not die?

Look at the rat, the rat has teeth.
Yet some people have no shame.
A man has no shame,
What is he waiting for, that he does not die?

Look at the rat, the rat has limbs.
Yet some people have no propriety.
A man has no propriety,
Why does he not die forthwith?

Zhong Da

Owl

Owl, oh owl!
You've taken away my fledglings,
please don't destroy my nest.
With extreme love and pains,
I toiled to hatch my young ones.

while it is not dark and raining,
I peck bark off the mulberry
To mend window and door of my nest.
And the children down the tree
May dare to bully me.

My claws are worn to the bone,
Gathering reed catkins far and wide.
And I keep them stored up.
My beak is sore and wounded,
Yet my nest is still unfinished.

My feathers are torn and sparse,
My tail has lost its gloss.
My nest is swaying and tottering
At the mercy of wind and rain,
I cannot help but cry in fear.

The Boat of Cypress Wood

Freely floats the boat of cypress wood,
Tossing about along the steam.
Eyes open, I can't sleep,
As if my heart was heavy with grief.
It's not that I've no wine to drink,
Or nowhere to enjoy visiting.

A Painful Reminiscence of a Dignified Soul

My heart's not like a bronze mirror,
Absorbing the reflection of everything.
I've brother, elder and younger,
But not one is trustworthy.
When I tried to pour out my grievances,
I found them furious with me.

My heart's not like a stone,
It can't be turned and moved easily.
My heart's not like a mat,
It can't be rolled up at will.
With dignity and honor,
I'll never flinch or yield.

My heart's weighted down with vexation,
Against me the villains bear a grudge.
Excessive distress I've been confronted with,
Too much indignity I've been treated with,
Meditating silently on this,
I beat my breast when the sad truth dawns upon me.

Oh sun, Oh moon,
Why are you so dim?
My heart stained with sorrow,
Cannot be washed clean like dirty clothes.
I reflected silently on this,
And cannot spread my wings and soar high.

After I sent out that two letters, I seemed to release some my indignations. I felt a little light-hearted,

While I kept close watch toward the destruction of the Cultural Revolution, I did not neglect my own affairs. Though I had great difficulties and met with many setbacks. I firmly believed a Chinese idiom: "Heaven never seals off all the exits—there is always a way out." I continued to strive to reach my goal. I kept in contact with my relatives, old friends and made new friends.

After two or three years endeavors, I finally got a potent help. I met a very distant relative named Sun Qianghua. He was a worker. He had been an activist during the first period of the cultural revolution. There were two opposite rebel factions in Zhenjiang. Sun joined one of the factions and became one of the leaders of it. After fierce fights his faction beat its opposite and formed the revolution committee in Zhenjiang. Sun was warm-hearted and promised to help me. He told me he had some friends who were working in the revolution committee of the city, he would contact them and ask them to help to transfer my registered residence to Zhenjiang.

A few months later Sun told me he did successfully win the approval of the public security bureau of Zhenjiang to enroll my name in the registered residence of the city. I was immensely delighted. It was a significant thing, because with my status I was eligible to apply for a petition to transfer my family to Zhenjiang. Now I started the second step of my mission, to find a job for my wife in Zhenjiang.

In August 1974 my wife with two daughters took her family leave to see me. Now I am a free man I can spend all my time to accompany them, leading them to visit the most famous scenic sites in Zhenjiang. Then I guided them to Shanghai to make a nice tour there. After spending twelve happy days they return to Fuling. And we are glad we add another daughter in the next year.

The struggle between Jian Qing and premier Zhou continued and got fiercer and fiercer. Jiang and her clique asserted categorically that the great duke is the great Confucian, though they did not say the great duke is Premier Zhou. They greatly extolled the old empresses Wu Zetian in China and implied that Jiang is the excellent modern empress. They conspired to organize a cabinet instead of premier Zhou and Deng Xiaoping. As Jiang clique was going too far, Mao was afraid that the people and the pragmatic leaders of the government and the Army would rebel. In July 1974 Mao pretentiously criticized that "Jiang Qing, Wang Hongwen, Zhang Chuengqiao, Yao Wenyuan was a small gang of four men; they opened two factories: one steel factory, one cap factory, for beating people with steel sticks and wearing big cap on people." In January 1975, as Premier Zhou could not fulfill all his work because his illness became worse, Mao promoted Deng Xiaoping to be the first vice premier, the vice chairman of the Central Military Commission of the CPC. With the time elapse and Zhou's disease getting worse and worse, Deng was taking charge of the work of the State Council In fact. As Zhou and Deng stressed the order and readjustment and opposed the ineffectiveness and the en-

A Painful Reminiscence of a Dignified Soul

gaging in factionalist activities. In March 1975 Jiang clique attacked the veteran cadres and criticized that empiricism is the chief danger of the Party. In November 1975 Mao started a campaign of "Counter attacking the trend of the reversing verdicts of the right deviation." He said: "Some of the comrades, mainly some senior comrades, still remain in the stage of the bourgeois democratic revolution in their thinking. They resist or even oppose the socialist revolution. Among them, I discern two attitudes toward the cultural revolution; one is discontentment, and the other is revenge, or denial of the cultural revolution." The campaign was directly criticizing and attacking Zhou Enlai and Deng Xiaoping, though he did not mention Zhou's name. But he openly criticized Deng that he was going to settle accounts with the Cultural Revolution.

Not long afterwards, a miserable news came, Premier Zhou passed away on January 8, 1976. Mao did not promote Deng Xiaoping as the premier, but appointed Hua Guofeng as an acting premier.

Premier Zhou's death caused a great shake in the country. People felt sad, shocked and lost. They mourned the death of the premier with great sorrow and tears. But Jiang clique was happy for they thought that their time has come to usurp the power. They did not allow people to mourn the death of Zhou, they forbade people to hold memorial ceremonies, to go to Tiananmen Square to express their mourning. But all their prohibition went to no avail. Defying their warning and suppression, people still held memorial ceremonies, went to Tiananmen Square and placed wreaths at the Monument to the People's Heroes.

On the day when remains of Zhou were to be cremated at the cemetery. Beijing residents lined up in the freezing cold along both sides of the boulevard from Beijing hospital to the cemetery to bid a final farewell to Zhou as the hearse of Premier Zhou passed by. Old and young alike tears filled their eyes. In all the other cities and countryside people were also spontaneous mourning Zhou with deep emotion.

On April 5, the Clean and Clear Festival, a time to sweep the graves and pay homage to the dead, more than one million people gathered at Tiananmen Square, where was decorated with thousands of wreaths and countless white flowers. The Monument to the People's Heroes was adorned with a great many poems and posters. While people mourned for the death of Zhou, they also expressed their exasperation to and protested against Jiang Qing and her followers. They wrote such poem to praise Zhou:

The spirit of our premier,

> The soul of our nation.
> Leave a fine reputation to posterity,
> Remain in our hearts forever.

They wrote such poem to accuse Jiang and her like:

> With grief we hear the ghosts cry out.
> While we weep the jackals and wolves laugh.
> Streaming tears we offer sacrifices to our hero.
> With our chins up we draw a sword out of its sheath.

They also shouted slogans, like "We will protect premier Zhou's fame with our blood and lives" "We are determined to knock down all the careerists and conspirators." When dusk sets in, the Square was still full of people and rife with activities. Jiang Qing watched the scene in the Great Hall of the People and was frightened. They reported to Chairman Mao and got his approval, they declared that this incident was one of a reactionary nature. At 11:00 pm that night, they sent militiamen, soldiers and policemen to detain people, arrest the suspicious "counterrevolutionaries" and drove everyone out of the Square. They loaded all the wreaths, white flowers and posters on two hundred trucks and drove away. The Square was cleaned.

The next day, April 6, people found all their wreaths and flowers were disappeared. They were angry and exasperated and asked the grabbers to return their wreaths to them. A conflict occurred between the people and the militiamen, soldiers and policemen. The people shouted slogans: "Down with those who oppose premier Shou!" "Return our wreaths and flowers!" "Release the people who are arrested!" Some people even directly condemned Jiang Qing. Many people sent new wreaths and white flowers to the Square and placed them around the Monument to the People's Heroes. The militiamen and policemen tried to drive the people out of the Square, but the hundreds of thousands of people just would not leave. The confrontation was sustained a whole day. Finally, at about ten o'clock that night the Jiang clique managed to send fifty thousand militiamen, three thousand policemen, and five battalions of the garrison troops into the Square, they drove the crowds to leave the Square with clubs, iron bars and the like. A great bloody suppression and struggle was carried out. Thousands of people were se-

A Painful Reminiscence of a Dignified Soul

riously wounded and many people were arrested. Jiang seemed to get a victory. But the people would never succumb to the suppression. As some people said: "Beloved premier Zhou, though the wreaths were disappeared in the Square, the wreaths for you are buried in our heart. Nobody can ever take them away. We will continue to struggle against those careerists."

Mao deemed the "April 5 incident" was stirred by Deng Xiaoping and dismissed Deng from all his posts in both the Party and the state on April 7, 1976.

Deng Xiaoping was purged a second time. The political situation of the country was in a great mess.

Only five months afterwards, on September 16, 1976, I suddenly heard a most shocking word that Chairman Mao died. I felt very strange. Yesterday all the media had still reported he was in good health, how could he be dead the next day! Was it a rumor? Yet all the people wore black armbands and the memorial meeting were held everywhere. I was convinced the news was a fact. I was extremely glad and gratified, the day I had long expected finally came. I could not set off fireworks to celebrate it, but I did buy a bottle of red wine and nice meal to celebrate it, though I had never drunk a drop of wine in my life. While I was walking on the street and saw all the people were voluntarily or forcibly worn black armbands on their arms, I felt it laughable for them to mourn a tyrant and a criminal. At the same time, I felt extremely proud for I was the single man who did not wear a black armband in public. My relatives warned me that it was dangerous not to wear it but I did not mind it. Sure enough, maybe some neighbor snitched on me, a policeman came to my home to interrogate me. He asked me sternly:

"Why didn't you wear a black armband? You are openly defying Chairman Mao!"

"I haven't a black armband. Everyone was issued a black armband by his unit. I have no unit, no one give me an armband." I answered quietly:

"You should buy one yourself. Why didn't you buy one?" He demanded.

"All stores had sold black cloth out. I could not buy one anywhere." I responded confidently, for newspaper had boasted that fact.

Finding there was nothing he could do about it, he warned me:

"Then you must stay at home, not go to the street."

"But I had to buy food, I could not live without eating a meal."

"Then you must go out as few as possible!" He had no alternative but to make some concession and left.

I was satisfied. In fact, I had a black armband which I had worn when premier

Zhou died. And I went out as often as usual.

With Mao Zedong's death, the Cultural Revolution was finally ended. What accomplishment was completed by the movement? A famous writer Qing Mu had such a comment: "This is really an unprecedented catastrophe. Millions of people endure great hardships. Millions of people die with deep resentment. How many families fall apart? How many books commit to fire? How many Scenic spots and historical sites are destroyed? How many graves of ancient sages are excavated? How many crimes are proceeded in the name of revolution?

Ye Jianying, the Minister of the Defense Ministry, revealed the number of the persecuted and the death in an enlarged Political Bureau Meeting: (1) 4,300 large-scare violent fights. The death toll is over 123,700; (2) 2.5 million cadres were denounced, over 302,700 cadres were illegal detention, over 115,500 cadres were abnormal death;(3) 4.81 million people in the city were labeled as all kinds of class enemies, and over 683,ooo among them were abnormal death; (4) in the country over 5.2 million landlords, rich peasants and their families were persecuted, and 1.2 million among them were abnormal death; (5) Over 113 million people were politically attacked in various degrees, and 557,000 among them could not be found, This is an official account, the actual number must be much larger than that.

Among the millions of victims there were many heroes and heroines who directly opposed the dictatorship and Mao bravely, such as:

Zhang Zhixin, a cadre of the propaganda bureau of Shenyang, Liaoning Province, was tortured and killed for daring to criticize Mao. She aired her view that "after the Great Leap Forward, Chairman Mao's scientific attitude grew weak, his sense of modesty diminished and his democratic style of work also weakened." She defended Liu Shaoqi, the president of PRC and Marshal Peng De Huai, who had been tortured to death. She criticized Mao's right-hand man, Lin Biao, accusing him of being an ultra-Leftist. She denounced the Small Cultural Revolution Leading Group. She also criticized Mao's wife, Jiang Qing, charging that she was ruining China's arts. She speaks her mind and she speaks the truth. Yet she was arrested on Sep. 18, 1969. She had been told that if she acknowledged her errors, she would likely remain a cadre, but she refused to recant. "You should not force me to deny what I think is right. It is impossible for me to surrender. It is better to live with honesty than with flattery. Whatever happens, I will remember that I am a Communist Party member and keep in mind the virtues of justice, truth and honesty." In prison She continued to write down her thoughts on toilet paper. She was

A Painful Reminiscence of a Dignified Soul

persecuted, tortured, and repeatedly raped by prison guards. In 1973, using the opportunity to criticize Lin Biao and Confucius, she said the real source of extreme leftism was Mao himself. Mao was responsible for what had happened at that time. She was accused of being an active counterrevolutionary and was sentenced to death in Feb. 1975. In preparation for the execution, the prison doctor slit Zhang's larynx so that she couldn't cry out her protest before dying. On the morning of April 4, 1975, she was paraded before her fellow inmates and then executed.

After the Cultural Revolution, Liaoning party secretary Ren Zhongyi declared her a "revolutionary martyr" She was posthumously rehabilitated. On March 31, 1979, the provincial paper published a long story "Devoting Her Life for the Truth" It received major nationwide publicity when Hu Yaobang authorized its republication in People's Daily.

Yu Luoke, a worker at the People's Machine Factory in Beijing, was a graduate of high school with excellent academic performance and character, but three times was not allowed to enter the university because of his bad family background—his father was a senior engineer, capitalist and was labeled as rightist. Under Mao's rule the bloodline theory prevailed and was practiced as a policy. The children of "five good classes" are to be trusted; while the children of the "five bad classes" are not trustworthy.

Yu Luoke was a bookworm, read extensively. He often wrote articles to criticize the "left" mistakes. At the beginning of the Cultural Revolution, the twenty-four-year-old Yu first published an article "the time to fight against mechanical materialism" against the article "The dismissal of Hai Rui", written by Wang Hongwen, a leader of the Cultural Revolution. In Oct. 1966, he wrote about 15,000-word article titled "On family background" criticizing the prevalent view that class characteristics run in families.

The article comments that the "five bad classes" often encountered unequal political treatment. They were "born criminals". Everyone's career hinges on his family background. Untold numbers of people died from such branding. The division of family had been a longstanding, widespread social problem. It involved not only the 5 percent of people designated as "five bad classes" but several times that number, including children of the bad classes.

The article argued that Since China is a backward country, the number of industrial workers before 1949 was only about 2 million, so that the number of proletarian families with the right pedigree is few. The enormous number of young people have a bad family background. They cannot join the army, enter university or hold important positions. Their "family background" decides everything in their lives. They become "sons of bitches" and the target of dictatorial government. It is injustice and cruelty. Anyone who is concerned with the destiny of the nation cannot ignore and fail to research this serious problem.

The article continued. The bloodline theory avers that the father has influence and his influence is above all else. In actuality, it is the opposite: social influence far exceeds family influence and family influence obeys social influence. From childhood a person enters the school, in which the word of the teacher is more authoritative than that of the parents, and the confluence of group education far exceeds that of private individual education; Instruction of leaders, messages of newspapers, books, literature, arts, customs and the work of cultivation all influence each individual. All these are called social influences, against which family influence cannot resist. The influence of society is much heavier than the influence of the family; One's worth is mainly lying on one's expression. Therefore, all revolutionary youth, no matter what their family background, must enjoy equal political treatment.

Yu's article was widely disseminated and had a huge impact. His bravery captured the hearts and minds of the youth.

Yu's article is all reasoning things out, not attacking the revolution, but this article was verdicted to be reactionary writing.

On Jan. 5, 1968 Yu was arrested by the police and On Mar 5. 1970 Yu was sentenced to death at the Beijing Workers Stadium and immediately executed. He was just 27 at that time.

On Nov. 21, 1979, the court ruled that Yu's condemnation as a counterrevolutionary and his executions had been a wrong interpretation of the law and should be corrected, and pronounced that Yu is innocent.

Lin Zhao joined an underground Communist cell at age 16 and wrote articles attacking brutality and corruption of the Nationalist Party. Three months before the founding of the PRA, she ran away from home in order to attend a journalism school run by the communists. In 1950, Lin was sent into rural areas to take part in the land reforms. In 1954 Lin enrolled at Beijing University to study literature and poetry. In Beijing University her quick wit and a strange incandescence attracted everyone. With the growing maturity in mentality and intelligence Lin began to question some views and policies of Mao Zedong and the Party. She be-

A Painful Reminiscence of a Dignified Soul

came a plainspoken criticizer during the Hundred Flowers Movement and was labeled a Rightist in 1958. She was suspended from her studies and punished to do menial work around the university.

Disillusioned with Mao and the party Lin became a prominent dissident. She continued her criticism, helped to publish an underground magazine and joined an underground student group. She was arrested In Oct. 1960 and detained for several years without trial. In prison she continued to criticize the party and Mao. She was subjected to the physical and emotional abuse, repeatedly beaten and tortured, handcuffed in painful positions for days on end, and forced to wear a tight rubber hood over her entire face with narrow slits for the eyes and mouth to prevent her outspoken criticisms. She wrote hundreds of thousands of words of prose, poetry, letters, notes, petitioning for democracy, freedom, civil reform, and the end of one-party dictatorship. Her writings vehemently criticized Mao; openly marked Mao as a big rotten egg, alone in those horrible times. She indicted the party for tragically misleading a generation of young idealists. She thought that we should embrace universal human values, join the mainstream of civilized nations. After jailer took away her pen she wrote with her blood. She pricked her flesh with a bamboo pick or hair clip, held blood in a spoon, then dipped a hairpin or a straw in the blood and wrote her words on her clothes or on white cloth torn from her bed sheets. She had a staunch will and stood firm on her beliefs. Even when her mother advised her to keep silence, she responded "Better to be destroyed than give up my principle." 1965 Lin was sentenced to 20 years' imprisonment.

During the CR the old sentence was converted to the death penalty for "serious crimes", which included: "1. insanely attacking, cursing and slandering our great CCP and our great leader Chairman Mao. 2. Regarding the proletarian dictatorship and socialist system with extreme hostility and hatred. 3. Publicly shouting reactionary slogans, disrupting prison order, instigating other prisoners to rebel and broadcasting threats to take revenge on behalf of executed counterrevolutionary criminals. 4. Persistently maintaining a reactionary stand, refusing to admit her crimes, resisting discipline and education, and defying reform." After Lin's final trial, she wrote: "This is an extremely reprehensible and shameful judgment...but just watch! The court of history will proclaim a verdict for future generations." She was executed in April 29, 1968. Lin's family was not made aware of her death until a Communist Party official approached her mother to collect a five-cent fee for the bullet used to kill her.

Lin's death caused me great grief. I admire her very much I also feel ashamed of myself extremely. My early life is similar to hers. Both of us took part in the revolution and joined the party fervently around 1949. Both of us criticized the party and were labeled rightist in 1957. Yet she is so brave and I am so cowardly. She is the quintessence of heroism; she lives a life with great aesthetic and moral value. She is a small young woman physically, but a giant soul spiritually.

In 1981, Lin was officially exonerated of her crimes and rehabilitated. Despite her rehabilitation, the Chinese government still not allow commemoration or discussion on Lin's life and writings. Many activists who attempted to visit Lin's grave were detained by government security officials.

Ding Zhuxiao and Li Qishun are two girl students who wrote a letter to the Revolutionary Committee, opposing the "Three loyalties" They wrote that "Our royalty is to the people, to the motherland, and to truth." For this "crime" they were executed at the age of 24 and 23.

These heroes and heroines bring about their own death with great fortitude; their bravery and firm faith will have stirred the heart of every Chinese. They are so simple, so pure. and sacrificed her young life in the pursuit of democracy and truth. Their death is their triumph. Their spirit will remain immortal. No lapse of time, no distance of space will cause their names to be forgotten and their sacrifices commonplace.

I had anticipated that after Mao's death, something important would certainly happen. As expected, only about one month after Mao's death, Hua Guofeng, Mao's appointed successor, felt threatened by the Gang of Four and arrested them with the support of marshal Ye Jianying and other members of the Politburo,

By the end of that year, I took the family leave to go to Fuling to visit my family with a light mind. We had a very happy days and were more confident that we could achieve our goal at last. One month later I went back to Zhenjiang.

On the train I got acquainted with a passenger named Wang Quangming. He sat by me in the same bench of the compartment. He was also returning to his working unit after visiting his family in Sichuan province. He was a cadre of Jiangsu Provincial government and now was doing manual labor at the May Seventh Cadre School in the countryside. He was quite talkative and sociable and had an open, warm heart, we often talked during the over thirty hours long journey. I told him frankly of my political affairs, including that I had been labeled a rightist. He did not disdain me and showed sympathy and respect of me. We found congenial with each other and had many common ideas and opinions and soon became good friends. We exchanged our name and address and promised to keep in contact afterwards. He assured me that he would help me to find a job. I thanked him heartily for his concern. When the train arrived in Nanjing, the capital of Jiangsu province, we got off the train and went to each other's destination.

Not long afterwards I received a letter from Wang Quangming. He told me that there was a junior high school attached to the May Seventh Cadre School, which needed an English teacher now, and asked me whether I would like to take that job. I was horribly delighted. At that time, I would like to take any job, and now I could have a job embracing my profession so quickly. It was beyond all my expectations. I replayed Wang's letter immediately, telling him I am happy to take that job and thank him profusely.

That school was located in a village called Qiaotou, about twenty minutes train ride to my native city Zhengjiang where I lived. It was very convenient to me. I began to pack my things and made all the preparations for the new job. Then I was waiting at home leisurely for the day school begins.

I moved to Qiaotou a few days before the school began. Contrary to my anticipation, the May Seventh Cadre School was not in a backward countryside, it nestles on a wide gentle hill slope surrounded by fields and was composed of many western buildings and apartments, which was formerly owned by foreign officers and residents that were driven out of China after the founding of the People's Republic of China. Usually the May seventh Cadre Schools were laid in remote, poor hinterlands, why this one was established in such a fine place? I wondered. A veteran cadre laughed at my innocence. He told me that "This cadre school was set for the province-level cadres themselves. The central committee of the party ordered us to build a cadre school for ourselves to remold our thought, we could not violate the order. but we had the privilege to choose the site of the school. Who would like to suffer themselves? This was called 'While the higher authorities have policies, the localities have their countermeasures'. I laughed too. It was good for me either. I lived in a comfortable two-story apartment of American architectural style. I was simply teaching English there, no need to work in the fields. In fact, even the "students" of the cadre school rarely did the farm work now. Mao Zedong had died four or five months, though the Cadre School was not disbanded right away, every "student" there was confident that the Cadre School would be dissolved early or later. They were just waiting that day to return to Nanjing, Wang Guangming and I still often met each other and had pleasant talks. He also promised me that after returning Nanjing he would help me and my wife to find a job there. I was glad that I was winning a devoted friend.

After I worked at the May Seventh Cadre school for about one year, I suddenly received a letter from an old colleague in the Youth Publishing House named Zheng Yanhui by the end of 1977. She informed me: "During the great cultural revolution, many editors were persecuted or transferred to other places and the Youth Publishing House was closed. All the editors and the office workers were sent down to the countryside to do manual work. After Mao Zedong's death, some policies were changed and they were called back to Beijing. The Youth publishing house resumed its work. As it had lost so many editors during the cultural revolution, it gravely lacked the qualified editors now." She asked me if I would like to return to the Youth Publishing House.

I was quite surprised by the letter. I had been expelled by the Youth Publishing House, and now it has asked me to come back. Was it true? I wrote back to Zheng Yanhui, asking her if it was the authority's idea or but her idea. She gave me a positive answer and told me the chief leader of the Publishing House had changed. The new leader was an enlightened female cadre. Considering edition was my old profession, I decided to quit the teaching job at the May Seven Cadre School and went back to the Publishing House. Wang Guangming and the leaders of the school understood my mind and situation, they congratulated on my new opportunity and I went back to Beijing in the early 1978.

Then I was working at the Youth Publishing House again. But as my cadre status was not yet resumed and my registered residence was not transferred to Beijing, I was not a regular member of the publishing House. The leader of the Publishing House went to the Organization Department of Beijing to apply for the transfer of all my family's registered residence, but the Organization Department replied that as the population of Beijing was too crowded, it could only approve the transference of my registered residence and refused the transference of my family's. Now I had to decide whether I was willing to return to Beijing alone and leave my family in Fuling.

I did not make the decision right away, for I was waiting for another opportunity. My friend Wang Guangming had been trying to find a job for my wife in Nanjing all the time. And my wife had a classmate Zhang Pingyi working at the tumor

A Painful Reminiscence of a Dignified Soul

hospital in Nanjing. She also promised to find a job for my wife. If they could get a job for my wife, I would prefer to return to Nanjing to reunite with them, for though I liked to do editorial work in the capital of our country, I did not want to be separated from my family for a long time.

During my stay in Beijing many significant things happened in China. Hua Guofeng, in order to vindicate his legitimacy for his position, stressed that "We must exercise whatever policies and whatever instructions set by Mao to the full extent." On the other hand, after Deng Xiaoping resumed his position as Premier of the State Council and Vice-Chairman of the CCP, he began to challenge Hua's legitimacy and gained greater power. He wrote an essay titled "The 'Two Whatevers' does not accord with Marxism". At the same time, under the support of Deng Xiaoping, Hu Yaobang, then the Minister of the Ministry of publicity, started a huge discussion movement on the article titled "Practice is the sole criterion in judging truth" published in Light Daily. The article negated the "Two Whatevers" as the fundamental theory, marked the key difference between Deng and Hua. The discussion movement shook off the bonds of the grave dogmatism and greatly pushed forward the development of ideological emancipation. Posters began to appear in the streets.

In western part of Beijing there is a place called Xidan, on the north sidewalk of the street there is a bus stop for several routes of buses. By the bus stop is a gray wall about 200 meters long and two meters high. As it was a really bustling, living place with endless flow of people, many people put up "big character poster" on the wall to attract great attention. The content of the posters on the wall varied greatly, from the appeals of those who had been persecuted, to all the criticisms, proposals, exposures of evildoers and scandals; Some people aired their views about the political and social issues of China, others demanded the purging of the poisonous remnants of dictatorship, called for democracy, and still more big-character posters demanded freedom of expression and publication. This wall caused a sensation in Beijing, thousands upon thousands of people were flocking to the Xidan Wall. Very soon the wall was well known as "Xidan Democracy Wall". In the latter stages it was mainly political commentary. Within this, the most discussed topics were democracy and law, advocating unofficial and democratic publishing, demanding freedom of speech, publicly evaluating Mao's merits and failings. The posters took many forms—poetry and stories, conversations, open letters. Some were signed with real names, others with pen-names, others were still completely anonymous. Some young people spontaneous formed non-official groups and produced publications. As more and more people came to read and put posters, the Xidan Democracy Wall soon attracted great attention of the leaders of the party. some supported it, some opposed it.

As most of the big character posters at that time were criticizing Jiang Qing clique, Mao Zedong, and Hua Guofeng, Deng Xiaoping was supporting the Democracy Wall movement, for it helped to strengthen his position. He had publicly praised Xidan Democracy wall. At a meeting with the Japanese delegates of the Democratic Socialist Party Deng said: "Writing big-character posters is permitted by our country's constitution. We have no right to deny or criticize the masses for carrying democracy forward by putting these posters. If the masses are angry, let them release their anger. The masses' comments are not all deeply thought-out, but we cannot demand complete correctness, and this is nothing to be afraid of." Following this, in a speech during Third Plenum of the Eleventh Central Committee, Deng reiterated, "The masses should be permitted to put forward opinions. Even if there are some harboring grievances who want to use democracy to stir up trouble, that is still nothing to be afraid of. we should deal with it appropriately in the belief that the great majority of the masses can judge right from wrong" He also warned: "A revolutionary party is one that is afraid of not hearing different voices. it is silence that is most to be feared." Marshal Ye Jianying also spoke highly of wall. He said The Third Plenum is a model of internal party democracy; the wall is a model of people's democracy." Under approval or acquiescence of the government, more and more people gathering in Democracy Wall and put posters there. Some people published unofficial journals, such as "Exploration", "Enlightenment", "Beijing Spring", "The Forum of April Fifth". Some activist characters even held demonstrations. There were bigger and bigger spontaneous gatherings. The movement was flourishing.

Apart from the posters there emerged a new genre of Chinese literature which was popularly called the "Scar Literature" or "trauma Literature" Which depicted the tragic experience and spiritual wound brought to people by the Cultural Revolution and the former cruel campaigns under Mao's rule. Those articles and novels were full of painful, depressing or horrific reminiscence of the cadres, intellectuals and students who had been persecuted, tortured, insulted, humiliated or exiled to the countryside. The true mood of those sufferers had been suppressed for many years, now that the present leaders gave the opportunities for public expression,

A Painful Reminiscence of a Dignified Soul

they vented their long pent-up emotions, telling out their sufferings and accusing the cruelty, hypocrisy of the officials and the wrong policies in public. The descriptions in those works were resonated with a large republic, attracting and touching millions of readers. But they also came under attack by the Leftists, who denounced them to be attacking the Communist Party and Chairman Mao, and exposing the negative aspects of the society.

Such phenomenon and situation gave me a gleam of hope: Maybe China will move toward democracy. Of course, I was not so simple as those young people. I was already fifty-two-year-old and I had witnessed many evils the party had done. I didn't have much faith in the party. I had not taken reckless action. Yet inspired by the enthusiasm of the writers of the posters and goaded by my responsibilities for the country, I went to the Beijing Library to collect some material and wrote a few anonymous small character posters put on the "Xidan Democracy Wall". My first article is:

One Party Dictatorship must be ended.
Dictatorship is a bad form of government. Absolute power is concentrated in a person who practices an autocratic rule. It destroys the elementary rights of the individuals and undermined the principle of liberty. And Mao's "One party dictatorship" is different from and much worse than the past dictatorship. All the former dictatorship had one dictator (king, emperor or monarchy) in the central government. In Mao's "one party dictatorship", while Mao Zedong, the first secretary of the central party, is the paramount dictator of the country, all the first party secretary of all the units, including all levels of government, mass organizations, factories, shops, schools, hospitals, residents' committees, etc. are big or small dictators with absolute power in their jurisdictions. Chinese people's lives, thoughts, actions are strictly controlled, supervised and suppressed by all levels' dictators so their sufferings, agonies, twinges, anguish, traumas are much greater than any other people under the autocratic rule. Of all forms of arrant autocratic control, this one-party dictatorship appears to have been the cruelest, hypocritical, execrable and demanding.

Under Mao's dictatorship, our country is infested with conflicts, struggles, violence, terror and extremism. Any different views from the party are forbidden. The recalcitrant and outspoken are singled out for vitriolic attack. Men of the most worth have been condemned and banished without a hearing. Sensible, pragmatic cadres have been treated as enemies. In order to eliminate his opponents Mao launches one campaign after another and each greater and extraordinary than the last. Maoist struggle session is like a kangaroo court. guilt is a foregone conclusion. Makeshift jail is set up every unit. Arbitrary torturing, random jailing, forced suicides are common, and execution takes place without any legal proceedings. All the suppression and evil doings caused at least thirty million abnormal deaths. All laws and regulations were trampled underfoot to pander to one single man's whims. Every single aspect of one's social life was supervised by the party. The atmosphere of cruelty and the pathetic sense of being hopeless hang over the whole country. To be revolutionary meant being aggressive and militant. Violence is the bedrock of the dictatorship.

Mao's dictatorship fools the people. It controls all the media and publications. The publicists use all their effort, all their energy, all their skills to produce lies, big words, braggadocios, empty promises and malicious slandering. Our perception and conception are limited to information that filtered out from the sensors. We cannot do things of our own volition. We are not allowed to seek and have a true, clear look of the past and present. Many felonies and evil doctrines have crept into the very habit of our thinking and of our lives. Dictatorship impairs the interest, dignity, honor of the people, spells the destruction of human thought and character, dismantles our spirit wholesale.

Mao's dictatorship destroys civilization. Gentleness, kindness, courtesy, dignity, humanity and self-esteem are insulted; cunning, intrigue, toadying, scheming are regarded as intelligent. It breeds the bullies, who flatter their superiors while abuse their subordinates; it instigates the opportunists, who try their best to ferret more and more "alien class enemies" so as to get political credit and gain rewards. People are forced to lie, brag, boast, slander. Teenagers are cheated to burn valuable books, destroy relics. Dulled conscience, cruelty, irresponsibility, and ruthless self-interest are rampant.

Mao's dictatorship spawned corruption. Giving, accepting or demanding brides; making appointments by favoritism; buying or selling access to offices; making fake medicine, fake wine, or counterfeit money; going through the back door are pervasive. Authority becomes a ticket to lucre and lust. All the lucrative posts have been known as the province of party elite's offspring. The special stores where brimming with high-quality, low priced merchandise, which were unavailable in local shops. The so-called "public ownership" was in practice nothing but a continuous flow of public resources into the private pockets of the power-holders. "Absolute power corrupts absolutely."

To continue the long trend of one-party dictatorship is to guarantee tremendous social, cultural, political and economic upheavals. We must put an end to that cruel, vicious system.

Later I wrote another article:

Morality Must Be Restored

Under Mao's rule, China's time-honored culture is almost extinct. There is a general and universal degradation of morality. Hypocrisy, chicanery, anarchy, intrigue scheme, deceit are pervasive all over the country. Many officials abuse their power, seek their own profit in public affairs and prostitute their honor for self-interest and power. Numerous leftists and opportunists frame up and persecute innocents. The lack of shame rendered rampant of all evils. Spiritual vacancy leads to a conviction crisis among the youth; the downheartedness, despondence, decadence, cynicism, nihilism, self-centered mentality permeates their life. The violation of the human conscience is commonplace.

Morality is a guide to lead life in the right direction. Both Chinese and western ancient philosophers stress the importance of morality and virtues. Confucius gives the first priority to the cultivation of the morality of men and inculcates people with the distaste for material gains. Socrates, a classical Athenian philosopher who is credited as one of the founders of western philosophy and as being the first moral philosopher of the western ethical tradition of thought, believes that intellectual virtues are the most valuable of all possessions, One must concentrate more on self-development than on material things. He preferred death for the sake of truth. When he is sentenced a death penalty, he solicits the judge to teach his children after his death: "If they seem to care about riches, or anything, more than about virtue, then reprove them." He sees "truth" is the foundation of morality.

Morality is not a mere individual's thing, it involves and relates to the harmony of the family, the stability of society and the survival of the nation. As far as 2,700 years age, Guan Zhong, a Chinese philosopher and chancellor, writes "Propriety, righteousness, honesty and a sense of shame are the Four Moral Principles of the country. If the Four principles are not spread, the country is perished." This teaching was observed for over two thousand years until the present time. When I was in high school, the government still promoted the four principles, only the Communist Party criticized them as feudal morality.

Washington, the founder of America, writes: "The foundation of our national policy will be laid in the pure and immutable principles of private morality" All the following governments paid great attention to private morality and fight against the immoral ideas and conducts. In the early years of 1930s America tumbled into the Great Depression, President Franklin Roosevelt decided that the Depression was not from the failure of substance but from bad morality—the rulers of the exchange of goods and the money changers abused their power and betrayed for profit the elementary decencies of life. He bravely challenged and beat them, undermined and abandoned the old admiration of worldly success, and moved the country toward an era of good feeling and good will. After successfully overcoming the crisis he proclaimed "I am justified in believing that the greatest change we have witnessed has been the change in the moral climate of America."

From all these facts we can see that only on the eternal basis of morality a normal, rational state can be established.

Degradation of morality is the root of the evils and crimes. We are facing this crisis now. To a crisis of spirit, we need an answer of the spirit. We must restore morality and place the highest value on the sound morality. The prevention and elimination of evil and crime is primarily based on morality and only secondly on institutions such as courts and police. The best moral sanction is that of conscience; the worst is the fear of punishment or going to hell. Shame, not guilt, is the primary force refraining people's behavior. Let us earnestly cultivate the old universal precious truths again— honesty, justice, kindness, love, pity, honor and courage; let us exercise forbearance, compromise, concession, gratitude; remove apathy, vanity, envy, prejudice from our heart; Let us pick our moral ethics anytime.

Not long after that I wrote a third article:

On Democracy

Democracy is the dream of human beings since the dawn of civilization.

Democracy is a historical trend and a universal value. The term "democracy" first appeared in Ancient Greek. Athenians established the first democracy in 508-507 BC. Democracy in its original sense means rule by the majority. A famous Greece historian Thucydides made a vivid description of its government: "Its administration favors the many instead of the few; this is why it is called a democracy. If we look to the laws, they afford equal justice to all in their private differences;

if to social standing, advancement in public life falls to reputation for capacity, class considerations not being allowed to interfere with merit; nor again does poverty bar the ways; If a man is able to serve the state, he is not hindered by the obscurity of his condition. The freedom which we enjoy in our government extends also to our ordinary life." It stresses legal equality, political freedom and the rule of law. Athens voting was normally by a show of hands or by ballots. They use bean or stone as ballot. Archaeologist had already excavated earthen vat for casting a ballot and the stone plate for recording the result of the voting. They used ballot to elect or remove official, to decide to go to war or to hold a negotiation, to levy taxes or not.

The Roman Republic was established in 509 BC. They believed that people should possess the right to manage and administer it. The most important right was the right to suffrage: "No one was deprived of the suffrage" except women, foreigners and slaves. And everyone was equally entitled to vote. The powers of sovereignty were entrusted to an elected representative. The Roman Republic was the first government in the world to have a Republic as a nation, and contributed significantly to many aspects of democracy. The Roman model of governance inspired many political thinkers over the centuries.

On the influence of the ancient ideology, the Charter "Magna Carta" was made in 1215 AD. Its main content is the protection of ancient personal liberties, promoting freedom of the individual against the arbitrary authority of the despot."

Greatly influenced by the "Magna Carta", Washington led the independent movement of America and in the Declaration of Independence, it proclaims that "we hold these truths to be self-evident: that all men are created equal and we are endowed with the unalienable right—Life, Liberty and the Pursuit of Happiness."

Today most democratic countries have imitated the Rome model and formed a republic government by the whole population.

The process of democracy was not smooth, it was repeatedly interrupted by the careerists, oppressors or dictators. They exercise autocracy and the arbitrary power to control the people. Yet after centuries of slavery, feudalism, theocracy, monarchism, and Fascism, they were eventually abolished or defeated. The historical trend proves that democracy has rendered more necessities and satisfaction for mankind and has more conformed to human nature. It is considered to be more desirable and welcomed by most people of the world. It is the right path we should take.

(2) The most important characteristics of democracy are liberty, equality, and

human rights.

Liberty is the inborn, perpetuated hope and the earnest longing of human beings. Liberty is self-government. Each man should be his own man, do things of his own will, decide his own destiny and not confined, determined by state or leaders. Naturally everyone wants to speak and act freely. Of course, freedom does not mean one can do whatever one likes. Freedom asks more than it gives, it demands one to have high sense of obligation and responsibility, to be a man of virtue, to do the right things, not evil things, to care about and respect others, to abide by reasonable rules and just laws. In entering into society individuals have to give up a share of liberty to protect the rest. Liberty is the most powerful, most enduring and toughest force in the world. Only liberty can allow people the moral and intellectual satisfaction, can unleash the energy, talent, genius of individual to the greatest extent, and create an infinite progress to improve human life. Only freedom can eliminate hatred, resentment, enmity and hostility and create harmony, tolerance and peace. And only freedom can expose the guises, crimes of tyrants and supply people courage and vitality to protest and fight against the oppressors. Pople's freedom and dignity are the strongest and toughest forces in the world. Without liberty there is no justice and equality.

In a democracy, people have Civil Rights of life, liberty and property. They have the freedom of speech, expression, belief, press, assembly, association and migration. They also have the freedom to strike, to demonstrate, to protest. Democracy is the best corrective mechanism which can check upon the administration of the government, eliminating corruption and intrigue, minimizing mistakes and wrong doings, and mitigate the danger of excess. The exercise of state power must be authorized by the people, thus avoiding violence in the changing of government and preventing the rule by cruel and vicious dictators. All these rights of the people are inherent with birth, not bestowed by a state or a leader. State or leader have no right to deprive or limit people's rights. Franklin Roosevelt said: "Freedom means the supremacy of human rights everywhere."

In a democracy, All the people have equal rights and equal standing in the society regardless of background, race, color, religion, sex, occupation, economic condition or political beliefs. Every person is equal in employment, public education, public accommodation and jury system. Any discrimination among the people and the segregation between races are prohibited. Democracy advocates Civil Rights for all and special privileges for none. Privilege is an execrable test of value, only by rejecting the privilege one can act justly, loftily. In a democracy, everybody has a say, not only the autocrat. No one is destined to be a master and no one to be a slave. Equality and liberty are the basis of civilization.

"Science and democracy together offer an ever-richer life and ever-larger satisfaction to the individual" (Franklin Roosevelt)

The features of democracy mentioned above show that democracy is superior to any other form of government. It is more humane, more advanced than any other social system.

(3) Unfortunately, we are now living under the despotic rule. we cannot say or do things at our own will. we cannot participate in political affairs and cannot criticize the mistake or wrong-doing of the Party. Any outspoken word would entail dangers. With the least complaint you were accused of blasphemy against the party. With the slightest deviation from Mao's word you were labeled counterrevolutionary. All Chinese people lay in thrall to the will of an emperor. All our rights and dignity is deprived by the party and the government.

We are taught that we must obey leaders absolutely. We are exhorted to emulate the simple screw, willing to be placed wherever the party needs us. We are not citizens, but Party's tools. As the suppressions are so severe and the punishment so cruel, most people endure the servitude and sufferings with a startling passivity.

Yet, we are not oxen or horses, nor inanimate things. we are human beings. Being a man, we must define what it means to be a human being; Every human being has his own rights, dignity, honor, ideas and feelings, we should stand upright, not succumb to oppressors. Furthermore, every human being is a social being who has an obligation and responsibility for himself and for others, and has a stake in the fate and future of his country and world peace. To restore our rights and for the benefit of the country, we should not tolerate the oppression any longer, we need the practice of democracy.

"Democracy is never a given delicious meal. Freedom is never voluntarily given by the oppressor; it must be demanded by the oppressed." (Martin Luther King). We must fight to earn the cause of democracy. The fighting is tough, arduous for the dictator and oppressors will never give up their power and prestige, they will suppress the people by all means, and torturing, killing are always their final argument to resort so we must have courage, patience, confidence and determination.

We can take various methods and forms to wage the fighting. At present, while the control relaxes a little, we can widely, openly put up posters anywhere, criticize the wrongs of the party and government at the meeting, promote democracy and hold demonstration. Even if the party tightened the control again, we should continue to do those right things secretly or so do bravely, openly for democracy.

Another important thing is that we must not help the party to suppress the people. We can refuse to criticize, persecute the innocent or expose others' so-called crimes.

In all the campaigns, there were millions of people, including many young students, wittingly or unwittingly help Mao do evils. Some Jackals even deliberately hold a candle to the devil. It is a terrible pity thing. And the cause of such miserable thing is the lack of democracy. We must take the lessons and never replay that thing.

Without democracy, China had no future. All of the people must be roused to take part in the cause. This is no time for any person to withdraw into some ivory tower and disregard the problem of the society and the agonies of the people.

In our struggle there will be full of twists and turns. We must consecrate all our mind, our energy, strength, knowledge and wisdom to reach our goal. We mustn't lose our heart and move forward constantly and consistently toward the ideal of the realization of democracy.

After I wrote those articles, I felt a little relieved. Though I am old and powerless I have done a bit for the country after all.

Except this new atmosphere, there was another important thing happened in 1978. Hu Yaobang, then the Ministry of the Organization Department of the Party, set off a movement to rehabilitate those wrongly purged cadres of all levels, setting free great numbers of them and reinstating them in their former offices. Afterwards Hu began leading a movement to rid of the labels of all the rightists in the country, five hundred and fifty thousand altogether. These movements were confronted by the leftists, so they were not going smoothly. Hu Yaobang, as the former secretary of the Communist Youth League, specially called the present leader of the League, saying "As the former secretary of the Youth League, I was responsible for wrongly delimiting so many rightists in the youth League. I hope you to correct the mistake as soon as possible. Thanks!". With the urge of Hu, soon afterwards Hu Qili, the present secretary of the Youth League, called all the rightists of the Central League in Beijing to the office by the end of 1978. I went there of course. In the meeting he formally declared the rehabilitation of our cases. Our salary and the membership

A Painful Reminiscence of a Dignified Soul

of the party were restored, but all our mental and material losses of the past twenty-two years could not be compensated.

The atmosphere of the meeting was harmonious. Hu Qili's manner was genuine and earnest. He made a sincere apology to us on behalf of the Central League. Some of us expressed their views and feelings. A writer Liu Shaotang said that he deeply thanked the Party which rescued him and gave him a new chance to turn over a new leaf. I did not like his speech. It seemed that he was currying favor with the Party, that he admitted he had made a great mistake and now the Party excused him. I looked down on such a character. My friend Liu Bingyan, the most famous correspondent at that time, also made a speech. He did not complain about his long terrible suffering in the Great Northern Wilderness, he did not thank the party, he only said: "Now we the five hundred and fifty thousand labeled rightists are formally rehabilitated. But there are equal or a greater number of quasi-rightists, who are not formally labeled as rightist, are still under surveillance all the time. This problem must be solved." I quite appreciated his word. While his own problem is solved, he still cares about other victims and appealed the emancipation of them. I did not air my view at the meeting, I just praised Hu Yaobang who was in charge of the work of rehabilitation of the rightist. I said: "I heard that Hu Yaobang had urged the Youth League to accomplish the work of rehabilitation before the Lunar New Year, so that they can have a real happy New year. I thank for his care and admire his enlightenment." The meeting was ended pleasantly.

While I was glad to be rehabilitated, I was greatly sad that my former leader Liu Zhong, the chief editor of the magazine "High school Student", could not attend the meeting. After we returned from the countryside to Beijing, Liu Zhong was unfortunately transferred to Changzhi Normal School in Shanxi Province. During the Cultural Revolution he was again persecuted, paraded and held in custody as a rightist by his students and rebels. Unable to bear the humiliation and tortures he fled the inhuman circumstances. Afterwards there had been no news whatsoever about him. His son and editor Huang Yi, Liu's loyal subordinate, tried all possible means to enquire about Liu's whereabouts, going to his native home Huangyan, his former workplace Shanghai, and visiting all his friends and relatives, but found no results. Some people said that they had seen Liu in his native land and Shanghai at the first stage of the cultural revolution and never saw him later. After the movement to rehabilitate the wrongly purged cadres and rightists made public to the country, we hoped that if Liu had hidden somewhere he would come back to receive the rehabilitation, but he still hadn't appeared anywhere. We had to presume that he had already gone to Heaven. He must have found no place to stay and left this ruthless world. He might jump into the sea near his native land or dropped himself in the Huangpu river in Shanghai. I feel deeply grieved with his passing away. I respect him. He is one of the path breakers in the field of children's literature of China. He has written 17 children's books with various types, including fairy stories, myth tales, dramas. Through these readings he carries out character education of the children. He is diligent in his editorial work and always works with scrupulous precision. He joined the Communist Party in 1947. Whenever I think of him, his careless clothed and bend down figure appear before my eyes. I lament the loss of an earnest writer and editor for our country.

At the beginning of 1979, one year after I was working in Beijing, I finally got good news from Nanjing. After having done a great deal of work Zhang Pingyi finally found a job for my wife at the Department of Public Health of Jiangsu Province. I was excited. Now I had to decide whether I should work in Beijing or go to Nanjing. I love Beijing and editorial work, but I love my family greater still. I decided to go to Nanjing.

My wife and daughters arrived in Nanjing in March, 1969. We were reunited again. For this reunion I had undergone six years of arduous exertion and numerous agonies, suffering from innumerable painful disappointment and sleepless nights, bearing countless untold weariness, anger, anxiety, frustration. Now my goal was finally reached. It was not an easy gain. I hoped my long miserable life ended here and a happy, peaceful existence would be permanent. But who can make sure of one's expectation? Fortune does exist, yet misfortune can also creep in anytime.

We had no house in Nanjing and my wife's unit could not provide dormitory, we had to stay at a hotel first. Then we sought to rent a house or a room. At that time almost every family only had narrow housing, no spare room to rent. There was no rent advertisement in the newspaper. We wandered about the street to look for the rent poster. We could not find a single rent poster. Finally, my friend Wang Guangming begged a friend to share a room for us. We moved from the hotel to that room. We purchased some furniture and articles of necessity for everyday life, and had our daughters enrolled in schools

After everything was settled down, my wife reported for duty at the Department of Public Health of Jiangsu Province. She didn't really like her job. She preferred to work as a doctor in a hospital, enjoying the satisfaction of curing patients instead of doing administrative work. I consoled her: "It was not easy to get a job for you in Nanjing. You can work here for the time being, maybe you can find a job in a hospital in the future." she responded: "I understood. I would concentrate my mind on my work. I would not let down my classmate Zhang Pingyi."

I began to look for a job for myself. My close friends Zhou Shacheng had an old friend who was the general editor of the People's publishing House of Jiangsu province. Zhou recommended me to him and he assigned me to work at the editorial department of the magazine Translation Garden.

In 1979 the political climate became chill significantly. Before that time, Deng Xiaoping, who was then still tussling to ensure his supremacy in the party, called people to "use your brains and liberate your thinking" to shake yourselves free of the Maoist line of the cultural revolution, to criticize Hua Guofeng's "two whatevers" He encouraged and supported the Xidan Democracy Wall and demonstration. He even went so far as to call on Jimmy Carter, the president of America then, that he supported the cause of human rights in China. But once his major rival Hua Guofeng had been at a disadvantage position, and the democratic movement strode forward, there appeared posters and articles criticizing Deng himself, he changed his bearing, betrayed his own word, and opposed the Xidan Democratic Wall. He began to wind down the publication of the posters and the "scar literature". He promoted four modernizations: "modernization in industry, modernization in agriculture, modernization in science and technology, and modernization in defense". A big character poster on Xidan Wall called for adding "The Fifth Modernization, Democracy and Others". Another poster was even more sharp-pointed: "Do we want democracy or a new dictatorship?" These articles enraged Deng. Not long after, Deng brought an end to the democracy wall and authorized the arrest of dozens of poster writers and editors of magazines who advocated democracy.

On March 30, 1979 Deng issued "The Four Cardinal Principles":

1. We must keep to the socialist road.
2. We must uphold the dictatorship of the proletariat.
3. We must uphold the leadership of the Communist Party.
4. We must uphold Marxism-Leninism and Mao Zedong Thought.

The Four Cardinal Principles soon sealed all channels of free speech and free expression. The bud of Democracy was nipped.

Different from Deng's ideas, Hu Yaobang had his own view about the democracy wall. He said: "It is the heartfelt voice of the people; I support anyone exercising their democratic rights under a socialist system. I hope everyone can enjoy the greatest freedom under the protection of the constitution. Despite the numerous comrades criticized me during the Central Work Conference and this people's congress, saying I was going behind the central government's back supporting a so-called democratization movement that violated the four modernization, and encouraging anarchy. Despite all that I still maintain my views." Regarding the arrest of the author of "adding the fifth modernization" Wei Jingsheng he said: "I respectfully suggest that comrades do not arrest people who engage in the democratic movement, still less those who merely show concern. Those who are brave enough to raise these problems, I fear, will not be put off by being thrown in jail. Wei Jingsheng has been held for more than three months, and if he dies, he will become a martyr of the masses, a martyr in the hearts of all." But Deng was the supreme leader of the country, Hu could not carry out his correct line.

In the early 1980, one year after our reunion, my wife found there was blood streak in her nasal mucus. At first, she did not pay much attention to it, thinking that it might be injured by her finger when she cleaned her nose. But when it appeared frequently, she began to feel uneasy. One day she decided to go to the hospital.

When I came home that evening, I noticed my wife sitting on a chair in our bed room brooding something with a pale face. I went to her and asked her what the doctor said. After keeping silent for a while, she reluctantly said with a wry smile; "Nothing serious wrong. It is only a slight wound." The smile was obviously unnatural. I felt nervous and I begged her to tell me the truth. She still kept silent. I held her hand and exclaimed: "No matter what happened we could deal with it all right. Tell me the truth, don't hide it." Suddenly she burst into a wild cry and could not speak. I stroked her shoulder tenderly and waited patiently for her composedness. I was conscious of the gravity of the matter. After a decent interval she finally confessed and said: "I have got a nasopharyngeal cancer." I was also shocked by her word; it was quite a bolt from the blue. But at once I forced myself composed, knowing that I mustn't fright her any more with my expression. I said: "As a proverb says 'Take unpleasant things calmly, now that they are here'. Worry helps nothing. You should have confidence that your illness can be cured. Let us forget it. I know you still haven't prepared supper. You need not make it tonight.

we can go out to have a nice meal." Since she also had no mood to make dinner she agreed. We took our children to set out. They were delighted and laughed to have a feast tonight. My wife held her youngest five-year-old daughter's hand, making a bitter smile. She must feel sad that she would leave them very soon and they did not know at all. We had a dinner with quite contrary mood: Our daughters were highly excited while the other two smiled with secretly misery.

At night My wife could not sleep, I mollified her but I knew how weak was my word at this moment. I talked no more, just asking her to go to sleep calmly and pretending to sleep myself. In fact, I could not sleep too. This was really an unexpected blow. I was seized by a horror: She would leave me soon! I would see her no more in a few years! the dearest of mine, the closest of mine, the heart and soul of mine. Can I bear it? I fell into a passion and tears welled up in my eyes. Then I thought of my fate. Thinking over my fate greatly increased my lament. Why my fate was so miserable and terrible. I reflected on my past, present and even the future at the same and one time: I had enjoyed very little parent's love; I lived alone in the countryside when I was twelve-year-old; I risked my life to take part in the so called revolution and helped Mao established his dictatorship; I was persecuted because I was honesty; I was labeled rightist and sent down to the countryside to do manual work; I was exiled to the countryside again because I sent the living expenses to my father-in-law; I bore the indescribable physical suffering of fake disease to escape the ugly cultural revolution; I underwent six years' hardest endeavor to remove my family back to the city. I had suffered enough misfortunes, setbacks, I had extremely tired. And only one year after I resumed a peaceful and happy life with my family, I had to face another mishap, a tragedy far exceeding all the past misfortunes: the terminal of her life journey is near now, which was completely beyond all my effort to avoid. Old regrets run like the endless Yangtze water; new grief pile up like clouds over the mountains. The sea has its shores, the river has its banks, but my sorrow is endless. How should I deal with the unbearable situation? Brooding over and over again, I could not decide what I should do. After immersing myself in the sad thought for a long time I was suddenly awakened by my senses that the complaining of fate and worrying about the future were no use to settle the present problem. I was aware that I must face the reality, I must calm, encourage my wife and help her to get the best medical treatment of her cancer. I decided that we must choose hope over fear, choose calmness over anxiety, choose optimism over pessimism, choose struggle over surrender. When I made this choice, the day was dawning.

Next day I accompanied her to go to the tumor hospital to make a further consultation. I hoped the doctor's diagnosis yesterday was a misdiagnosis. We visited a senior doctor. He made a thorough examination and affirmed the former diagnosis. He prescribed some medicine for her and advised her not to be frightened. Science and technology are developing fast, cancer can be conquered very soon. We thanked the doctor and returned home.

At night we had a candid, hearty talk. She admitted that from the very moment she knew she got a cancer, she was afraid and downhearted all the time, having an unexplainable distressed mood and feelings which could hardly bear. She did not really fear death, but heavily dreaded how our children and I would suffer. She said that she did not want to tell her parents of her disease. They were over eighty years old, could not bear such heavy a blow. The most frightful thing the old men fear is the white hair men pay their last respects to their black hair descendants. After she finished her word, I expressed that I completely understand her feelings. It was quite natural. I myself also had the same emotions. The question is how should we deal with them. I believed that we must set a bridle on those feelings, because they haven't any use. On the contrary, they have many negative effects. Many patients who got a fatal disease were haunted by fear, which only accelerated the speed to their last day. Fear reduces our confidence and the capacity of our body's immunity and self-repairing function. Fear of cancer hurts a person ten times more than cancer hurts him, so we must get out of fear, responding to our adversity with cheer, patience and courage, facing our new challenge with perseverance. Let things progress of their own accord. What we need is to take medical treatment actively, keep a quiet and peaceful mind, relying our hope on science. There are more than ten thousand doctors and scientists are engaged in the fighting of conquering the cancer all over the world. Early or later they will triumph. let us live an ordinary life as usual, forget the word "cancer". She replied me with a faint smile: "Of course what you said is right, but knowing something is easy, practicing something is difficult. I'll try my best to keep the right mood and practice the right thing, but you don't expect too much." I thanked her for her cooperation. We went to sleep with a little lighter heart than yesterday's.

From then on, she takes regular medical treatment, I take good care of her rest and nutrition and rarely mention the word "cancer".

In 1980 Hu Yaobang was elected as the general secretary of the central com-

A Painful Reminiscence of a Dignified Soul

mittee of the Communist Party, Zhao Ziyang was elected as the premier of the State Council. I welcomed the great news. Hu had been our old leader. When I worked at the Youth Publishing House in the 1950s, he had come to our office to inspect our work several times. He was amiable and easy of approach, he especially venerated knowledge and talents. At that time our publishing house just annexed a private bookstore, the Enlightenment Bookstore, which had many old editors. During that period of the "ideological remolding", the young editors usually look down the old intellectuals. Hu instructed us: "you must respect those old editors. They are all erudites." He patted an old editor's shoulder and continued: "like Gu Junzhen, he has written many popular science books. you must learn from them." Hu also concerned our livelihood. Once he asked us about our housing condition. We told him of our difficulties and Hu urged our director to solve the problems as fast as possible. After Mao Zedong's death he became one of the top leaders of our country, he had managed to rehabilitate millions of wrongly persecuted capitalist roaders and rightists. He was really an excellent leader. Zhao Ziyang was also a broad-minded, enlightened, courageous, and patient leader. he had long worked as the party secretary of Canton province and Sichuan province and greatly improved the situation there. More important he bravely reformed some ultra-leftist agriculture system, prominently increased the agricultural products, so there was a widely disseminated word among the people "wanting for grain and seeking for Ziyang".

Unfortunately, Deng Xiaoping only resigned ostensibly, superficially, he still remained the paramount leader of the party, holding court from behind a screen. In addition, Deng also established a Central Advisory Commission. The body was a selected group of senior party members. Its mission was supposed to provide "political assistance and consultation" to the central committee of the party. In fact, it had more authority unofficially than the Central Committee. The core of the Central Advisory Commission was composed of party members with over forty years' service in the party—the "eight elders", including Deng himself. Despite its mission was only giving advice, its power surpassed that of the politburo standing committee of the party. Therefore, Hu Yaoband was a mere nominal general secretary of the party, and Zhao Ziyang a nominal premier of the state council.

The setting of the Advisory commission further proved the gravity of the bureaucratism of China. There were so many overlapping organizations in our country. In other states there are usually two central leading groups; a central government and a central legislative body. In China there were five central leading groups: the central committee of the party, the central people's government, the national people's congress, the Chinese people's political consultative conference, the central advisory commission. It was really a tragic laughingstock: so much people's blood and sweat sent so many bureaucrats to the leading position and paid their way. Were such people's paying and sacrifice worth it?

Anyway, though Hu Yaobang was a nominal general secretary of the party and Zhao Ziyang was a nominal premier, their appointment was a good thing. That meant the second generation of the party was stepping in the top arena of the country. At least they could share part of the power of the elders. The situation of China made great changes. All the People's Communes are cancelled and the township governments were established. Production had been restored and developed. The party and the government began to emphasize reform and open the door to the world. They took a policy of active participation in the world market and welcome foreign business that wanted to invest in our country, and they allow the existence and development of the private economy. In 1980. the first Chinese-foreign joint venture was born in Beijing. At the same time, the first private-owned restaurant appeared in Beijing. Then four cities (Shenzhen, Zhuhai, Shantou and Xiamen) were set as special zones experimentally.

With the continuity and development of the policy of opening-up to the outside world and developing diverse sectors of the economy, more and more foreign countries and Taiwan, Hong Kong invested large capital into our country and there appeared more and more foreign and private enterprises and shops in China. Our economy developed rapidly.

Hu Yaobang emphasizes to establish both socialist material civilization and spiritual civilization. Answering his call, the Youth League promoted some activities: pay attention to five things: good manners, courtesy, hygiene, order, virtue; realize four beauties: beautiful mind, beautiful language, beautiful behavior, beautiful environment. He also called the people to break through the constraints of long-standing dogmatism and personal worship. In fact, he meant that people must emancipate their mind from Mao Zedong thought. He denied all the cases created by Mao in his 27 years' rule. After all the capitalist roaders and rightists were rehabilitated, the over twenty million landlords, rich peasants, counterrevolutionaries and bad elements were all rehabilitated under the leadership of Hu Yaobang in 1984.

Zhao Ziyang is also an enlightened leader. He ensured that "socialist democracy will gradually move toward systematization and legalization. This is the most basic guarantee that we can prevent a replay of the cultural revolution and achieve long term peace and stability." He emphasized the importance of reforms and had undergone and deepen many reforms, including wage reform, price reform, housing policy reform, personnel system reform, economic structure reform, etc. But constrained by Deng Xiaoping and conservative elders, he could not carry out the real political reform.

On December 18, 1984, Premier Zhao Ziyang and Prime Minister Margaret Thatcher signed the Joint Declaration of the Government of the United Kingdom of Great Britain and Northern Ireland and the Government of the PPC on the Question of Hong Kong. It declared: While national unity and territorial integrity shall be upheld and a Hong Kong Special Administrative Region (HKSAR) shall be established. China will resume the exercise of sovereignty over Hong Kong from July 1, 1997. The HKSAR will enjoy a high degree of autonomy except in foreign and defense affairs and will be vested with executive, legislative and independent judicial power. The current social and economic system of Hong Kong will remain unchanged. All the rights and freedoms will be ensured by law in the HKSAR. And all the policies stated in the Joint Declaration will remain unchanged for 50 years. This policy is called "one country, two system"

After Mao Zedong's death, there were not so many campaigns, social situation became relatively more peaceful. Yet, though Deng Xiaoping did not show delirious personality cult like Mao, he was also a dictator, left the people no less in thrall to the will of an emperor. He persisted in Mao's one-party dictatorship and his "Four Cardinal Principles" He pledged "we absolutely won't carry out western-style separation of powers, with periods of elected office." He advocated reform and open policy, but he only emphasized the changes in the economic field, he did not make the paralleled reform in political, social and cultural fields. He was tough and obstinate, forbidding any opponent voices and suppressing any challenge to his authority. Deng Xiaoping declared that we'll build socialism with Chinese characteristics.

Under the yoke of Deng's "Four Cardinal Principles" people don't have the liberty of speech. The word "liberty自由" is a commendatory term, an ideal of human beings. But this word was not allowed to appear alone in Communist China. When the party leader and the media wanted to use it, they added a prefix or suffix to it, such "liberalism自由主义", "liberalization自由化". Then these words become derogatory terms, criminal terms in China. Whenever people criticize the party, promote liberty, democracy and further reformation, demand greater respect for human dignity and freedom, or ask for a reconciliation of socialist dictatorship and humanist ideals, the leftists will condemn them to advocate bourgeois liberalism. They would start the political campaign "Anti-spiritual pollution" to curb western liberal ideas among the people. In 1982 Deng called to build up China's "socialist spiritual civilization" to prevent the unwanted societal impacts of bourgeois liberalism. He criticized humanism as "un-Marxist", saying it "leads youth astray" He emphasized the need to combat spiritual pollution brought about by liberalization.

Hu Yaobang, the secretary of the central committee of the party then, has a different opinion from Deng. Hu stressed that in order to realize four modernization we must carry out an all-round, comprehensive reform, break down all outmoded convention, abandon all the trite practice, put an end to all the old style of work and deepen the reform in anyway. In a meeting to discuss principles he said that speech has no forbidden region, any viewpoint can be expressed, any field can be involved; ideology must be thoroughly liberated without any misgivings; He insists on a parallel process of political reform. He is always willing to act on behalf of the people and push on the political reform heedless of his personal safety. But confined by Deng Xiaoping he cannot carry out his idea and policy freely. He can only try his best to boycott or limit the activities of the leftists, to check each "Anti-Bourgeois liberalization campaign" to a certain degree and to protect those intellectuals who dare to speak out their true views within his power.

Any reform without political reform is sham reform, cannot resolve the fundamental issues. It is simply a matter of using the guise of "reform" to maintain the one-man dictatorship. It can only allot privilege to a few cronies and develop corruption, lead to an enormous wealth disparity, encroach on the liberty of the individual, deprive the right of the people, and cause great degradation of morality. The corruption and inflation continued and expanded. People were angry and exasperated.

In early 1982. I was transferred to the Academy of Social Sciences of Jiangsu Province. I was assigned to work at the Information Department of the Academy as the chief editor of the magazine "The Information of Foreign Social Sciences". There were nine persons in our Department. Most of us were editors. Each editor was responsible to collect and translate articles of social sciences in different languages, Japanese, Russian or English. Our director was an economist named Cheng

A Painful Reminiscence of a Dignified Soul

Jiming, who had also worked in the Central Committee of the Communist Youth League years ago. We had been fellow colleagues so we felt very close with each other. He is a very warm, able man conversant with English, Chinese and economics, and his mind is also rather liberal, so we can speak and work more freely without much misgivings. He gave me a lot of help. Our magazine was published every month. Apart from editorial work each editor also engaged in research of a social science. My object of research is sociology.

In order to control people's minds, Deng Xiaoping continued the political study in every Saturday afternoon. In fact, people had no interest in it at all. During those studies, people could only repeat or praise what the party said. We could not express our true views. Usually the political studies became a pure idle talk for a mere killing of time. I liked to speak with frankness, but I had suffered heavily in the past for out-speaking and I had four children and a sick wife now. I did not have enough courage to criticize the wrong policies and activities. Nevertheless, I could not bear completely shutting my mouth, so sometimes I would play at the limit of what Party was permitted. For instance, once in a political study I said:

"At present the corruption has become rampant all over the country. Angst of the question runs deep among the people. The party and the government must not cover them and must take sternest measures to stop it. Otherwise the four modernization could not be realized. I am really worried about it." I criticized the awful situation but People cannot blame me that I am attacking the Party.

A colleague made a joke on me:

"You are so concerned with the problem; I'll recommend you to be the party secretary of The Discipline Inspection Commission of Jiangsu Province or the chief judge of the court of the Province."

I replied: "Even if they assigned me to the position, I would not take the job, because China hasn't the judicial independence. I cannot make my own decision; I have to obey orders of the superior party secretary. I do not want to be a puppet."

Here I criticized the party obscurely. Even though someone might not like my word, they cannot denounce me for what I say is the fact and my word is not too sharp.

In another case I asked:

"We are asked to practice the communist morality. But what is the communist morality? In capitalist countries, there are people who sacrifice their own lives for the sake of others, which is capitalist morality; in old China, there was a moral maxim: "Propriety, righteousness, honesty and a sense of shame are the four moral principles of the country, if the four moral principles are not magnified, the country will perish." which is feudalistic morality, we should not practice. Then what morality should we do? what is the communist morality? As far as I know about it, the communist morality is that we must believe communism, we must love and respect Communist Party, and we must absolutely listen and obey whatever the party says. Is it right?"

Nobody answered my question.

I also often used the satire or oblique words to express my discontent of the party. And since the leader and all the colleagues of my editorial department except one, were not leftists, I didn't encounter troubles.

My wife constantly took treatment at the Nanjing Tumor Hospital calmly and patiently. For a long time, her disease did not seem to be improved, nor appear to be clearly worsened. To make a further effort, in 1982 I escorted her to Shanghai to take treatment. She took her youngest daughter to accompany her. I arranged them to stay at the home of one of my nieces and took her to go to the Shanghai Tumor Hospital. The doctor confirmed that she had cancer and planned to take radiotherapy. But he warned us that after the radiotherapy her nose might be indented and asked us whether we will take the radiotherapy or not. My wife said if the disease could be controlled or cured, she didn't mind the disfigurement of her face.

After one month of treatment in Shanghai she returned to Nanjing. She stopped the treatment for some time. Her cancer did not improve. She went to the Nanjing Tumor Hospital again. The doctor continued her radiotherapy. During that time the doctor also took a surgical operation with general anesthesia for her. She suffered a lot and I also had an anguished heart. Her disease continued to be exacerbated

For making a last effort, I decided to take my wife to Beijing Tumor Hospital, the best one in China. On November 21, 1984 we took a plane there, stayed at the dormitory of the Youth Publishing House. Next day I escorted her to visit a senior doctor of the Tumor Hospital. The doctor was very kind and made a thorough examination. He decided to take chemotherapy. Each day I convoyed her to go to the hospital and accompanied her to go to the places she wished to revisit again, such as the Summer Palace, the City Wall, etc. She always lingered those places long and was loath to leave, knowing she would never see them again. I understood her feelings and satisfied all her demands. In the evening, when she went to bed, I began to polish the articles and edited the magazine till midnight, for my magazine had to be published each month. My wife knew my tiredness and expressed her gratitude to me again and again. I told her that was the least I ought to do and asked her to feel at ease in it. One month later, the doctor told us the period of treatment was finished. we returned to Nanjing by a plane on December 25th. Before leaving I bought some flower seeds and chemical fertilizer for her, I knew she liked to plant flowers. She was very glad and surprised, asking me "How can you think of such trifling thing? Thank you for your care."

My wife's disease did not seem to turn better. In fact, the doctor had secretly told me "The present medical skill was still not good enough to cure cancer. It can only postpone the process of the cancer." My wife was disappointed and wanted to give up treatment. I persuaded her to continue to go to the hospital, telling her, "You should always hold hope, maybe someday a new effective method or drug will be invented." In fact, I anxiously expected that wonderful thing every day. She went on her treatment and the doctor continued to give her radiotherapy. But all the cures were to no avail. With the lapse of time she became weaker and weaker, felt fatigued all over the body. Her eyesight declined sharply and blurred, the most unbearable thing was the pain of the nose and head. As her health turned very bad, I asked a long-term leave to take care of her at home in early 1985.

In May 1985 she was unable to go to work. On the last day she left her office, she cleared her desk, burned all the useless papers in the courtyard, bade farewell with tears of her colleagues and the office building, where she had worked for six years. At home she secretly wrote her testament, which she did not show us right away, only handed me on her deathbed. Every morning after four children went to school, I made food for her. Most of the time she lay in bed, but each day I would help her go out for a short walk or go to the hospital. We believed that a certain exercise was helpful. Some time she would find something to do to while away her time.

One day she collected all her photographs and stuck them on a photograph album. I sat beside her to help her. Pictures of her whole life, from childhood to middle age. Some were her single picture, some were with her family or friends, some were group or graduation pictures. Each picture evoked painful memories of her life. Sometimes she would made relevant explanation to me: when, where or why she took the picture. With infinite grief she stuck one picture after another. Sticking pictures was a very light labor, but she was too weak to adhere to that work long. Only sticking half of her pictures, she stopped and staggered to the bed. She sprawled on it and was sick at heart. I felt equal grief at the same time, and I felt even greater grief later, for she could not finish that work herself until her last day. Looking at the have stuck picture album each time I could not help but feel heartbroken.

One night there was a grand concert in a gymnasium, I took her to go there to enjoy it. The singers were all very famous and they sang beautiful songs. The stage light was bright with many colors. That was the most brilliant performance that had never shown before. She usually liked music very much but her body could not sustain her that night. At the half of the concert she told me she was too tired and wanted to go back home. I felt sad that she became so faint that could not enjoy a perfect performance. We walked out of the theatre to the bus stop. Suddenly a bus came near the stop. My wife wanted to catch the bus and ran to the stop. I did not seize her in time. She ran only three or four steps, her right knee failed to support her and she fell at a tree by the road. I felt a great pang that she had become so frail and feeble. The tree became my memento forever. Whenever I passed the tree, I would touch it and stare at it for some time. Once I passed there with my eldest daughter, I pointed at the tree and said "This is where your mum fell…" Before I was finished, I wept and so did my daughter.

As she often had sharp pain, living meant enduring tortures for her, she often tried to commit suicide. One day she took out a small bottle of strong painkiller, a deadly drug, and wanted to swallow them all. Fortunately, my youngest daughter happened to enter the room and seized the bottle hurriedly. She cried, muttering "Mom, you'll leave me alone?" My wife stroked her hair, said sorry to her, and promised that she would not do it again.

But the suffering was so severe that she could not bear it. Not long afterwards, in one afternoon she went into the small bedroom and locked the door from inside. My youngest daughter followed her but could not come in. She knocked on the door but her mother would not open it. My daughter was horrified and immediately drew a chair to the door and through it climbed up the transom window above the door. Seeing her mother clinging to the window and preparing to jump down, she cried at the top of her voice with tears "Mom, Mom, You mustn't, mustn't …" Her mother stared at her and hesitated for a long time. Finally, she stepped down the window and opened the door. Mother and daughter hugged tightly with tears streaming down like torrents. When my daughter told me the events, I felt as if a knife were piercing my heart. It was not I hadn't dissuaded her, but her unbearable

A Painful Reminiscence of a Dignified Soul

pain and her depth of despair forced her to do that thing.

For her recreation, I begged a friend working in Nanjing Daily to buy a 14-inch black-and-white television through back door. At that time color television was very expensive. A 20-inch color television would cost my two year's salary. I could not afford to buy one. She liked the television and watched it every night. But as her body was very weak and her eyes were deteriorated rapidly, she usually watched half of the play and had to go back to bed to rest.

Not long afterwards, as her cancer cells proliferate to eyes, her left eye became blind and her right eye's eyesight became weak. I took her to see an eye doctor. The doctor suspected that her eyes were hurt by radiotherapy. I had the same suspect. Her nose had received radiotherapy for long time. Though each time she took nose radiotherapy the doctor would cover her eyes with something. But some radioactive rays might still penetrate the covering to the eyes. After so many radiotherapy, the hurt could be very severe. The eye doctor said her eyes might be difficult to be cured. My wife was deadly frightened that her right eye would blind too and she could not see her dearest kin again. Impulsed by an instinctive emotion she kneeled down before the doctor and said "I begged you to cure my eyes." I pulled her to stand up. The doctor sympathized her deeply and promised to do his best. Her desperate action made me feel woeful. I saw how sharp a contradictory feeling was torturing her: On the one hand, she wanted to end her life immediately; on the other hand, she was so loathing that she could no longer see her dearest persons again. When a person is at the critical point between life and death, how pathetic and miserable one is! I sighed with painful emotions.

Now she had no energy to go outside. Each day I held her to walk around the room as an exercise. The distance she could cover became shorter and shorter. One day her right knee suddenly bent without any strength to support her. I carried her to the bed. From then on, she could no longer walk. One month or two afterwards she was paralyzed from the waist down.

On Sep. 9, 1985 she could not swallow food. The last solid food she ate was a morsel of pear. I could only feed her with liquid food, like milk, porridge. For three days she had not eaten any solid food and could not pass feces and urine. Her abdomen swelled as big as a drum. She groaned ceaselessly. On Sep. 12 I called my unit for help. My leader sent a car to my place. Two of my colleagues helped to carry her into the car and we drove to the tumor hospital. In the emergency room the doctor immediately began to perform catheterization and enema operation on her to excrete feces and urine. For two days her abdomen distention gradually subsided. Then she was transferred to a ward. It was not a regular ward in the hospital. It was a temporary ward set in an old family house near the hospital. Its facilities were very bad. My wife was very angry for such an arrangement.

Each morning, I cooked oatmeal in milk at home, carried it to the ward. I helped her clean face and fed her the porridge. As she had difficulty to eat, she had to received infusion every day to supplement nutrition. She could not discharge urine herself; we must insert a tube into her urethra to induce it. This is a technical job, which should be performed by a nurse. But the nurse was loath to do it. She taught me how to do it and left the work to me. My wife's nose often flowed pus and blood, I needed to wipe them off with a handkerchief anytime, so I was busy. When there was nothing to do, I would sit by her bed and had a chat with her. She missed her father and sisters very much and wanted to see them one last time. She also talked and worried about her daughter's study and future. She was very grateful to me, telling me: "I read in a medical magazine that 'If a cancer patient can last five years, it is regarded to be fully cured in medical profession.' I have lasted almost six years. It is all depending on your care. You look after me meticulously, escort me to Shanghai, to Beijing for medical treatment. And now you cook and feed food for me and clear away all the filthy thing. I really find no words to convey my thanks to you." I replied "Don't mention it! It is my duty. I did not do a mite more than I ought."

One day she even talked about my future. She said:

"After I pass away, I want you remarry again. Our children are all at school, they cannot take care of you. You are approaching sixty-year-old and very busy. You need a woman to help you."

"Thank you for your concern." I replied "But it is too early to refer to the question."

"I really want you to consider the question. I am not a woman of nursing jealousy. You need remarry. Otherwise I would worry about you. The only thing you must take care of is not let our children be ill-treated by stepmother.

I saw she was seriously discussing the question and I wanted to dispel her worry, so I considered the problem. suddenly I thought of a suggestion:

"Your younger sister's husband died one or two years ago. She is a widow now. If I marry her, she will surely not ill-treat her nieces. What do you think?"

She thought for a while and said:

A Painful Reminiscence of a Dignified Soul

"My elder sister married your elder brother, I married you. Is it destined that all my three sisters surnamed Zhang must marry your family surnamed Da? I don't like the idea."

"Well, I will not do things you don't like. I can guarantee I will not marry a woman who has children, I will only marry a woman who has no children or who has not got married. then she will treat our children as her own. You can set your mind at ease."

She seemed to be satisfied with my promise. Our discussion ended there.

One morning I went to the ward and saw that she was crying. Her patient mates told me she had excruciating pain and cried for a long time. They consoled her but she was still crying and said she wanted to die quickly. I fed her some painkiller immediately and soothed her. Gradually she quieted down. She complained "The Heaven was too unjust, all my life I have behaved well, always tried to help others, to be perfect in doing everything, why should I be treated so terribly."

I agreed with her complaint. The Heaven is indeed too unjust. So many evildoers are living comfortably and so many good and honest people are suffering terribly. I soothed her tenderly and told her good news that her father sent us a telegram, saying he will come to see you soon. She appeared full of mixed feelings: happy, surprised, worried, and anxious. she had always been longing to see her father a last time, but she was afraid of her father's coming now. She said her father is already ninety-year-old, how can he bear such a long, arduous journey, in case there is an accident happened on him I will be guilty. Considering the safety of her father, with a bitter smile she urged me to send an urgent telegram to her father at once. persuading him not to come. I pitied her for her painful contradictory feelings and could not offer any better opinions. I just rushed to the telegraph office right away.

Another morning, after I fed her egg drop soup and meat broth and wiped her mouth, we started some small talk. Suddenly she asked me a question:

"There is something I need your help. Will you help me?"

"I will help you to do whatever you need. Did I refuse to help you anytime in the past? Never. Just tell me what you want. Don't hesitate. I will help you." I pledged.

"Is it true?"

"Every word."

"I am too weak to take my life away myself now. Please you use a scissors to cut my throat to help me to get rid of the sufferings and worries. I beg you."

What a demand! How could I expect she need that help! I replied:

"I cannot do that."

"You pledged to do anything to help me."

"You want me to become a murderer and to be sentenced a death penalty?"

She could not find any words to respond. I continued:

"Don't think of death any more. I beg you. I wish you to be alive as long as possible, or live forever. It is true. If you pass away, all your troubles will end and you will be relieved in peace, but I will have an endless suffering all the rest of my life. Whenever I remember you, whenever I see the thing you left, my heart will be seriously hurt. It will be very hard for me to bear.

She kept silent. We gazed at each other's eyes fill with tears.

From Oct. 6 on, she could hardly speak and often had a coma. Her face became expressionless. I felt sad and regretted that I hadn't had more talks with her when she was still conscious. On Oct. 11th, in her semi-consciousness, she murmured over and over again: "I want to go back home. I want to go back home. I don't want to die at this shabby ward." We persuaded her not to move. But she insisted on going back home. She refused to drink water and have any food and to receive infusion, she wanted to starve to death. We could do nothing but satisfy her desire. With a handcart my daughters and I pushed her back home.

All the process of the movement she had no sense at all. When she regained her consciousness, she blamed us: "Why you still not move me back home?" I told her she was already at home. She suspected we cheated her. I held her hand to touch our bed frame. She believed she was in her own bed again and was contented. But she still did not like to have food. I reminded her that only two days later was her birthday and we were going to celebrate it. She seemed a bit delighted and received food and infusion again. On Oct. 14th her spirits seemed a little high, she was aware that day was her birthday. At night my daughters and I stood before her bed, congratulated her birthday, and sang "Happy birthday to you... ..." Then I fed her food; the birthday cream cake, egg soup, mashed chestnut, soft-shelled turtle broth, etc. I even dipped some wine in her mouth. My daughters sang some sprightly songs and had a few dances in between. It was the one and the only time during the last few months, she seemed forgotten her distress and was delighted and even beamed smile from time to time. It may be the temporary flourishing before passing away. She enjoyed the happy hour until eleven o'clock, then she said:

A Painful Reminiscence of a Dignified Soul

"Thank you all! I am really tired. I have to rest now. Good-bye!" Everyone, including her, reluctantly ended the meaningful birthday party.

We lived in the dormitory of the Department of Public Health. It is a big building with forty-eight families within it. Our neighbors take it a taboo to have a person died in the building, they reserved a sickbed in the hospital for the cadres of the government of Jiangsu province and asked us to move my wife there. The next day of her birthday I called an ambulance to send her to the hospital. She did not protest for she did not know she was moved. At the hospital she could not eat anything and even found it difficult to drink water. Each day she had infusions to keep her alive. Most of the time she was in a stupor. I also slept on a camp bed beside her bed. Each time our daughter came to see her, I would ask her, "Do you know who is coming to see you?" At the first three or four days he could still say their name. Gradually she could not recognize them one after another. On Oct. 22 afternoon I asked her, "Do you know who I am?" She slurred my name with very low voice; "Da Zhong". That was her last word. From then on, she spoke nothing, sensed nothing, knew nothing. She no longer groans, no long feel pain, no longer seek suicide. She became quiet, waiting for her last day.

Each day I kept staring at her disfigured face and body: the caved nose, the eroded left eye, the twitching mouth, the shrunken cheek and the drained color, the flat breast and buttocks, the bag of bones. The only unchanging thing was her pitch-dark hail, without a white one. If it was not for the cancer, she would surely live till one-hundred-year-old. While facing all these unbearable scenes, I felt a kind of sadness which is beyond any description. My mind was full of her former image and the past events: the bright-eyed, flower-like charm, the cool slim face and form, the apple-blossom color. I taught her the revolutionary songs when she was a child; I met her at the Beijing railway station; the simple wedding ceremony, we lived two thousand kilometers apart painfully for eleven years, half of our marriage life. A heavy weight fell on my heart: The mortal was nearly being refined away. The living limbs and trunk would turn into ashes in no time. I stroked her hand all the time, I pressed my cheek on her cheek from time to time, trying to give her some last warm. She seemed still able to perceive my caress, for she would nod appreciation slightly occasionally. On her last one or two days, she sometimes shook her head frailly. What was it meant? Nobody could tell. Probably he was still complaining about the unjust Heaven, the cruel Communist Party. The cause of her disease was certainly as much psychological as physiological. The twisted life greatly reduced her immunity. If she was able to live a normal life, she could not get a cancer.

The knell finally tolled. On Oct. 24 afternoon two o'clock and twenty-four minutes, she had a cough, but she could not cough out phlegm which clogged her throat, her breath stopped. I rushed to seek a doctor for an emergency treatment. He came and made an examination and declared that she was dead. Two workers came and carries her body to the mortuary immediately. It was a very small dark room with a wooden board bed. I called a daughter at home through public phone and asked her to inform other three daughters. At the same time, I called the funeral parlor for their service. Soon afterwards my four daughters came. We all felt sad and did not know what to say, only stared at her body, stroked her hands or face from time to time with tears. Looking at her pale face I was mournful she would never come back to bless me with her smile.

At about seven o'clock a truck from the funeral parlor came and stopped at the door of the hospital. Two workers came to the mortuary, they threw her body into a big cloth bag, dragged the bag on the ground to the truck, then flung the bag over the back of the truck. Their actions astonished me. I was very angry and wanted to protest but I dared not speak out. If they refused to carry the body and left it here, how could I do. I controlled my temper and kept silent. Throughout the world, even in the most backward country, people always carry a dead with a stretcher. But in China, under Mao's rule, all man's dignity, pride, and value were deprived. We kept staring at the truck till it disappeared and then we staggered home with a mournful feeling of losing our most beloved one in the world.

Five days later, my family and some relatives, friends and colleagues gathered at the funeral parlor to bid a last farewell to my wife. Everyone had a stern expression, wore a black armband round their left arm and a small white flower on their breast. The workers of the funeral parlor pushed into the hall a cart on which my wife's body lay. I stared at it long and stroked her hand and cheek the last time, and murmured a final farewell to her with a melancholy thought that this dear flesh body would soon become a wisp of smoke floating into the air. I lamented for her leaving us so early; she was only 47 years old. Unable bearing the parting, I asked a colleague to take several pictures of me and the body.

Then we all stood before the body, made three deep bows to it to pay our last respects to her. Then I delivered a short eulogy on her:

"Dear wife Runshu, we are coming here to see you off today. Wish you have a good journey to the Heaven. Your life is a perfect life. You have always taken good care about your career and your patients. Your blood still flows in several patients' bodies. You are loved and respected by all your patients. You are a most tender wife, always take good care of your husband. you are a merciful mother, always treat your daughters kindly and sternly. We have always felt congenial and close with each other. You always have a positive attitude for life and an outgoing personality; no matter how hard the situation is, you keep calm and composure, treating all difficulties with patience, courage and determination. All these attributes made you a special, wonderful person. I will miss you dearly all my life, and when you miss me, always come to my dream and prolong the dream as long as possible. Now you are on the way to the paradise where you will get a peaceful and happy life forever without any worry and grief. Wish you have a good journey! Goodbye! My dear wife Runshu."

After the simple ceremony the worker pushed the cart to the crematorium. I thanked and said goodbye to all the attendees. My daughters and I were waiting outside the funeral parlor. Looking at the heavy smoke spiraling upward, in which her soul is floating to the Heaven, I feel extremely miserable. After a long time, a worker came to us and handed me a cinerary casket. With a heavy heart I held it with my two arms and returned home with my daughters.

At home, I set up a mourning room. A big picture of my wife was put up in the middle of a wall. Under the picture was a table, on which place my wife's cinerary casket. Before the casket was a burner, in which we offered incense as a tribute to the dead. By either side of the burner we kindled two candles. On the other three walls hung several large, oblong sheets of silk with inscriptions for funeral, presented as a gift by her father, sister and our relatives and friends. On the ground laid several funeral wreaths with elegiac couplet presented by myself, my daughters and friends. My elegiac couplet is:

> "Beloved and virtuous wife, bitterly cold rain and wind pressed you leave away."
> "Poor and pity daughters, cried loudly and wailed softly called mom to return."

My daughters' elegiac couplet is:

"A simple and frugal life left an excellent example."
"A diligent and vigorous work conveyed a fine mode."

Each day we went to the mourning room to offer our condolences and bow to the picture, usually lingering long time there.

A few days later the flowers were withered, I placed the casket in a big green trunk, together with it I packed many memorable things, such as towels and handkerchiefs she last used, the enamel mug with which she last drink water, her graduation dissertation of the university, her photograph album, a pair of her braids I cut off when she was young. a beautiful small boat she made of shells when she took a rest cure in a sanatorium by the seashore. a worn bed sheet mended by her with hundreds of stitches, etc.

I also distributed some things left behind by their mother among the daughters, asking them always remember their mother who had served and cared for them for so many years. I also made a suggestion that every year at the time 2:24 pm October24, wherever we are and whatever we are doing we must stand up and pay a three-minutes silent tribute to our dearest person. It is one of the most simple and meaningful memorial way.

Parting with one's dearest spouse is really the most painful thing, which cannot be expressed by any words, which cannot be cut off from the feelings, which cannot be soothed by any reasons, which makes people unbearable. I often thought of leaving this world and following her to the Heaven. I had many pain-killer drugs; I could do the thing easily. But I knew I still had great responsibility upon me. I had four daughters, who were still all in schools, the youngest was only nine-year-old. If I left them, how could they live on? I could not do that. Her haggard, pathetic face always reverberated and lingered long in my brain. Many nights my eyes still envisioned her lovely form, my ears still rang with her soft sweet voice. One whole night I could not sleep at all; with my eyes wide open, with my mind full of her image I compensated her for the knitted brows of entire life, for the intimate care of her husband, anticipating the reunite in another world. My grief dragged on day after day, week after week.

Though Deng Xiaoping and the leftists sternly prohibited people to air their opposing views, people's voices could not be completely smothered. There were more and more brave persons who came to challenge the one-party dictatorship, among them Fang Lizhi was an outstanding one.

Fang was an astrophysics professor and vice president of the University of Science and Technology of China. He was very popular among the students. He was invited to make lectures in many universities and wrote essays in popular magazines. Many of his essays and lectures expressed his liberal views on politics and criticized the leftist dogma of the party. His main viewpoints are as follows:

"The so called "extending democracy" is very mistaken. Democracy is not bestowed on and extend to people by the government or the leaders. The power rests with each individual. Each person fulfills his obligations as a citizen of the country, and in turn he is due his rights. People have the right to mind their country's business, and to demand the dismissal of unfit leaders. It is people who maintain the government, paying taxes in return for services. People are not the docile tools of the country. In Western countries, a would-be official needs a number of recommendations prior to being nominated, and then the nomination must undergo general scrutiny. Relying solely on the recommendation of cronies is not acceptable. Democracy was indispensable to progress and symbolized a society's level of development. Democracy, education and intellectual freedom are its absolutely indispensable prerequisites. If we fail to achieve democracy, China will hardly become a truly developed modern country.

"Marxism belongs to a certain epoch of civilization which is over. Marxism is no longer of much use. It is a thing of the past. It helps to understand the problems of the last century, but not those of today. It is like a worn dress that must be put aside. Socialist movement has included many different streams. There have been diverse approaches of socialism. The Swedish Social Democratic Party practice the socialism, caring for their citizens essentially from cradle to grave. The Swedes acknowledged the existence of classes and class conflict, but they sought to reconcile these conflicts through compromise and mediation. Half a century later Sweden eliminated a class, but it wasn't the bourgeoisie—it was the proletariat! The bulk of its population became middle class. Yet China remain clung to archaic beliefs. The Party propagated feudalism under the guise of Marxism. Our socialism comes from endorsing the obsolete ideas, ideas without basis in either theory or fact. What we have done here is neither progressive nor socialistic. On the contrary, it has been feudalistic."

"The Four Cardinal Principles are wrong. It is a sort of strait-jacket that prevents China from developing into a democracy. To carry out reform we need openness not restrictions, we need open in all directions. It is not enough to import things from Western, in order to become truly modern, we have to import the spirit of Western civilization. Open expression of public opinion is a key indicator of democracy. Respect for the opinion of your opponents is a crucial requirement. In a democracy you must recognize the existence of opposing viewpoints and permit those views to be expressed. Every individual possesses certain rights, human rights. Democracy is based on recognizing the rights of every single individual. Yet human rights are a taboo subject in China. The rights in the Chinese constitution should be "actual rights" and not just on-paper rights."

"The intellectuals are the main force for pushing society ahead. They should assert their independence and assume greater social responsibilities and exerts influence. They ought to play a big role. They are not the "Stinking Ninth", the last of the "Nine Bad Categories". Mao described the dependency of the intellectuals on the party with the words "the hair clings firmly to the skin" It is completely wrong. They are independent, not the tools of someone. The students at school might not to open their mouths too wide but to study diligently. Those, however, who have completed their studies successfully, must open their mouths."

"People's Congress delegates should represent the people, and now they are considered some kind of flower vases. The people's representative is an honorary post, a model worker. The People's Congress should become a legitimate legislative body and vehicle for public opinion."

"The propaganda hails our leader as an emperor. It is wrong. Hu Yaobang is an enlightened leader who had once said that not one portrait of Mao should be hanging in China. Yet today the one still hangs on Tiananmen Square."

Another famous person who dared to speak was Liu Binyan. He was my friend and his wife Zhu Hong had once worked with me at the same editorial department, so I knew him very well. Honest is a salient virtue in his character. He has a clean and unruffled conscience, speaking his mind and the truth. He was of an inquiring disposition. seeing the world through his own head and heart and not following the herd. After the founding of the People's Republic of China he worked as a reporter and editor for China Youth Daily. In 1956 he published "On the bridge worksite" which exposed the corruption and bureaucratism, the superior decided every trivial matter and the initiative spirit of the cadres and workers were suppressed. He also wrote an article "The inside story of our newspaper" which described the restriction and control of the press by the censorship. The two works were the first pieces to criticize the Party at that time and had a powerful nationwide impact among readers. Because these articles violated the taboo laid down by Mao in 1942 in his article "Talks at the Yan'an Forum" that writers should extol the bright side of life and not expose the darkness, Liu was labeled a rightist and expelled from the Communist Party. He was punished to do manual labor and other inferior work for twenty years.

After he was rehabilitated in 1979, he worked as a reporter for the People's Daily. He did not change his original ideal and character, with a devotion to socialism and a deep love for the people he insisted to express the fact honestly. He continued to probe and investigate bureaucratism, injustice and corruption of the party high and low. He strongly criticized Communist Party officials for abusing their power and suppressing people's rights. He blamed the party Leftists for their 20 years of misrule, distorting the true meaning of Communism. Marx's basic tenet is that the prerequisite condition of the realization of communism is a high level of material development. We aren't economically mature enough to build a communist society. Our so-called socialism was not true socialism. He advocated reform and emphasized the need of legal and political institutions to protect liberties, particularly the freedom of the press. He produced an extraordinary series of reports, exposing the gross depravities of the officials. In 1979 he published an article entitled "In Between Men and Monsters", in which he told the story of a party secretary named Wang Shouxin in Heilongjiang Province who had made a great fortune from bribery. The article made a great sensation in the country, because it reflected a universal phenomenon. People could see corrupters like Wang Shouxin around them but did not dare to say. Now there was someone to speak out their mind they were glad and wanted all those corrupt officials who had not been brought to justice should be exposed and punished. But the bureaucrats and the leftists did not like the report, they criticized that it calumniated and harmed the Party. His another most influential article is "A Second Kind of Loyalty", in which he reported two young men's story. They risked their lives to advise Chairman Mao to correct his mistakes. One young man named Chen Shizhong wrote a letter to Chairman Mao, criticized him point-blank that he could not hear any different opinions and advised him to correct his mistakes. Another young man named Li Yuxian wrote a letter to Chairman Mao, pointed out the mistake of the Great Leap Forward and the People's Commune and made many suggestions to correct the mistake. Both of the brave youths were suffered all kinds of persecutions and almost lost their lives. Liu Binyan praised their behavior as "A Second Kind of Loyalty", they were not anti-party, but were loyal to the party. In my opinion, Liu is also using this article to justify his behavior; his exposes of the dark side of the society is beneficial to the party and the country, not to oppose the party. Liu's articles had a powerful nationwide impact among readers. He built up a sound reputation as a reformer and a corruption watchdog. His works made him a household name among Chinese readers and cemented his reputation as "China's conscience". In 1985 when the Chinese Writers' Association elected its leader, Liu received the second-highest number of votes.

Wang Ruowang was also a famous prolific essayist and literary critic. He was imprisoned for political reasons by both the Nationalist Party and the Communist Party. He wrote an article mocking Jiang Jieshi for allowing the Japanese to seize three northeast provinces and was imprisoned for three and a half years. After his release, in order to "fight evil, autocracy and oppression" he went to Yanan and joined the Communist Party at nineteen years old. During the Yanan Rectification Campaign he was persecuted for writing articles to discuss dark and unsavory aspects of life in Yanan and was banished to Japanese-occupied Shandong Province as a low-level Communist agent. After the founding of the People's Republic of China, he returned to Shanghai, where he worked at the East China Bureau Propaganda Department. He became a co-editor of a prominent local newspaper. In 1956, after Mao encouraged writers to criticized the Communist Party, he published articles criticizing the Party. Because of these articles he was labeled a rightist and was forced to work at a labor camp in the countryside. His wife, Li Ming, was also persecuted for her association with him. Refusing to condemn her husband, she also lost her job and suffered a mental breakdown. During the Cultural Revolution Wang was imprisoned for four years. After he was rehabilitated, he continued to exposed the dark reality of the party and agitated for greater human rights and democratic reforms. In one of his books he recalled that the Communists' political prisons had been much more cruel than Nationalist Party's political prisons, and he asserted that, although both Jiang Jieshi and Mao Zedong practiced dictatorship and used hunger as a weapon against their political opponents, Mao was more systematic and ruthless. He suggested in an article that the common people of China should have the right to conduct public discussion with the leader of our country. He openly opposed the "Four Cardinal Principles" He believed that Chinese socialism was "feudal or semi-feudal in essence" he even wrote an article titled "One Party Dictatorship can only Lead to Tyranny". Because he was the oldest of the three protest leaders, Wang gained a reputation as "the grandfather of Chinese dissidents"

The three men were the main targets of the three campaigns of "Anti-Spiritual Pollution" launched by the government in 1981, 1983, and 1987.

In those years the corruption and cronyism within the government and party were rampant. People were angry and exasperate and complained. Some accusations of corruption even targeted the children of Deng Xiaoping. At the same time the inflation was serious, which led to large increases in living cost. In the middle of the December of 1986, many college students started demonstrations. The first demonstration was held in the city of Hefei, the location of the University of Science and Technology of China, in which Fang Lizhi was the vice president. Soon the demonstration spread to a dozen or more cities in China, including Shanghai, Nanjing, and Beijing. Students demanded the elimination of corruption curbing inflation and greater economic and political freedoms. All the student's demands got no answer. On the contrary, Deng Xiaoping deemed that the student movement was instigated by the liberal intellectuals and declared on December 30, 1986, two weeks after the student demonstrations: "The disturbance made by students is the result that the leadership hasn't taken a clear-cut stand against bourgeois liberalization for many years. We must resolutely uphold the 'Four Cardinal Principle' with a clear-cut stand." He cracked down on the demonstrations and directed Hu Yaobang to expel Fang Lizhi, Liu Binyan and Wang Ruowang from the party. Hu wanted to protect the intellectuals and refused Deng's demand. Because of the refusal, Hu was dismissed from the position as General Secretary of the Party in Jan. 16, 1987. and replaced by premier Zhao Ziyang. Hu was perceived as being excessively liberal and overlooking the spread of the "bourgeois liberalization" by Deng and the conservative "Eight Olders" Soon afterwards, Deng launched a movement of crackdown on "bourgeois liberalization". The illegal dismissal of Hu Yaobang's position effectively ended the power of the second-generation leader of the Party. The relatively enlightened atmosphere created by Hu Yaobang was finished.

After the death of my wife I was always troubled by the painful remembrance of the past. Everything around me was full of her presence, continually reopening the wound. The bed she had slept might still remain her dead cells;

the quilt that had covered her might still have her smell. I could not bear to see the stitches in my garment. Her photos and letters often induced my tears. I was torn by nostalgia. The Xuanwu-lake Park, the Daybreak Cinema, the top of the old city walls where we had enjoyed our happy hours, were now turned into miserable places I was afraid of visiting again. The deeply-attached feelings accumulated in long period could not be dispersed and lingered in my mind unremittingly. As miserable memory always causes great pain, once I had a fantastic thought: "The science and technology is developing fast, I hope it will soon be able to locate which part of the brain stores the happy memories; which part of the brain stores the miserable memories, and man can delete the memories from the brain as he wishes. In that case, I can go to the hospital and ask the doctor to remove the miserable memory from my brain so that I can reduce my pain." But not long after that, a second thought came to my mind: "Even though the science and technology can do that job, I will not remove those miserable memories. They are painful but also very precious. They hurt you and also sweeten your heart with their great value." In order to relieve my gloomy mood, I considered to make a trip.

I could not go far away for I had four children at home, I had to choose a beautiful scenery or historical sites near Nanjing. There are many famous scenic sites near Nanjing, such as the West Lake in Hangzhou; the Chinese classical gardens in Suzhou; the Daming Temple in Yangzhou, an ancient famous monk Jianzheng of which had gone to Japan to preach Buddhism. Because of this each year there are many Japan Buddhists coming to China to visit that Temple. but all of them I had already visited I did not want to repeat the trip. Later my eldest daughter recommended the "Old Drunkard Pavilion" to me. Her school had organized a trip there. It is in Chuzhou County, only one-hour train ride away from Nanjing. It was crowned as one of the best four ancient pavilions in China. It was built by Ouyang Xiu about one thousand years ago.

I had read something about Ouyang Xiu and I respected him. He was a famous statesman and writer. He was a reformist and was courageous. He sought to political reform and criticized the political practice fearlessly. His moral courage and outspoken words offended the authorities and was banished to Chuzhou County as the magistrate there. He drank wine to drown his sorrows and called himself "Old drunkard" I like my daughter's suggestion.

On a sun shining Sunday morning I took a train to Chuzhou. The train started and gathered speed to its capacity. I looked out through the window, the gray cottages receded from my sight fast along with trees and fields. Within a span of an hour we arrived at the Chuzhou train station. I walked along a gentle meandering road which led to the deep of the mountain where the Old Drunkard Pavilion lies. On either side of the road, ancient trees towered into the sky. The leaves were gone from the trees, yet there were few withered leaves still clinging to the branches, rustled mournfully from time to time. The fresh morning breeze caressed and cooled my face. The azure sky is so pure and balmy that I often took deep breaths of clean air. Influenced by the marvelous confluence of nice weather and beautiful scenery and my light mood, all my worldly worries ceased at that moment.

Finally, I reached the Old drunkard Pavilion. The pavilion is small and exquisite, deep and quiet, and full of poetic and artistic conception. In the Pavilion the floor was covered with grey bricks, and a statue of Ouyang Xiu was placed there. Around the walls were chairs. The building has a profound cultural background and unique and quaint architecture structures.

What left me the deepest impression was the stone tablet, on which carved another famous writer Su Shi's hand writing of the full text of "The account of the Old drunkard Pavilion.", which was written by Ouyang Xiu, recording the event of the pavilion. This prose is one of the most celebrated works in Chinese literature.

The text writes:

"Chuzhou is surrounded by mountains, and all its peaks, trees and valleys at its southwest are especially beautiful. What looks very luxuriant in trees and grass, deep and quiet pretty in scenery is the Langya Mountain. Walking about two miles in the mountain, people can gradually hear the murmur of a running stream flowing out between two peaks. It is the Niang Spring. Winding along the path of mountain ridges, people can find a pavilion close to the spring like the wings of birds. It is Old Drunkard Pavilion. Who did it? He is Zhixian, the Buddhist monk in the mountain. Who named it? He is the prefecture chief by his alias. The prefecture chief coming here and drinking together with his visitors. He is always drunk after only drinking a little and his age is the oldest in all, so he often called himself the Old Drunkard. The Old Drunkard's delight does not reside in wine but in the mountains and waters. He holds the joy of mountains and waters in his heart and finds the expression to it in wine.

Noticing the mists in the trees go off at sunrise and the caves grow dark at sunset when the clouds return back the horizon, this change from bright to gloomy is the morning and evening in the mountains. In spring, wildflowers bloom and send out a faint fragrance. In summer, the fine trees are very beautiful, luxuriant and shading. In autumn, the wind blowing, the frost condensing, the sky is high and clear. And in winter, water fails down and rocks appear. Those are the four seasons in the mountains. Climbing on the mountain at morning and turning down at evening, the scenery of the four seasons are various and the joy is also endless.

As carriers singing on the road and pedestrians resting under trees, the preceding people shouting the following responding, the old bending down and the children being held, all walking to and fro ceaselessly. They are the Chuzhou people touring about. Fishing by the stream, the stream is deep and the fish are fat; Making wine by the spring water, the water is fragrant and the wine is clear and mellow. Delicious dishes made by the mountain specialties and the vegetables picked up from the wilderness put on the table in a jumble, that is a banquet which is held by the prefecture chief. The joy of the banquet and drinking doesn't reside in the string and wind instruments but in hitting the bull's eyes in succession, play chess in victory and toasting with each other. Sometimes sitting down, sometimes standing up and sometimes uproarious talking and laughter, they are the guests of the banquet. However, who is the man with his grey hair and dropped down among all the people? He is the drunken prefecture chief himself.

Thereafter, when the sun sets to the west in the mountain, people and their shadows move scattered and disorderly. Then the prefecture chief begins to return and all his guests follow behind. The forest is shaded and concealed, the song of birds floats up and down. The tourists have gone and then the birds stay joy. However, the birds only know the joy of the mountains and trees, and they are unaware of the people's joys. People only know the joy of their tour when they followed the prefecture chief, but they may be unaware of the prefecture chief's joy. Who can enjoy together with all his guest when he is drunk and can state the story when he is sobered? He is the prefecture chief. Who is the prefecture chief? He is Ouyang Xiu who came from Ruling."

"The account of the drunkard pavilion" seemed to describe how Ouyang Xiu and his guests sought pleasure through a feast. In fact, under the cloak of happiness was hidden the great sorrow of Ouyang Xiu. In the first paragraph of the essay he wrote "The Old Drunkard's delight does not reside in wine but in the mountains and water." This sentence indicates that he is not fond of drinking. The aim of his drinking is to enjoy the mountains and waters, and the aim of his sightseeing of

A Painful Reminiscence of a Dignified Soul

the scenery is to drown his sorrows.

In the third paragraph of the essay he wrote "Sometimes sitting down, sometimes standing up and sometimes uproarious talking and laughter, they are the guests of the banquet. However, who is the man with his grey hair and dropped down among all the people? He is the drunken prefecture chief himself." This sentence indicates that while all the guests were in great excitement, the oldest man alone drank to the state of drunk so that he can forget his grief.

In the fourth paragraph of the essay he wrote "People only know the joy of their tour when they followed the prefecture chief, but they may be unaware of the prefecture chief's joy" this sentence indicates that his guests might think he also savors the joy of the tour as they do, but they are unaware of his true feelings and frustrations. The last word of the prose is "Ouyang Xiu is the prefecture chief who came from Ruling" which expressed his regret and sorrow that his lofty aspirations were unrealized and he was banished.

In short, through this prose he was just pouring out the whole store of his pent-up psychic traumas in a guise of gratification.

I have great sympathy with Ouyang Xiu, along with great admiration and respect. While I was sitting on the chair against the wall of the pavilion, stared at his statue, a torrent of thoughts rushed into my mind, redolent with the present situation of China. Ouyang was punished because he had different political views, but the emperor still gave him a lower ranking job as the prefecture of Chuzhou. How did Mao Zedong, the last emperor of China, treat his subjects who had different views with him? Millions of them were denounced, beaten, humiliated, exiled. Tens of thousands were even persecuted to death. Even his closest colleagues, like the president of the country, the minister of national defense and two marshals were driven to an end of death though they were willing to resign their positions. Compared with all the precedent emperors in China's history, emperor Mao's barbarity and atrocity certainly comes first on the list. With a mind of sadness, I heaved a deep sigh and left the pavilion on my way home.

Halfway down the mountain road I felt tired and took a rest at a wayside resting place. At the same time, I picked up a foreign magazine from my plastic bag. I wanted to find if there was any article in it that could be used in my magazine. In the resting place there were also many college students, who were reviewing their lessons for the final examination. Their school is near here. At that time very few people could get a foreign magazine to read, so my reading attracted some students' attention. Suddenly a female student came to me and asked:

"Excuse me! From where you bought the magazine? I also want to buy some"

"It isn't my magazine. It's the one my unit ordered from Foreign Language Bookstore" I answered.

"What is your unit?"

"The Academy of Social Science of Jiangsu Province"

She seemed to be admiring my job and continued:

"I am an English teacher at a junior high school. I am sent by my school to the Normal College to engage in advanced studies. We are going to have the final examination, and I happened to have some problems on English grammar. Would you mind explaining these questions for me?"

"I am glad to try it."

We began to discuss the questions she raised. After the discussion was finished, she said:

"Thank you very much! All my questions were solved. Your explanation is very clear. May I venture to ask, can I borrow some foreign magazines from you? and if I have other questions in the future, will you still help me?"

"I am willing to do what you ask for."

Then she left me her name and address and I gave her mine. Her name is Zhi Qing. After saying goodbye to her I resumed my way home.

Not long afterwards, my new friend Zhi Qing came to see me. She told me her semester had finished and she was going to return home now. She asked me whether I could lend her some English magazine to read during the winter vacation. I found one magazine to her and gave her a copy of the periodical "The Information of Social Sciences of Foreign Countries" which I edited. Then I invited her to be seated, offered her a cup of tea and began to chat. She introduced her affairs first:

"My home is at Fengyang County, Anhui Province. My father is working at tax bureau of the county, my mother is a high school teacher. Both of them were in the Liberation Army before and were discharged from active military service to Fengyang. After graduating from high school, I was sent down to the countryside as an educated youth. I stayed there for seven years. After Mao Zedong's death, I returned to the city in 1980. I failed the college entrance examination and studied English on my own at home. Then I was assigned to teach English at a junior high school. As I haven't received a regular teaching in English, I was sent to the Normal College to improve English last Summer."

I laughed and said: "You are also one of the educated youths who had been exiled to the countryside to receive reeducation from the poor peasants. You must have suffered a lot. I have great interest to know how they think and live in the countryside, will you tell me something about your experience in the country?"

She laughed too and replied: "Of course I would like. It was a special and magnificent experience. While we lost many precious things, we also gain some valuable things. It was a long story. I will tell you gradually later."

Then I told her something about my family: "I have four daughters. All of them are at the school. the eldest one is studying at Nanjing University, her major is English, the second and the third are at high school, the youngest is at a primary school. My wife died of cancer not long ago. She was a doctor."

She was surprised. She expressed her profound condolences on my wife's death and felt great sorrow and concern for me. She consoled me:

"It is really an unfortunate thing for you to be bereaved of your spouse, you must be very, very sad. But for your health and your daughter's sake you have to restrain your grief and accord with the sad fact. I know your life must be very hard, your work is heavy and you have to take care of four daughters. If you need any help, just tell me, I will do my best to light your burden."

I thanked her for her concern. Then she was going to go back home. I said "it is near noon time; you can stay and have lunch here. It's an ordinary meal. My third daughter is a good cook." She smiled, fearing it is not polite to refuse, she agreed with my invitation. It was during the winter vacation; all my daughters were at home. I introduced each of them to Zhi Qing, she had a few talks with them and watched my daughter cooking the meal in the kitchen. The lunch was prepared soon, four dishes and a soup. The dishes were nice and Zhi Qing praised my daughter's skill. We enjoyed the meal together happily. After lunch Zhi Qing bid farewell to us to go to the railway station.

After Zhi Qing returned to her college next term, she often came to see me and help me, bringing unique sweets and foods of Chuzhou to us, taking my youngest daughter to the Nanjing Cultural Palace to ride the bumper car or helping us to arrange something. We had lots of talks. The content was very wild: The discussion of English questions; the situation of our country; our past experience and our hope of the future, etc. We became good friends.

One day she began to tell me how she had been indoctrinated and misled by the party since her childhood and her life in the countryside:

"I entered primary school at six-year-old. The first time I went to school I was very excited. Our classroom was large and bright with blank white wall. A huge rectangle blackboard was against the front wall, and over it in the middle was a portrait of Chairman Mao, staring down on us beatifically. At the back of the classroom hung a red large-character maxim composed by Mao: "Study hard and make progress every day." Chairman Mao's portrait and words left me a deep impression.

Our school stressed political education, the first lesson on the first day was learning the song 'The east is red'. The teacher told us: 'This song is praising our great leader Chairman Mao. It is Mao who has led Chinese people to overthrow the reactionary Nationalist Party and to found the new China. You are the children of Mao's era, growing under the red flag. You must love, respect and listen to Chairman Mao and the Communist Party.' After finishing her word, she introduced the text of the song to us: 'The east is red, the sun rises. China has got a Mao Zedong. He seeks happiness for the people. He is the great salvation of the people.' The first thing I learned in school was to love, respect and listen to Chairman Mao.

Our teacher encouraged us to join the Young Pioneer. She told us that young pioneers are models and vanguards of the children, who love chairman Mao and our country, study hard and behave well.

For proving ourselves and for pride sake, most of us demanded an application. One week later our teacher announced that ten applicants out of the thirty at our class were accepted. I was among them. We were elated and ecstatic. But those who were not accepted seemed to be disappointed. The teacher consoled them that this was not the only chance for being a young pioneer, they could strive to win the honor on the second or third round and must not lose heart.

The next afternoon, all the new recruits of the school were gathered on the playground, then led by a band of young pioneers who were beating dumb, we entered the auditorium and stepped on the stage for the ceremony. All the teachers and students in the auditorium were warmly applauding to greet us. The headmaster congratulated us and addressed: 'Today is your great day. From today on, you will begin a new life and wear a red scarf every day. The red scarf is the emblem of the young pioneer. It signified a corner of the national flag and the blood of the revolutionary martyrs.' Then the old pioneers came on to the stage to put the red scarves on our necks and taught us how to knot it. At last, facing the red flags we raised our right hand by the ear with a tightly grasped fist and took the oath. The main text of the oath is "We are the successors of the communism. We are determined to follow the teachings of the Communist Party. Always be ready to contribute all our strength for the cause of communism.'

The ceremony was so grand, so solemn that I was extremely excited. With the red scarf tied around my neck, my heart was jumping. It was the first emotional experience I have ever had.

The teacher told us that before liberation, China was a feudal, semi colonial country, people's lives were miserable, exploited by landlords and capitalists, suppressed by Nationalist Party and foreign countries. if the revolutionary martyrs had not shed their blood for building the new China, we would be lack of food and clothes and we might not be able to sit in a classroom. In new China the people have become the master of the country and the officials are the servants of the people. All the people are equal and live a happy life. Our motherland was a huge garden and the children were flowers in the garden. The teacher also said, though fortunate be our lot, we must not forget that two thirds of the world's population are still living in 'deep water and scorching fire'. In the capitalist countries, workers are exploited by the capitalists. Their lives are very poor and hard. We should help them and have the mission to liberate all the oppressed people in the world. Moved by teacher's talk, A classmate collected pennies to donate the starving children in America. Her compositions were filled with impassioned words and sympathy. She was honored and praised as "Mao's Good Child" We were also taught that we have a duty to support the people in Asia, Africa and Latin America who were struggling against their colonial powers; and we should exalt the spirit of heroic self-sacrifice and the ideal of communism, to place the interests of the party and the revolution above everything, even our lives.

Through the teachings, textbooks, and school activities in our primary school, we were believing Mao's system of morality and attracted to communist cause which promised an egalitarian society and a best life. At that time, we were sorry we hadn't fought against the reactionary and missed the chance to become heroes; and now our chance had come, we can take part in the revolution and build a beautiful communism for our country and the world.

In 1965 I graduated from primary school. I and classmate Meng Ying entered the same junior high school. She and I were good friends. For six years at primary school, we often had intimate talks, exchanging our secrets and hearsays, sharing our joys and problems. We also often played table tennis together. We were very glad that we would remain classmate another three years.

In May 1966, Mao started the Great Cultural Revolution. We were excited, jubilant and exhausted. The movement exhilarated us. In the past we dared not to question our teachers or criticize our leaders. We were taught to obey leaders absolutely; we are mere screws of the machine and the docile tools of the party. Suddenly we could say whatever in our mind now. We could rebel and criticize even the officials in the central committee of the party. We thanked Mao for allowing us to speak out. He praised us: 'You are the morning sun, you are the hope of the country, you are the future of the country.'

Big character posters criticizing teachers and academic authorities were springing up like mushrooms in our school. Very soon Red guards appeared. Most of the first red guards were sons and daughters of high-ranking cadres, they usually dressed in old army uniforms, wore broad leather belts and military caps as a sign of their revolutionary purity, as well as a proof of their impeccable background. Almost all students wanted to join the red guards because nobody wanted to be 'unqualified', 'backward' and 'non-revolutionary'. I was then only twelve years old; I knew little things and didn't have much to say, but we had grown up believing that life's purpose was to serve the revolution. I felt I had the responsibility for the country, I had to take part in the cultural revolution, to realize communism, to protect Chairman Mao, so I always followed the red guards to do all the revolutionary work.

We thought we were real revolutionaries. it was our turn, our moment, our chance, our duty to move away from the established order and create a new china. We were guarding Mao's thought and the party's principle, and above all, we were guarding the communist ideology.

We were passionate about ideals and vowed to launch a fierce war against anyone who dares to resist the Cultural Revolution. We believed that through the revolution we would wipe out bureaucracy, corruption and privileges from government officials and academic authorities. We would build a new society in china where everyone would enjoy equality and happiness. We would build an exemplary society for the entire world.

We marched along the street, fist in the air, shouting political slogans. singing the 'Red Guards' Battle Song' composed by the Central Conservatory of Music.

We are Chairman Mao's Red Guards,

A Painful Reminiscence of a Dignified Soul

We steel our red hearts in great winds and waves,
Absolutely firm in our proletarian stand,
Marching on the revolutionary road of our forebears.

We are Chairman Mao's Red Guards,
Shoulder the heavy task of our age.
We arm ourselves with Mao Zedong thought
To sweep away all pests.

We are Chairman Mao's Red Guards,
Vanguards of the cultural revolution.
We unite with the masses and plunge into the battle,
To wipe out all monsters and demons.

Dare to criticize, dare to repudiate, dare to struggle,
Never stop making revolutionary rebellion,
We will smash the old world,
And keep our state red for ten thousand generations!"

We took revolutionary actions on the streets: cut long hairs, cut high-heeled shoes, destroy signboard with feudalist flavors. We went to the homes of the capitalist roaders and academic authorities to clean four olds.

Once we entered a restaurant and our team leader declared: "Chairman Mao taught us 'Waste is a great crime,' you must not abandon food at ease, you must finish all the food you ordered. In addition, everybody should be equal, the eaters should not be served for everything by waiters or waitresses, you must take your own food from the counter and carry the used dishes back to the kitchen. Everyone who have meal at this restaurant must observe these rules. Otherwise we reds will take revolutionary actions."

I saw some eaters who had ordered too much food Knitted their brows now. They could not eat them all, but they dare not leave the leftovers on the table. They knew the red guards would pour food down their throat by force. Looking at their ugly face I smirked.

In another case, we went to a Buddhist temple, we ordered the monks to shout the slogan: "There is no Buddha, we only believe Chairman Mao". One monk refused to call the slogan, we strung the monk by his feet and hung him from a tree.

A red guard beat him with a stick. Each time he hit the dangling victim; the body spun. It is really a funny sight. We were all laughed with our mouths shut.

While I followed the red guards to take revolutionary actions, I often had an inner conflict of ideas and emotions. On the one hand I determined to believe Mao's word and to be a revolutionary firmly; on the other hand, I also heard many invectives, lies, slanders, smears, untrue words and saw many rude, uncouth, ferocious, barbarous behaviors. When I saw children fight their parents or students beat their teachers fiercely, I felt uncomfortable and sick to my stomach, but Chairman Mao and the leading team of the CR encouraged them. I was confused, puzzled and bewildered.

I was struggling to cope with the contradiction of my mind fiercely: Whether I lack the firm stand of the revolution and the deep faith in Mao's thought or there was something wrong with the conduct of the cultural revolution. Should I loyally follow the party and Mao's call to be the red successor to the revolution or obey my own emotions, feelings, ideas? After a long period of consideration, I decided to walk my own way: Be less energetic toward the revolution and gradually retreat from the movement. Wait and see how the cultural revolution will develop and then decide my attitude.

I also had another contradictory mind and met a difficulty.

At that time, the 'blood lineage theory' became very prominent. According to that theory, one's family background determines what kind of person he is. There were slogans like 'If the father is a hero, the son will also be a hero, if the father is a reactionary, the son will be a rotten egg.' 'If a person is a dragon, his son will be a dragon; if a person is a rat, his son can only dig a hole.' The children with bad background were to be called 'dog bastards' and were often discriminated, disparaged, humiliated, spat or beaten.

My devoted friend Meng Ying, whose father is a revolutionary cadre and her grandfather is a landlord, was categorized in the good family background before the cultural revolution. During the Cultural Revolution her father was labeled a capitalist roader. Meng suddenly became a child with bad family background. She was often criticized, discriminated now.

We were repeatedly taught that 'Everyone must clarify class lines. It is a test for everyone. It will distinguish stone from gold and separate the fish eyes from the pearls' Should I still keep a good friendship with her?

One day Meng Ying was criticized. A red guard screamed hysterically at her:

A Painful Reminiscence of a Dignified Soul

'Your grandfather is a landlord. You must remold yourself seriously.' Meng replied: 'He was a landlord, he took rents, I haven't, he lives in the countryside, I have nothing to do with him.' The red guard cried again 'You see, she said she has nothing to do with her grandfather, she need not remold herself! She is openly denying the class struggle.' Another girl uttered: 'Chairman Mao taught us: In a class society everyone is a member of a particular class, and every kind of thinking, without exception, is stamped with the brand of a particular class' There is no doubt that your grandfather's reactionary class stand had influenced your father's mind and therefore your father became a capitalist roader. Your father would certainly instill some idea into your heart, how can you think you need not remold your ideology? In addition, your family hire a housekeeper, plant flowers, raise goldfishes, which reveals your bourgeois lifestyle.' Meng justified: 'My mother's health is very poor, so we have to hire a housekeeper......' Before her word was finished the red guard cut her short with a ruthless wave of her hand. 'Shut up! Nobody asked you to talk. You just listen. Hiring housekeeper is definitely exploitation'. Meng lowered her head, kept silence with tears, listening whatever they shouted about.

One afternoon after school I saw two female red guards running toward Meng, spitting on her face, throwing her books out of her bag in a great mess, knocking her down to the ground. Her glasses went flying in the air. her hair disheveled and her face was scratched. The sight shocked me and I saw terror and sadness in her eyes. I wanted to go and help her but I dared not, fearing the enthusiastic red guards criticize me for losing class stand.

Meng was a lively, brisk girl, eagerly hankers for knowledge, strain every nerve to his studies and was elected a 'Three Good Student'—superior in study, virtue and physical culture. Now she has changed into a different person. She wanted to be left alone and avoid any classmates. When she met me, she bent her head and strode away quickly. She looked languished and emaciated. Sometimes she stared blankly ahead, a withering stare of emptiness and sorrow. All her smile, song, vigor, passion, fervor and enthusiasm deserted her. She was in a pitiable, wretched plight.

Seeing her sad face and thinking of her miserable situation, I felt ashamed and guilty. She and I were seven years' close classmates, yet when I saw her being attacked by others with my own eyes and I did nothing at all. I was really a mean, petty and cowardly brat. I always wish to say sorry and apologize to her and help her in some way, but I could not find the right word to say, and I felt so powerless and inadequate that I could not find any means to help her. I delayed the apology for a long time. Finally I could not bear the pain of being guilty and feared that Meng might be hurt and scarred by my betrayal of her, I decided to see her at once, believing I need not say any fine words; my going to see her is proof that I do not forget or betray her.

One day I went to see her. First, I made a sincere apology to her. I said: 'I am sorry I haven't talked and contacted with you for a long time, and when the red guards hit you, I haven't come out to help you. It is wrong, I have failed to be your good friend, I am filled with guilt that I have hurt your heart. I beg you to excuse me. I am apologizing to you from the bottom of my heart, please believe me.' She replied me right away: 'You need not apologize at all. I have never been unhappy or complained you. During the campaign even daughters were forced to fight against their parents. You do not join them to criticize me is already not an easy thing. I thank you and I am afraid the enthusiasts would criticize you for being sympathetic with me.' I was greatly relieved by her word which was the best reward for my apology. We restored the devoted friendship and exchanged some intimate words. I encouraged her not to lose her heart, 'If we are sure we are not doing anything wrong, we are not inferior to others in any respect, it is alright. let them say what they like.' She said: 'I don't mind their criticism and bully. But according to this theory of inheritance and policy, I am afraid I would have no future. I cannot enter university. The rest of my life would not be what I had imagined. I had had many beautiful dreams. I dreamed of being a scientist and inventing some beautiful things; or being a doctor in a white coat, with a stethoscope dangling from my neck, curing and saving lives one after another; But all these dreams would never be realized. The world is cold, Life is hard, so hard that I could hardly breathe sometimes. I felt like leaves being ripped from a tree in a storm, drifting and swirling in the air without knowing where to go.' I consoled her: 'Don't be so sad and pessimistic. Everything is changing. Maybe Chairman Mao and the party would realize the mistake and correct it. She thanked me for my concern with a bitter smile.

Not long afterwards the Cultural Revolution turned from the criticism of capitalist roaders and the elimination of the four olds to seizing power through faction fighting. It was no longer a cultural revolution; it became a political struggle. I had more and more doubts and questions. I did not understand much of the policies and theories, I could not definitely judge the right or wrong, but I hated the fighting

A Painful Reminiscence of a Dignified Soul

among the people.

I did not take part in either of the two factions. I stayed among the so called "faction of free and unfettered persons(逍遥派)" I lived a leisurely and carefree life and I was no longer a revolutionary. Later facts proved that my selection was correct.

In 1969, All the old governments were overthrown and all the new revolutionary committees were established. The red guards had done the work Mao wanted them to do and had no use any more, they were sent to the countryside to receive reeducation from the poor peasants.

In 1971, When I graduated from high school, it was my turn to receive the reeducation. My teacher told me I belonged to the category now, a category of settling down in the countryside. He said it was an unalterable decision from the central government. He also said many words of encouragement, such as "Go where Chairman Mao's finger points", "The countryside is a vast expanse of heaven and earth, where you can realize your great aspirations." Some enthusiasts were inspired. They were eager to devote themselves to the great cause. Some were hesitant. Most were unwilling to go. I was in a dilemma: I did not want to be regarded as a backward element; yet I loathed to part with my parents and the city. My parents hated to bereave me and tried to keep me at home, but my father's office criticized him and forced him to let me go. My fate was sealed. My father remained speechless and my mother wept her eyes out.

The parting day finally came. My family saw me off at the railway station. The platform was a sea of heads floating around. I managed to get through the crowd and onto the train. I pushed my way with my elbows and squeezed toward my seat by the window, from which I saw my family among the crowds and shouted: "father, here I am!" They pushed their way to my place. My father reached his hand to mine and we clasped tightly, for each of us could not be sure whether we could see each other again. My mother looked extremely faint and my sister held her arms tightly. I asked them to leave because the longer they stayed the more bitter we grew. But they remained motionless. The train whistle sounded. My father was pushed away from the window by the station guard. When the train pulled away, all the crowd, including my family, moaned or cried. My tears welled up. It was a moment, however strong one was, who is weak now. It was a moment; which memory will take root in heart."

With this word Zhi Qing's eyes were wet and continued "I have told you a long story, you must be tired. I'll stop it here. I will tell you my life in the countryside next time. Is it Ok?" I nodded my head and said: "You have made a very true and moving description. Your story of the children and juvenile is a miserable story. You have been cheated and have done many foolish things. I feel sorry for you. Now is near lunchtime, you can rest for a while." After lunch, she went back to her college.

A week later Zhi Qing came to see me again and continued her story:

"When we arrived at the village, we were met by many peasants, young and old. The village head led us to the village committee. He told us: "We are now building a big cottage for you, when finished you will move in there. Now you can live in peasant's home temporarily. Then he assigned each student to a family.

This is a poor village. There was no electricity, no gas, no running water and no agricultural machinery. almost all the work was done by hand. We carried water from the well by our shoulder with a bamboo pole and two buckets. I had been prepared that life in the countryside would be very hard, but I didn't imagine it would be that difficulty.

I lived in an old female peasant's cottage. She seemed to have an affection for me and treated me as her own daughter, often caressing my hand with her rough hand and helping me to do chores. Our relationship became intimate.

I like the common peasants, they are simple, honesty. still preserved the Chinese traditional moral values: benevolence, compassion, faithfulness. Their heart is pure and clear. They respect those who have knowledge. One of our fellow students, whose father was a so-called counterrevolutionary, was humiliated and bullied in the city; but he is respected here as an intellectual. Another example: On a hot day when we hoed the soil in the corn field, I sweated so much that I was soaked wet. I tried to identify myself with the peasant. A young woman said to me: 'Don't be so hard on yourself. You can't be like us. We are used to such hard labor since our childhood; we grew up in the countryside.' All other women agreed with her. They were so kind to us but the party always force the peasants and us to work day and night regardless of our health. They are happy thought poor. They had an abundant sense of humor. They relaxed their tense lives through singing love songs and joking with the opposite sex. Unlike some residents in the cities, whose human nature is distorted and their individual feelings and sensitivity were all denied by their authorities.

When the clay house was finished, we moved in. The house has a thatched roof, two big rooms and a kitchen. We four girls lived in one room; the four male students lived in another room. We were glad to live together, for we had more common languages and feelings. We had to prepare our meals ourselves. Most of us had never cooked meal before, only a girl who knows how to cook and taught us girls the skills. The male students were responsible for carrying water and collecting firewood and lighting a fire. The village leader also offered a vegetable garden to us. We planted cabbage, lettuce, eggplant, green beans, cucumbers, etc. there.

Our farm work is hard. We worked from before the sun rise until the sun set, with an hour break for lunch. There were no weekends. We worked for seven days a week, unless we were sick or it was raining hard. Every day we started our work with the production team leader allocating jobs. We do different work according to the seasons. We planted rice, corn, sweet potatoes, vegetables and raised pigs. When we worked, we all made our best endeavor to demonstrate that we were diligent and not mocked as lazybones or backward elements. We also hoped that through our hard work we would be assigned a job in the city or enrolled into a college or Liberation Army.

In the first year, several times I had worked quite exhausted. The first is when I transplanted rice seedlings.

The day has not yet broken, stars still sparkle in the sky, we search our way to the rice seedling field. In order to double the product of rice the village plant rice twice a year, so we have to plant the first rice in early Spring. The temperature before daybreak is still very cold. When I step my right bare foot into the water of the rice seedling field, I cry and retract it at once. It is freezing. The cold-water cuts to my bone and goose-fleshes rise all over my body. I pluck up my courage and clench my teeth and step my feet into the water again. My feet are numb with cold. I begin to lift rice seedlings, tie them in bundles and place the bundles by my side. Once in a while I stand up, stretch my stiff back. Finally, the seedlings are all picked up and the seedling bundles stand the whole field. Then the male peasants carry the seedling bundles to the plowed and soaked rice fields. We also walked there to plant the seedlings into the field. We bend doubled and take backward steps, separating a few seedlings from the bundle held in the left hand and stick them into the mud with the right hand. The lines of seedlings extend fast and straightly like a beautiful green design. We are pleased with our fine work. When we plant the seedlings to the end of the field and step onto the field ridge, I see two leeches snuggling against my leg. I am horrified and hurriedly pull the slimy leech out, but the harder I pull, the deeper the leech sucks into my skin. I am frightened and the woman beside me comes to help. She slaps my leg hard near the leech and the leech retreats. She taught me the right way to remove the leech. She also told me that we cannot kill the leech by snapping the leech into two, for the broken parts of the leech would turn into two leeches. Transplanting rice shoots is really a very hard job because one has to bend so much. At the end of the day, even the toughest peasants complain about not being able to stand up straight. One may well imagine how our students would feel that day.

Another busiest time of the year for the peasants is the 'double rush', rush harvesting and rush planting. We have to harvest the first crop of rice and immediately plant the second crop. We get up early in the morning and go to the field to harvest the rice. Under the bright rising sun, the yellow rice stalks look like a golden sea. We are proud at the sight of the ripened rice—the reward of our labor and sweat. We all throw ourselves into the battle of harvest. With sickle in the right hand, grabbing a handful of stalks with the left hand, we cut them at the roots, fling them aside. Taking one step forward, working on the next handful, we slog ahead. We all bend double over the rice and wield our sickles mechanically, thinking of nothing but finishing our harvest quickly. The sun rises higher and higher and exerts its fierce power. We are soon sweating, but We are so busy that we have no time to wipe the sweat that is dripping and hurting our eyes. Our outerwear are soaked. At noon, lunch is sent to the rice field. We gobble our lunch in a few minutes and rush back to work. In the mid-afternoon our backs seem about to break. Some people are forced to kneel in the field and inch forward. I am exhausted, every muscle, every joint in my body is aching. I straighten my back from time to time and persevere in cutting stalks with set teeth till the sun is slanting. The day's work will end with each person carrying the rice stalks back to the village threshing ground. With my last bit of strength, I tie a great lot of rice stalks together into two sheaves with ropes. Then I shoulder a pole with two huge loads of rice stalks at both ends of it and stagger to the threshing ground. My shoulder aches and my legs tremble under the heavyweights of the load. Each step is a great effort. When I finally reach our destination, I throw my burden and hurry back home. After wolfing down a couple of cold corn buns and gulping down a cup of water, I throw myself onto my bed and fell fast asleep oblivious to my sweaty, filthy body and the dirty clothes. Next morning the village bell wakes me. Hurriedly having my breakfast, sharpening my sickle on a stone hastily, I throw myself into the harvest battle again. By the third day, all the rice is cut, we are all exhausted. But we cannot rest, we have to go through next hard toils, threshing rice stalks and planting a second crop of rice. The season of 'rush harvesting and rush planting' is indeed a hard time.

Thought our labor was hard, we also had happy times in the village. For example, after a backbreaking work of the day, bathing in the river was a greatest fun. We rushed toward the river with our soap, towels and clean clothes. We untied our braids, rolled our sleeves and trouser legs up high, and jumped into the river's embrace. As soon as we dipped ourselves into the cool water, our fatigue from the day's work was gone. I beat the water with my limbs comfortably, propelling myself forward or backward. When swimming, I'm in the moment enjoying the full, pure pleasure, free of all the fret and mope. Water caressed my body, calmed my mind. Sometimes we splashed water at each other for fun. We were cleansed and refreshed in the moonlight. After washing we spread plastic sheets on the grass and flung ourselves upon them. The dark dome of the sky was dotted with innumerable dazzling stars. We stared the boundless expanse of the sky and the brilliant stars with various fanciful thoughts. We are closer to nature and further away from the worldly affairs than most of the people now.

By the end of the year we'll gain the reward of our labor. A working-points recorder kept the number of points each individual earned, and the earnings were distributed according to the value of the accumulated points. The value of work point was decided by the good or bad harvest of the year, usually a work point was three or four cents. The presence of us city students diluted the value of the points, for the village did not need additional laborers. Without us they could produce the same crops, so the peasants didn't want us and viewed us as a burden. But they could not refuse to accept us, for they were ordered by Chairman Mao that they must 'welcome' the students from the city.

In China's Lunar New Year, we were allowed to visit our family in the city. It was the happiest time during the year, enjoying the affection between blood relations with our family. When we returned to the countryside, we carried delicious food as much as we could bear to satisfy a craving appetite in the countryside. We also took many gifts to give the party secretary for reasons known to all.

After one year in the village I basically learned the farm work, from planting and fertilizing to weeding and harvesting. Afterwards each year we worked day in and day out, month in and month out, year in and year out, repeatedly sowing and reaping along with the cycles of the spring and autumn. Our lives were hard and monotonous, we gradually lost our enthusiasm and anxiously craved for leaving the countryside as quick as possible. Many rusticated students began to complain. I have heard a lot of complaints; some revealed it to me privately, some grumbled in public. For instance:

"Under the veneer of empty revolutionary rhetoric 'The countryside is a vast land for great achievement' we came to the countryside, but what we achieved on this vast land except the hard labor with tons of sweats and buckets of tears? What is the purpose of Mao sending us here? I felt I was an outcast. My life has just started. Yet it is already all over. We are not allowed to complain and protest, we can only privately sing songs of misery, songs of exasperation, songs of desperation, songs of nostalgia and songs of regret."

"Mao called on us to wage war against the remnants of traditional society and pernicious influence, both Chinese and foreign. He blocked all the true information and created lies. His instruction maimed, disabled, and handicapped an entire generation of young people and made us criminals. Now the God I had enshrined in my mind was tumbling, the fervent idealism was shattered. My ignorance cost me dearly, and what remained was only frustration, disillusionment and bitterness."

"From childhood on, we were indoctrinated by Chairman Mao. He controlled everything we see, everything we hear, everything we read and learn from kindergarten to senior high school. He instructed us that communism is the most ideal social system and took advantage of our innocence and passion, our love of our country, our ardent longing for freedom and justice to take part in the revolution. We were all made idiots and clowns. What he asked us to do is to realize his ambition. We made a great mistake. 'One wrong step leads to eternal remorse.' We had to swallow the bitter fruit of following Mao's word blindly.

Some students made repentance:

"Under Mao's rule we grew up drinking wolf's milk; we were taught to hate and persecute every class enemy ruthlessly, believing 'torturing the class enemy the bitter, the more firm is my class standing. I subjected so many 'class enemies' to brutal mental and physical attacks. All my accusations against them were entirely false, groundless. Sometimes they pleaded for mercy but I had no mercy in my heart. Now all the old memories flooded back and I felt regret and guilt. What broke my heart most was the trembling, faltering sound of the singing which I forced my teacher sang: 'I am a cow ghost and a snake spirit. I am a criminal against the party and the people. I am guilty. I deserve a thousand times of death.' Whenever I think of this, the remorse and repentance nibbles my conscience bitterly. Perhaps that will be something from which I will never be free as long as I live. My guilt will haunt my mind all the time."

A student even made a list of how many victims had been beaten and tortured, how many families and churches had been ransacked, how many books and valuable things had been destroyed by him and his red guard team. His behavior was unusual and courageous because it underscored his willingness to admit his mistake and bear the responsibility. While so many people who had done the same guilt still felt free of the pangs of conscience, his conscience was not so easily numbed. I admire his frank and dauntless spirit.

There is another tragedy that makes me very, very sad. One of our educated youths doesn't want to waste her youth in the country. Considering her future and a life-long interests, she prepares to sacrifice her temporary pain to exchange a chance to leave the countryside.

She was cheated by the apparent sympathy of a villain, the brigade leader. He said he would recommend her for entering a college. One evening she went to his home to get the college registration form, he asked her for a favor. She promised to offer him expensive liquor and cigarettes, a watch or anything else. However, he told her that he wanted something spiritual. Later, he raped her after making her drink some wine.

She swallowed the insults and suffered the indignity, waiting for the day to enter college. But later the brigade leader told her that his recommendation was not approved by his superior. In fact, that was a pretext, he was going to hunt another victim.

She was totally destroyed by the strike. She sacrificed her virgin yet still could not leave the countryside. One night she secretly swallowed a lot of deadly drugs without telling anyone of us. Next morning all others got up but she did not wake. Her body was cold, her eyes were closed tightly, her lips had turned purple. We were all horrified and felt sharp pain in our heart. A young life slips away. The short song ends, the flower withers, the moon wanes, the soul floats into the sky. I mourned for her and pledge 'I will miss you forever and think about you always. Now you have God's care and is no longer suffering. We are still suffering in this world. Now is your turn to look after us from the Heaven.'

After Mao's death the sufferings of the educated youth were attached attention by the new leaders. Finally, all the settled down educated youth were instructed to return to the cities in 1980. The exile cost me seven years of prime, golden youth, doing manual work in the fields instead of studying at college.

Before I left the countryside, which I had urgently wanted to leave, now looked attractive. While I lost something in the rustication, I also gained some things valuable here: I could endure hardships and stand hard work; I learned perseverance and resilience to accommodate the difficult conditions. When I stared at all the things and people which had accompanied me for a long time, my heart ached. Giving a last look at the rice paddies, the heavy hood of gray vapors gathered about the summits of the luxuriant mountains, and the drab cottages of the peasants, I bid a final farewell to them reluctantly.

Back in the city, I was no longer the carefree teenager I was when I left home. In the highly competitive urban environment, I found the life journey of us educated youth were not easy. we have less knowledge; our ages were in the second half of the twenties. We were in the difficulties to get a job and to get married. The majority of us were in the underprivileged group. I could not find an ideal job. I decided to review my lessons at home for the college entrance examination. I failed the test. I was not disheartened and continued to study English on my own. Finally, I got a job teaching English at a junior high school."

Zhi Qing stopped her stories here. Her experience caused me great sympathy for her and a deep thought about the settled down educated youth. The fate of a whole generation of youth was controlled by a dictator. More than seventeen million youth were forced to leave their dear parents and exiled to the remote countryside. In the whole history of human society, in all the countries of the world had never seen such a cruel thing.

The relationship between Zhi Qing and I was getting closer and closer.

One day I went to Chuzhou to visit Zhi Qing. She met me at the train station. That morning her complexion seemed especially ruddy and lovable. My heart was vibrated a bit with admiration. She led me to her little room and asked me to sit in front of her desk, on which were some candy and cake. She sat in another chair by me and we began to chat. While we were talking, I noticed there was a delicately framed picture on the left top corner of the desk. I took it and had a look. It is a woman's photo about forty-year-old, not very pretty, but very decent, graceful, with a mouth wearing a subtle smile like Mona Lisa's, and a pair of vacant, staring eyes hiding some faint misery. The picture is small, about one and a half inch by

A Painful Reminiscence of a Dignified Soul

one inch, black and white, the color of the figure is already faded with the elapse of time. I asked Zhi Qing: "Is the woman your mother?" She said "She is my mother, but not blood-mother. My blood-mother gives me a body; she gives me lots of intellectual assets. She teaches me mathematics, nurtures me with her example, influences me with her ideas and feelings. She is dead."

"It's a pity. She died so young. You must miss her very much."

"Yes, she is always in my mind. I have kept her photo on the desk for nearly twenty years. I still take it as my guide when I am sailing the boat of my life on the rough sea. When I feel weak, it gives me strength; When I lose heart, it encourages me; when I am sad, it cheers me up. When I cannot bear the terrible storm and want to abandon the boat, it scolds me and demands me to brave the storm and strive to reach the calm water of my destination."

I was touched by her word and said: "While you value it so highly, why didn't you take it to a photo-studio to enlarge it, color it? The modern advanced technology can do these things easily and well."

"I have considered it, but I hesitate and never go to the photo-studio. I cannot bear to change it. This photo, though small and faded, is the one she had looked at, her hand had touched with. It may still have remained her finger prints and smell on it. I often feel it, kiss it, sniff it, I loath to part with it."

"You are really a good student. You love and respect your teacher so deeply."

"Yes, I love and gratitude her profoundly, Yet I also feel the deepest sorrow and shame for what I have done toward her. Sometimes, when I look at the photo, my heart is pierced with bitterness and my tears cannot help but stream down."

I felt strange and questioned her:

"Why?"

"Because, because I have hurt her. In fact, it is I who killed her. I am the murderer of her." With this word she burst into tears.

Her words did surprise me, horrify me, I did not know what to say. I just patted her shoulder instinctively and said: "Be calm! Be calm!"

Gradually her composure was recovered. She narrated the whole story to me in detail:

"In the autumn of 1965 I entered high school. I was happy to learn many new teachers and classmates. Among the teachers, mathematics teacher Long Zhenghua was my favorite and she was always kind to me. Long was a decent, middle-aged lady. She was a single, not married, so she put all her endeavors in teaching and treated the student as her child. One day it was raining hard after school, she lent her umbrella to a small girl while she herself went home wet. She was energetic, never tired of teaching. One afternoon she took a long time, almost losing her voice, trying to explain a question to me. When she finally helped me to understand that question, she smiled silently. She was glad that I was assiduously in learning math, never ignoring a question. Sometimes she was ill, she still came to class despite her fever.

Later I heard some talks about her. She was a graduate from law department of Central University in Nanjing before the founding of PRC and worked at the court of law as a judge for one year or two. She had been criticized during the campaign of suppression of counterrevolutionary, but had not been charged and sentenced any crime for having no evidence. She quit her job at the court and returned to her native land to accompany her mother and worked at our School as a math teacher. Her mother was categorized a landlord during the Land Reform. As she still was a suspect of counterrevolutionary and the Party's political line became more and more left-leaning, Long was regarded as a person who had serious historical problem. She was discriminated and we were warned to keep distance with her. I was in a puzzle: I love and respect her, yet I had to hear party's word.

In 1966, the Cultural Revolution started. The red guards suspected everyone and began to distinguish the enemy from the people. They regarded teacher Long as a class enemy.

One day they began to denounced teacher Long. She was escorted to the stage of the auditorium and a red guard questioned her severely:

"You had worked at the court of Nanjing. Nanjing was Nationalist Party's capital city then. The court is the state apparatus of suppressing people. You must have done many crimes; you must profess your crimes honestly and thoroughly. Our party's policy is 'Leniency to those who acknowledge their crimes and severity to those who refuse to admit' You should understand. Now tell us what crimes you had done."

"Yes, I had worked as a judge at the court, but I had worked there for only one year or two, I had made few sentences. And I made the sentences according to the law, not according to my own ideas. I did not make crimes." Long answered.

Her answer offended the red guards, incurring a gust of roar. A red guard cried:

"What you accorded with is the law of nationalist government. It is a reac-

A Painful Reminiscence of a Dignified Soul

tionist law. The fact that you practiced the reactionist law was a crime. You must profess what sentences you had made by using those reactionist laws."

"I have only investigated and tried few cases. Most cases were sentenced as minor crimes and I cannot remember them for they were things almost twenty years ago, only one case was a severe one. The criminal is a bandit, who had robbed and killed many People. I sentenced him a death penalty according to the law and the chief judge of the court approved it."

A red guard shouted out angrily: "Nationalist Party always call communists bandits, always kill communists, you still dare call him a bandit." He rushed to Long and gave her a hard hit. Long fell down the floor.

"He is not a communist. He is a bandit." Long stood up and disputed.

"You lie!" Some red guards pushed and kicked her again.

Long insisted that the criminal is a bandit. The beating continued. During all the beatings, Long did not make a single cry or scream. I saw her just biting her lower lip hard. Most red guards stayed still and some of them seemed to try to dissuade the beating but hesitated. Finally, the leader of the red guard stopped the beaters, asked teacher Long make a deep self-examination and declared the end of the meeting.

Long was left on the stage. She was badly battered, blood seeping from her face and limbs. She staggered to her room.

Afterwards, the rebels held another struggle meeting against Long. The red guards beat and humiliated her and she sternly denied their accusations

During those struggle meetings, I did not make a word. There was no way I could picture teacher Long as a class enemy. One day after the meeting a teacher came to see me. She asked me: "Why didn't you report Long's guilt in the meeting? You are Long's favorite. She must have many intimate talks to you." I said "she did not tell me any secrets." and kept silent. I did not believe teacher Long is a criminal. As if reading my mind, she smiled and said: "You are too naive. She is a wolf in sheep's skin. You should know, only 'Raging flames refine the real gold.' During the class struggle you must firmly keep your class stand. You must persuade her to admit her crime. You must express your loyal to the party and Chairman Mao."

Next morning, she asked me and two classmates to accuse Long and persuade her to admit her crimes. We went to Long's room. To express our firm class stand we demanded her to admit her crimes firmly. She denied our demand and said she did not commit any crimes. We accused her to tell lies. In spite of our repeated demand, she did not say any more word. We finally left her.

Next day an unexpected tragedy happened. Teacher Long hanged herself dead in her room. The rebels threw her corpse over the wall of the school onto the hill slope and asked teacher Li Haogu, the leader of the Mathematics Teaching Section, to inform her mother with the things left behind by her.

Her death shocked me terribly. Her death proved her innocence and I had accused the innocent. She had helped and loved me so much and I blamed her with stem words. I felt ashamed, I felt guilty.

I went to see the teacher Li Haogu. I told him I was very sad for Long's death and I asked him to let me see the things left by Long. Teacher Li was also very sad for her death. He understood my feelings and show me her watch, bank certificate and a letter to her mother. I read the letter with great sorrow and made a copy of it. Teacher Li said he was not going to send all the things to her mother right now. He did not want to hurt her mother's heart suddenly. He thought that when her mother hasn't got her daughter's information for a long time she would certainly suspect if her daughter is still alive. By that time tell her the death of her daughter, she would be less shocked. I admired teacher Li's idea. He had a great consideration about her mother's mood.

I could not sleep well that night. I read the letter again. The letter is as follows:

Dear mother:

Sorry I haven't written letters to you for a long time, for I haven't any good things to tell you and I don't want to worry you with my sad things.

When I was young, I studied law in order to do justice for the people in the future, and I became a judge after graduating from the university. I am proud of my work. But only one year or two later, I am deemed as a criminal suspect during the "campaign of suppression of counterrevolutionary" I was investigated and criticized. As they could not find any evidence I was not sentenced as a criminal but I have always remained a criminal suspect. In high school, I exert my best endeavor in teaching work and love my students, yet I still have been discriminated

A Painful Reminiscence of a Dignified Soul

and regarded as a suspect counterrevolutionary. No one dares to make friends with me, no one takes care of me. I am all alone. I am a human being I need friends, need love, need warm talks, need compassion, need consolation, but I cannot get them, I have to stay alone. I suffer from the loneliness and discrimination for sixteen years. Facing such a cold society I feel sad and melancholy. only sometimes get some enjoyment from my teaching and students.

Since the start of the Cultural Revolution, I am not merely regarded as a criminal suspect, but a criminal. I was listed in the group of "class enemies". The rebels hold struggle meetings, force me to profess I had killed communists. I vindicate that I have never been a criminal, but they blame me to lie, beat me, insult me, humiliate me. Even the students, including my favorite, do not believe me and demand me confess my crimes. I do not complain to them, they are juvenile, only twelve or thirteen-year-old, they have been taught they must love and obey the order of the party, they are also victims, but their words do grieve me a bit.

I have endured the discrimination, cold and apathy for too long a time. I am a human being, I have my honor, dignity and majesty, I cannot bear such an insult and humiliation. My tears have run out all, my heart is bleeding, I no longer want to live in this world, full of hate and hurt. I want to stop the anguish and pain. I want to go to a place where there is no cruelty, only calm, love always. I wish to die a free woman, rather than to live as a slave in a prison.

I am now thinking of the village I was born, the clean flowing water of the river, the emerald green of the mountains and your warm, dear care of your baby daughter. I'll leave them behind forever soon.

I am sorry I can no longer do my filial piety to you. I can only provide you a happy life in the next life. Please excuse me, your selfish daughter. Bye, my dear mother.

Here leave you a 700 RMB deposit certificate of the bank

and a watch. Those are my only valuable properties.

Your daughter Long Zhenghua

I read that paragraph again and again: "Even the students, including my favorite, do not believe me and demand me confess my crimes. I do not complain to them, they are juvenile, only twelve or thirteen years old, they have been taught they must love and obey the order of the party, they are also victims, but their words do grieve me a bit." My heart perceived the heaviness of the weight; I realized the gravity of my guilt; She treated me well and my reward is sharp word. How much pain she must suffer from my infliction. I sensed I was the last straw that broke the back of the camel. My guilt pressed on me like a stone slab. I felt as if a dog had bitten my conscience. I felt dazed with grief and shocked with sobs till late at night.

After I graduated from high school and went to the village, I always put her photo on the left top corner of the desk. I stared at her and often apologized to her.

In 1980, under the leadership of Hu Yaobang, all the past frame-ups and false and erroneous cases during the cultural revolution have been reviewed or rehabilitated. I decided to go back to my high school to see how they treated teacher Long's case.

I visited teacher Li Haogu at his home. I told him the aim I came back the school. We had a frank, intimate talk, pouring out our minds. I said "I have always felt guilty. Teacher Long is so kind toward me, help me so much, but I bite the hand that feeds me. I am the one who hurts her the most. I want to remedy my fault, but I can find no way to do that. if I can exchange my life for her returning the world, I will not hesitate to die. As I grow old with time, my anguish is deepened, my guilt torments my conscience. My irremediable guilt has weighed me more and more heavily." Teacher Li consoled me: "At that frenzied time, even the adults had done many foolish, wrong things, you were only twelve years old then, how can you see things clearly?" He asked me not to blame myself too much. He also said that he had made a much greater mistake than any of us. Long and him were working in the same mathematics teaching section, having a great deal of contact and knowing each other very well. He loved her, but because of her bad background he was not brave enough to court her. He felt very sad all these years and had a deep regret. He thought If he had proposed marriage to Long, the tragedy

A Painful Reminiscence of a Dignified Soul

might have been avoided. He also said, the day after Long's dead body was thrown out of the wall of the school, he had secretly gone to the hill slope to look for her corpse. He wanted to think of some way to bury it somewhere, but he could not find the body. It was disappeared. Where is it now? It remains a mystery.

I asked him whether he had sent Long's left things to her mother and how had her mother felt after she knew her daughter's death. He told me:

'I have seen her mother long ago. I tell her I am Long's colleague. She is surprised and asks me how is her daughter. I say I will tell you her situation, but you must keep calm; otherwise I will not tell you the fact. She says 'I will keep calm. In fact, I have thought of all the possibilities of her situation: she was forbidden to contact me, a landlord; she was confined in jail; she might be beaten to death by the red guards. Please tell me the truth.' Then I handed her daughter's letter, the bank deposit certificate and the watch to her. She reads the letter with tears. After reading the letter, she bends over the desk sobbing. I keep consoling her and advise her that she mustn't follow her daughter's way. For a long time, she becomes a litter composed. She thanks me and sobs out her grievances and feelings: 'I understand what she had done. Her agony is too heavy to bear. Passing away is an extrication for her. I will always remember her; I will not do the extreme thing like her. Don't worry! Please.' Then I want to leave. She asks me to stay for lunch, I decline the invitation politely, saying 'Don't stand on ceremony.' I promise to come to see her later from time to time. She saw me off at the door of her home'

'What a pity! The poor old creature.' I let out a sigh with deep emotions. 'Do you know how she is living now?'

'I did go to see her and send something to her occasionally. Her life is hard but she is still able to keep her head above water.' he replied.

Teacher Li also told me the political situations of the school in recent years. After Mao's death and the end of the cultural revolution, most of the rebels and red guards, except the few ultra-Leftists, realized they were cheated and became the paws of Mao in his power struggles. they regretted they had persecuted so many innocents. The order of school has been restored and students pay more attention to studies, for the college entrance examination has been resumed. According to the instruction from the central committee of the party, this year our school began to examine and distinguish the cases, in which the people were unjustly, falsely, or wrongly charged or sentenced. Almost all those people who had been denounced were rehabilitated. Most teachers were mourning for teacher Long's death and suggested to hold a memorial meeting to honor her. Two or three teachers who had persecuted Long cruelly opposed it, arguing that the party had claimed that memorial meeting should not be held for those who commit suicide, particularly if the suicide was clearly for political reasons. But since the cultural revolution was formally negated by the central committee of the party, the political atmosphere became much milder, so the leader still decided to hold the meeting a few days later. The school had already informed her mother and elder sister to attend the meeting.

I decided to stay there till the day when the memorial meeting held. The meeting was held in the auditorium of the school. In the middle of the platform there was a table, on which laid a great picture of teacher Long. In front of the picture was a brown box containing her hat, clothes, because there was no her cinerary casket. By both sides of the table stood many wreaths. All the teachers and students were present at the meeting, wearing a black mourning armband on the left arm. Long's mother and several Long's former students were also participating in the meeting.

At nine o'clock in the morning, the chairperson of the meeting called the meeting to order. First, he asked all the people present to stand up in solemn silence. Next, he asked us to make three bows to the photo of the deceased. Third, he asked us to pay a three-minutes' silent tribute to teacher Long. Then he asked us to be seated again and invited the party branch secretary to deliver a memorial speech. The secretary praised Long as a model of the teacher, having an exceedingly loving heart and sense of responsibility. She organized teaching course serious and helped students earnestly and patiently. He said her passing away was a tremendous loss of our school and brought us great grief and wound. He did not rehabilitate her case for she was not formally charged any guilt, and he did not mention her suicide and the cause of her suicide. Then the chairperson invited Long's colleagues, friends, students to make speeches. A teacher, who had persecuted Long most fiercely, also made a speech. He said he and Long were good friends and he cherished the memory of Long very much. He did not make the least apology to Long. His speech was downright farcical. I despised him.

Teacher Li and I also made a speech. I said:

'I came here from thousands of miles away to attend the meeting, not only for commemorating teacher Long, but also for offering my deepest apologies for my fault. Twelve years ago, while teacher Long was at her most difficult time, I was

A Painful Reminiscence of a Dignified Soul

not helping her, consoling her, but condemning her. Teacher Long was my dearest, most respected teacher then. She often gave me remedial courses when I had difficulties. She often encouraged me to study hard and take good care of me, treating me like her child. When the cultural revolution started, she was charged with many crimes, being tormented fiercely. Though I did not know whether those charges were the facts or not, I thought that I must believe the party and obey my teacher's instruction. I went to her room with two classmates and abused her seriously. Her miserable death woke me up to the reality and realized my mistake. I have suffered from my betraying my conscience ever since, and felt pain extremely. Now she was officially rehabilitated, so despised the long distance I came here to express my apology to her. Some people advised me not to blame myself too much for I was very young at that time. Indeed, I was too young then, yet one is never too young to have vanity. At that time, I was afraid people would look down upon me, regarded me as a backward element. I had to admit my mistake and guilt. What tortures me now is the problem: If I owe an obligation to a living person, I can always think of some way to square accounts. But the person I have wronged is already dead, how can I atone for my crime? I know I can never make amends; I have to bear the guilt for the rest of my life. The only thing that can lighten my burden and soothe the wounds of my heart is to do my best to practice what teacher Long had taught me: to study hard, to be honest, to have a noble ideal, to be a doer not a speaker. I wish all of you to supervise what I do in the future. Thank you all."

After the meeting Teacher Li invited Long's mother and I to have lunch at a restaurant. He ordered several delicious dishes, but Long's mother had no mood for the food. She complained: 'Taking part in daughter's funeral for a mother is already a very sad thing, and I cannot even visit my daughter's grave. Where is her body? Where is her sour?' She was filled with an ineffable sorrow and bewailed her deceased daughter exceedingly. My heart ached, but I could not find an effective word to comfort her. Some human misery is unable to be assuaged, at such times silence seems preferable to hollow condolences. We just urged her to have meals. After having a few food, she thanked teacher Li and bid farewell to us to go back home. Teacher Li and I also went to our own places.

After returning my lodge, I kept thinking about the poor old woman's word: 'Where is Long's body?' Her dead body was thrown on the hill slope and the next day it disappeared. I know there is a habit in Tibet called "celestial burial(天葬)". They throw the dead body of the deceased on the top of mountain to feed the vulture. But in our place there neither vulture nor fierce beasts. Long's body could not be eaten by birds or wild animals. It also could not be decomposed and destroyed by the weather within a day, so I guessed that there must be somebody or the policeman who collected the body for the sake of goodness or protection of the environment. I decided to make some search for the body.

I began to visit some peasants who lived near the hill slope where Long's body lay. I entered a peasant's home and started the talk with an old woman: 'I am a former student of that high school at the top of the hill. During the cultural revolution a female teacher was persecuted to death. The rebels threw her body on to the hill slope outside the wall of the school. Now the teacher is rehabilitated by the authority. We have held a memorial service for her, and now we are going to find out where her body was laid. Did you see the body at that time or know where the body is placed now?' The old female peasant said that she felt very sad for the poor teacher but she did not see or hear anything about the body. I thanked her and left.

I went to the second, the third, the fourth peasant's home and asked the same question and got the same answer. I felt a little disappointed and even wanted to give up the search. But the pathetic face of Long's mother reverberated and lingered in my brain, my feet involuntarily entered into the fifth peasant's home.

The owner is a very old peasant with deep crow's feet at his eye's corner and white whiskers around his cheek. He warmly accepted me and listened to my narration patiently. Like other peasants he said he knew nothing about the body. But I noticed that when I asked 'Did you see the body at that time?' his face muscles contracted slightly. I grew some doubt. I continued to explain: 'I am really her student. I love her. I am not from the police or other office to investigate something about it. In addition, though she was regarded as class enemy at that time, she is now rehabilitated. There isn't any problem about her. If you knew anything about the body, please tell me.' He still insisted on his ignorance. But all his attitude and speech were unnatural. I believed he must know something about it and begged him again and again to tell me the truth. He kept silence for a long time and finally moved by my streaming tears and tell me the fact:

'You are really a benevolent girl and full of gratitude for your teacher. I'll tell you the truth. During the cultural revolution, people condemn and fight each other all the time. The tragic sight was really unbearable. One day I went to the hillside to pick up firewood. Suddenly I saw a woman's corpse. I was horrified and returned home immediately. I am afraid I'll be suspected to be involved in the case.

A Painful Reminiscence of a Dignified Soul

At home I cannot but think of the woman. How pitiful is the woman, killed in her prime age. And even no people send her body to the crematory or bury her. They are not human beings. I often go to the hill slope to collect firewood. How can I bear to look at that dead body? How can I bear to look at that dead body rotted day by day? Suddenly an idea burst into my mind: maybe I can perform an act of mercy, burying the body somewhere. The Buddha will commend me and bless me sometimes. I am happy with the idea. On that evening, with the help of my son we carry the body to my home. I dare not bury it in the hill slope, fearing others blame me to sympathize a class enemy. We dig a deep pit in our backyard, wrap the body in a mat, put it in the pit, and then cover it with earth. Later I planted a peach tree on it. That is the whole story. I hope you do not tell it to anyone else. I do not want others to comment whether I have done a philanthropic act or I have done a wrong thing.

I was deeply touched by what he had done. He was really a kind-hearted old man. I gave him my heartfelt thanks and asked him: if I want to offer sacrifices and pay respects to teacher Long tomorrow morning, will he permit me. He allowed me to do what I wish to do.

Next morning, I bought some fruit, food and a bunch of flowers to the old peasant's home. I put them in front of the peach tree. Then I made three bows before the sacrifice, mourned in silence for a long time and delivered a few memorable words: 'Dear teacher Long, I have come here to see you, to express my love and respect to you. I am glad I finally find your last place. I deeply regret that I have hurt you so much, I have been devoid of gratitude and I have made a great guilt. I have come to apologize to you. Please excuse me. I will do my best to follow your example and teachings. Wish you a happy life in the Heaven; wish you continue to take care of me. Goodbye teacher Long.' After I finished my word, I went to the peach tree. I touched the tree affectionately as if I touched her hand.

After my memorial service I returned to the old man's room. I thanked him again and said: 'You are really kind-hearted and have a great mercy. You have done a charitable deed. You will certainly get the great reward from Buddha later.' He answered: 'She had suffered great pain and was treated as a beast. I pity her. They are not human beings. I am a man; I do a thing a man ought to do.'

I was a little relieved after I had done all the memorial things. I returned to my home.

After hearing the narration rendered by Zhi Qing, I like her more and more, a really lovable woman, kind, frank, honest and having a heart overflowing with gratitude for benefactor. I think if I am not too older than her, I will ask her to marry me and my passed away wife in the Heaven will feel at rest that I remarry one who will not ill-treat our children.

We have more contact and always have heart-to-heart talks.

One day I started a talk:

"When Mao was alive, he advocated communism and always talked beautiful words, such as serving the people, equality, morality. After his death, people found that Mao's doctrines were false fallacies, his practices had caused great disasters, his Communism is but a Utopia; They also found that Mao is really a base man full of greed and lust. Most people lost all the faiths. Their ideologies and moralities were in a state of "double vacuum" They are angry they have been cheated out of all their lives. They no longer believe any preaches and moralities; they only think of self-interest. The fashion nowadays is all for money and power. They regard having great money to be the most important and happiest thing. Do you also think so or agree with their views? Tell me your true ideas."

"I admit I like money. Money can improve our life, can help us to do good things. But I don't think it is the happiest thing. Happiness lies not merely in the possession of money; It lies in having a harmonious, perfect family, in gaining a prominent accomplishment in one's career, in making great contributions to the country and the world, etc. A man's real worth depends not upon his wealth, rank, or fame but upon his character and virtue. It is the spirit that matters most in one's life."

"You are right. I agree with you. True happiness should be measured in other than material things." I answered.

"Then, what do you think is the happiest thing in one's life?"

"I do not know what is the happiest thing, I only know the 'Three Hearts'— a heart of love爱心, a heart full of conscience良心, a heart of a child童心—have made me happy. Since my childhood, my teachers taught us 'All love me and I love all' 'love of mankind' 'with love your heart is perfect' The well-known writer Bing Xin has a famous word 'Once one owns love, one has everything.' The books tell me 'Love constitutes the pivot of our life.' "Love is the most precious thing in the universe" 'loving, giving, helping, cherishing and contributing is the happiest thing.' Following these teachings, I highly value the feeling of love. I love everyone, I lead a thrifty life and share lots of my money to help those in need, I always eagerly make efforts to help others. At the same time. I abide by Gandhi's preach

A Painful Reminiscence of a Dignified Soul

'By the law of love we are required not to return hatred for hatred, violence for violence, but to return good for evil.' and Martin. Luther King's word 'Darkness cannot drive out darkness; only light can do that. Hate cannot drive out hate; only love can do that. We must meet the force of hate with the power of love; we must meet physical force with soul force.' So I do not hate anyone. Even people wrongly denounce or persecute me, I do not hate them. I would be angry but I can excuse or pity them for they are but poor victims of evil doctrines. Since I only have love and no hate, I always feel happy.

I have a good conscience. Conscience is an inner feeling, guiding to the rightness or wrongness of one's behavior. I don't want to hurt my conscience any time. When I do something, I will consider whether my behavior catch up with my conscience. I never wrong others. Even though the party always force us to expose the 'faults' of our kins, friends and colleagues, I have never denounced a single one in my life, which makes me feel calm and proud. I also always sincerely feel grateful for other's care and favor, and always seek ways to double return their kindness. All these conducts give me great satisfaction and happiness.

I highly admire child's heart. Child is always pure, true, simple and honest, knowing nothing of lie, cheat, intrigue, calculation, flattery and boast. I try hard to keep my child heart unstained. I have never tricked anyone, flattered anyone, or do any evil things, so in my memories there isn't any reminiscence of repentance. Without painful regret is a great happiness.

In short, the 'Three Hearts' give me peace, consolation, stimulation, happiness and good health, and bear me up through all dark periods. With these hearts, honor or insult would not disturb me, I would treat them slightly just as the blooming and withering of flowers; Fame and profit would not impact me, I would indifferently look at them just as the gathering and drifting of the cloud in the sky. I try hard to be calm amidst excitement, patient under trials, never unduly elated by success and depressed by defeat. I keep a greater tolerance and an easygoingness about other's attitude, manners and way of life. Though my lot is rather bad and my life is full of twists and turns, I have still been very happy. I hope everyone to keep the "Three Hearts".

"You can always feel happy? That's good. I have been thinking you might always be unhappy because you suffered so many misfortunes. Your mental attitude is excellent, I admire you and I'll learn from you.

After about one year's communication between Zhi Qing and I, we have deeper and deeper understanding and affections.

One day we made a tour to the Yellow Mountain. It is widely believed as the most beautiful mountain in China. We took a bus there first and then walked up the mountain. The landscape is really entrancing. There are many lofty and steep rock peaks in the mountain, which have no soil. But there are still many pine trees on the rock. The pine trees here are variants of the ordinary pine. They grow in areas very high above sea level with special natural environment. The pine trees have short and thick needle leaves and peculiar shapes. Some pines grow horizontally or slantingly on the steep slopes. I wondered how can the pine trees grow on the rock A worker there explained that when their seeds drop into cracks in the granite and then germinate. Their roots can secrete some acid matter which corrode the rock and transfer them into nutrients to be absorbed by the tree. Finally, the pine trees tenaciously bore into the rock. I am stunned by the great life force of the pine trees.

In order to strengthen our nerves, we decided to climb the Tiandu peak, which is one of the three main peaks of the Yellow Mountain and the most perilous one. When we were near the top of the peak, we had to pass a Carp Back, which is a stone bridge, ten-odd meters long and only one meter wide. On both sides of the Carp Back are over one thousand feet high cliff and the deep valley. Looking at the narrow "Heaven Ladder" we were fear-ridden and dare not cross it. But there were travelers behind us, we could not retreat. We had to pluck up courage and step up cautiously, hold the cables along the path tightly. Finally, we crossed the Carp Back and gradually reached the summit of the peak. Standing here we feel like in a fairyland. From a distance, the tens of steep peaks, the grotesque rocks and the peculiar shaped pine trees come hand in hand amidst the sea of clouds. Usually clouds are in the high sky we have to raise our heads to look at. Now the clouds are below our place, we bent our heads to enjoy the strange, fascinating sights. The clouds were flying with the wind, now rising, now dropping, now gathering, now drifting; like a sea of billowing waves.

After staying on the top of the peak for some time we went down along another narrow path. We appreciated the landscape and talked about our impressions. I said:

"While the magnificent scene gives me great enjoyment of beauty, it also causes me some reflections. I remember an ancient poem written by Bai Juyi.

A Painful Reminiscence of a Dignified Soul

    Mounting on high
    I begin to realize the smallness of man's domain;
    Gazing into the distance
    I begin to know the vanity of the carnal world.
    I turn my head and hurry home
    Back to the court and market,
    A single grain of rice falling
    In the grain barn.

Today I experience such feelings myself. In the endless time and space of the universe, the life of a man is really like a dust in the sky. The process of a man's life is the same as an ant's life—birth, old and death. Mao thinks he is a great emperor, yet he also has a death as a common people. Why so many people struggle for power and profit all their lives, even conduct things that are extremely cruel and inhuman. The world is indeed too complicated, repugnant and intrigued. I am a mediocre person, have no interest to compete with others, only want to do my proper share for the common good."

"You are too self-abased," Zhi Qing said, "you can do some excellent things."

"I am not self-abased. Large part of my life has been wasted under Mao's rule. There isn't much time left for me. My deepest desire now is the realization of democracy in China and the creation of a new family again."

She remained silent for some time. Suddenly she asked me a question: "What is your age?" I was a little surprised but soon I was conscious why she asked that question. I smiled and said:

"Age should not be considered merely by the count of years. There are many kinds of ages: physical age, psychological age, feature age, spiritual age, and so on. There are persons who are in forties but already lie on deathbed because of many diseases. On the contrary, some old people over eighties years can still walk fast and vigorously: Some young man looks much older than his actual age because he is always pessimistic and disheartened. But some men live to the advanced age of 90 still full of vigor and in high spirits. As for my age, I think, if judged by my life experience, I might be in the sixties, for I have seen so much of the world, I have tasted all the sensation of bitter, sweet, salt, sour of life; if by counting the years I have lived I am in fifties; If judged by my appearance, I can be regarded in forties; If judged by my health, I seem to be in thirties; if judged by my spirit, I am in no way different from what I was at the age of twenty. If there is a demonstration against the Communist Party now, I would certainly take part in it as I did against Nationalist Party about forty years ago. Vigor will incline, vitality will decay with the passing of time. Time will wear body but cannot wear spirit. Spirit is a state of mind . it can be unchanged.

My answer must be quite out of her expectation and imagination. She did not answer my question. I guessed she must be thinking if what I said was likely. I was confident she would agree with my description. She knew I had undergone more painful vicissitudes of life than ordinary people; She had said I looked young and we had a photo taken together which showed no big gap between our ages; She also knew I had won the fourth place in the competition of a long distance race in the old men's sports meeting of Jiangsu Province government. The first three winners were all the members of the Geological Prospecting Team, who had always trekked up mountains and down dale all year round. Of course, they would run faster than I.

After a long time of silence, she said:

"You are really like what you say. You can certainly live until one-hundred-year old. Now I'll tell you a secret of mine. Since we get to know each other, I have always admired you very much. You are amiable, frank, honest, trustworthy and intelligent. When I know you have lost wife, I have great sympathy for you and I think you need a woman to help and accompany you. I want to be such a woman, but I have always been troubled by the distance of our ages. What you say today has dispelled my misgivings. There are also many couples who have large distance of ages, like Lu Xun, Xu Beihong, etc. so I am going to marry you now, do you think I deserve to be your couple?" With this word her cheeks were suffused with blushes. I was extremely delighted with her word and said: "It is I who is not worthy of your company. You always help me, take care of me, I am very grateful to you. I also love you very much, but I also have the same problem: the gap of ages. If you are willing to marry me, of course I am excited. But you have to carefully consider the disparity of our age. You must not act on the impulse of the moment, lest you regret in the future. You can think of the question more thoroughly, then make a final decision. Do you think my opinion is right?"

She agreed with my opinion and said, "I will think the question over again. But believe me, my feeling is true."

We ended the Yellow Mountain trip with a double happiness.

A Painful Reminiscence of a Dignified Soul

In a couple of weeks, she told me she had considered the question over and over again. She believed that my body is very stout and we could live together at least for thirty or forty years, and thirty or forty years' happy life is enough for a person, so she was determined to marry me.

We went to the civil administration office to get a marriage certificate. We got married on November 17, 1986.

During these two or three years the situation of my family had great changes. In the Summer of 1986, my eldest daughter graduated from Nanjing University and was assigned to work at the English newspaper "China Daily" in Beijing. My youngest daughter, an eleven-year-old girl, was admitted to Shanghai Dancing College and went there to learn ballet in the fall of 1986. My second daughter graduated from high school in 1987 and went to work in Shenzhen, Guangdong Province, a special economic zone in China. Next year my third daughter graduated from high school and went to work in Shenzhen too. My wife Zhi Qing graduated from the Normal College in 1987. She returned to her junior high school and worked there for one year as a reward to the school, in 1988 she was transferred to Nanjing and got together with me. After so many years toss and turn, I finally have a normal, happy family again.

After the party general secretary Hu Yaobang was dismissed in January 1987, the Central Committee of the Party passed the resolution about "Improving and strengthening the ideological and political work of the institution of higher learning". The Party highly enhanced the control of the ideology, expression and speech. The whole country was engulfed in silence. But the taciturnity was not succumbing. The exasperation was accumulated in the taciturnity and waited for the chance to explode.

On April 15 1989 Hu Yaobang suddenly died of a heart attack. Hu was a reformer who favored complete economic overhaul and political reform and was deeply cherished by the people. Students had great sympathy with Hu and believed that Hu's death was clearly related to his forced resignation. Hu's death provided the impetus for students to gather in large numbers. In university campuses, many posters appeared eulogizing Hu, calling for a revival of Hu's legacy. Spontaneous gatherings to mourn Hu began on April 15 around Monument to the People's Heroes at Tiananmen Square. Student gatherings also began in Xian and Shanghai on April 16. On the night of April 17 four thousand students of Beijing University and Tsinghua University marched from the campus towards Tiananmen Square.

They joined forces with those already gathered at the Square. As its size grew, the gathering gradually evolved into a protest. Students drafted a list of pleas for the government:

1. Affirm Hu Yaobang's views on democracy and freedom as correct.
2. Admit the campaigns against spiritual pollution and bourgeois liberalization were wrong.
3. Publish information on the income of state leaders and their family members.
4. Allow privately run newspapers and stop press censorship.
5. Increase funding for education and raise intellectuals' pay.
6. End restrictions on demonstrations in Beijing.
7. Provide objective coverage of students in official media.

From April 18, some students also gathered at the Great Hall or Xinhua Gate, the entrance to Zhongnanhai, the seat of the party leadership to demand dialogue with the leadership. On April 20, a group of workers formed the Beijing Workers' Autonomous Federation not under the central leadership. Three students knelt on the steps of the Great Hall to present a petition and demanded to see Premier Li Peng. However, they were refused to enter the Great Hall.

On April 23, forty students from 21 universities formed the Beijing Students' Autonomous Federation in a meeting. The Federation called for a general class boycott at all Beijing universities. The situation became more serious and volatile. Zhao Ziyang stressed to hold open forms of dialogue with students. Premier Li Peng promoted to condemn protestors and to take more serious action. Zhao left Beijing for a scheduled state visit to North Korea on April 23. In Zhao's absence, Li Peng and the leader of Beijing municipality framed the protests as a conspiracy to overthrow China's political system and took firm action against protesters. On April 25, Li Peng's hardline stance was endorsed by Deng Xiaoping. On April 26, the party's official newspaper People's Daily issued a front-page editorial titled "It is necessary to take a clear-cut stand against disturbances." The editorial effectively branded the student movement to be an anti-party, anti-government revolt.

The editorial enraged students, the next day of the publishing of the editorial, almost one hundred thousand students marched through the streets of the capital to Tiananmen Square, breaking through lines set up by police, and receiving wide-

A Painful Reminiscence of a Dignified Soul

spread support of the residents.

As Zhao Ziyang returned from North Korea, he asked the press report the movement positively. He said that the student's concerns about corruption were legitimate, and that the student movement was patriotic in nature. He was even willing to withdraw the April 26 editorial on his own account as the General Secretary of the Party. But Li Peng, backed by Deng Xiaoping, refused to retract the editorial.

As the protests developed, the authorities veered back and forth between conciliatory and hardline tactics, exposing deep divisions within the party leadership.

On May 13 students on Tiananmen Square pledged a hunger strike unless granted a meeting with government officials. Thousands suffered dehydration and exhaustion. The hunger strike galvanized support for the students across the country. Protests of varying sizes were occurring in almost all the big and medium cities. From May 17-18, around a million Beijing residents from all walks of life held demonstrations. Including many party, government organizations and factories. In Nanjing there were also great demonstrations. Our unit, the Academy of Social Science, also held a demonstration. The student movement also attached great attention to the world, many foreign governments urged Beijing to exercise restraint.

Facing the intractable situation Deng Xiaoping decided to move troops into Beijing to declare martial law. Zhao Ziyang's concessions-based strategy was thoroughly criticized. Zhao announced that he was ready to take leave, he could not bring himself to declare and carry out martial law as the general secretary of the party. He was in fact deprived all his power.

In the early morning of May 19, Zhao Ziyang went to Tiananmen Square and made a speech with a bullhorn to a crowd of students, urging the students to end the hunger strike. He said; "Students, we came too late. We are sorry. You talk about us, criticize us, it is all necessary. The reason that I came here is not to ask you to forgive us. All I want to say is that students are getting very weak, it is the 7th day since you went on hunger strike, you can't continue like this. ……You are still young, there are still many days yet to come, you must live healthy. ……You are not like us, we are already old, it doesn't matter to us anymore." This short emotional speech is his political swan song. He confirmed that students' criticism is necessary. He was sorry he came too late. He was apologizing to the students and expressed that anything doesn't matter to him now. From then on, he was put under house arrest for 17 years till his death.

On May 20 Li Peng declared martial law and mobilized as many as 300,000 troops to Beijing. When the army was entering the city, they were blocked at its suburbs by throngs of protesters. Tens of thousands of demonstrators surrounded the military vehicles, preventing them from advancing. Protesters lectured soldiers and appealed to them to join their cause, they also provided soldiers with food, water, and shelter. Seeing no way forward, the authorities ordered the army to withdraw on May 24. The army retreated to bases outside the city. Students still refused to withdraw from the Tiananmen Square and Li Peng continued to refer to the protesters as terrorists and counterrevolutionaries. And the final assault against the protesters began on the evening of June 3. The protesters and residents blocked the incoming army as they had done two weeks before. But this time the army fired at the protesters with automatic rifles and the tanks rolled into the city. As the battle continued between the army and the crowds along the road, the firing became indiscriminate, killing both protesters and innocent bystanders. The massacre went on till the morning of June 4. They finally reached and cleared the Tiananmen Square. The students on the Square were forced to withdraw. The imposition of martial law plunged the city a bloodbath. On June 6, spokesman Yuan Mu said at the press conference that about 300 civilians and soldiers died, including 23 students from universities in Beijing. Other estimates of the death toll have been higher than the figures announced by the government. After the massacre the government made widespread arrests of protesters and their supporters. The suppression of June 4 is a watershed event of the end of the policies of liberalization practiced by Hu Yaobang and Zhao Ziyang in the 1980s. The one-party dictatorship has remained. The bud of democracy was brutally snapped.

The massacre of June 4 roused me great indignation. I had taken part in the demonstration against Nationalist Party, they did not dare to open fire on us; but the Communist Party, which claimed to be the savior of the people, dared to open fire from rifles and roll tanks over the students. It is too cruel and barbarous without human nature. I am ashamed to be a member of the party, so I decided to risk anything to quit the party. When I was labeled as a rightist and expelled from the party in 1957, nobody dared to contact me. But this time many party members praised me. A female party member in forties-year-old told me, she also wanted to quit the party, but having teenage children still, she could not do that. The party had betrayed the people and completely lost the faith of the people. The date of June forth became forever etched in my memory.

At that time, I was already sixty-one-year-old. My life will soon be ended. My prime time from 21 to 60 was all elapsed to work under the one-party dictatorship. Much of my time was wasted. Fortunately, I have received fine traditional education in my childhood and youth. I have been able to distinguish what is right and what is wrong. I haven't become the accomplice of the oppressors and never condemned or persecuted any so-called class enemies. I retired according the policy. I lament my declining physical strength and powerless, but I firmly believe that our younger generation will surely abandon the dictatorship and build a democratic China in the future.

I am eagerly looking forward to the great glorious day.

Epilogue

AFTER I RETIRED IN 1989, I had full confidence that in the next twenty years the one-party dictatorship would certainly be ended, Mao Zedong's crimes would surely be acknowledged. However, thirty years after the June 4 massacre, democracy is still not realized. On the contrary, the one-party dictatorship seems to be strengthened; Mao's portrayal is still hung on the Tiananmen gate tower and printed on the banknote (RMB).

Mao's successor Deng Xiaoping knew clearly that he himself hasn't enough prestige and power to force all the people to obey him. He has to rely on Mao's one-party dictatorship to control the country. One party dictatorship is in fact one-man dictatorship. Party is not a living thing. It cannot speak or write. There must be a man to speak for it. If he kept the one-party dictatorship, his word is the party's word. Then he can practice the dictatorship in the name of the party and people have to obey him.

By making use of Mao's one-party dictatorship, Deng Xiaoping consolidated his power. Before his death he handed over his power to another Maoist Jiang Zemin. Jiang is a vulgar, selfish, greedy politician. For maintaining his power, privilege and profit he firmly kept Mao's one-party dictatorship. He hung on in his leading post for 16 years (from 1989 to 2005). Even after he left office he still acted as a director of his successors. For this reason, the democracy cannot infiltrate into China even now.

As Deng and Jiang practiced capitalist market economy under the system of one-party dictatorship, and as all the political power and material resources were grasped in the hands of officials, they and all the party officials could easily use their power and position to get money. As a result of it very soon corruption became rampant and seeped into virtually all levels of government and all organizations throughout the country. They pursued and gained great private profits at the expense of the interest of the people and caused an enormous wealth disparity. In an online opinion poll in 2010 by the People's Daily, 91% believe "All rich families in China have political backgrounds" People complain "There is no official without corruption (无官不贪)" Toward the problem of corruption Jiang Zemin has always taken an acquiesce attitude, so the corruption became increasingly intense. Only when Xi Jinping assumed the leadership of the party in 2012 and took severe measures to check corruption, the situation became a little better.

Apart from the corruption, the quality of the people has greatly declined. From leaders, officials to the common people, most of them lose their old intrinsic ideological, ethical, and cultural traits. They are only concerned with money, power, fame, lust, car, house now. In the past, China had been called "the land of courtesy and propriety" and now has been called "the land of savage and barbarity". According to "The ranking of global citizenship" published by the United Nations, the quality of Chinese citizen has ranked 160ths in the world for many years and the last in one year.

In order to keep their power and profit, Deng and Jiang have to constantly, strictly hide the true history, hide the evil, harm, cruelty and viciousness of Mao and one-party dictatorship. and forbid people to listen or read any different and outside information. They spared no efforts to praise Mao's "merits" and the high value of one-party dictatorship all the time. Their twenty-odd year rule brought about two great results: first, the rampant corruption and the declining quality of the people; second, most people, especially the young generation, are being cheated; they esteem Mao and believe that one party dictatorship is a good and necessary system. They do not know the true history. Cultural Revolution is a ten-year-long disaster, but Some young people want to start a second cultural revolution.

China is still greatly exacted by the dead hand of the bygone Mao's tradition.

The situation and the miserable, possible prospect frighten me. If Mao's evil influence still lingers on, his portrait hangs on the Tiananmen gate tower forever, all the following generations will suffer from the totalitarian rule and live as slaves. And if China's leader can extend one party dictatorship to other countries in the future, the world will suffer from it.

A Painful Reminiscence of a Dignified Soul

In order to end the dictatorial system in China, I think, we must first let people know Mao's true features and deeds. We must eliminate the poisonous influences of Mao Zedong, move Mao's portrait out of Tiananmen gate tower and the banknotes. China can have hope only when it negates Mao's political line.

Mao has died over forty years. People who know the true facts under Mao's rule have become fewer and fewer, if these old people do not leave their words in the world, the true modern history will fall into oblivion and China will never become a democratic country. The heavy weight of responsibility pressed me to do something. Though I am already ninety-year-old and I am not a writer, I decided to overcome all the difficulties to state some facts happened during the period of Mao's era, so that the deceived people can know some true history. That's the reason I write this book.

With the finish of the book I think I must contradict some argument about Mao Zedong.

Many Maoists argue that Mao has done many great deeds: turning China From a semi-feudal and semi-colonial society to a modern country; unifying China by defeating the separatist warlord regimes; ending the imperialist control over China; making China a world power and Chinese people stand up proudly in the world.

Their argument is not the fact. They are deceived by the communist Party. It is the Revolution of 1911 led by Sun Yat-sen which overthrew the Qing feudal dynasty, not the Communist Party.

In the aftermath of that Revolution China did have once fragmented by many warlords. In 1928 the National Revolutionary Army led by Chiang Kai-shek launched the Northern Expedition(北伐). The Nationalist forces advanced northwards and secured a series of decisive victories against the warlords. In December 1828 the last warlord of Manchuria(东三省) announced to accept the authority of the nationalist government in Nanjing and China was reunified so the unification of China is Ching Kai-shek's deed, not Mao Zedong's deed.

China became a world power before the founding of the PRC. On October 30, 1943 the government of the Republic of China, the United States, the United Kingdom, the Soviet Union signed on the "Four Power Declaration" at the Moscow Conference(莫斯科会议). The main clause of the Declaration is that the four nations recognize the necessity of establishing at the earliest practicable date a general international organization (the United Nations) based on the principle of the sovereign equality of all peace-loving states. At that time China is already generally recognized to be a great power in the world, and the Republic of China is one of the four founders of the United Nations and one of the five permanent members of the Security Council of the United Nations. How can you say it is Mao who makes China a world power?

In November 22-26, 1943 a conference was held in Cairo, Egypt. The Cairo Conference(开罗会议) outlined the Allied position against Japan during World War Two and made decisions about postwar Asia. The meeting was attended by President of the United States Franklin Roosevelt, Prime Minister of the United Kingdom Winston Churchill, and Generalissimo Chiang Kai-shek of the Republic of China. One clause of the Cairo Declaration is "all the territories Japan has stolen from the Chinese, including Manchuria, Formosa （台湾), and the Pescadores(澎湖列岛), shall be restored to the Republic of China". And in fact, the Republic of China had taken back those places in 1945, so it is Chiang Kai-shek who recovered the lost territory, not Mao Zedong.

People's Daily bragged that Mao Zedong had performed four meritorious deeds for our country and people: 1, Founding a nation—The People's Republic of China; 2, Founding a Party—The Communist Party of China; 3, Founding an army—The Chinese people's liberation army; and 4, Establishing Mao Zedong thought. The editorial created great lengthy words to vindicate its arguments. All of its words are rubbish, no worth refuting at all. I can use very simple words to prove that all the four things Mao had done were wrong doings or crimes.

First, Mao did not found a nation. China has existed for over five thousand years. Mao only usurped the former state power and gave it a new name. He called it "New China". If this so-called New China is really better than the "old China" - the Republic of China in Taiwan, Mao's work can be praised. But when we compare and evaluate the situation in all the social, cultural, political, and economical spheres between the two China, everyone finds that the New China is much worse than the old China. In this case, how can one boast that the founding of the PRC is a meritorious deed. It was but Mao's crime of usurpation and damage of China.

Second, Communist Party of China is not founded by Mao Zedong. It is founded by Chen Duxiu, Li Dazhao. There were many former leaders in its early days. Mao Zedong only usurped the leadership in 1943, twenty-two year after the founding of the Communist Party of China. After seizing power, Mao betrayal its original fine ideals and built a dictatorial party. All the things the party led by Mao had done were negative: the Yan'an Rectification Movement around 1943; the

A Painful Reminiscence of a Dignified Soul

launching of civil war in 1946; the campaigns of suppressing and eliminating counterrevolutionaries in 1950, 1954; the campaign of anti-rightists in 1957; the Great Leap Forward from 1958 to 1960; the Great Cultural Revolution from 1966 to 1976. All these campaigns caused tenths of millions death of innocents. Is it meritorious deed? We need such a dictatorial Party?

Third, Mao's aim of founding an army is to seize power, as he himself admitted "power grows out of the barrel of a gun" This army has fought two great wars: The first was the civil war(1946-1949), which caused the death of about two million innocent Chinese youth on both sides. The second was the War of Resist US Aggression and Aid Korea, which claimed a death toll of about half a million of our compatriots. Is it worthy to wage the two wars? Do we have an obligation to support the dictator of North Korea? If Mao competed with Chiang Kai-shek through peaceful means, all those meaningless sacrifices would be avoided. Founding this army is Mao's crime not a merit.

Fourth, the so called "Mao Zedong Thought", in my opinion, can be summarized in one sentence: "Struggle between proletarian class and the bourgeois class must be carried on endlessly" And he alone is the representative of the proletarian class. All his views and actions are correct and all the different views and actions belong to the bourgeois. During his thirty-three-year ruling period he proceeded successive struggles to purge, eliminate and execute his opponents, whose number mounted over tens of millions, including the president of the country. Is this thought and its practice meritorious? There is not a leader, all over the world and history, who titles a thought with his name. Have you ever heard a "Washington thought"? "Chechier thought"? Or "Li Shimin(李世民) thought"? "Kang Xi(康熙) thought"? No one has heard that. Only Mao Zedong undertake the glorious task to proclaim his thinking as a school of thought.

Some people think that Mao was not as culpable as Stalin and Hitler, but he was worse than the two. The horrors of the Gulag and the Holocaust have long been known throughout the world, yet the far crueler tragedy happened in china has not been acknowledged by the world and Chinese people itself. It is a great pity.

I must shout at the top of my voice to make a proper comment on Mao Zedong:

Mao is the basest, shameless, most vicious dictator throughout the world and history. His character is very bad.

He possesses a demoniac personality and a heart of granite. He creates a reign of mass terror characterized not only by deprivation of all basic human rights, but also by arbitrary torturing, random jailing and summary executions. He is a sadist and had a blithe indifference to anyone's feelings, as relentless as a wolverine. In the past, when a dictator wants to kill his opponents, he just beheads them or gives them a shot. The victims only suffer a few minutes. But when Mao wants to kill his opponents, he will torture them physically, mentally for months or years until their death. He takes delight to see his victims humiliated, suffered and enjoys his triumph over them. According to his own word "Qinshihuang (the first emperor of China) only buried 460 scholars, but we buried over 46,000 scholars, one hundred time more than them." In cruelty he is supreme, unchallenged and unparalleled in scale in history. His cruelty is so severe and fierce as to render it unbelievable to mankind.

He is greedy and wildly ambitious. He is insatiable for power. He strives to become emperor of China first. Then his ambition has daily puffed up. He wants to eliminate all the so called "capitalist, revisionist and reactionary" countries and spares no efforts to procure the crown and throne of the king of the world. He dreams to destroy "the old world and build a new world."

He is a megalomaniac. He thinks he is omnipotent and omniscient to do everything, as if he is a celestial immortal descended to earth. He believes he is eternally correct and infallible. He is the king, the state, the people, determining the pros and cons of anything. He is greater than the law and can overthrow the law. There isn't the least minimum of checks and balances to curb his power. Even in the old dynasty, the emperor has "imperial admonisher(谏官)" in the court, whose duty is to point out the emperor's fault frankly and plead him to correct it. But the modern emperor Mao cannot hear any different voice. If anyone has the temerity to point out his fault, he will severely punish or deaden the critics or advisers.

He is sly, insidious, tricky and cunning. He always masks his true face and real goals to confuse and paralyze others. His ostensible kindness and frankness always cover a devious scheme. He solicits criticism from the people, with which as means to entice "snakes(critics) out of their lairs." He has an incomparable capacity to weigh up people and situations: when to wait, lurk, feint, and withdraw and when to hit obliquely or attack fiercely. He can exile cadres and students to the country with beautiful convincing pretext that the victims would bow in gratitude. His role in all the tragedies is indirect. He is not involved in executing opponents, but in fact he does arrange their death. He kills with a borrowed knife. Some Dictators are good at pretending to be kind and hurt others in the dark; some dictators are good at killing openly, and Mao shares both the virtue of crafty and cruelty in highest measure. There is a mixture of the tiger and the ape in his character. He assumed a Marxist guise to bluff, ensnare the youth. He controls people by disguised hooks or military crooks. Stratagem is his specialty.

He is sham, hypocritical, and shameless. He always tells lies. His deeds do not square with his promises. He says we must establish coalition government; we will establish a democratic system of America style and practice "Lincoln's Gettysburg speech" and "Roosevelt's four freedom." yet he practices severe dictatorship. He names our country "The People's Republic of China". Republic is a system of government by the whole population, through elected representatives. But our people are never allowed to take part in the affairs of the government and to elect their leader. He uses this beautiful name and governs the country in an utterly opposite way. He speaks of materialism, but in fact he is the most idealistic. Materialism believes that physical matter is the fundamental reality and that all things can be explained and done by the physical matter. Matter precedes the idea. But Mao says and does anything as he likes or follows his whims, never considers the material conditions. He speaks of objective law, but it is he who shows the least respect for objective law. He frequently accuses others of fermenting conspiracies, but he is the greatest manipulator of conspiracies. He has never really served the people; he has just harnessed and threatened people to his selfish purpose. He committed all unspeakable crimes in the name of revolution, justice, equality, freedom.

The damage wrought by Mao are embodied in every fibre of our social and potitical beings. He can never be identified anything other than a criminal. He has committed many serious crimes, such as

1. Mao abolishes China's fine traditional culture completely and destroys the glorious civilization which the world has known. His rule has caused a general degradation of morality of the people. To recover the destroyed economy is relatively easier; to recover the destroyed morality is much harder. I think it may take several generations' time. That is why I deem the destruction of morality as Mao's greatest crime.
2. He usurps the power of the President of the People's Republic of China and establishes an illegal Committees of the Revolution. This coup caused millions of deaths of the officials and common people, including the pres-

ident of China Liu Shaoqi.
3. He starts a Great Leap Forward, using unscientific, fallacious method to lead industrial and agricultural production, which causes countless waste of resources and an unprecedented famine which claims a death toll of over thirty million.
4. He cheats and instigates millions of youngsters, who are still physically, mentally weak and vulnerable, to do evil deeds, torturing or killing innumerable innocents, destroying myriad treasures and relics. He hurts, ruins the mind and spirit of a whole generation.
5. He launched many political campaigns, like the Suppression of Counterrevolutionary Campaign, Elimination of Counterrevolutionary Campaign, Anti-rightists Campaign, etc. which hurts or killed at least ten million of innocents.
6. He was the maker of civil war and aid North Korean War. The two wars wound and kill millions of our compatriots, only destroying a legal government and surviving the dictatorial country North Korea.

The Communist Party leaders believe they can hide the facts and deceive the people forever. It is impossible. As Lincoln said, "You can fool all the people some of the time, and some of the people all the time, but you cannot fool all the people all the time." We must reveal all the facts to Chinese people. I hope all the true patriots who want to save China to enthusiastically participate in the great work.

First, I hope the old people of my age come out to relate more true history to the younger generations.

Second, I hope those people who had persecuted the innocents come out to bravely admit their faults and apologize to their victims. Their narration can help young people to understand how they were fooled by Mao to do those mistaken things. There were millions of people who were cruelly treated under Mao's rule, so there must be millions of persecutors. Yet we rarely see persecutors to admit their faults. I only read two persons' repentance and apology in the newspaper. One is Chen Xiaolu, the son of marshal Chen Yi; the other is Song Bingbing, who had hung armband of red guard on Chairman Mao's arm. Why so many persecutors keep silent?

I read a book titled "A comrade lost and Found—A Beijing Story"

The book is written by a Canadian named Jan Wong. In 1972, In the high of the Cultural Revolution, she, a 19-year-old girl, came to China as one of the first two Westerners permitted to study at Beijing University. She was an inexperienced enthusiast girl and a Mao's worshipper then. One day in 1973 her acquaintance Yin Luoyi asked Wong to help her to get to the U.S.A. At that time Wong had no interest in the West and believed that China was a proletarian paradise. She reasoned that the workers and peasants had paid for Yin's university education, she should stay in China and help develop the country. Wong did not know how dire the punishment for "thought crimes" were then, she promptly reported Yin to her communist professor. Yin was subsequently expelled and Wong lost all trace of her. Years later, Wong became a foreign correspondent and knew more and more real situation of China. In 1994 as she browsed through her old diary, she found she had ratted Yin to the Party. She realized she had thoughtlessly destroyed a young woman. From then on, she kept thinking about Yin: what had happened to her? She must have suffered terribly. Perhaps she was dead. Wong even thought that if yin was dead and had a daughter, she would help her daughter to come to Canada if she wanted. Guilt over Yin's plight continued to plague Wong and Yin's fate haunted Wong all the time. She can't keep unloading her guilt on Yin. She resolved to track down Yin and made an apology to her. Three decades later, In August 2006, the fifty-three-year-old Wong boarded a plane to return to Beijing. She wanted to find out what had happened to Yin. Was she still alive and, if so, what horrors befell her as a result of her betrayal? That is not an easy task. She tried all possible means to find out Yin's information. She consulted the archives, but it hadn't Yin's thirty years records; She searched the telephone directory, but there wasn't the name Yin Luoyi; She pestered her old friends and professors, but most of those old rebels would rather forget or remain silent about their tragedies and betrayals. She even tried to contact private detectives. But all her efforts were to no avail. Fortunately, a Yin's classmate, who had been forced to denounce Yin and regretted for her conduct, help Wong to find Yin's situation. After suffering many years' persecution, Yin was rehabilitated and returned to Beijing. She had married a professor and just live at a dormitory of Beijing University. Wong visited Yin at her home and made deepest apologies to her: "I am so sorry for what I did. I have wrong you for telling the teachers that you wanted to go abroad." Yin said: "Don't be sorry. What happened to me wasn't merely because of you. I was accused of many, many crimes. You only added to the weight of my crimes. I don't blame you. Everyone who knew me was forced to denounce me. Never mind." Yin's tone isn't accusatory, she does not hold Wong accountable. Wong admitted her guilt frankly: "I was not under pressure to criticize you. I did not have to rat you out. No one made me. No one would have even known about your desire to leave the motherland. I voluntarily turned you in. I betrayed you casually, nonchalantly, thoughtlessly." Wong laid it out as bluntly as she could and made apology over and over again. She waited for a rebuke, reproach, or something. Yin seemed surprised and said with genuine feeling: "I didn't know you had told them on your own. I thought you were forced to tell the thing to the party." "Let me put it this way. You didn't have that much power. You didn't have enough influence to ruin my life." "It wasn't your fault. We were all crazy in that era." "I will never forget you, it must be fate that has brought us together again" They had intimate talks and became good friends. The day before Wong's leaving, Yin called Wong, saying, "You know, the day after our first meeting, I was wounded in the heart. I didn't know you had told them about me on your own, without anyone asking you. I felt very sad. But Now I am so happy we have found each other." Wong also felt so lucky to have eventually found Yin with unexpected results, to have received her forgiveness and her journey allowed her to soothe old wounds and seek clarity and catharsis.

I am deeply touched by Wong's story. A foreigner, when she recognized her mistake, painstakingly travelled halfway around the world to probe her victim and make a sincere apology to Yin. How brave, lofty she is! I hope those misled wrongdoers follow her example. All of them are about seventy-year-old now. I wish their conscience and reason will lead them to do some worthy things to smooth over their fault.

Third, I hope the descendants of the party leaders and high-ranking officials can make a clear distinction between right and wrong, virtue and vice. They are commonly called the Second Red Generations or the Third Red Generations. "Red" is regarded as a symbol of goodness, righteousness in China. They should make a consideration and judgment whether their and their father's ideologies and deeds are really "red" They should affirm what is right and negate what is wrong. Hu Yaobang negated Mao's wrongdoing and rehabilitated all the victims persecuted by Mao. He is a real "second red generation" Zhao Ziyang boycotted the June 4 massacre, he is a real "second red generation" Premier Li Peng, who advocated the June 4 massacre, is not a "second red generation" he is a black generation, a traitor to the people and the nation. Jiang Zemin, who continued to practice the one-party dictatorship. He is not "red" He is "black", too. There are many second

A Painful Reminiscence of a Dignified Soul

generations who suppress the people cruelly or use their privileges to embezzle hundreds of millions of RMB. Can they be called the "Second Red Generation"?

There are many wise, noble, worthy descendants of the dictators, such as Alina Fernandez. She is the daughter of Fidel Castro, the fifty-years' dictator of Cuba. She is an activist, a family woman and a rebel all at once. Fernandez becomes increasingly critical and rebellious towards the political climate. She has been critical of the government of Cuba. She has a radio show called "Simply Alina in Miami, Florida" devoting Wednesdays to Cuban politics. She plays a key role in a movement of political dissent in the 80s and is forced to flee Cuba at age 37, using false papers and a wig. She resides in the United States. She made a lecture at Oakland University. She spoke about her experiences growing up in Cuba and ultimately fleeing the country. The lecture provides an intimate account of her father, how the country changed after the revolution and of the potential for a reformed Cuba. She gives a really rare insight into Cuban life and politics. She writes her memoir, Castro's Daughter: An Exile's Memoir of Cuba, describing her life in Cuba and the changes that occur over nearly four decades. Fernandez shows great courage and speaks up for what she thinks is right what is wrong.

Hussein Khomeini, the grandson of the founder of the Islamic Republic, Ayatollah Ruhollah Khomeini, is a liberal cleric. In strong contrast to his grandfather's politics, Hussein Khomeini has spoken out against the Islamic Republic System. He strongly advocates the end of the religious despotism practiced by his grandfather and father. He has denounced the Iranian government as the "dictatorship of clerics" He calls for a referendum to decide how the country should be governed in the future. He has also advocated for a non-classical interpretation of Islamic law applied in the country. He hopes "the rule of law would be established" in Iran and "people, political activists, and leading figures of the Iranian Revolution would be treated with wisdom and prudence." He is sympathetic to American neoconservatives, and has lectured at the American Enterprise Institute. He calls for the overthrow of the Islamic Republic. He calls for American destruction of the Islamic Republic by invasion on the Al-Arabiya television station, saying "freedom must come to Iran in any possible way, whether through internal or external developments." This position is even more extreme than that of the fiercely anti-regime Iranian exiles, who oppose military action while urging the US to back a domestic uprising. He expects the realization of democracy in Iran and appealed to America to promote democracy throughout the world more firmly and strongly. Since returning to Iran, he has been under house arrest. He is praised as a "courageous foe of his grandfather's theocracy."

Kim Han-sol, the open-minded great-grandson of Kim Il-sung, the founder of North Korea, provides a stark contrast to his forefather's regime. He expresses guilt for his family role in the suffering of the North Korean people. He criticizes the despotic system of North Korea in various messages on YouTube, Twitter. He opposes "dynastic Succession". He said "I would like to engage in more humanitarian projects, work to contribute to building world peace, especially back home because that is a really important part of me." He is now exiled in foreign countries over fears that his uncle Kim Jong-un, the present dictator of North Korea, could have him assassinated. He sees North Korea is a prison, concentration camp. He said "I have always dreamed that one day I would go back and make things better, and make things easier for the people. I also dream of unification" He feels guilty about having enough to eat when his people in North Korea are starving. Being asked whether he preferred democracy or communism, He said he preferred democracy. His father Kim Jong-nam died after a toxin was applied to his face in a Malaysian airport. Who assassinated him is still a mystery. Kim Han-sol is under protection at his mother's house. When he is living in exile, he says he becomes more exposed to different cultures and opinions. He says that he has made friends with Americans and South Koreans. These are countries which we have been having conflicts with and in a lot of tension, but we turn out to be really great friends. That just sparks the curiosity for me." He studies social sciences in foreign countries.

Sergei Khrushchev is the son of Nikita Khrushchev, the former Soviet leader who had pledged to bury US. Yet his son went to the United States in 1991 and worked there, teaching a class at Brown University. He also becomes a citizen of the United States of America, vowing to defend the capitalist lifestyle. In an interview with The Associated Press, he said he hoped his father would be supportive of his new American citizenship. "After all," he says, "it's not as if I'm defecting." After taking the oath of citizenship he said: "I'm feeling like a newborn. It's the beginning of a new life." Some Russians see betrayal in his move. He replies: "You are still living in the Cold War. It is a different Russia." In an interview with a correspondent, he confidently remarks that in the Soviet Union the bureaucratic debates and policy formulations are always controlled by the most dominant personalities. There are many bureaucratic struggles within the Soviet Union's

A Painful Reminiscence of a Dignified Soul

leadership. He speaks a great length about the various struggles he had observed within the Kremlin.

Even Alliluyeva, Stalin's daughter, has fled from her country. Unable bearing the life living in a prison without iron window, Alliluyeva leaves Soviet Union for India on the pretext of burying the cinerary casket of her husband, an Indian communist, then approaches the United States Embassy in New Delhi. After she states her desire to defect in writing, the United States Ambassador offered her political asylum in the United States. Upon her arrival in New York City in April 1967, she gives a press conference denouncing her father's legacy and the Soviet government. She says that her father had the power to send anyone to prison. She lectures and writes in US. In the United States she is widely known as "the red princess escaping to the West" She launches an unbridled attack against Soviet Union and Stalin. In 1978, Alliluyeva becomes a US citizen. She describes herself as "quite happy here". In 1984, 58-year-old Alliluyeva has some money problems and the Soviet Union promises her a better retiring treatment and medical treatment, she returns to Soviet Union. But soon after that she complains "In these cold days of 1984 in Moscow, I feel as if I am sinking into dark waters—as it is sometimes in a nightmare." She writes to a friend: "I feel sad again—as long ago in my native cruel Russia, I have to force myself to silence, force myself to false behavior, to hide my true thoughts, and to bend my head down before the fist of false authority. All that is too damn sad. But I shall survive." Two years later she moves back to the United States again. She lives in the United States for over forty years. She has a strong character; she is not willing to be controlled by any person. In her whole life she expresses her extreme exasperation against her father. She regards her two elder brothers and herself are all victims of her father. It is her father who destroyed her life.

These sensible, virtuous descendants of the dictators are real red generations. But in China I still haven't seen any descendants of our dictators and high-ranking officials to criticize the wrongdoings of their elders. Most of them follow their elders' way to suppress the people or to seek money through corruption. It is a shame. They think they are "Red Generations" but is depriving people's civil rights Red"? Is opposing democracy Red? Is suppressing dissidents Red? No! They are "Black, I hope that more and more so-called "Second Red Generations" can make a clear distinction between right and wrong, virtue and vice, can honestly examine whether their lives are "Red" or "Black". They should recognize that democracy, freedom and human rights are universal values of human beings and world tendency. If our genuine red descendant can comply with the will of the people and transfer dictatorship into democracy, his meritorious deeds will go down in history.

Finally, I hope that all Chinese people should not be contending as a blind and a deaf-mute. The party force you to listen to a single voice, pull the wool over your eyes, you must try your best to get different information. You can listen to VOA, BBC etc., buy books from Hong Kong, Tai Wan or foreign countries. You can also get information through "over-the-wall(翻墙)software". Even from "Sogou search engine" or "Sina search engine" in China you can get little true facts about "the Great Leap Forward" "the Great Cultural Revolution" etc. When you know more views and facts you can make your own choice. And I believe most people will choose the right one.

I also hope you are not contending to be docile tools or slaves. One party dictatorship is a political monopoly. In economics, monopoly is a crime. It will be punished by the law. Monopoly is an evil thing. It stifles competition. It forcibly seizes all power for one group's profits. In China there are 1,400 million people. The Communist Party has about 80 million members. The party only allow its members to be the leaders of all levels of government, factories, mines, academies, universities, schools and hospitals. And all the other 1,320 million people are deemed not qualified to do those jobs. Is this system reasonable? Do those 1,320 million people have less capacity, competent, talent, wit, quality than that 80 million party members? The number of non-party members is 16 times the number of the party members. We can endure the 1/16 people ride on the back of the 15/16 people? All the Chinese people, whose rights have been deprived by the party, must rise up to regain their rights and freedom. If everyone has the moral, political awakening, then the dictator will have no army and police to suppress the people so the awakening of the people is the most important prerequisite for the realization of democracy.

This book is a record of some facts of my life and history, having no shade of untruth or exaggeration. All the names of the people in this book are true except "Zhi Qing". Zhi Qing(知青) in Chinese means the educated students who are exiled to the countryside by Mao. I use that name as the embodiment of the miserable generation of the youth. Zhi Qing's story described in this book is not a single student's story but many students' thinking and experience.